Pennsylvania Trout Streams and Their Hatches

By Charles R. Meck

BACKCOUNTRY PUBLICATIONS
THE COUNTRYMAN PRESS, INC.
WOODSTOCK, VERMONT

AN INVITATION TO THE READER

With time, access points may change, and road numbers, signs and land-marks referred to in this book may be altered. If you find that such changes have occurred near the streams described in this book, please let the author and publisher know, so that corrections may be made in future editions. Other comments and suggestions are also welcome. Address all correspondence to:

Fishing Editor
Backcountry Publications
P.O. Box 175
Woodstock, Vermont 05091

Library of Congress Cataloging-in-Publication Data

Meck, Charles R.
    Pennsylvania trout streams and their hatches / by Charles R. Meck.
        p.   cm.
    Includes index.
    ISBN 0-88150-142-5 : $14.95
    1. Trout fishing—Pennsylvania—Guide-books.   2. Fly
fishing—Pennsylvania—Guide-books.   3. Insects, Aquatic—
Pennsylvania.
    I. Title.
SH688.U6M43   1989
799.1′755—dc20   89-34606
                                                            CIP

Published by Backcountry Publications
A division of The Countryman Press, Inc.
Woodstock, Vermont 05091

Line art by Donald M. Whitesel, Jr.
Cover and text design by Leslie Fry
Maps by Richard Widhu, © 1989 Backcountry Publications
Printed in the United States of America

Dedication

To Shirley, Lynne, and Bryan, who have been so understanding of my devotion to fly-fishing.

April 12, 1990

To

Chuck

Have a year of great fly-fishing! I hope you enjoy the book and have a great year. Best wishes!

[signature]

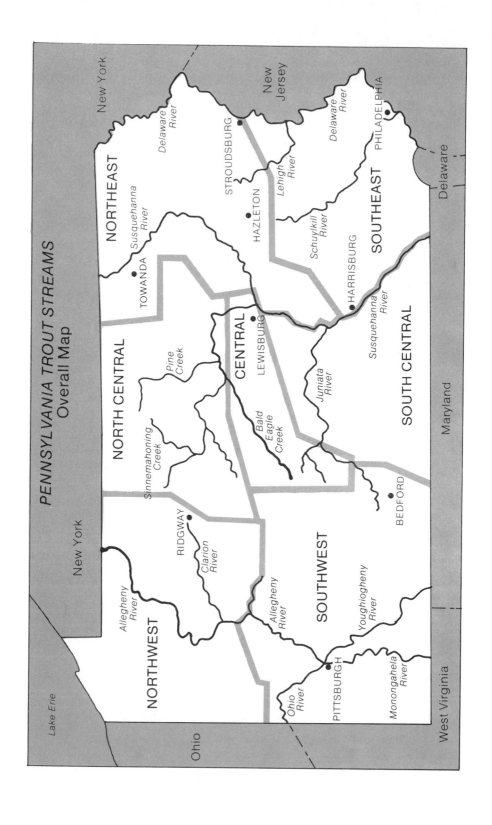

PENNSYLVANIA TROUT STREAMS
Overall Map

Contents

Acknowledgments

How does one get an idea for a book? Often the beginning is a combination of sources culminating in a manuscript. *Pennsylvania Trout Streams and Their Hatches* is a direct result of a request by John Randolph, editor and publisher of the highly regarded *Fly Fisherman* magazine. Several years ago John asked me to develop a story about Pennsylvania's top ten streams for a special edition of his magazine. As a result of that article, and subsequent requests by the Pennsylvania Trout Unlimited Council to present a talk on the streams of the Commonwealth, I developed the present manuscript. Thanks to John for giving me the opportunity to write for his magazine, and to the state TU Council.

Many others have assisted in the project. In southwestern Pennsylvania Russ Mowry, Ken Igo, and Tim Shaffer helped with the hatches and took time to reacquaint me with trout streams I hadn't fished for twenty years. Ken furnished the hatches for the Loyalhanna Creek. Bob Forr of Everett, Carl Dodson of Martinsburg, and Nelson Hamil of Altoona aided on the hatches of Yellow Creek. Bob Davis of Big Run supplied some of the hatches on the Little Mahoning Creek. Nate Rascona and Ken Sarver of Somerset, John Sanner of Rockport, and Tim Shaffer of Latrobe helped with the hatches on Laurel Hill. Art Gusbar of Friedens and Pat Docherty of the Corps of Engineers supplied data on the Youghiogheny; Bob Beck of Altoona helped with Canoe Creek; Danny Deters and Ed Gunnett, both of Williamsburg, assisted with Piney and Clover Creeks. Tony Stair and Bob Bryant of Hyndman guided me on Brush Creek and Wills Creek. Thanks also to Howard Bach of the Western Pennsylvania Conservancy for helping me locate fly-fishermen in the southwestern area.

In north-central streams Jack Mickievicz helped tremendously with the hatches and background information on the Genesee Forks, Ninemile Run, and the upper end of Pine Creek. Pete Ryan and Vic Howard of Coudersport assisted with the hatches and background on the Allegheny River, and Stewart Dickerson of Shinglehouse assisted with the hatches on the Oswayo Creek. Tom Finkbiner and Mike O'Brien helped with the hatches on Pine, Slate, and Cedar Runs. Dennis Renninger of Hillsgrove and John Plowman of Mechanicsburg helped with the history and hatches on Elk Creek, Hoagland Branch, and the Loyalsock Creek. Curt Thompson of Wharton assisted with First Fork and East Fork. Rich Meyers of Pottstown helped with the hatches on Young Woman's Creek and Phil Baldacchino with the hatches and history on Kettle, Cross Fork, and Hammersley Fork. Jack Bush of Erie, Don Foltz of Lincolnville, Marshall Young of Union City, Tony Palombo of Hermitage, Ted Fauceglia of Sharpsville, Bob Davis of Big Run, and Tom Greenlee of Tionesta assisted with hatching information and stream background on northwestern streams. John Salandra of Brockway enlisted some of the better-known fly-fishermen in the Brockway area, including Mike Veltri, Hank and John Foradora, Brent Rearig, Dick Koval, and Blackie Veltri.

In the southeast Joe Petrella of Downingtown, Wayne Poppich of King of Prussia, Barry Staats of Media, Mary Kuss of Haverford assisted in the suburban streams around Philadelphia. Dick Henry and Ellwood Gettle of Lebanon, and Larry Gasser of Fleetwood helped with orientation and the hatches on the Tulpehocken. Thanks to Frank Plucinsky of the Tulpehocken Trout Unlimited chapter for use of his emergence chart. Desmond Kahn, Jim Leonard of Delaware, Ken Depoe, and Don Whitesel helped on Lancaster County streams. Joe Kohler of Allentown assisted with the hatches on the Little Lehigh, Cedar Run, and Monocasy Creek.

In the south-central region Jim Gilson of Port Royal, Reed Gray and Dennis Sieber of Lewistown, and Steve Bullich of Reedsville helped tremendously with Honey, Tea, Kishacoquillas, and East Licking Creeks. Gene Macri gave me hatches and other data on Falling Springs, Big Spring Run, and Yellow Breeches. Dan Meckley, John Taylor, and Brian Berger assisted with York County streams. Ed Lehman, Steve Frey, and John Fetterhoff aided in the Fulton County area. Phil Stewart helped with Blacklog and Standing Stone Creeks.

In the northeast Bob Dibble of Wyalusing helped on the Mehoopany, and Don Baylor on the Brodhead and Big Bushkill. Mike Marinelli and Jay Kapolka assisted with the Pohopoco and Mud Run. Bob Sentiwany of White Haven helped in identifying hatches on Hickory Run, Haines Creek, the Lehigh River, and the Delaware River. Rick Eck of Honesdale helped with the hatches on the Dyberry. Barry and Cathy Beck of Berwick helped with Fishing Creek. John Churnetski and Lee Eckert of the Wyoming Valley area helped with the hatches on the Lackawaxen.

Al Gretz gave me some names of Trout Unlimited members through-out the state who might help with some of the hatches. Alvin Grove of State College also furnished some names.

Thanks to the Cortland Line Company and Lora Hall for her fine cooperation in supplying high quality fly line.

Thanks also to Ralph Frankenberger for developing photographs for the book; to Albert Nakpil of Penn State University, who aided me countless times with word processing for the book; Rod Bond of Harrisburg, who made sketches of the maps included in the book; and to the Pennsylvania Fish Commission for their assistance. Edward Miller, Edward Manhart, and Richard Snyder of the commission gave considerable assistance.

Finally, thanks to Carol Kersavage for her untiring effort in editing the manuscript.

One

INTRODUCTION TO
Pennsylvania Streams and Rivers

Pennsylvania has much to offer the fly-fisherman, whether he or she is an expert or a novice. Picturesque mountain streams; scenic, uncluttered, secluded valleys; limestone springs teeming with brook, brown, and rainbow trout—Pennsylvania has them all.

You don't have to travel far to enjoy excellent trout fishing in our state. There are fantastic streams near some of Pennsylvania's major cities. The Little Lehigh and Cedar Run flow through Allentown; the Tulpehocken is near Reading; French Creek is near Phoenixville, and Valley Creek near Philadelphia; Clark, Stony, and Fishing Creeks are found just north of Harrisburg; Clover Creek and the Little Juniata River are near Altoona; the Loyalhanna is not far from Pittsburgh; and on and on.

Pennsylvania boasts 10,000 miles of trout water classified as either wild-trout or stocked waters. They range from two- or three-foot-wide streams to large rivers like the Delaware, Youghiogheny, and Clarion. Many display a diversity both in the insect life and the number of trout they contain. Many of the more fertile waters are the highly alkaline limestone streams common in central Pennsylvania near State College, Altoona, and Lewistown. But other streams with a high degree of alkalinity can be found in the Lock Haven area, around Allentown, Chambersburg, Lebanon, Carlisle, and McConnellsburg. And don't exclude Pennsylvania's north-central streams from your fly-fishing plans. Many of these large streams, most flowing from north to south, contain plenty of early- and midseason hatches and teem with trout eager to take the proper imitation.

You'll find special regulations on more than 100 miles of the streams and rivers in Pennsylvania. The Pennsylvania Fish Commission has enhanced dozens of streams by earmarking specific areas of them with these special rules. You'll see these special regulations, where they apply, highlighted at the beginning of the stream descriptions in Chapters 3 through

9. Special regulations include catch-and-release, fly-fishing only, trophy trout, and delayed harvest. All are designed to maintain an optimum trout population in the regulated area. A delayed harvest area, for example, by setting a late opening date for trout season, assures the angler that the section will hold a good supply of trout until the middle of June. In trophy trout waters, only fish over fourteen inches may be taken—and in very limited numbers. Make certain you check the latest regulations in the Summary of Fishing Regulations and Laws booklet you receive when you buy your fishing license.

The streams and rivers of Pennsylvania have an abundance of insect activity; hatches appear on the waters throughout much of the fishing season. Some years you can begin the season with a hatch like the Quill Gordon, Blue Quill, or Hendrickson in April and end the season in October with a Slate Drake or Blue Dun. Between the beginning and ending days appear many abundant, spectacular hatches of mayflies, stoneflies, caddis flies, crane flies, midges, ants, and other assorted insects straying too near the water. Hatches appear and many trout rise even in July and August on streams abandoned by fishermen because the waters were thought to be void of fish.

In the upcoming chapters we'll explore much of the aquatic life and the streams and rivers of Pennsylvania. For it is with precise knowledge of the hatches on specific waters that the novice and expert angler can enjoy the rewards of a more complete sport—fishing on streams when a hatch of insects appears and being adequately prepared with the proper imitation. We'll examine suitable patterns—whether they are wet flies, dry flies, or nymphs—for the major hatches on Pennsylvania streams.

Pennsylvania boasts many of the world's finest anglers. The dean of fly-fishermen, George Harvey, has fished the state's waters for more than a half-century. George has popularized fly tying as well as fly-fishing with his *Techniques of Fly Tying and Trout Fishing*. He is a legend in the nation's history of fly-fishing. The state also has other notables who have contributed much to the sport. Fly-fishermen like Charlie Fox, Ed Koch, Jim Bashline, Ed Shenk, Don DuBois, Joe Humphreys, and Alvin Grove claim the Commonwealth as their home.

For all its riches in water, fish, and fishermen, however, Pennsylvania has problems. An immediate concern for all the Commonwealth's citizens is the number of miles of posted trout waters in the state. Just twenty years ago Penns Creek was open anywhere below PA 45. Now much of the property below Spring Mills and above Coburn is posted. Once the state declared some of its waters as wild trout zones some property owners closed fishing on their land. Big Fill in Blair County was open to public fishing over its entire length just ten years ago. Now some of the property just above Centre County's Bald Eagle is posted against trespassing.

There's much you can do to prevent further erosion in the number of streams available to you. Enjoy your stay on the stream, but also respect the property owner's rights. Take everything home that you brought to the stream. Patrol the stream, and keep it clean. Several years ago a friend brought his son along on a trip with me to Falling Springs near Chambersburg. When we went back to the car to grab a sandwich, the boy tossed his bag near the stream. I asked him to pick it up and place it in a nearby container.

How many streams have you seen with scars of recent fishermen? Vince Gigliotti and Terry Carlsen regularly take garbage bags with them so they can collect debris left behind by careless sportsmen. We all should be prepared to do the same. Annually, just before Christmas, I regularly take gifts to some of the farmers and landowners who have allowed me to hunt on their land and fish on their water. You'd be surprised how much goodwill these small gifts create.

Let's look at the chapters in the book and how they're organized. Chapter 2 examines many of the mayflies, caddis flies, and stoneflies found on the streams of the Commonwealth. Unless and until you become familiar with these insects, when they appear, and on what streams, you probably won't be prepared to fish the great hatches of Pennsylvania. Chapters 3 through 9 explore in detail some of the better streams and rivers of Pennsylvania, arranged by region. Some of these regions overlap, but the index will help direct you to specific waters.

Maybe I've omitted some of your favorite streams from the book. It's impossible to know all the hatches and sections of all the streams and rivers of the Commonwealth. To include them all would require several volumes, and several decades. I hope that those streams I have included will provide you with many hours of good fly-fishing and many hatches successfully matched.

Some of the streams and rivers I describe may have declined or improved in trout or insect populations since this book was completed. A few years ago Spruce Creek received a shot of liquid manure that killed thousands of trout in the stream for miles. Almost annually someone or something deposits contaminants in the Little Juniata River. On some occasions contamination follows a train spill, on others a truck accident, and too often it's intentional. As Pennsylvanians and as avid fishermen we must guard our natural resources jealously so that not only we, but also future generations, can enjoy the solitude and rewards of pure water.

Chapter 10 suggests some tying descriptions to match many of the hatches and spinner falls found on Pennsylvania streams. Whether you tie or buy your imitations, this part of the book will be useful.

Chapter 11 includes a wish list of suggestions that can make Pennsylvania streams and Pennsylvania trout fishing even better. Why place restrictions of various kinds on fishing some of the Commonwealth's streams? Chapter 11 examines this question. Why should you join a local chapter of Trout Unlimited, Federation of Fly Fishermen, or the Izaak Walton League? Chapter 11 tells you why.

When you travel many of the back roads of Pennsylvania in search of fine fly-fishing, large trout, and excellent scenery and solitude, take plenty of fly patterns along. As we'll see shortly, you'll be fishing over some great mayfly, stonefly, and caddis fly hatches.

Have a great journey!

Two

INTRODUCTION TO THE
Hatches of Pennsylvania

It's the opening of another trout season in Pennsylvania. If you already fly-fish, are you prepared for the great hatches on many of the state's streams? Do you know where and when these hatches appear? Do you know what imitations match what hatches? How about those of you who are just starting? Does the complex know-how of fly-fishing seem too much to learn? Is it worthwhile fishing the hatches? If you are prepared with the proper pattern and appear on a stream when the hatch will appear, does that really improve your chances of success? You bet it does! Let me give an example with an incident that occurred just two years ago to a newcomer to fly-fishing.

Dave Butts, of State College, had never been fly-fishing, but he was eager to learn and pleaded with me for almost a year to take him out. During a January blizzard we planned a trip to the Little Juniata River for the upcoming May. Every time Dave saw me, he reminded me of our approaching fishing excursion. Dave had no fishing tackle, and I suggested he use mine. Then he could decide whether he liked the new sport before he spent money on waders, a rod, reel, line, and other fly-fishing necessities.

Dave had never cast a fly prior to our May 21 trip.

The long-awaited evening finally arrived, and we were on the river. Dave donned a pair of oversized waders and one of my old Orvis fishing vests. Like a child anticipating Christmas morning, Dave anxiously headed for the river hoping to witness the hatches I promised would appear that evening. We hiked upriver a half-mile, over a railroad track, up a hill, then down to the water. Almost as soon as we saw the river clearly through the brush, Dave saw trout rising. Before we could even tie a fly on the tippet, brown trout rose to a good supply of Light Cahills.

Less than five minutes after he entered the river, Dave was thrashing the surface with his Light Cahill but he encountered immediate problems.

First he had difficulty casting any distance with that confounded fly on the end of his line. Second the dry fly mimicked a wet fly and sank for him every time. Third he had a problem covering a rising fish.

Soon, however, the dry fly seemed to behave properly and floated. Next Dave covered rising trout, casting a few feet upriver from the surface feeders. I turned away from Dave for a short time to watch a dozen or so trout feeding below at the tail of the pool. Soon I heard a yell, looked up toward Dave, and saw a slack line.

"Missed that one," Dave shouted.

The Cahill hatch peaked, and dozens of the duns remained on the water. Trout rose out from Dave—upstream and downstream. Possibly two dozen trout filled the pool with splashing rises. Dave's casting techniques had improved considerably, and he successfully covered a constant riser just a few feet above him on the second cast. Another strike, and another slack line.

"Missed another one," Dave bellowed as he cast to another fish within his limited casting range. On the next cast Dave dropped his Cahill just a foot above and in line with a third riser.

Another yell from Dave. When I looked up I saw the ultimate reward— a tight line. I knew my novice had hooked his first trout on a fly. If you want to know the joy that a successful fly-fishing event produces, accompany a beginner on his or her first successful fly-fishing trip.

By now it was 8:30 P.M., and Dave had already landed three Cahill-eating browns. Only sporadic Light Cahills remained as any evidence of the fantastic hatch that had appeared just an hour before. Almost as a signal when the last hatch had waned, it was time for the next hatch of Sulphur Duns to make their highly predictable appearance. I quickly tied a size-16 Sulphur on Dave's line, and he cast to possibly twenty trout now rising in the pool. Thousands of Sulphurs filled the air, with more on the surface. What a fantastic hatch! The Sulphur hatch lasted for more than a half-hour that evening, then ended as quickly as it had begun.

The Little Juniata had one other event to display before hatching activity ended that evening. Around 8:30 spinners of Sulphurs that emerged as duns the evening before returned to the stream with their bright-orange egg sacs to deposit the next generation of that mayfly species. For another half-hour the river was alive with trout rising everywhere— in the pool, in the riffle above, and at the tail. We hastily tied a Sulphur Spinner imitation on Dave's leader, fumbling with the clinch knot in the half-light near dusk. Almost every cast brought a strike to Dave's spent-wing imitation.

It was now near 9:00, and still some trout rose to the diminishing supply of adult naturals. Dave pleaded with me to stay for a few more casts, but I reminded him that we had to head back to the car about a half-mile away and I didn't want to stumble through the undergrowth in total darkness. That evening—the first evening Dave ever fly-fished—he caught and released a half-dozen trout. Granted, for an accomplished fly-fisherman, catching a half-dozen trout under the conditions Dave and I found that evening would have made just an average evening. But for someone who had not cast a fly or caught a trout on a fly, that night's fishing was quite an accomplishment.

As we headed back to the car, Dave kept asking when we could return for another exciting night of fishing. This is what success produces—not a dying interest in the sport, but an everlasting devotion to fly-fishing.

Why did Dave experience immediate success on the Little Juniata that night? First he fly-fished over trout actively feeding on a plentiful supply of naturals. Second I knew which mayflies would appear and at about what time, and I had prepared for the occasion with an adequate supply of imitations to copy the hatches and spinner fall. Third we didn't elect to fly-fish over a natural that was too small, but rather used fairly large mayflies copied with patterns on sizes 14 and 16. And finally, we selected hatches like the Sulphur and the Light Cahill, which are surprisingly predictable in their appearance. With a little knowledge of the hatches of Pennsylvania you will experience the same type of success whether or not you are an accomplished fly-fisherman. Dozens of the state's other great trout streams have equally superb hatches and would likely result in success similar to what Dave and I experienced. That is, if you take some time to learn a little about the hatches.

Mayflies, Caddis Flies, and Stoneflies

Many words may be foreign to the beginning fly-fisherman: hatch, spinner, dun, spinner fall, nymph, natural, and so on. To understand why trout take wet flies, dry flies, and nymphs, it's essential to have a basic understanding of the biology of the aquatic insects on which they feed and so come to understand these terms. Let's first look at a typical life cycle of a mayfly.

Mayflies of different genera lay their eggs in different ways. Some sit on the water to deposit the fertilized eggs, others drop the eggs while flying above the water, others sit on the water for a short period and deposit their eggs and then take flight again. Some (like most of the genus *Ephemerella*) carry their eggs in a ball or sac under the female's abdomen and drop them into the water. After depositing eggs the female mayfly *spinner* (the adult capable of mating) usually dies, often on the surface of a stream.

In the stream the eggs take several weeks to hatch into nymphs (the larval form of the mayfly). These nymphs usually have specific habitats.

Some closely related mayflies live in loose gravel (*Ephemera*); some live in mud or silt (*Hexagenia*); others live under rocks (*Stenonema, Epeorus*); some species live on or in aquatic weeds (some *Ephemerella* species); and others swim freely about the bottom of the stream (*Isonychia*). Not only are scores of nymphs specific in their habitat, but also many kinds are particular in the velocity of the water where they live. Slate Drakes (*Isonychia*) usually inhabit fast-water sections of a stream. Hendricksons (*Ephemerella subvaria*) are found in all types of water, but Yellow Drakes (*Ephemera varia*) customarily occupy slower areas, usually pools of a stream. Other nymphs, like the Speckle-Winged Dun (*Callibaetis*), regularly inhabit ponds and lakes.

Most mayfly species live under water for about 340 days as nymphs, although there are numerous exceptions. As the nymph feeds and grows, it regularly sheds its skin or exoskeleton and develops a new one. Some species, depending on size and length of time they live as nymphs, go through five or ten of these transformations, called instars.

A year after the eggs were fertilized, the nymph begins to move toward the surface. At or near the water's surface the nymph splits its skin dorsally and appears on the surface as a mayfly *dun*, or *subimago*, an immature, non-mating adult. (There are exceptions here, however, like *Epeorus*.) The mayfly dun rests on the water for a split second to several minutes, depending again on the species and on the weather, before flying away. Abnormally cold weather, especially in the spring and fall, delays or prevents the dun from taking flight. These conditions are of special importance to the fly-fisherman.

If and when the dun or subimago escapes, it flies toward a branch to rest. On extremely cold, miserable days many duns struggle to rocks or debris on the shoreline and remain there. In a couple hours to a day or more the dun again goes through a transformation, loses its outer skin (pellicle), and becomes a *spinner* (also called an adult or imago) with glassy, clear wings. This spinner is a mating adult. Often, in the evening, male spinners form a swarm over the water, waiting for females to join them. When the females enter the swarm, they are impregnated by the males. Females then move toward the water's surface and deposit their fertilized eggs, and the cycle begins again. Mayflies live out of the water as air-breathing duns and spinners usually less than five days. Thus the name for the order of insects that contains the mayflies is Ephemeroptera, which comes from the Greek for short-lived.

This is a very generalized description, and there many exceptions. For example, some mayflies like the female White Mayfly (*Ephoron*) never change into a spinner but mate as a dun. A few species remain as nymphs for two years (some *Ephemera* species), and many life cycles last only a few months (some *Baetis, Pseudocloeon*, and others). This latter type, with multiple broods, may appear as many as three times a year.

When the term hatch is used in this book, it usually refers to duns emerging on the surface. When the nymph splits its pellicle or skin near the surface and changes into a dun, it is referred to as an emerger. *Spinner fall* is that time when females (and in some instances males) return to the water to deposit eggs and fall onto the surface spent, or with wings out-stretched. Natural refers to the nymph, dun, or spinner of a species.

Caddis flies (Order Trichoptera) and stoneflies (Order Plecoptera) are similar to the mayfly in their development. Stoneflies and mayflies, however, lack one stage of the complete insect life cycle and are therefore considered to have incomplete metamorphosis. Caddis flies pass through this phase, called the pupa or resting phase (diapause). This period usually lasts several weeks. Caddis fly larvae, like mayfly nymphs, are specific in their habitat. Unlike stonefly and mayfly nymphs, however, caddis larvae lack the tough outer shell called the exoskeleton. Therefore, some caddis (but not all) construct a protective shelter or case. Caddis flies can be grouped according to the type of case they build. Some, like the Green Caddis (*Rhyacophila*), are free swimmers on the bottom and construct no shelter. Other important Pennsylvania caddis, like the Grannoms (*Brachycentrus*), build a case of twigs. Still others build a cover in the form of a net (the Little Black Caddis), and the Dark-Blue Sedge(*Psilotreta*), common on many Pennsylvania waters, makes a case of coarse stone fragments. The nymph turns into a pupa inside its case.

Stonefly nymphs take one to three years to develop, depending on the species. When they do emerge, mating by male and female usually takes place when they are resting on some surface rather than while they are in flight.

You can see by the brief description of the life cycles of mayflies, stoneflies, and caddis flies that the nymph or larva of a species is available to trout almost every day of the year, whereas the adult is available for only about a week. Nymph fishing by a skilled angler will usually outperform fly-fishing using dry flies—*when there is no hatch.* During a hatch the dry fly reigns supreme, except when few trout rise to the supply of naturals on the surface.

The Hatches on Pennsylvania Streams

Several years ago a fly-fisherman called me from Massachusetts and asked if he could fish with me and see some of those hatches I had written about in *Meeting and Fishing the Hatches.* John and I met on a central-Pennsylvania stream, Spruce Creek, in mid-May. We were on the upper section of Spruce Creek near the town of Baileyville. In this area Spruce is extremely small, only about ten feet wide. Within an hour of our initial meeting a concentrated Sulphur hatch appeared on the surface. Streambred browns almost anticipated the hatch and began rising just as the hatch began. Thus John saw his first hatch of mayflies. Many people react similarly, telling me that they have never experienced the great hatches and spinner falls that writers describe. After ten years of fly-fishing this was the first hatch that he had ever seen.

Why don't more fisherman fish the hatches and spinner falls? Are such occurrences rare? Are hatches found on only a few, select Pennsylvania streams?

Much of the general neglect of hatches by fishermen comes from a lack of information. Many fisherman are amazed at how predictable the mayflies' appearance can be. Fish the Little Juniata, Spruce, Spring, Falling Springs, and many other streams on an evening in late May, and you'll see a Sulphur hatch. Fish Spring Creek, West Valley Creek, or one of hundreds of other streams on a mid-July morning, and you can be certain that there will be a Trico hatch. A knowledge of the hatches—on what days they might appear, at what time of day, on what stream or river, and what to use to copy the hatch—all combine to transform a frustrating fishing experience into a successful trip.

In any discussion of the major hatches on Pennsylvania streams according to the time of year that they appear, there are a few disclaimers to remember. These concern the life cycle of mayflies, caddis flies, and stoneflies. Some species have more than one brood a year; that is, they lay their eggs, develop as nymphs, and hatch two or more times a season. Some of the mayflies have more than two broods. Although hatches are generally predictable, emergence dates vary from year to year by as much as a few weeks. Dates shown in the charts in this book are approximate average dates of the first appearances of the insect in central Pennsylvania. Hatches occur earlier in the southern part of the state and later in the north.

Time of day a species will probably appear is also given. This often varies because of weather. For example under normal April weather conditions, the Hendrickson hatch on the Bald Eagle Creek in central Pennsylvania appears on the surface from 2:00 to 4:00 P.M. Two years ago, in a particularly warm April, Hendricksons appeared on the first day of the season, April 19, almost a week ahead of schedule for that stream. Not only did the Hendrickson appear prematurely in the year, but also it emerged earlier in the day than what is customary. On that opening day with an 80-degree air temperature, the Hendrickson arrived on the surface a good three or four hours ahead of schedule. By 10:00 A.M. the surface was filled with duns. Some years earlier, on the same stream, the Hendrickson hatch appeared after 6:00 P.M..

In Chapter 10 possible body colors for imitating various duns and spinners are suggested. Body color often varies considerably from stream to stream. Look at the Green Drake on Penns Creek and compare it with the same species found on Kettle Creek or Cedar Run. On Cedar the Green Drake's underbelly is white, whereas on Penns and Kettle it is a dark cream. Body size also differs from stream to stream. The Green Drake on Penns Creek is a good two to three hook sizes larger than the same insect found on Cedar and Kettle.

Finally, if you've fished the hatches for any length of time, you already know that not all insects are found on all streams. Maybe your favorite stream has only one, two, or three major hatches all season. That's true for the lower end of the Bald Eagle. Yet it's a terrific trout stream—if you fish when one of the three species appears.

How to Read the Charts

Use the emergence charts in this chapter only as rough guides. Many deviations occur in the dates listed, the times of day certain species appear, and insect coloration and size. Furthermore, although a hatch is listed for certain streams (in Chapters 3 through 9), it may well not be included in the charts. Let's examine some of the events that can change emergence dates and habits.

Column one lists the common name for the dun and the spinner of a species, with the dun listed above, the spinner below. Common names on the chart vary from region to region. Those listed are probably used most often.

The second column lists the scientific name of the mayfly, stonefly, or caddis fly species. Several hundred species of these insects are common on Pennsylvania streams and rivers; therefore it's impossible to detail all of them. Included are most of the hatches you'll meet on Pennsylvania waters.

In column three the approximate average first date on which the species appears is given. Dates provided are average dates for central Pennsylvania. Remember, these dates vary by as much as two weeks.

The fourth column suggests the time of day at which the dun appears on the surface or the spinner fall occurs. Again, these change from day to day and year to year.

The final column suggests the best hook size to imitate the species. This too varies from stream to stream for the same species. A good rule of thumb is that most Blue Quills (*Paraleptophlebia* species) can be copied with a size-18 hook, many Little Blue-Winged Olive Duns and Blue Duns (*Baetis* and *Pseudocloeon* species) are effectively imitated with a size-20, and most Sulphurs with a size 16-hook.

THE EARLY SEASON HATCHES—APRIL TO MID-MAY

Common Name	Scientific Name	Average Date	Time of Day	Hook Size
Mayflies				
Little Blue-Winged Olive	*Baetis tricaudatus* (*Baetis vagans*)	April 1	11:00 A.M.	16–20
Rusty Spinner			Afternoon	
Blue Quill Dark Brown Spinner	*Paraleptophlebia adoptiva*	April 18	11:00 A.M. Afternoon	18
Quill Gordon Red Quill Spinner	*Epeorus pleuralis*	April 20	1:00 P.M. Afternoon	14
Hendrickson or Red Quill Red Quill Spinner	*Ephemerella subvaria*	April 21	2:00 P.M. Afternoon or early evening	14
Black Quill Early Brown Spinner	*Leptophlebia cupida*	April 25	2:00 P.M. Afternoon	14
Great Speckled Olive Dun Great Speckled Spinner	*Siphloplecton basale*	April 20	1:00 P.M. Afternoon	14
Little Blue Dun Rusty Spinner	*Pseudoclocon* species	May 1	Afternoon and evening Afternoon	20
Sulphur Dun Sulphur Spinner	*Ephemerella rotunda*	May 12	7:00 P.M. Evening	16

Caddis Flies				
Little Olive Caddis	*Hydropsyche bronta*	April 10	Morning and afternoon	16
Little Black Caddis	*Chimarra atterima*	April 15	11:00 A.M.	18
Grannom	*Brachycentrus numerosus*	April 20	Morning and afternoon	12
Cream Caddis	*Psilotreta* species	April 25	Morning and afternoon	14
Green Caddis	*Rhyacophila* species	May 1	Morning and afternoon	14
Dark-Brown Caddis	*Deplectrona modesta*	May 15	Morning and afternoon	12
Stoneflies				
Little Black Stonefly	*Capnia vernalis*	March 1	Morning and afternoon	16
Early Brown Stonefly	*Strophopteryx fasciata**	April 10	Noon	14
Great Brown Stonefly	*Phasganophora capitata*	April 20	Morning and afternoon	12
Light Stonefly	*Isoperla signata*	May 8	Afternoon	14

*Also copies *Taeniopteryx nivalis*

The April Grays

Another trout season has begun in Pennsylvania. Is this the year you devote entirely to fly-fishing? But wait, you say, productive fly-fishing doesn't begin until late in May. Ask those frustrated anglers on several opening days when Blue Quills, Quill Gordons, or Hendricksons have appeared. Ask them if they would have exchanged their spinning rods for fly rods.

If they wouldn't, they're in error. As soon as the water temperature approaches 50 degrees insect activity begins, and trout can be caught. Usually this occurs first in the southeastern part of the state. On hundreds of occasions I've witnessed not just one hatch the third or fourth week in April, but rather two, and often three hatches appearing concurrently. Dozens of streams, especially those in the north-central region like the Loyalsock, Cedar Run, Slate Run, Cross Fork, and Kettle Creek, contain all three April hatches.

Fishing often is extremely variable on these first days of the fishing year, however. Early spring produces cold water which in turn might delay the predicted hatches. But fly-fish on your favorite stream that contains the early hatches, and you can experience an early bonus.

I like to fish the Loyalsock or Lycoming Creeks from April 20 to 25, especially after the water has had time to moderate. When the water temperature is above 50 degrees (preferably above 52 degrees) the three gray hatches of April emerge rapidly. Fly-fish when the air temperature is below 60 degrees and the sky is cloudy, and you have all the ingredients for a successful trip. On several trips to the Loyalsock in Lycoming County I have experienced just those favorable conditions.

When I checked the water temperature on the upper end of the Loyalsock's fly-fishing only section around 10:00 A.M. it registered 52 degrees. It was April 22, and I felt confident that a hatch would occur. Little did I realize that three separate species would appear. By 11:00 A.M. Blue Quills, struggling desperately to become airborne, rode the surface from the pool to the riffle below. Few if any of the duns took flight, but only an occasional trout rose to the first surface food of the year.

Shortly after 12:30 P.M. the first Quill Gordon appeared. Several trout, awakened by this larger food supply, started to rise for the stunned duns. Not one of these duns appeared to escape the combined misfortunes of cold air and high water to take flight. Trout went on a feeding frenzy, with dozens of fish feeding. Cast after cast hooked trout on a size-14 imitation. The hatch seemed to last for hours. Stunned duns from miles above still drifted past me at 2:00 P.M., and trout still rose to the bonanza from upstream. A third species, the Hendrickson, then complicated matters by appearing on the surface. This last species didn't emerge in the numbers the other two had, probably because this was just the beginning of the Hendrickson hatch. The next few days might produce a greater number.

Little Pine Creek in north-central Pennsylvania also contains the three April Grays. Often, from April 20 to April 25, the three emerge simultaneously. Fred Templin and I have had countless memorable trips to Pine and Little Pine Creeks. Once we hit Little Pine on the third week in April and fly-fished over all three hatches. As is often the case in April, the water level was high on Little Pine, and it seemed almost impossible to fish with anything smaller than a Muddler or Woolly Bugger. About 11:00 A.M. a sporadic hatch of miniature Blue Quills appeared in the eddy of a swollen pool in the Carson Flat section. Even with the runoff from a recent late-spring snowstorm, trout began to feed on these small, dark-gray naturals. Not only did they rise in the back eddy protected by a huge fallen hemlock, but now they began rising in the riffle above and throughout the pool. Blue Quills appeared on the surface by the hundreds, not by the tens as they had before. Shortly after noon a second, larger, gray fly appeared in amongst the smaller mayflies. Some trout still fed on the smaller Blue Quill, while others switched abruptly to the Quill Gordon. Which trout was taking which fly? Have you ever felt that you should have prepared for fishing with two fly rods complete with two imitations?

By 2:00 P.M. surface action subsided and Fred and I moved upstream to the next fairly slow pool—and just in time. The Hendrickson had already begun to emerge. It seemed like trout captured any natural that rested before struggling to become airborne. Almost all of the surface feeders readily took the imitation, with isolated refusals.

What a day! Three hatches, rising trout, few refusals, and not one other fly-fisherman to enjoy the event. Maybe the cold weather or the high water kept them away.

I prefer dry fly-fishing, but many early-season excursions depend on the proper weather and water conditions; poor conditions limit dry fly-fishing. How many of these early trips with high water have been saved with a wet fly or nymph copying one of the April grays? Just before and during hatches in April the Hendrickson Nymph has rescued me from many a barren day. On other days and other streams, like the Mehoopany in northeastern Pennsylvania, a Quill Gordon wet fly has worked.

More than it affects any other mayflies, weather affects the hatching activity of the April grays. A few days of extremely cold weather when the Quill Gordon or Hendrickson appear can produce a sparse hatch the next year. Even though one or all of these April mayflies inhabits a stream, the density of the species varies significantly because of the hazards of early-spring weather.

It's April and the season has just begun. Will you be ready for the April grays with plenty of size-18 Blue Quills, 14 Quill Gordons, 14 Hendricksons and Red Quills, and some size-14 Black Quills? Or will you, like so many other fishermen, become frustrated at the first hatch of the season because you're ill prepared?.

Caddis Time

April has ended, and the first spring hatches are a thing of the past. Annually there's a dearth of hatches during the first two weeks in May. Usually the last mayfly species of the early season to appear is the Black Quill around the end of April. The next species, the Sulphur, doesn't emerge for about two weeks. What do you do now? Those early-May days are prime times to fly-fish for caddis. Look at the Little Juniata River, Spring Creek, or the lower Bald Eagle—all three have excellent Green Caddis hatches appearing around May 5. Visit Pine Creek around May 1, and you'll likely encounter the concentrated but often frustrating Cream Caddis hatch. Thousands of these caddis flies appear in the air throughout the day on Pine Creek. Or visit Penns Creek or Big Fishing Creek in the latter part of April, and you'll probably encounter a Black Caddis or a

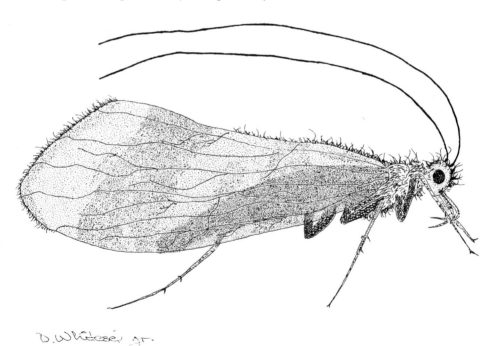

D. Whitese, jr.

Caddis Fly

Grannom hatch. All of these heavy caddis hatches appear in a relatively short time from late April through mid-May.

Maybe you've become frustrated with caddis hatches. Often when caddis are in the air, I cast about violently with a dry-fly imitation, like the fluttering caddis, trying to tempt a trout to the surface. More often, however, trout are feeding on the emerging pupae as they try to escape to the surface. Look, for example, at the splashing rises so evident during caddis hatches. These rises are a certain sign that trout are chasing emerging pupae, not the adult.

A series of events on the Little Juniata River changed my thinking on fishing a caddis hatch. As usual I tied on a Green Caddis dry fly, as thousands of the naturals fluttered past me. Few trout rose, but I continued to cast. Suddenly, my dry fly sank and became a wet fly submerged just a few inches beneath the surface. As my Green Caddis made its first swing or arc as a wet fly, I noticed a swirl at the fly. On the next cast I deliberately fished the pattern wet and twitched it slightly as it made its swing. This time another swirl at the fly, and then a strike. I fished the rest of the afternoon and evening with that dry fly converted to a wet fly, caught dozens of trout, and missed countless others. On many casts with the Green Caddis I had multiple strikes.

I went home that evening to my fly-tying vise and tied a few dozen emerging Green Caddis pupae patterns which have changed little since that initial success. I tied the pattern on a size-18 hook with a body made of gray-green ultra translucent nymph dubbing and a couple turns of a dark-brown grouse hackle to imitate the legs and wings of the emerger. The pattern continues to be one of the most effective on Pennsylvania streams in early May.

Caddis flies aren't limited to the north-central streams of the state. They appear in considerable numbers on many others. Bowman Creek has a fishable Grannom hatch in May and a Spotted Sedge later in the same month. Valley Creek in the southeastern part of the state near Valley Forge has an excellent Green Caddis hatch early in March and April. And Oil Creek in northwestern Pennsylvania has a tremendous caddis population.

If it's May it's prime caddis time. Caddis patterns are effective through most of the season, however. In July and August when you see splashing rises and some caddis on the water, switch to a pupa imitation. Possibly the best time to fly-fish on the lower Bald Eagle is July or August in the morning. Riffles which the night before seemed to be void of any remaining trout come alive for a half-hour or so when a Green Caddis makes its appearance. Although a number of caddis species select the early part of May to appear, don't forget your caddis patterns for the entire season—caddis time is almost any time during the fishing season in Pennsylvania.

THE MID-SEASON HATCHES—MAY 15 TO JULY 1

Common Name	Scientific Name	Average Date	Time of Day	Hook Size
Mayflies				
Sulphur Dun	(see early season)			
Gray Fox	Stenonema fuscum	May 15	Afternoon	12–14
Ginger Quill Spinner			Evening	
Pale Evening Dun	Ephemerella septentrionalis	May 15	Evening	14–16
Pale Evening Spinner			Evening	
Pale Evening Dun	Hexagenia aphrodite	May 18	Evening	16
Pale Evening Spinner			Evening	
March Brown	Stenonema vicarium	May 18	Morning and afternoon	12–14
Great Red Spinner			Evening	
Light Cahill	Stenacron interpunctatum*	May 23	Evening	14
Light Cahill Spinner			Evening	
Chocolate Dun	Ephemerella bicolor and needhami	May 25	Late morning and early afternoon	16
Chocolate Spinner			Afternoon and evening	
Green Drake	Ephemera guttulata	May 25	Evening	8–12
Coffin Fly			Evening	
Brown Drake	Ephemera simulans	May 25	Evening	10–12
Brown Drake Spinner			Evening	

Fly	Scientific Name	Date	Time	Hook Size
Light Cahill Ginger Quill Spinner	*Stenonema ithaca*	May 25	Evening Evening	14
Dark-Green Drake Brown Drake Spinner	*Litobrancha recurvata*	May 25	Afternoon and evening	6–10
Slate Drake	*Isonychia sadleri and bicolor*	May 25	Evening	12
White Gloved Howdy			Evening	
Cream Cahill Cream Cahill Spinner	*Stenonema modestum*	May 25	Evening Evening	14 or 16
Blue-Winged Olive Dun	*Drunella (Ephemerella) cornuta*	May 25	Late morning	14
Dark-Olive Spinner			Evening	
Blue-Winged Olive Dun	*Drunella (Ephemerella) longicornus*	May 25	Early morning	16
Olive Spinner			Evening	
Pink Cahill Salmon Spinner	*Epeorus itreus*	May 25	Evening Evening	14–16
Sulphur Dun Sulphur Spinner	*Ephemerella invaria*	June 1	Evening Evening	16–18
Dark-Blue Quill	*Serratella (Ephemerella) deficiens*	June 1	Evening	18–20
Dark-Olive Spinner			Evening	

* Includes *S. interpunctatum interpunctatum* and *S. interpunctatum canadense*.

Common Name	Scientific Name	Average Date	Time of Day	Hook Size
Blue Quill	*Paraleptophlebia mollis*	June 3	Morning and afternoon	18
Dark-Brown Spinner (F) Jenny Spinner (M)				
Iron Blue Dun Blue Quill Spinner (F) Jenny Spinner (M)	*Leptophlebia johnsoni*	June 5	Late morning Evening	16
Little Blue-Winged Olive Dun	*Baetis levitans*	June 5	Afternoon and evening Evening	20
Rusty Spinner				
Little Blue-Winged Olive Dun	*Dannella (Ephemerella) simplex*	June 15	Morning and afternoon Evening	18–20
Dark-Olive Spinner				
Blue-Winged Olive Dun	*Drunella (Ephemerella) lata*	June 15	Morning and afternoon Evening	16
Dark-Olive Spinner				
Light Cahill Light Cahill Spinner	*Heptagenia marginalis*	June 15	Evening	14
Cream Cahill Cream Cahill Spinner	*Stenonema pulchellum*	June 15	Evening	14–16
Sulphur Dun* Sulphur Spinner	*Ephemerella dorothea*	June 15	Evening	18

Common Name	Scientific Name	Date	Time	Hook Size
Yellow Drake Yellow Drake Spinner	*Ephemera varia*	June 20	Evening	12
Blue Quill Dark-Brown Spinner	*Paraleptophlebia guttata*	June 25	Morning Morning and afternoon	18
Golden Drake Golden Spinner	*Potamanthus distinctus*	June 25	Evening	12–14
Pale Evening Dun Pale Evening Spinner	*Heptagenia* species	June 25	Evening	16
Caddis Flies Spotted Sedge	*Symphitopsyche slossanae*	May 23	Afternoon	14
Dark-Blue Sedge	*Psilotreta frontalis*	June 5	Evening	12
Stoneflies Yellow Sally	*Isoperla bilineata*	June 5	Afternoon	14
Little Green Stonefly	*Alloperla imbecilla*	June 5	Afternoon	16
Great Stonefly	*Phasganophora capitata*	June 5	Afternoon and evening	10
Great Brown Stonefly	*Acroneuria lycorias*	June 15	Morning and afternoon	12

* This species is often called the Pale Evening Dun.

If you had to select just one week of the entire fishing season in which you could fly-fish, which week would it be? For me, in central Pennsylvania it would be May 25 to June 1. Why? Within that span of a week you'll witness Sulphur, Light Cahill, Green Drake, Brown Drake, Slate Drake, March Brown, Blue-Winged Olive Dun and Gray Fox hatches—and many others—on Pennsylvania streams. Don't expect all these hatches on all your favorite streams: fly-fishing is often easier if the water is not congested with multiple hatches. When it is, selecting the proper imitation is often arduous. Look at Penns Creek as an example. Droves of enthusiastic fly-fisherman head there for the acclaimed Green Drake hatch and Coffin Fly spinner fall. The majority of these avid anglers come away from their experience disappointed. Often, at the end of May, when these hatches are in their prime on Penns, so too are several other hatches. Sulphur duns and spinners, Ginger Quills, Light Cahills—all these appear at the same time as the Drake.

In late May many Pennsylvania streams display at least two or three hatches—the Sulphur, Light Cahill, and the Green Drake. The north-central and northeastern streams exhibit Blue-Winged Olives, March Browns, and Gray Foxes during the day, and Brown Drakes, Gray Foxes, Slate Drakes, and Green Drakes in the evening.

We'll examine in some detail two of the largest mayflies to appear at this time of the year, the Green Drake and the Brown Drake.

It's Brown Drake Time

The Brown Drake is alive and well on at least nineteen Pennsylvania streams. It has been fifteen years since I first witnessed this superb hatch on Pine Creek. I was totally unprepared for the hatch and the events that followed.

On June 3 several of us decided to try our luck on the lower end of Cedar Run in Lycoming County. About 7:00 P.M. large male spinners began appearing overhead in an undulating flight so common for some species. This impressive but unfamiliar spinner dumbfounded all of us with its unexpected appearance that evening. What was it? Could it be an enlarged version of the March Brown adult—the Great Red Spinner? Within a half-hour the gorge on the lower end of Cedar filled with layers of male and female spinners. We moved down to the mouth of Cedar where it enters Pine Creek.

The water on Pine above Cedar Run felt warm to the touch and was in the low 70s. Just below Cedar, Pine registered 68 degrees, evidently reduced by the cooling effects of this moderate-sized tributary—perfect for the massive spinner fall that was about to unfold. This was to be the greatest spinner fall that any of us had ever seen. By 8:00 P.M. thousands of fertilized females, laden with eggs, moved upstream past us in unison, just a few feet above Pine's surface. The females were so profuse that all of us heard a humming from the movement of their wings. We were still perplexed. What was this hatch? We all agreed that it had to be an abnormally large Great Red Spinner.

Now the spinners touched the water. We tied on Great Red Spinners with spent wings and started casting to more than fifty trout rising in the eddy just below Cedar Run. Trout nearby gorged themselves on this huge supply of food, sucking in three and four spinners at a time. By now thousands of spinners descended to the surface. I captured a spent spinner nearby and examined it. It definitely was not a Great Red Spinner; it was, in fact, a species I had seen only once before, on the Beaverkill in New York State. Three of us fished in total confusion that evening—we had hundreds of trout rising around us but could catch only a few of them on the Great Red Spinner and later on an Early Brown Spinner imitation.

I collected a few male spinners to take home with me to identify later. The wings looked heavily spotted or barred under my stereo microscope. This suggested that the species was member of the Genus *Ephemera*, closely related to the Green Drake and Yellow Drake. It was, in fact, the Brown Drake (*Ephemera simulans*). I vowed never again to visit Pine Creek without a good supply of Brown Drake imitations, so I tied a dozen to resemble both the dun and spinner.

It wasn't until two seasons later that I next encountered the Brown Drake. I had told Greg Hoover stories about the tremendous hatch on Pine Creek and he was anxious to see it. Greg did a graduate paper on the Green Drake on Penns Creek and is one of the most knowledgeable entomologists in the East. We arrived on Pine Creek, two miles below Cedar Run. Dana and Dave Poust, of Waterville, and Tom Finkbiner, of Slate Run, told us that the hatch had begun just two days ago. We started fly-fishing early in the morning on May 28 over the heavy Blue-Winged Olive Dun hatch so common on Pine. Olive duns appeared on the water until well after 10:00 A.M. Shortly after the hatch both Greg and I noticed a small number of female Brown Drakes appearing over the water. The few turned into hundreds by 11:00 A.M., and trout fed on them under an overcast sky. Both of us were surprised at this freak appearance, since the normal time for the spinner fall is near dusk. We quickly tied on appropriate patterns and cast toward a dozen or so trout feeding on this larger mayfly. The pattern worked. No disappointment like the last encounter with this species—the trout freely took the imitation.

Near dusk thousands of the Brown Drakes appeared over the water in their egg-laying ritual. One problem developed, though—the water temperature had risen above 70 degrees from the hot late-May day. Spinners fell, but only a dozen or so trout rose to them, and those that did rise seemed to do so lethargically. Greg complained about the few trout that rose to the tremendous spinner fall.

Water temperature, however, is only one of the obstacles to successful fishing with the Brown Drake. At best the Brown Drake appears on Pine for four days; at worst it appears for as little as three. On numerous occasions I have missed the hatch and spinner fall completely because of their brief appearance. Before you travel to Pine Creek for the Brown Drake, check with someone near the stream on the status of the hatch.

Another impediment to making the Brown Drake the prime hatch of Pennsylvania is the temperamental nature of the species. Even when duns have emerged, I have waited in vain a day or two later at dusk for the spinners to return to the water. They never did one spectacular evening on Pine Creek. Male spinners formed a swarm around 8:00 P.M., and females entered the swarm to mate. Females normally should have flown back to the stream and deposited their eggs. On occasion these females fly back to the trees and not to the stream, canceling any chance for a great evening of matching the spinner fall.

A final barrier to fishing the Brown Drake hatch successfully is its limited distribution. Brown Drakes appear on First Fork, East Fork, Cross Fork, Kettle, and Pine. I have heard reports that some Brown Drakes exist on Thompson Creek in Crawford County, Neshannock Creek in southern Mercer County, and the upper part of the Delaware River above Equinunk in Wayne County.

The extensive Green Drake hatch on Penns Creek is fairly predictable. Once the species begins appearing on the lower end near Weikert, hatching activity moves upstream four to six miles each night until it reaches Coburn. Not so with the Brown Drake, although there is some evidence to substantiate the claim that the spinner fall extends a day longer in the Cedar Run area than near Slate Run, six miles downstream.

The past few years the Brown Drake hasn't emerged in the numbers it once did on Pine Creek. Tom Finkbiner at Slate Run bemoans the loss of this great hatch on the stretch from Blackwell downstream to Waterville. Tom feels that acid water from nearby mines, entering from Babb Creek at Blackwell, has caused the decline of the Drake.

With all of its shortcomings, the Brown Drake has the potential to be the most sensational hatch you'll encounter in your life. For in a short period of time you'll witness an explosive hatch or spinner fall and large trout, some over twenty inches long, gorging themselves on the large mayfly. At the same time you'll find scant competing fly-fishermen, and best of all, if you've prepared for the hatch and spinner fall, you'll probably experience a productive, rewarding evening on a spectacular stream.

Even though the hatch on Pine Creek has declined, there are at least eighteen other Commonwealth streams that harbor the Brown Drake. Pick your stream from those below, and be prepared for the hatch of a lifetime.

SOME PENNSYLVANIA STREAMS WITH BROWN DRAKE HATCHES

1. Allegheny River (Coudersport area)
2. Oswayo Creek (spotty)
3. Neshannock Creek
4. Cool Spring Creek (Mercer County)
5. North Fork, Red Bank
6. First Fork, Sinnemahoning
7. Driftwood Branch, Sinnemahoning
8. Pine Creek
9. Kettle Creek
10. Delaware River
11. Raystown Branch, Juniata River (Everett area)
12. Loyalhanna Creek
13. Little Mahoning Creek
14. East Branch, Mahoning Creek
15. Callen Run (Jefferson County)
16. Slippery Rock Creek (upper end)
17. Thompson Creek
18. East Fork, Sinnemahoning Creek
19. Ninemile Run

Three Weeks with the Green Drake

Mayflies catch but a fleeting glimpse at an above-water environment. That's why they're called ephemeral. Many live as adults only two to five days. Some mayfly species emerge just a few days on a stream and then are gone for another year; others appear on a stream for a week or more. A scant few, like the Trico, emerge for two or three months, and some species emerge several times every year. The Green Drake often exists above water on a particular stream for less than a week. Would you like to stretch the length of the Green Drake hatch from less than a week to two or three weeks?

Twenty years ago Dick Mills and I began fishing the great Green Drake hatch on Penns Creek. We had a friend in Millheim near the stream who called us every time the hatch appeared. Dick Mills, Tom Taylor, Lloyd Williams, and I fished that hatch for some years but always returned home to the Wilkes-Barre area disillusioned. Why? Normally we'd encounter a tremendous hatch of duns or an impressive Coffin Fly spinner fall, but rarely did we do well during the excitement. Certainly trout rose for the surface food, but they routinely refused our imitations.

Many anglers contend that the only really heavy Green Drake hatch exists on Penns Creek. The Green Drake is part of the mystique of that stream. The species, however, is abundant on a surprisingly large number of Pennsylvania streams. It is so common that you can start in south-central

Pennsylvania the third week in May and continue to fish over the same species a couple weeks later on some of the northeastern and north-central streams.

For several years Ed Gunnett, of Williamsburg, recounted stories about a fantastic Green Drake hatch on a local stream. He promised to alert me when the hatch next appeared. We met on Canoe Creek at 6:00 P.M. on May 23 to witness this impressive hatch. When we arrived we scanned the water at a pool just a few miles upstream from Canoe Creek Dam. Already hundreds of Green Drake duns were in flight, and trout cruised the pool catching laggards.

Canoe Creek is a small, unimpressive trout stream. With its brush-covered banks and narrow pools, even skilled flycasters find it difficult to cover rising trout. Further, by the third week in May the water level was a mere trickle compared to its spring flow. Small pools and shallow riffles produced difficult fly-fishing.

By 7:00 P.M. dozens of Green Drakes, as large as the Penns Creek version, thrashed on the surface in an attempt to make their heavy bodies airborne. In each miniature pool trout rose to these massive mayflies. The Green Drake that evening had the stage all to itself; only a handful of Sulphurs appeared. There was no confusion about what the fish were taking, so my son, Bryan, and Ed tied on Green Drake dry flies. Just about every trout that rose to a natural that evening took the copy.

Canoe's Green Drake hatch is different from the same hatch on Penns. The number of Drakes on the water that evening was sufficient to bring trout to the surface, but it wasn't excessive, as it often is on Penns Creek. After a trout captured a Green Drake, it might be a minute before another dun passed overhead, giving a fisherman plenty of time to cover the trout with an imitation. There were few other mayflies on the surface that evening, a second advantage to fishing the hatch.

In pool after pool Bryan and Ed caught trout on the Green Drake dry fly, some of the trout exceeding fifteen inches on this small, heavily fished stream near Altoona. Duns emerged for more than two hours that evening, while trout rose in concert with the hatch.

Four days later, on May 27, Bryan and I headed to three small but extremely productive streams vacated by most of the early-spring anglers. These three—Vanscoyoc, Big Fill, and Bald Eagle creeks—have some incredible hatches in late May, and one of these is the Green Drake.

Afternoon fishing in late May is frequently unrewarding if no hatch appears, but Green Drakes typically emerge on these heavily canopied streams during the afternoon. We selected a slow manmade pool about 200 feet long and 10 feet wide on Vanscoyoc Run to watch for the Drakes. By the time we arrived at the pool, Drakes were already in the air. Bryan tied on a Green Drake imitation, and I captured some of the escaping duns. Some of the duns were much larger than others. The smaller dun was the

Green Drake. The larger mayfly was a good two hook sizes bigger than the Green Drake—it was a Dark-Green Drake (*Litobrancha recurvata*). Green Drakes and Dark-Green Drakes appeared to emerge in equal numbers for the next hour—in the middle of a hot late-May day. Trout after rising trout in that small pool took Bryan's imitation. Some of the trout measured over fifteen inches long—from this heavily fished but fertile stream.

On May 29 of the same year I arrived on Pine Creek below Cedar Run just in time for a combined hatch of Brown and Green Drakes. For every four or five Brown Drakes emerging there was one Green Drake. That same evening the Green Drake emerged on Penns just below Coburn.

A week later, on June 5, I fished the same hatch on the narrows on Big Fishing Creek above Lamar. Although Big Fishing Creek is just twenty miles north of Penns, the Drake appears a good week or two later. The water on Big Fishing Creek is much cooler than on Penns, and this delays the emergence for about a week. The hatch on Big Fishing Creek is not as concentrated as it is on Penns; therefore you don't have to contend with as many naturals on the water, and fishing with the Drake seems to be more rewarding.

What a great year! Fly-fishing continued good over Green Drake hatches longer than two weeks on several different streams in central Pennsylvania. On May 23 the hatch appeared on Canoe Creek, later on Vanscoyoc, Pine, and Big Fill creeks. A week later it appeared on Big Fishing Creek. Until ten years ago I was one of those anglers who thought you had to fish Penns Creek to meet a decent hatch of Drakes. Not any more.

With a reasonable awareness of which streams harbor this large burrower and when the mayfly normally appears on each stream, you can extend your Green Drake season, as I did. I began fly-fishing over the

Stony Fork Creek near Wellsboro holds many of the early-season hatches. This stretch produces spectacular hatches of early Blue Quills and Quill Gordons.

Drake on May 23 and concluded it on June 8—seventeen days devoted to fishing over the giant of the East, the Green Drake. How can you extend the time you fly-fish over the Green Drake hatch? Select a couple of the more than fifty Commonwealth streams listed below that contain this giant hatch. Check with local fly-fishermen to see when the hatch appears on those streams, and carry a good selection of nymph, dun, and spinner imitations.

SOME PENNSYLVANIA STREAMS WITH GREEN DRAKE HATCHES

1. Brush Creek (Somerset County)
2. Big Fill
3. Phoenix Run
4. Ninemile Run
5. Hammersley Run
6. Pine Creek
7. Kettle Creek
8. Big Fishing Creek
9. Elk Creek
10. Yellow Creek
11. Spruce Creek
12. North Fork, Red Bank
13. Little Mahoning Creek
14. Lehigh River (above Francis Walter Dam)
15. Honey Creek
16. Kishacoquillas Creek (West Branch)
17. Delaware River
18. Bear Creek (Elk County)
19. Driftwood Branch, Sinnemahoning Creek
20. First Fork Sinnemahoning Creek
21. East Fishing Creek
22. Lost Creek
23. Willow Creek
24. Loyalhanna Creek
25. Canoe Creek
26. Vanscoyoc Run
27. Little Sandy Creek
28. Caldwell Creek
29. Thompson Creek
30. White Deer Creek
31. Allegheny River
32. Oswayo Creek
33. Mill Creek (Potter County)
34. Huntington Creek (Luzerne and Columbia counties)
35. Spring Creek (Warren County)
36. Hayes Creek (upstream)
37. Cove Creek
38. Little Juniata River (around Barree)
39. Cedar Run
40. Slate Run
41. Little Pine Creek
42. Cross Forks
43. Town Creek (Bedford County)
44. Oar Creek (Bedford County)
45. East Branch, Mahoning Creek
46. Big Mill Creek (Elk County)
47. Callen Run (Jefferson)
48. East Fork, Sinnemahoning Creek
49. Grays Run (Lycoming County)
50. West Branch, Pine Creek
51. Millstone Creek (Jefferson County)
52. Young Woman's Creek
53. Genesee Forks (Potter County)
54. Penns Creek
55. Elk Creek (Centre County)
56. Hemlock Creek

THE LATE-SEASON HATCHES—JULY 1 TO OCTOBER

Common Name	Scientific Name	Average Date	Time of Day	Hook Size
Mayflies				
Pale Morning Dun Pale Morning Spinner	*Centroptilum album*	July 15	Morning	22
Little White Mayfly	*Caenis* species	July 15	Evening	28
Little Blue-Winged Olive Rusty Spinner	*Baetis* species	July 15	Afternoon Evening	20
Trico	*Tricorythodes* species	July 15	Morning	24
Slate Drake White-Gloved Howdy	*Isonychia harperi*	July 23	Evening	12–14
White Mayfly	*Ephoron leukon*	August 15	Evening	14–16
Big Slate Drake Dark Rusty Spinner	*Hexagenia atrocaudata*	August 18	Evening	8
Slate Drake White-Gloved Howdy	*Isonychia matilda*	August 25	Afternoon and evening	14
Little Blue Dun Rusty Spinner	*Pseudocloeon* species	September 25	Afternoon	20
Caddis Flies				
Green Caddis	*Rhyacophila* species	July 10	Morning	14
Terrestrials				
Winged Ant	*Monomorium* species	August 25	Afternoon and evening	18–20

The angling crowds of spring have gone. The waters of most of Pennsylvania's trout streams are low. Many of these waters have become marginal habitat with temperatures too high for any trout population. On the bright side, most of the anglers who crowded the streams and rivers in spring have gone, and the waters are clear. The fact is that there are hatches in these weeks, too, and many trout remain in some of Pennsylvania's better streams.

By and large late hatches are meager. With the addition of the Trico on scores of waters, however, you find a small but dependable hatch that continues daily for a few months. Other hatches continue to appear into the late season. Hatches like the Cream Cahill, Light Cahill (*Heptagenia marginalis*), Yellow Drake, and at least two Blue-Winged Olive Dun species (*Drunella* [*Ephemerella*] *lata* and *Drunella* [*Ephemerella*] *cornuta*) persist throughout much of the late summer and into autumn.

This is also the time to use patterns mimicking some of the common terrestrials. Terrestrials like ants, beetles, grasshoppers, and crickets make up much of a trout's diet in July, August, and September. And many Commonwealth streams experience a hatchlike influx of winged ants in late August.

The Trico on Freestones

Fifteen years ago I had the great pleasure of fly-fishing with Barry Beck and Vince Marinaro. Barry has an excellent fly-fishing shop near Benton and is one of the finest fly-fishermen I have ever known. Vince had written several books including the classic *A Modern Dry-Fly Code*. At the same time, Vince was visiting Barry at his country home, next to Fishing Creek in northern Columbia County. It was a muggy July evening, and Vince reminisced about the great Trico hatch present this time of year on Falling Springs.

"I wish we could fish over a Trico hatch tomorrow," Vince remarked, "but I doubt that there are Tricos on any of these freestone streams nearby."

Dick Mills and I indicated that Bowman Creek in Wyoming County, just twenty-five miles away, had a respectable Trico hatch that we had been fishing for the past few years. Although Bowman Creek is quite productive, it is considered a typical freestone stream with little or no dissolved substances (such as calcium) and a pH (a measure of acidity and alkalinity) near or just below 7. Vince pleaded with us to go to Bowman the next morning so he could witness his first Trico hatch on a Pennsylvania freestone stream. Vince and countless others had associated a Trico hatch with limestone water.

We arrived at the fly-fishing-only stretch of Bowman the next morning before eight o'clock. Trico duns had already emerged, and a swarm of male spinners began to form above the riffle at the head of the so-called Barn Pool. Vince waded across the stream so he could get in a good position to view the hatch and spinner fall and to wait for rising trout. His wait was brief, for in ten minutes several browns began feeding on the first female spinners to fall spent. It wasn't long before Vince caught his first trout on a freestone Trico fall. The spinner fall often doesn't last very long on those hot, humid mornings so common in late July. By the time the fall had ended about a half-hour later, Vince had hooked a handful of trout on his size-24 imitation. He was elated at his success and at the surprisingly heavy Trico spinner fall on this freestone water.

If you plan to fish the Trico on one of the more than fifty streams in Pennsylvania that harbor this species, there are a few important points to

John Randolph with a holdover brown trout taken during a Trico fall on the Bald Eagle below Milesburg.

remember. Since male and female are dissimilar in body color and tail structure, carry imitations which copy both sexes. And keep in mind that this is one of a handful of species where both sexes fall to the surface spent. The female, after entering the swarm of males, drops to the surface, lays her eggs, and dies on the water, usually spent—that is, with wings outstretched. Unlike the majority of other species the male spinner also dies over the water.

It seems that the longer the Trico fall occurs, the more difficult the trout are to deceive. Use the same Trico spinner imitation in September that you employed in July, and you'll likely catch fewer fish. Trout seem to be unusually capable of selecting the natural from the copy as the season progresses. I have had innumerable encounters with Trico spinner falls on dozens of Pennsylvania streams over the past twenty years. I've encountered them on northwestern waters like Thompson Creek; on north-central waters like the Loyalsock, Pine, and Kettle; and on southeastern streams like West Valley Creek, just outside Philadelphia. Heavy Trico hatches also develop on central-Pennsylvania streams like Spring, in Centre County, and on the upper end of Clover Creek, near Martinsburg in Blair County.

Yes, Tricos are abundant throughout Pennsylvania. If you want to determine whether or not your favorite stream possesses a Trico spinner fall, examine it on a late-July or August morning preferably between 7:30 and 9:00. Look ten to twenty feet above fast water at the head of a pool for small, undulating mayflies moving in a swarm. On streams like Elk in the central part of the state, some anglers confuse the spinner of the Blue Quill (*Paraleptophlebia guttata*) for the Trico. The Trico, however, is much smaller (size 24 as compared to a size 18 for the spinner of the Blue Quill). In addition Tricos eventually move to the surface of the stream, whereas the larger mayfly undulates for hours.

If you haven't found the Trico on your favorite stream, don't give up your search. Check another part of the stream. The hatch may occur farther up- or downstream. Elk Creek, Clover Creek, and the Little Juniata River are good examples. All three have Trico hatches, but only in selected areas of the streams. Explore the entire stream thoroughly before you conclude that the hatch is missing from the stream.

Elk Creek in Sullivan County contains plenty of holdover trout and a good native brown trout population. The stream joins the Loyalsock just above Hillsgrove. On a recent August morning I witnessed an excellent Trico spinner fall on the lower three miles of this freestone stream. A major tributary to Elk, Hoagland Branch, also has the Trico on its lower mile.

Spend some of those summer mornings on your favorite freestone stream in Pennsylvania—it might just contain a terrific Trico hatch and spinner fall. After all the Trico is more abundant on Commonwealth streams than most anglers realize.

SOME PENNSYLVANIA STREAMS WITH TRICO HATCHES

1. Penns Creek
2. Elk Creek
3. Big Fishing Creek
4. Loyalsock Creek
5. Bowman Creek
6. Delaware River
7. Oswayo Creek
8. Allegheny River
9. Yellow Creek
10. Thompson Creek
11. Caldwell Creek
12. Spring Creek
13. Spruce Creek
14. Bald Eagle Creek (below Milesburg)
15. West Valley Creek
16. Tulpehocken Creek
17. Donegal Creek
18. Big Spring Run
19. LeTort Run
20. Yellow Breeches Creek
21. Falling Springs Creek
22. Slate Run
23. Little Juniata River (spotty)
24. Clover Creek
25. Piney Creek
26. East Fork, Mahoning Creek
27. First Fork. Sinnemahoning Creek
28. Kettle Creek
29. Cross Fork Creek
30. Hoagland Branch (Sullivan County)
31. Elk Creek (Sullivan County)
32. Allegheny River (below the Kinzua Dam)
33. Little Lehigh Creek
34. Cedar Run
35. Little Bushkill Creek
36. Monocacy Creek
37. Lackwaxen River
38. Towanda Creek
39. Buffalo Creek (Union County)
40. Loyalhanna Creek
41. Fishing Creek—lower section (Columbia County)
42. Spring Run (Fulton County)
43. Big Cove Creek (one mile below Big Cove Tannery)
44. Genesee Forks
45. Ninemile Run (Potter County)
46. Brodhead Creek
47. Pine Creek (Lycoming County)

White Mayflies in August

Hatches appear early and abundantly on the Little Juniata River. As early as May 1 I've seen Yellow and Green Caddis bring brown trout to the surface. By mid-May, Sulphurs dot the evening surface of this productive river. The last week in May, Light Cahills blend with the Sulphurs emerging. The river has a dozen popular and productive mayfly and caddis fly hatches. By the time August appears, you're certain the Little Juniata holds no more surprises. But wait!

John Randolph, Bob Panuska, and I met Allan Bright and Terry Moore at Spruce Creek Outfitters one late-August evening. The five of us decided on the spur of the moment to fish the Little Juniata. We proposed to hit

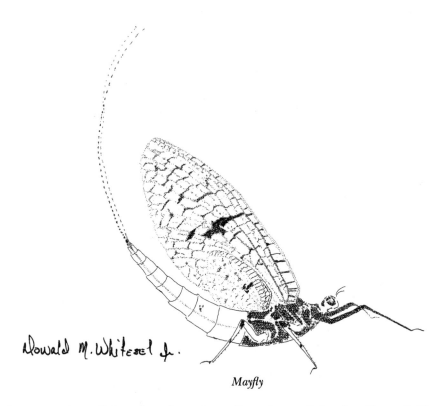

Mayfly

a lower section of the river just above Petersburg. John is editor of *Fly Fisherman* and just a year before asked me to write a story on the return of this river. Now, a year later, he had a chance to experience this rejuvenated trout stream and some of its late-season hatches.

The past summer had been unmerciful to the Little Juniata, and to all Pennsylvania streams. Extreme heat and drought brought trouble to many of them. Trout kills were common throughout the state. The Little Juniata, however, survived—no, more than that, it thrived. Water temperatures on this large stream rarely exceeded 75 even while air temperatures rose above 100.

The five of us arrived on the water at 6:45 P.M. Already a good number of Slate Drakes emerged near the edges. Eddies carried dozens of *Isonychia* nymphal shucks upstream past us. Before I decided what fly I'd try, Allan Bright had already caught several trout on a Slate Drake imitation.

But we hadn't come to see the Slate Drake appear. I hoped John and Bob would get a true impression of the diversity of this stream and see some of its White Mayflies. That mayfly already had appeared for more than a week—but spottily and with very mediocre results.

By 7:45 P.M. we noticed a few *Ephoron* moving in their characteristic flight a foot above the riffle. Within a half-hour thousands of these White Mayflies had emerged and began their mating ritual. These mayflies seemed to tantalize the trout by flying just a few inches above the surface. Trout up to fifteen inches long lost their timidity and leaped into the air to capture an errant dun or spinner. Now dozens of trout in the pool below and upstream in the riffle tried to capture mayflies. Bob Panuska had more than ten trout feeding in front of him, and three of these appeared to be near fifteen inches long. Many of the rises occurred over the riffle at the head of the pool.

The action continued well past dusk. Thousands of mating duns and spinners still darted just inches above the surface, and trout still rose to the food. What a fitting ending to a match-the-hatch season on the Little Juniata River!

Few anglers realize that the Little Juniata holds this late-season hatch. When anyone mentions the White Mayfly, most fishermen immediately think of the great hatch on the Yellow Breeches in south-central Pennsylvania.

The Yellow Breeches holds dozens of hatches that emerge throughout the fishing year, but this stream is best known for a single species—the White Mayfly. Many anglers who fly-fish the Breeches do so only in late August, when this water is teeming, both with these pale insects and with fly-fisherman.

Park near the Allenberry Inn in late August after 5:00 P.M. and you'll witness a carnival atmosphere similar to the festival that occurs on Penns Creek when the Green Drake appears. Fisherman discuss their strategies, including what flies they're using, all the time trying to work their way onto the stream where they have room to cast freely. It's like opening day on a well-stocked stream. Fly-fishermen, elbow to elbow, try casting to rising trout.

But there are several other trout streams in the state that display a White Mayfly hatch in late summer. The Bald Eagle near Julian has a respectable hatch, but the water temperature of this marginal stream often doesn't cooperate when the hatch appears. Several times I've recorded 75-degree water in late August and quit before the hatch appeared. The lower—and cooler—end of the Bald Eagle at Curtin contains a few White Mayflies. One August 22 I fished over enough spinners to catch three trout on the imitation. The hatch is not heavy, however.

Spruce has a sparse hatch of White Mayflies on its lower reaches. Credit Joe McMullen for the presence of the late-August mayfly on that stream. For years Joe has driven to the Yellow Breeches during the hatch, brought back fertilized eggs, and deposited them in his section of Spruce Creek. The hatch isn't heavy there, either, though.

The greatest White Mayfly hatch of all is on the smallmouth hotspot of the East, the North Branch of the Susquehanna River and the main stem around Harrisburg. On this river over twenty years ago I had my first encounter with the White Mayfly. Hatches of pale mayflies on this north-eastern Pennsylvania river are so heavy and concentrated around August 1 that some of the steel bridges between Wilkes-Barre and Scranton must be closed because the masses of crushed insects make the roadways slippery. Smallmouths gorge themselves for about a week on these mayflies, and a size-14 White Wulff takes plenty of bass. The hatch begins in early July around Harrisburg and toward the end of July near Tunkhannock. The hatch is earlier on the river because of the warmer river temperatures, which cause the nymphs to mature a bit faster than they do in the cooler trout waters of the Commonwealth.

There are other trout streams that contain the White Mayfly. Start checking some of your fishing spots around August 15—even earlier if the stream you're checking has warmer summer temperatures or is located in the southern half of the state. Look for the hatch on moderate to large trout streams which contain some slow water.

Keep exploring the Commonwealth's waters in late August, and you might meet a bonus end-of-the-season White Mayfly hatch. I've listed ten streams and rivers that contain good numbers of White Mayflies. Bob Panuska of Miami, Florida, recently wrote a note thanking me for the great fishing weekend when the White Mayfly appeared. He ended his letter: "I'll never forget that night on the Little Juniata River. It seems to me that's what fishing's all about."

SOME PENNSYLVANIA STREAMS WITH WHITE MAYFLY HATCHES

1. Little Juniata River
2. Yellow Breeches
3. Lehigh River (Lehigh Tannery area)
4. Raystown Branch, Juniata River (Everett area)
5. Yellow Creek (Loysburg Gap)
6. Bald Eagle Creek (just below Julian)
7. Neshannock Creek
8. Sandy Lick Creek
9. Slippery Rock Creek
10. Delaware River

Terrestrials on Pennsylvania Streams

Clayt Dovey's an experienced angler, a great fly-fisherman, and the producer of outdoor programs for WJAC-TV in Johnstown, Pennsylvania. He and his wife, Adelle, have roamed the world for unique and unusual fish-and-game stories. Clayt comes back to Pennsylvania each year to do some fly-fishing. Recently he and Dick Mayer, of Johnstown, invited me to join with them on Wayne Harpster's property on Spruce Creek. Trico spinners fall in good enough numbers in early September on this productive limestone stream to bring big browns to the surface.

Fishing over a Trico spinner fall this late in the season can bring mixed results, and most of the large trout seemed to refuse our lifelike imitations. The Trico spinner fall lingers longer in September than in July and August, and we fished over rising trout until early afternoon without much success.

Clayt had some success with a beetle, so I tied one on too. I fished the beetle in the home pool where Jimmy Carter fly-fishes frequently. This stretch, although it has large browns, is difficult to fly-fish because of the overhanging hemlocks on the far shore. Besides, since it's so close to the cabin, it's fished regularly by all the guests. On one of the first half-dozen casts I plopped the beetle just inches from the far bank under the cover of a heavy evergreen branch. The beetle floated a foot or two before a large shadow followed, then sucked in the small terrestrial. The lunker thrashed, shook from side to side, went deep, then seemed to sulk under the undercut bank. With a gentle nudge on the nine-foot Western graphite rod, the brown headed toward me away from the rooted bank. Fifteen minutes later I netted the heavy fish and removed the beetle pattern from its mouth. With the release of that heavy trout all three of us quit fishing for the day. What a way to end the day—releasing a twenty-two-inch brown on a size-16 beetle imitation!

Sparse hatches are the order of the day in July, August, and September. Don't fish on those days without a good supply of ants and beetles. These and other terrestrials, like the grasshopper, have saved numerous late-summer trips. The Poly Beetle is a must for those hatchless summer days. It is extremely easy to tie, taking less than a minute per pattern, even when tied by a relative beginner. Chapter 10 gives a quick but simple tying description for the beetle.

Some New Mayflies on Pennsylvania Waters

Many of the mayflies present on Pennsylvania streams have been thoroughly described by Schwiebert, Marinaro, Wetzel, Caucci and Nastasi, or by one of many other writers. Some species, however, remain out there yet to be identified.

When Will Flowers worked at Florida State University and later at Clemson, he identified many mayflies for me. In 1975 and 1976 I sent Will more than thirty male spinners that I was unable to identify. One of these was a dark-brown mayfly that appeared on Big Fishing Creek in Clinton County. The hatch looked somewhat like the Hendrickson, but it was darker and emerged around the middle of April. Will tentatively identified it as a subspecies of *Ephemerella subvaria*, the true Hendrickson. In *Hatches II*

(Winchester Press, 1986) Caucci and Nastasi confirm that observation, indicating that they have discovered several Hendrickson subspecies.

Another hatch appeared that same year on Bowman and the Mehoopany in Wyoming County, on the Bald Eagle in Centre County, and on dozens of other Pennsylvania streams. This hatch, a Blue-Winged Olive Dun tentatively identified as a subspecies or a new species, resembles *Drunella* (*Ephemerella*) *cornuta*. There's so much confusion about Blue-Winged Olives. Most anglers put any olive-colored mayfly into this category. But dozens of these mayflies have unusual body colors ranging from pale to dark olive, and they may vary in size, from size 14 to 20. The majority of these Blue-Winged Olives belong to the genus *Drunella*.

Many of the so-called Blue-Winged Olives of Pennsylvania remain to be identified. A new species emerges in abundance on Pine Creek in Lycoming County. Fish this great stream in mid-June around 11:00 A.M. and you'll meet this hatch. Fishing for trout at this time of the season can be unrewarding because the water temperature rises rapidly when June approaches. But on one occasion several years ago in mid-June the water temperature registered a respectable 68 degrees. At the section several of us refer to as the Cemetery Pool, I was surprised to see a number of trout rising. Tiny three-tailed olive mayflies emerged in heavy numbers and seemed to be in no hurry to take flight. In a small section of slow water with a riffle above, probably two dozen trout fed on these small, lethargic olive duns.

I collected a half-dozen male duns, put them in Styrofoam cups with some vegetation in each, and placed the cups under the shade of several sycamores on the bank. I then tied on a Little Blue-Winged Olive often used to copy many of the *Baetis* hatches. The pattern has the same proportions as the emerging mayfly but a much darker olive than the natural. The trout had a seemingly inexhaustible supply of real mayflies, and they refused the pattern time after time until the hatch diminished in intensity. Then for about a half-hour trout took the pattern infrequently.

The captured male duns metamorphosed into male spinners within a day. The species (*Dannella simplex*) had not been mentioned in fishing literature before. This species, however, may be widespread on diverse streams and rivers of the Commonwealth.

Another Light Cahill, *Hexagenia marginalis*, begins appearing in early June and continues throughout the summer into September. The hatch and spinner fall are predictable. The hatch is very sporadic, and duns escape rapidly from the surface, leaving scant time for rising trout. The spinner presents a different story. Mating adult females appear over fast water about 8:00 P.M. and remain there, sometimes almost motionless, for a half-hour or more. These spinners sometimes seem suspended above the surface just a few inches. Because of their habitual flight pattern they are inconspicuous. I hadn't noticed them until I saw trout coming completely out of the water in a series of riffles on the Bald Eagle near Julian. There trout fed actively on these hovering egg-laden adults. Oddly, trout refused the Light Cahill imitation completely on this occasion. The natural had a pale-olive cast to the cream underbelly, but that shouldn't have made a big difference.

I finally lay down on the bank parallel to some fast water to see how the trout were feeding on these insects. The mayflies were at first motionless, but after a while they would move rapidly up- or downstream. I tied on a spider pattern with long hackle and a cream body. The longer hackle kept the dry fly floating higher on the water. That's all the trout needed.

Most of the state's waters contain at least one species imitated by the Slate Drake. There are about a half-dozen closely related species that use the same common name. The duns are very similar, and most of them have dark-gray bodies, slate-colored wings, pale-gray tails, and dark-brown front legs with the rear pair cream. It's not difficult to identify this group of Slate Drakes. The group has not been given the credit and importance it deserves, however. Other than the Blue-Winged Olives, Blue Quills, and Tricos, no mayfly appears for as long or in the same numbers as the Slate Drake. Hatches appear as early as late May, and species continue to emerge well into October on Commonwealth streams and rivers. These late hatches often become the last hatch before winter approaches.

Occasionally fall Slate Drakes share the spotlight with another tardy species, the Blue Dun (a *Pseudocloeon* species). When you meet a hatch of Slate Drakes in early fall you can experience some great fly-fishing, because your choice of patterns is simplified. The rewards of matching a late Slate Drake are many. Often the mayflies that emerge do so in a cool above-water environment, slowing down their escape considerably.

Greg Hoover identified the Great Speckled Olive (*Siphloplecton basale*) on Clark Creek, and Rich Meyers identified a spinner fall of Great Red Spinners (*Stenonema pudicum*) on Young Woman's Creek recently.

These are just some of the hatches you'll encounter on your fishing trips throughout Pennsylvania's streams and rivers. Are there other hatches to be discovered on Pennsylvania waters? You bet!

Three

STREAMS OF
Northeastern Pennsylvania

The streams of northeastern Pennsylvania are found in a diverse area. Fly-fish on the Pocono streams in late summer, and you'll experience coffee-colored, often marginal waters. Look at the Brodhead Creek and the Lehigh or the Lackawaxen River. These and many more waters have suffered from the ravages of population growth and natural disasters. Hurricanes Diane in 1955 and Agnes in 1972 devastated the area. The flooding and resulting channelization destroyed much of the habitat for natural reproduction of trout and aquatic insects. In particular the Brodhead, Lehigh, and Lack-awaxen lost the great Green Drake hatches they had prior to 1955.

But time and the efforts of many dedicated environmentalists have assisted in the recovery of some streams. The Brodhead Chapter of Trout Unlimited has made habitat improvement an important goal on the local streams. The Lehigh River has regained the once-dominant Green Drake, along with a healthy population of streambred brown trout. With man's help the northeastern streams will recover and continue to provide many enjoyable hours of fly-fishing.

Fishing Creek

Catch-and-Release—1 mile; from the confluence of the East and West Branches of Fishing Creek at Grassmere Park downstream to the lower Gary Cook property line.

Barry Beck has grown up fly-fishing on Fishing Creek in Columbia County. He's fly-fished this unusually cold freestone stream since Dwight Eisenhower ran our country. Barry knows every pool, riffle, run, and pocket that this twenty-seven-mile stream contains. His experiences on Fishing Creek have contributed to making him one of the top fly-fishermen in the

United States. Barry now shares his secrets of the stream and the trout it holds with others less experienced through his guided trips to Fishing Creek. But this is only half the story. Barry's wife, Cathy, although fly-fishing only a little more than ten years, has also gained prominence as a top angler. In June of 1988 Cathy landed a record trout on a fly on Fishing Creek. The monster measured 28 inches long and weighed 8¼ pounds. Cathy caught the lunker holdover on one of Barry's creations, the Wooly Bugger. Barry and Cathy operate Beckies' Fishing Creek Outfitters just two miles from the stream.

How do you fish—and succeed—on Fishing Creek? Barry says "you have to have patience, learn the water, and learn the stream. It's a stream with some important hatches. You have to know these hatches."

What happens on Fishing Creek when there's no hatch to match? Barry often resorts to an ant pattern. More often than not Barry's changed those frustrating days when nothing seems to work into productive days by using the terrestrial.

Barry agrees that Fishing Creek probably is the coldest freestone stream in Pennsylvania. Even after record summer heat, with twenty-four days of 90-plus temperatures, Fishing Creek registered a reading of 63 late in the afternoon on the catch-and-release area near Grassmere.

Many July and August evenings I have fly-fished this excellent stream just above Benton when the Yellow Drake appeared in good numbers. On many of those hot summer evening trips I had to vacate the water and stand on a nearby bank to warm myself. Water temperatures in the upper half of Fishing Creek remain low all summer, even though water flow lessens considerably. As is commonplace with freestone streams, Fishing Creek evolves into a low, clear trout water late in the season, but it always seems to retain its remarkably low temperatures. Barry believes the stream remains cold because it contains unlocated springs along its entire length. These springs, plus a good canopy at its headwaters, keep Fishing Creek cool downstream to the town of Forks, where the warmer Huntington Creek enters.

Several tributaries combine just north of Central, in southern Sullivan county, to form Fishing Creek. Diminutive streams like Elk and Painter runs, Sullivan Branch, West Branch, and Quinn Run merge within a few miles to form an outstanding trout fishery. From Central the stream flows south to Grassmere, where a mile-long section has been set aside as a catch-and-release area. Coles Creek flows into the main stem two miles below Grassmere. Below Coles Creek two more tributaries enter from the east, Raven and Huntington creeks. Fishing Creek is quality freestone fly-fishing from above Grassmere to Forks.

Fishing Creek above Grassmere is a small, gravel-filled wild trout stream with plenty of streambred brown and brook trout. From Grassmere downstream the creek receives several in-season stockings of trout. Much of the water below Forks is put-and-take, with occasional heavy trout.

Hatches on Fishing Creek are extremely localized. Take for example the Yellow Drake that first emerges in mid- to late June. If you're at one of the manmade pools above Benton on a late-June or early-July evening, you'll see an extensive hatch of Yellow Drakes, but fish any other type of water on Fishing Creek, and you'll probably see few of these mayflies. Just a few miles above Benton is "Mom's" pool. This slow section is about 100 yards long and four to five feet deep. Fish this slow section or any nearby pool or eddy, and you'll see plenty of Yellow Drakes. The Yellow Drake emergence, unlike those of its sister species the Brown Drake and Green Drake, lasts for several weeks. Position yourself before the hatch on Fishing Creek and wait for it to appear. Fishing over this mayfly at dusk is short but explosive and often productive.

Another major hatch on Fishing Creek, especially below Benton, is the Sulphur. The Sulphur also appears for several weeks and is heavy enough in sections to produce many rising trout. Pattern size is important with this species. The hatch on Fishing Creek can be matched by a size-16 or -18 imitation. Sulphurs emerge from about the middle of May until mid-June. The best time on Fishing Creek is the third week in May.

Fishing Creek has other hatches. There are some caddis and stoneflies and a good supply of March Browns usually about the third week in May. Blue Quills are also somewhat abundant with appearances in April and again in June and July. Blue-Winged Olives appear in heavy numbers on the stream in late May. Barry Beck has said that few anglers fish this prolific hatch. Tricos appear on the stream below Stillwater, but few anglers fish this late-season hatch on the stream.

Wading is relatively easy. Some of the stream's artificial pools contain cool water all summer long, and neoprene waders might be a good choice. Below Coles Creek PA 487 parallels much of the stream. Secondary roads above Coles Creek closely parallel the upper area.

Photo by Barry Beck

Cathy Beck with a record brown trout caught on a fly on Fishing Creek. The lunker measured twenty-eight inches long and weighed 8¼ pounds.

The Freestone Fly Fishers have accomplished much on the catch-and-release area of Fishing Creek. They recently placed more than forty tons of limestone in the stream for dams and deflectors. The 130- plus members would like to increase the size of the catch-and-release area.

Best Times to Fly-fish:

April 20–May 1
Blue Quill: #18, morning and afternoon
Quill Gordon: #14, afternoon
Hendrickson and Red Quill: #14, afternoon

May 15–June 20
Sulphur Dun and Spinner: #16, evening
March Brown: #12, morning and afternoon
Blue-Winged Olive Dun: #14, morning
Pink Lady: #14, evening
Light Cahill: #14, evening
Little Green Stonefly: #16, afternoon and evening

June 20–July 10
Yellow Drake: #12, evening
Little Blue-Winged Olive Dun: #20, morning and afternoon
Light Cahill: #14 and #16, evening
Blue Quill: #18, morning and afternoon
Gray Caddis: #16, afternoon and evening

July 15–September 30
Slate Drake: #12 or #14, evening
Blue Quill: #18, morning and afternoon
Trico: #24, morning (lower end)
Cinnamon Caddis: #14, afternoon and evening

Bowman Creek

*Fly-fishing-Only Project—1 mile; from the vicinity of PA 292
downstream to near the confluence with Marsh Creek.*

When I think of fly-fishing, Bowman Creek merits a special place in my memory. More than twenty years ago, when I first devoted an entire season to this newfangled type of angling, I came here. Why did I start on this stream? Out of frustration more than anything else. Crowded streams in the Wilkes-Barre area the first couple weeks of the season motivated me to look for open space. Bowman Creek contained a fly-fishing-only section on its lower end. I fly-fished an entire morning of an opening day in total seclusion—not one other fly-fisherman appeared on the one-mile stretch. I enjoyed this solitude; it was almost like having my own private stream.

Lloyd Williams, of Dallas, and Dick Mills, of Lehman, shared those first few years of fly-fishing experiences on Bowman. Lloyd used only three patterns all season long, while Dick and I faithfully matched the hatch on this prolific freestone stream. Early in the year Dick and I matched Blue Quills, Hendricksons, and Grannoms. The first couple weeks of the season you'd find Lloyd flinging a Muddler Minnow or a Wooly Worm. By late May Dick and I copied the March Browns or Blue-Winged Olives so common at that time on the stream. Lloyd, from mid-May on, used the Royal Coachman. Lloyd did well with his unorthodox methods. At the end of a fishing excursion Dick and I would carefully pack our rods away. Lloyd broke his rod and left the Wooly Worm, Muddler, or Royal Coachman attached. His argument was that he'd be ready instantly for another fishing trip to Bowman. Besides he had the fly already attached to the tippet. On one midsummer trip Lloyd landed a twenty-four-inch brown trout on the Royal Coachman. I know—I netted the fish for him.

Conditions changed, and the number of fly-fishermen on Bowman increased over the years. The fly-fishing-only section is no longer our personal domain. Now dozens of fishermen frequent this once-secret section daily.

You might think that after June, when all the insects appear, Bowman would not have further hatches the rest of the season. But a local fly-fisherman, Tom Bean, of Noxen, told me about the great Yellow Drake hatch near the end of June about three miles upstream from the fly-fishing only stretch. On this new water, an impounded area about 100 yards long, I first fished while a heavy Yellow Drake appeared just at dusk.

Bowman is a stream for all summer, with a respectable Trico continuing daily into September. Hatches and spinner falls of this species appear as early as the middle of July. Vince Marinaro saw his first freestone Trico hatch on this stream twenty years ago. Fish the lower half of the stream any July or August evening, and you'll see hundreds of Slate Drakes emerging. Yes, Bowman has hatches—great hatches—throughout much of the season. From July through September don't overlook terrestrial patterns like ants, crickets, and beetles. These imitations have worked well on this stream. Bowman is a splendid stream with plenty of native, holdover, and stocked trout—and all within a few miles of the Wilkes-Barre/Scranton area.

Bowman Creek flows from Red Rock Mountain northeast toward Tunkhannock. Splash dams formerly used for timbering in this upper area once provided the Wilkes-Barre area with ice. For the first ten miles the stream is isolated except for an abandoned railroad bed. This wilderness section has water with some tannic acid from the numerous beaver dams and swamps the stream drains in its headwaters. Only brook trout thrive in these upper reaches.

From Stull downstream through Noxen the stream is easily reached by blacktop roads. Until the early 1960s the tannery in Noxen added brown effluent to the stream; the hole where the tannery water entered is still called the Lye Hole. From this point downstream the stream is stocked several times annually.

Until Bowman crosses PA 309 it is relatively small. Below that point the water enlarges to a thirty- to forty-foot-wide stream harboring an abundance of good hatches. Good fishing can be found from Noxen downstream past the fly-fishing area almost to Tunkhannock, where Bowman enters the Susquehanna River. The stream in the lower six miles contains plenty of deep pools with productive riffles and runs. The Evans Falls section, three miles above the fly-fishing-only stretch, contains a deep pool with a twenty-foot falls above. This area has been posted against trespassing for the past fifteen years. Locals have named some of the other areas on Bowman. The Barn Pool in the fly-fishing stretch remains a favorite match-the-hatch section for anglers.

Bowman Creek in its drainage area contains tributaries that harbor native brook, brown, and rainbow trout. Few other streams in Pennsylvania can boast tributaries with all three streambred populations.

Major flooding in 1972 caused many problems on Bowman. The high water changed many productive pools into riffles and runs and vice versa. The Soil Conservation Service channelized sections of the stream after the flood. Some of these devastated areas still suffer from this impulsive, irresponsible treatment. In recent years the Endless Mountains Chapter of Trout Unlimited, in cooperation with the Pennsylvania Fish Commission, undertook several projects to improve the stream. The chapter, as part of an "adopt-a-stream" policy, sponsored a project to prevent further erosion on some of the banks of the stream. Unfortunately the chapter is now defunct.

Abundant down-wing hatches like the Grannom, Spotted Sedge, Dark-Blue Sedge, Yellow Stonefly, Light Stonefly, Green Stonefly, and many others complement the list of mayflies found on the stream. Fishing caddis hatches on Bowman often requires wet flies rather than dry-fly patterns. Emerging caddis pupa patterns for the Grannom and Spotted Sedge work effectively in mid-May.

Throughout much of its length Bowman has acceptably cold water all season long. Even though it is a freestone stream and suffers from a declining water flow in the summer, temperatures remain fairly hospitable for trout. Bowman's trout population consists of brook trout, especially in its upper reaches; some streambred brown trout, most notably in the lower third of the stream; and a combination of stocked species in the middle section. Some of the tributaries, like Sugar Hollow Creek and Roaring Run, contain good populations of streambred rainbows. Marsh Creek, which enters the main stem at the lower end of the fly-fishing-only stretch, holds streambred browns. Several other small tributaries upstream also harbor brown and brook trout. Beaver Run enters Bowman at Noxen, and Leonard Creek enters two miles downstream. The main stem from Evans Falls downstream three to four miles holds trout year-round. Some of these measure more than twenty inches long and weigh up to five or six pounds.

Bowman Creek is easy to fish, from the point of view of access. PA 309 parallels much of the lower half of the stream. Wading is fairly easy on this freestone stream. The bottom is composed of small stones with a scattering of larger rocks and boulders. Bowman has plenty of productive riffles and pocket water and some deep pools. Many of the hatches, like the Sulphur and Blue-Winged Olive Dun, emerge from the riffles.

If you like pristine conditions, fishing a medium-sized freestone stream with plenty of hatches, and a good trout population, then try Bowman Creek. Much of the lower end is accessible, with superb fly-fishing water.

Best Times to Fly-fish:

April 18–May 5
Blue Quill: #18, morning and afternoon
Quill Gordon: #14, afternoon
Hendrickson and Red Quill Spinner: #14, afternoon and early evening (spinner)
Early Brown Stonefly: #12, morning and afternoon

May 8–June 1
Grannom: #12, afternoon
Light Stonefly: #12, afternoon
Spotted Sedge: #14, afternoon
March Brown: #12, morning and afternoon
Gray Fox: #14, afternoon
Light Cahill: #14, evening
Green Drake: #12, afternoon and evening (spotty)
Blue-Winged Olive Dun: #14, morning
Pale Evening Dun: #16 and #18, evening
Dark-Blue Sedge: #12, evening
Slate Drake: #12 or #14, evening

June 20–July 5
Yellow Drake: #12, evening (on slower pools)
Slate Drake: #12 and #14, evening

July 15–September
Trico: #24, morning (lower end)
Slate Drake: #12 and #14, evening

Clark Creek

*Delayed Harvest Fly-fishing Only—2 miles; from Pennsylvania Game
Commission parking area on PA 325 downstream to PGC access road
at the Iron Furnace.*

Greg Hoover lives in Halifax, just a half-hour from Clark Creek. He
recently made a study of the Green Drake on Penns Creek. Greg is an
entomologist working for the Pennsylvania State University, and he's past
president of the Pennsylvania Entomological Society. He fishes Clark Creek
about twenty times a year. Several years ago, in late April, Greg recognized
a new hatch on the stream. He identified it as the Great Speckled Olive
Dun (*Siphloplecton basale*).

I visited with Greg that same year and we fly-fished over a decent hatch
and spinner fall of this species a year later. The hatch and spinner fall
bring Clark Creek trout to the surface for this early-season mayfly. Fishing
over this new species, we both caught trout. Greg feels that many of the
fly-fishermen who see the hatch believe it's a Quill Gordon. The body of
the Quill Gordon, however, is much darker than that of the Great Speckled
Olive.

Greg fishes Clark Creek frequently from mid-March through August.
From July on he feels the stream gets extremely difficult to fish with its
typically low, gin-clear water. The largest trout he has caught on Clark was
a twenty-two-inch brown trout.

Clark holds a fair number of early hatches, including some Black Quills.
Greg feels that three of the best early-season hatches are the Early Brown
Stonefly, Hendrickson, and the March Brown. Don't expect the intensity
of these hatches to measure up to those on the Loyalsock or the upper
Allegheny, but be assured that they can provide residents of the Harrisburg
area with ample opportunities to match the hatch.

Dick Henry, of Lebanon, fly-fishes on Clark from early April until
September. He's seen a decent hatch of Blue-Winged Olive Duns on occasion and a few Sulphurs on the water. Dick cautions that neither hatch
in heavy numbers. He suggests that the two most important mayfly hatches
on Clark are the Hendrickson and the March Brown. Dick feels terrestrials
work well on this stream. "When leafrollers are on the water," he says, "the
trout often go wild, and nothing but a leafroller imitation will take them."

Clark Creek reminds me of so many other isolated valley streams, like

East Licking Creek, Blacklog Creek, and many others. It begins near Tower City and flows southwest for twenty miles before entering the Susquehanna River near Dauphin. The city of Harrisburg maintains the DeHart Reservoir about ten miles upstream from its mouth. Above the dam Clark is a small stream running from ten to thirty feet wide. The state stocks the area above the dam with plenty of trout. Fly-fishing in this upper stretch presents plenty of problems with dense bushes and brush on the banks. Below the dam the stream widens to thirty to forty feet. Water released from the bottom of the reservoir keeps Clark fairly cool downstream throughout much of the summer. The flow is slow, and the bottom contains a mixture of sand, gravel, and rocks. The stream flows just ten miles north of Harrisburg. PA 325 follows its entire length.

Greg Hoover spends several weeks on Clark Creek each year. Greg first identified the Siphloplecton *hatch on the stream.*

Clark contains a two-mile delayed-harvest fly-fishing-only section. Even after the middle of June you can find trout in this section. The stream contains a good supply of stocked trout, some holdovers, and possibly a few native trout.

Best Times to Fly-fish:

April 15–May 5
Early Brown Stonefly: #12, morning and afternoon
Little Blue-Winged Olive Dun: #20, morning and afternoon
Blue Quill: #18, morning and afternoon
Black Quill: #14, afternoon
Great Speckled Olive Dun: #12, afternoon

May 15–June 5
Sulphur Dun and Spinner: #16, evening (spotty)
March Brown: #12, morning and afternoon
Blue-Winged Olive Dun: #14, morning (spotty)
Light Cahill: #14, evening
Slate Drake: #12 and #14, evening
Dark-Green Drake: #10, afternoon and evening

June 5–July 1
Little Green Stonefly: #16, afternoon and evening
Yellow Stonefly: #14, afternoon and evening

June 20–July 10
Yellow Drake: #12, evening
Slate Drake: #12 and #14, evening

Lackawaxen River

Jerry Lewis has lived on the Lackawaxen River since 1929. He remembers well how productive this great river was prior to 1955 and Hurricane Diane. He recalls stories of enormous Green Drake hatches and Coffin Fly spinner falls that occurred in back of his house in late May and early June. "That's when the lunker browns surface fed," Jerry says. "In one evening fly-fishing over the Green Drake, I caught a half-dozen trout—all over twenty inches long."

Those memorable days have vanished. Many of the once-deep, productive pools and gravel stretches essential for the Green Drake nymphs have been buried by silt and debris from several floods. The Drake is only a faint reminder of the once-dominant hatch that filled the late-May air.

Now only a few Drakes appear. Will the hatch ever regain its prominence?

Annually John Churnetski and Lee Eckert, of the Wyoming Valley, and Carl Laurer, of Emerson, New Jersey, meet at Jerry Lewis's home near Rowland for the opening of the trout season in Pennsylvania. Some of these mid-April days have been cold and blustery with flurry-filled, leaden skies. Even on days when the temperature barely rises to 47 degrees, however, Hendricksons often appear. On those early days of the season John, Lee, and Carl select patterns like the Quill Gordon (wet and dry), Hendrickson (wet, dry, and nymph), and the Little Black Caddis (wet and dry).

The river begins in northwestern Wayne County near Pleasant Mount. It travels southeast about twenty miles to the town of Honesdale, where it picks up additional volume from another trout stream, Dyberry Creek. The Lackawaxen then flows south-southeast for eight miles to Hawley, where Middle Creek enters the main stem. Just downriver the Lackawaxen adds water from Lake Wallenpaupack, then flows east for fifteen miles in Pike County to the town of Lackawaxen, where it enters the Delaware River. There's about forty miles of good trout-fishing water on the Lackawaxen, some excellent hatches, and a good supply of trout—even some holdovers. US 6 follows the river from Honesdale to Hawley, and PA 590 and a paved secondary road parallel the river below.

If you enjoy fishing large water and don't mind plenty of anglers nearby, try the Lackawaxen, especially when the enormous Hendrickson hatch appears around April 23.

Best Times to Fly-fish:

April 15–May 5
Blue Quill: #18, morning and afternoon
Hendrickson and Red Quill: #14, afternoon
Early Brown Stonefly: #12, afternoon
Quill Gordon: #14, afternoon

May 15–June 5
Blue-Winged Olive Dun: #14, morning and afternoon
Gray Fox: #14, afternoon
March Brown: #12, morning and afternoon
Green Drake and Coffin Fly: #10, evening (spotty)
Sulphur Dun and Spinner: #16, evening

June 15–July 1
Blue-Winged Olive Dun: #16, morning and afternoon
Yellow Drake: #12, evening

July 15–September 1
Trico: #24, morning

Hayes Creek

Bob Sentiwany and I stopped at Hayes Creek (also called Black Creek) where it crosses PA 534. We hiked upstream along a path that follows the creek. As we walked under a heavy canopy of evergreens, Bob boasted about the excellent trout the water contained. The upper end held plenty of brook trout, and the lower end, a good supply of streambred browns. We saw several pools over five feet deep, and each held several native trout.

Yellow and Green Stoneflies emerged from many of the pools, and trout rose to a few that didn't become airborne immediately. Hayes, however, contains much more than just two stonefly species. March Browns emerge in good numbers the last week of May. Earlier, in April, you can fish to rising trout when Blue Quills, Quill Gordons, and Hendricksons appear.

Hayes begins at Pocono Mountain Lakes. Discharge from the top of the lake plus effluent from sewage-treatment facilities below warm the stream unnaturally in June, July, and August. Temperatures then approach and exceed 70 degrees. The stream flows southwest under the Pennsylvania Turnpike and I-80 and then into state game lands for two miles before it joins the Lehigh River. Halfway between I-80 and PA 534 Fourth Run enters the main stem. This branch adds plenty of cool water but also some tannic acid to the main stem.

Most of the upper part of Hayes flows through private land. The lower two miles remain open only because the stream flows through state game lands. There are 1½ miles of open water above PA 534, and a half-mile below. Get on the stream on PA 534, then hike up- or downstream.

If you enjoy small-stream fly-fishing on water that contains some good hatches and high quality streambred trout, then you'll enjoy fishing Hayes Creek. This stream could be made even better if the state placed a catch-and-release policy on it.

Best Times to Fly-fish:

April 15–May 5
Early Brown Stonefly: #14, morning and afternoon
Blue Quill: #18, morning and afternoon
Quill Gordon: #14, afternoon
Hendrickson and Red Quill: #14, afternoon

May 15–June 10
Gray Fox and Ginger Quill: #12 and #14, afternoon and evening
March Brown: #12, morning and afternoon
Light Cahill: #14, evening
Slate Drake: #12 and #14, evening
Little Green Stonefly: #16, afternoon and evening*
Yellow Stonefly: #14, afternoon and evening*

*Continue well past date listed

Hickory Run

*Catch-and-Release—1.5 miles; from Sand Spring Run downstream
to the mouth.*

Hickory Run lies halfway between Hayes Creek and Mud Run. PA 534 gives access to this stream also. Below the highway are three miles of top-notch small stream catch-and-release water. Hickory ranges from fifteen to twenty feet wide, with plenty of narrow riffles and small pools teeming with streambred browns and brookies. It holds some hefty trout. Bob and Mary Lou Sentiwany operate the AA Pro Shop just a few miles away. Bob's largest trout on Hickory Run measured nineteen inches long and weighed about three pounds.

Bob's concerned about the number of poachers on Hickory Run. In some areas there are only a few posters noting that the lower end contains a catch-and-release area.

Like Hayes Creek and Mud Run, Hickory contains a good supply of aquatic insects. Plenty of March Browns appear, albeit sporadically, the last week in May. The Hendrickson presents some decent fly-fishing in late April, especially if Hickory's temperature rises above 50 degrees. If you meet these or any of the hatches listed you'll experience some fantastic fly-fishing to rising trout.

Hickory begins just east of the Pennsylvania Turnpike and flows southwest through Saylorsville and into Hickory Run State Park. From PA 534 downstream to the Lehigh River the stream contains a catch-and-release area. Bob Sentiwany says the best fly-fishing on the stream is located just before it enters the Lehigh. Hickory warms above 70 degrees in the summer; a dam on a branch, Sand Spring Run, causes the thermal problem. The state stocks both the main stem and Sand Spring Run upstream from PA 534.

Best Times to Fly-fish:

April 15–May 5
Early Brown Stonefly: #14, morning and afternoon
Blue Quill: #18, morning and afternoon
Quill Gordon: #14, afternoon
Hendrickson and Red Quill: #14, afternoon

May 15–June 10
Gray Fox and Ginger Quill: #12 and #14, afternoon and evening
March Brown: #12, morning and afternoon
Light Cahill: #14, evening
Little Green Stonefly: #16, afternoon and evening*
Yellow Stonefly: #14, afternoon and evening*

*Continue well after date listed

The Lehigh River

The Lehigh River was a great trout fishery. In the 1930s, '40s, and '50s the river teemed with trout and hatches, especially the great Green Drake hatch. This hatch and many more disappeared after 1955, because of indiscriminate spraying and because of damage from floods caused by Hurricanes Agnes and Diane. Later the hardy Hendrickson still appeared, but mainly to lethargic, nursery-reared trout.

Guess what? The Lehigh has returned with gusto. Just a year ago the Green Drake reappeared in a hatch abundant enough to bring heavy trout to the surface. This year the hatch reappeared for the second consecutive year—in numbers to rival past hatches. The Drake at present emerges upstream from the Francis Walter Dam. The Hendrickson hatch this past April proved to be the heaviest in past memory.

Recently I revisited the stream with Bob Sentiwany. We headed behind Bob's fly shop in the Lehigh Tannery area. The lower end of the stocked area, from the Francis Walter Dam to just below Lehigh Tannery, presents large-water problems similar to those on some large western rivers. In this section footing is treacherous, and wading only several feet is an experience. Here the river ranges from 100 to 150 feet wide. Tobyhanna and Bear creeks enter just above the dam and add considerable volume to the river. As we cautiously waded into some deep pocket water we noticed a half-dozen trout surface feeding on a variety of Cahill spinners and microcaddis. The last time I had fly-fished the Lehigh, twenty years ago, I saw few insects and fewer trout.

Bob and I headed upriver to a section just below the dam to look for feeding trout. Here the Lehigh contains deep pools and mile-long riffles. The locals call this section Devils Elbow. Although most of this water remains open to fly-fishing, access is difficult. In color the water below the dam resembles weak tea, because of the infusion of tannic acid, mainly from the Tobyhanna.

As Bob fished I collected dozens of March Brown duns. This species appears on the Lehigh in massive numbers.

At the upper end of the Lehigh Falls Club's posted water (one mile below Lehigh Falls and PA 115), there's some excellent pocket water. When we arrived there we saw a dozen trout feeding on caddis. The splashing rises to these insects indicated the fish were taking the down-wing naturals. I captured a couple caddis, examined the tan body and size, and selected a size-16 Tan Caddis imitation. Bob tied on the same pattern. For the next hour the frenzied feeding continued. Bob's first trout proved to be a seven-inch streambred brown. The next trout that sucked in his caddis was a six-inch native brook trout.

In another few minutes Bob took a hefty brown trout that looked like a native. In a little more than an hour the two of us caught some small and medium-sized trout up to fifteen inches long. Most were holdover or streambred trout. By 8:00 P.M. the Lehigh proved it has returned as a prime trout stream. A smorgasbord of insects appeared in the air: several Coffin Flies, thousands of Ginger Quills, March Browns, Light Cahills, and assorted other mayflies and caddis flies hovered in the air above us.

Access to areas just above the dam is difficult. You'll also see some private water in this area. If you plan to fish any section of the river, it's a good idea to check with Bob Sentiwany at Lehigh Tannery. He can tell you what's hatching and where to fly-fish.

The Lehigh begins in southeastern Pike County, then flows southwest to White Haven to form the boundary between Luzerne and Monroe counties. A few miles upstream from White Haven is a relatively new flood-control project, the Francis Walter Dam. It's a shame that the dam, which possesses a bottom release, is not more accommodating to the fantastic cold-water fishery it could provide downstream. If releases were planned in summer, the lower end of the Lehigh would become a productive trout stream and bring in thousands of fishermen to boost the local economy.

Access to the river is relatively easy from Gouldsboro to Thornhurst, via a parallel secondary road. Much of the water in this area is open to fishing. When the Lehigh reaches White Haven, about thirty miles downriver from Gouldsboro, it becomes an impressive river. You'll encounter many whitewater rafters in this section, especially on weekends. PA 940 follows the Lehigh on its lower end and crosses the river at White Haven. From White Haven to Lehigh Tannery a secondary road and PA 534 approach the water.

Bob Sentiwany shows off a native trout caught on the Lehigh River above White Haven during a Light Cahill hatch.

The Lehigh has many long, deep pools with riffles above. It picks up volume from numerous small creeks, and many flow though bogs and open ponds. Some side streams contain brook trout, but many are posted against trespassing. Streams like Lehigh, Ash, Buckey, Wolf, and Trout runs, as well as Choke Creek, one of the larger tributaries that flows into the main stem around Thornhurst, flow into the Lehigh. Two major tributaries, Tobyhanna and Bear creeks, enter the main stem at or near the dam.

The Lehigh has regained some of its hatches. Sections of the river now hold plenty of holdover trout, and above the dam there's good evidence of a healthy streambred population of brook and brown trout. The Lehigh has returned.

Best Times to Fly-fish:

April 20–May 5
Early Brown Stonefly: #12, morning and afternoon
Blue Quill: #18, morning and afternoon
Quill Gordon: #14, afternoon
Hendrickson and Red Quill: #14, afternoon

May 15–June 15
Sulphur Dun and Spinner: #16, evening
Gray Fox and Ginger Quill: #12 and #14, afternoon and evening
March Brown: #12, morning and afternoon
Blue-Winged Olive Dun: #14, morning
Light Cahill: #14, evening
Slate Drake: #12 and #14, evening
Green Drake and Coffin Fly: #10, evening
Tan Caddis: #16, evening
Black Caddis: #14, evening
Pink Lady: #14, evening
Chocolate Dun: #16, morning and afternoon (spinner, evening)

June 15–July 15
Slate Drake: #12 and #14, evening
Light Cahill: #14, evening

August 15–August 31
White Mayfly: #14, evening (lower end)

September 15–October 10
Slate Drake: #12 and #14, evening
Blue Dun: #20 and #22, afternoon

The Delaware River

Bob Sentiwany and I arrived at the Delaware at 11:00 A.M. hoping for a Blue-Winged Olive hatch. From noon until 7:00 P.M., however, the river looked barren and almost void of trout. Few trout rose to a plentiful supply of Little Blue-Winged Olives and Black Caddis. All the signs had been

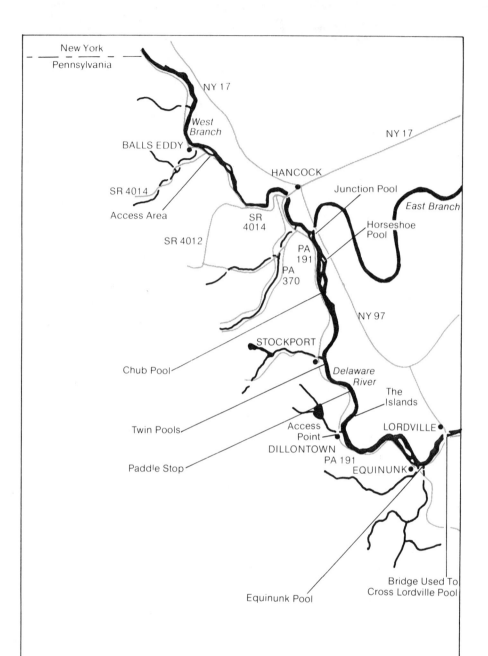

New York
Pennsylvania

NY 17

West
Branch

NY 17

BALLS EDDY

HANCOCK

Junction Pool

East Branch

SR 4014

Access Area

SR
4014

Horseshoe
Pool

SR 4012

PA
191

PA
370

NY 97

STOCKPORT

Chub Pool

Delaware
River

The
Islands

Twin Pools

LORDVILLE

Access
Point

DILLONTOWN

PA 191

EQUINUNK

Paddle Stop

Equinunk Pool

Bridge Used To
Cross Lordville Pool

From a map by Bob Sentiwany

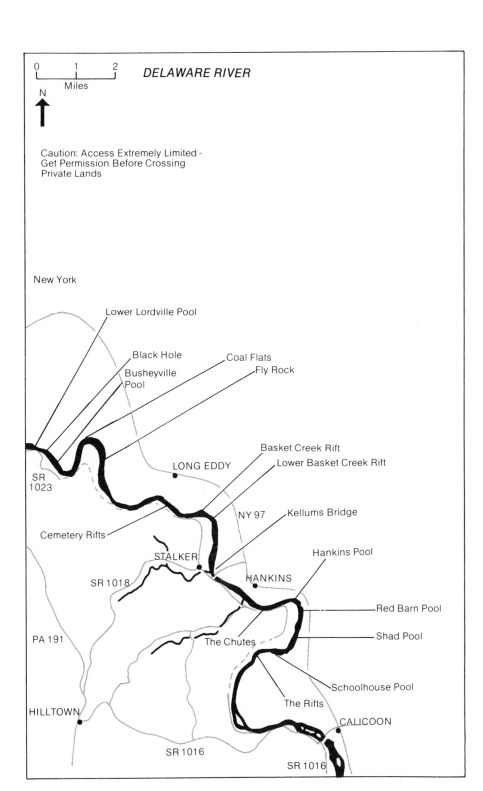

DELAWARE RIVER

0   1   2
Miles

N

Caution: Access Extremely Limited -
Get Permission Before Crossing
Private Lands

New York

Lower Lordville Pool

Black Hole   Coal Flats
Busheyville   Fly Rock
Pool

Basket Creek Rift

Lower Basket Creek Rift

LONG EDDY

SR
1023

NY 97   Kellums Bridge

Cemetery Rifts

Hankins Pool

STALKER

SR 1018   HANKINS

Red Barn Pool

PA 191   Shad Pool

The Chutes

Schoolhouse Pool

HILLTOWN   The Rifts

CALICOON

SR 1016

SR 1016

favorable. The leaden skies above the river shaded the water all day, and the air temperature on that early-June afternoon stayed below 60 degrees— perfect to delay mayflies from escaping from the surface too rapidly. Nevertheless not much happened on the river near Callicoon, so Bob and I drove upriver to fish the West Branch near Hancock.

About 7:00 P.M. insect activity began to increase. First a few Gray Foxes appeared, then dozens, then hundreds. Many of these duns hit cold air, now near 50 degrees, and rested on the water—unable to take flight immediately. Soon a few trout responded to the lethargic, drifting duns. Within minutes the barren waters boiled with ten heavy trout rising in front of me. Bob and I switched to Gray Fox imitations and took a half-dozen trout—none particularly heavy. The rises to duns soon changed to the typical splashing rises to caddis.

"They're taking the Black Caddis," Bob yelled.

We both hurriedly tied on Black Caddis patterns and cast in the general direction of more than twenty surface-feeding fish. Both of us tied into several heavy browns and rainbows with the down-wing pattern before the action subsided.

By 8:30 P.M. the splashing rises in the riffle in front of us ended. Bob looked downriver to the tail of the pool. Here maybe a dozen trout sipped in an assortment of Ginger Quill, Light Cahill, and White-Gloved Howdy spinners. Bob switched to a Cahill Spinner while I watched. He hooked three trout on the spent-winged imitation. Dusk arrived, and we had to leave the river. A slow start, but what a day! What abundant hatches and spinner falls! What heavy trout! The true Delaware River revealed itself that day. It reminded me more of several of the great western rivers, like the Kootenai and Bitterroot rivers in Montana, than a typical eastern river.

That day of fishing the Delaware made me a believer, as a similar day had for Bob twenty-six years before. Bob Sentiwany first fly-fished on the Delaware in 1962. He heard reports at his sporting goods store in Lehigh Tannery about huge rainbows. After his first encounter with the Delaware he was hooked. He now makes the two-hour trip to the river ten to fifteen times a year.

The Delaware's West Branch flows south, forming the eastern border of Pennsylvania. Just below Hancock it joins the East Branch to form the main stem. There's great trout fishing on the river from the northern part of the West Branch down past Callicoon, New York. Bob feels that many of the trout near Callicoon migrate upriver when the water in that area warms. The West and East branches add these migrating trout to their already abundant supply. Check the temperature before you begin fishing. The river's flow and water temperature depend on releases from the Cannonsville Reservoir on the West Branch and the Downsville Reservoir on the East Branch.

In the early '80s this part of the country suffered from a severe drought. Dams released meager water volumes for several summers. Fishing on the Delaware suffered tremendously. Bob Sentiwany recalls seeing hundreds of dead trout floating down what water there was in the river. Fishing suffered again in 1985 with another water shortage. Since then the water releases have been steadier and more predictable, and trout fishing has been outstanding. A frightening reality about the Delaware and its future as trout water is that it depends totally on the water releases from upstream reservoirs.

Once on the Delaware you can wade up and downstream without trepidation. Getting access to the river, however, is a major problem. The Pennsylvania Fish Commission provides only two access areas in thirty miles of water, and New York has only one. It seems both states ignore additional access areas because those in Pennsylvania would be frequented by New York residents with New York licenses and vice versa. You can fish from the New York side of the Delaware with your Pennsylvania license. Why don't New York and Pennsylvania sell a stamp to fish on the Delaware and use the proceeds to purchase additional access on both sides of the river? Make certain that you have permission to park and cross any landowner's property on the Delaware.

Although much of the Delaware is inaccessible, the section of the West Branch that borders the Commonwealth can be reached by a paved secondary road that runs north along the river. PA 370 crosses this state route (SR 4014) just on the Pennsylvania side near Hancock. There's an access area designated by the Fish Commission upriver a few miles at Balls Eddy, and the fishing in that vicinity is excellent. Downriver from Hancock, Pennsylvania, PA 191 parallels the Delaware for about ten miles to Equinunk. Just above Equinunk at Dillontown there's a second access point. From that point downriver, the main stem is difficult to get to until you reach the bridge crossing the river to the town of Callicoon.

Trout fishing on the Delaware has always been portrayed as a difficult task. It is when there's no hatch to match and when there's a multiple spinner fall at dusk. It can be when several duns emerge concurrently. That early-June day on the Delaware Bob Sentiwany and I saw hatches of Pink Ladies, Gray Foxes, Slate Drakes, Sulphurs (*Ephemerella dorothea* and a *Heptagenia* species), Light Cahills, and Little Blue-Winged Olive Duns. We noted spinner falls of Ginger Quills, White-Gloved Howdys, and Light Cahills. And we saw at least two caddis species, a size-14 Black Caddis and a size-16 Brown Caddis, appear. When we matched the naturals we caught trout.

You'll often be frustrated fishing a spinner fall at dusk. What spinner is on the water? Check the fast water at the head of a pool before dusk and note the species in the air. Of course a knowledge of the hatches and spinner falls and of when they occur helps. Take plenty of caddis patterns with you with body colors from black, brown, olive, green, tan, and gray in sizes ranging from 12 to 18.

Hatches are extensive on the river, the first appearing at the beginning of the trout season or even before, with the advent of the Little Blue-Winged Olive Dun (*Baetis tricaudatus*). The Hendrickson hatch is possibly the heaviest hatch on the river, but weather conditions at the end of April are often less than ideal. By late May the rivers display many hatches, including the Gray Fox, March Brown, Green Drake, Brown Drake, and Blue-Winged Olive Dun. Interspersed throughout the season on the river are a plethora of Blue Quills (*Paraleptophlebia* species). These seem to appear daily throughout the season.

If rainfall for the season has been average or above, and the flow from the Delaware dams is normal or above normal, then July and August can be productive months on the river. Tricos hatch every morning on the Delaware, but trout sometimes fail to rise to the spinner fall. The Delaware is wide at spots, and many of the "eddies" are impossible to cover by wading. Unlike the Little Juniata River, Slippery Rock Creek, the Clarion River, and the lower Lehigh River, however, the bottom of the Delaware presents few wading problems.

The Pennsylvania Fish Commission adds fingerlings to the native population of browns, rainbows, and occasional brook trout. If you enjoy fly-fishing over large streambred trout that often rise to massive hatches you'll enjoy fishing the Delaware River.

Best Times to Fly-fish:

April 20–May 5
Little Blue-Winged Olive Dun: #20, morning and afternoon
Blue Quill: #18, morning and afternoon
Quill Gordon: #14, afternoon
Hendrickson and Red Quill: #14, afternoon
Grannom: #12, morning and afternoon
Olive Caddis: #14 and #16, morning and afternoon
Gray Caddis: #14 and #16, morning and afternoon

May 12–June 15
Tan Caddis: #14, morning and afternoon
Sulphur Dun and Spinner: #16 and #18, evening
Gray Fox and Ginger Quill: #12 and #14, afternoon and evening
March Brown: #14, morning and afternoon
Green Drake and Coffin Fly: #10, evening
Light Cahill: #14, evening
Brown Drake Dun and Spinner: #12, evening
Chocolate Dun and Spinner: #16, morning and afternoon (dun), evening (spinner)
Pink Lady: #14, evening
Slate Drake: #12 and #14, evening

June 15–July 15
Sulphur Dun and Spinner: #16 and #18, evening
Golden Drake: #12, evening
Cream Cahill: #14 and #16, evening
Slate Drake: #12 and #14, evening

July 15–September 30
Cream Cahill: #14 and #16, evening
Blue Quill: #18, morning and afternoon
Trico: #24, morning
White Mayfly: #14, evening
Slate Drake: #12 and #14, evening
Blue Dun: #20 or #22, afternoon

Mehoopany Creek

Bob Dibble of Wyalusing will tell you that the Mehoopany Creek is full of contradictions. It is a productive stream at times and barren at others. It exemplifies what fly-fishermen think of as pristine water, yet it sometimes has problems in its headwaters with acidity. At times it displays fantastic hatches like the Blue-Winged Olive Dun around the end of May. At other times it's void of any hatches whatsoever. Hit the Mehoopany on one of its better days with a fantastic hatch appearing and you're in for a memorable day of fly-fishing.

The Mehoopany begins in the southwestern end of Wyoming County and flows northeast fifteen miles before it enters the Susquehanna River. Above Forkston the Mehoopany picks up several fine small tributaries loaded with brook trout up to twelve inches long. Opossum, Somers, Henry Lott, South, Stony, and Kasson Brooks flow into the main stem within a few miles of one another. Some of these tributaries are difficult to reach but can be rewarding to fish with their plentiful supply of native trout. The main stem above Kasson Brook holds plenty of native brook trout also, but you have to hike in to enjoy the fishing on the upper Mehoopany and its tributaries.

The upper end of the Mehoopany above Forkston usually contains cool water all season. From Forkston to the Susquehanna, however, the water temperature often rises above 70 degrees during June, July, and August, reserving fishing for the cooler hours. The North Branch flows into the main stem just downstream from Forkston. The pool formed at this junction holds trout throughout much of the season. A hundred yards below this junction pool lies another deep pool with a good trout population.

The Mehoopany contains plenty of small-to-medium-sized boulders throughout. You'll also find pools spaced 100 or more yards apart between many unproductive riffles. PA 87 parallels the lower end of the Mehoopany and most of the North Branch. A secondary road from Forkston to Lopez takes you to the upper half of the stream.

The Mehoopany has several heavy mayfly hatches and plenty of stoneflies and caddis flies. Probably the heaviest hatch is the Blue-Winged Olive Dun, which appears for a week in late May or early June. The duns emerge anywhere from 8:00 to 11:00 A.M. depending on the weather. The mating adults of these mayflies, the Dark-Olive Spinners, mate in the evening. Add to this hatch some Sulphurs, Light Cahills, and March Browns, and you'll see that you can meet some exciting hatches on the Mehoopany.

The best hatches and largest trout extend from Forkston downstream about five miles. On that stretch in early May you can see Light Stoneflies and the Tan Caddis. In early June, in addition to Blue-Winged Olives during the day, you can see Light Cahills, Olive Spinners, Dark-Blue Sedges, and Slate Drakes in the evening.

Best Times to Fly-fish:

April 18–May 5
Blue Quill: #18, morning and afternoon
Quill Gordon: #14, afternoon
Hendrickson and Red Quill: #14, afternoon
Green Caddis: #16, afternoon and evening
Tan Caddis: #16, afternoon and evening
Brown Caddis: #16, afternoon and evening

May 5–May 20
Light Stonefly: #12, morning and afternoon

May 25–June 15
March Brown: #12, morning and afternoon
Blue-Winged Olive Dun: #14, morning and afternoon
Light Cahill: #14, evening
Slate Drake: #12 or #14, evening
Little Green Stonefly: #16, morning

June 15–July 10
Little Green Stonefly: #16, morning
Slate Drake: #12 or #14, evening
Blue Quill: #18, morning and afternoon

July 15–September 1
Trico: #24, morning (spotty)

Towanda Creek

In June 1972 Hurricane Agnes devastated much of northeastern Pennsylvania. In its wake it left many flooded towns and cities and devastated many trout streams by scouring the streambeds. Towanda Creek exemplifies the destruction caused by this violent storm and its aftermath. Before the catastrophe Towanda contained a decent hatch of Green Drakes—now the hatch appears sporadically. Many local fly-fishermen in the Canton area avoid the creek today. Harry Jenkins lives next to the stream but rarely fishes it. Larry Thoren's home also borders the waters, but he seldom enters the water. Both fly-fishermen and many others in the Canton area travel forty to fifty miles to fly-fish on Pine or Kettle Creeks rather than stay at home and fish the Towanda.

But Towanda Creek has some good hatches and an adequate supply of trout for the early season. Try this stream after the first couple weeks of the season, you'll encounter few anglers and even fewer fly-fishermen.

Best Times to Fly-fish:

April 15–May 3
Tan Caddis: #14, morning and afternoon
Hendrickson: #14, afternoon (spotty)

May 15–June 10
March Brown: #12, morning and afternoon
Green Drake and Coffin Fly: #10, evening (spotty)
Brown Drake: #12, evening (spotty)

July 15–September 1
Trico: #24, morning

Mud Run

Fly-fishing-Only Project—2.6 miles; in Hickory Run State Park

What a name for a stream! You'd expect to see a slow, meandering, mud-filled creek flowing through intensively farmed land. The name doesn't appropriately describe Mud Run. Located in the eastern end of the scenic Poconos, Mud Run almost defies you to reach it. A trip to the stream is both rewarding and frustrating.

Mike Marinelli, Jay Kapolka, and I gathered our fishing gear and headed toward the lower end of the section open to public fishing on Mud Run. Jay had prepared us by saying that we had to hike some distance—

maybe a mile. We headed down an old path made by fishermen next to a private section owned by the Jervis Corporation. We crossed several small swamps and walked directly into a thick stand of ten-foot-high rhododendrons. After almost a mile of hiking, we still heard no stream. Finally, about fifteen minutes later, we headed down a steep, boulder-filled decline by crawling on our hands and knees until we finally reached Mud Run.

What a fantastic, spectacular sight—Mud Run in all its magnificent, hurrying splendor! A high, roaring waterfall above us fell into a deep, rock-filled pool below. This was the true Mud Run. Even when on the stream it defies you to walk up or downstream. High cliffs and huge boulders prevent you from any easy approach to the tan-colored pools. On this section of Mud Run wading is truly hazardous.

Mike, Jay, and I leapfrogged upstream, each of us casting in a pool or two. Only a few Hendricksons appeared while we fished, but all three of us elected to use Red Quills. In each sizable pool we caught several trout. All of them appeared to be streambred browns and brook trout ranging in size from six inches to a foot long. Obviously the state doesn't stock these trout. How would anybody reach this lower section to stock it? After fighting rapids, rocky cliffs, boulders, and deep water for three hours, we headed back to the car. To reach the car we again had to climb the steep mountain of boulders and cross through the rhododendrons.

Access to Mud Run is extremely limited. Only three or four hiking paths take you to the stream. The upper section lies in an organized camping area of Hickory Run State Park off PA 534. The state stocks only this upper section by using a private dirt road to the stream. Pools and riffles in this upper end don't compare to the lower end. The middle section lies just west of where the Northeast Extension of the Pennsylvania Turnpike crosses PA 534. There's a Fly-Fishing Only sign to show you the way to the stream.

Mud Run flows northeast in Carbon County, entering the Lehigh River near Lehigh Tannery, where Bob and Mary Lou Sentiwany run AA Pro Shop. Bob knows all of the hatches on Pocono streams well, and Mary Lou ties outstanding fly patterns. Bob says the abundant March Brown hatch on Mud Run brings up some heavy trout.

There's more to fly-fishing than casting and catching trout. You'll enjoy spectacular scenery on this stream, and if you don't mind hiking in, you'll love Mud Run.

Best Times to Fly-fish:

April 15–May 5
Quill Gordon: #14, afternoon
Hendrickson and Red Quill: #14, afternoon
Grannom: #16, morning and afternoon

May 15–June 15
Green Caddis: #16, morning and afternoon
March Brown: #12, morning and afternoon
Sulphur Dun and Spinner: #16, evening
Light Cahill: #14, evening
Green Drake and Coffin Fly: #10, evening (above PA 903)
Slate Drake: #12 or #14, evening
Little Green Stonefly: #16, morning, afternoon, and evening

Pohopoco Creek

Many people call Pohopoco Creek "Big Creek." Others attempt to call it by its proper name, although no two fishermen seem to pronounce it the same. The Pohopoco doesn't resemble the stream I first fly-fished thirty years ago. At that time no reservoir interrupted Pohopoco's upper and lower sections. Also thirty years ago all of the stream was open to fishing.

The Army Corps of Engineers created a dam about three miles upstream from the Pohopoco's confluence with the Lehigh River. The Beltzville Reservoir, with some sections over 100 feet deep, contains a bottom release. Because of the foresight of the Corps of Engineers this release keeps the two miles of open water below the dam cool all summer. Water temperatures below the dam remain in the 60s in July and August. This lower section contains some heavy trout, many holdovers, and plenty of trout planted by the state. The stream here ranges from fifty to seventy feet wide.

The reservoir contains some large brown trout. Jack Reichelderfer, of Pocono Gateway Sporting Outfitters, said that trout up to thirty inches long have been caught in the dam.

Above the dam the stream narrows to about thirty feet. From the upper end of the dam to Kresgeville much of the stream remains open to fishing but receives no state stocking. This section depends on streambred trout. From Kresgeville upstream, however, there's about eight miles of stocked water. The stream is open and stocked above Effort. Middle and Dotters creeks, two main tributaries of the Pohopoco, also receive stocked trout.

Mike Marinelli and Jay Kapolka of Levittown and I fly-fished the unstocked water of Pohopoco Creek in early May two years ago. In this section of the stream the south bank harbors a heavy canopy of rhododendrons, while the north bank has alders and hemlocks. Our dry flies seemed to attach to an alder, hemlock, or rhododendron as often as they rested on the surface.

When we approached the stream shortly after noon, we saw several Quill Gordons fly toward the far bank. Smaller, size-22 Blue Duns (*Pseu-*

docloeon) emerged frequently as we waded upstream. All of us tied on patterns to match the afternoon's hatch of the Blue Dun. As we approached the first sizable pool, possibly six trout rose to Blue Dun naturals on the surface. Both Mike and Jay caught trout on the Blue Dun and later on a size-16 Tan Caddis. Well after the Blue Dun hatch ended, the Tan Caddis continued to emerge, but trout rose only sporadically to the hatch. Trout refused to rise because the water temperature that afternoon only reached 48 degrees. Mike and Jay caught several streambred brown trout from six to ten inches long. They seldom catch trout in this section much larger.

The Pohopoco contains many good hatches throughout the season. The Blue Duns and Quill Gordons of April give way to Tan Caddis and Grannoms in early May. Later in May, Slate Drakes, Light Cahills, and Blue-Winged Olive Duns appear. If you plan to be on this stream in late May or June, make certain you carry a good supply of Blue-Winged Olive Duns in sizes 14 and 16.

The Pohopoco presents some difficult wading because of its rocks and boulders. It has some deep debris-filled pools with productive riffles above. US 209 parallels much of the stream east of Lehighton. Jack Reichelderfer knows the stream and its hatches. Stop in at his store in Lehighton and check conditions with him before you fish the "Big Creek."

Best Times to Fly-fish:

April 1–April 20
Little Blue-Winged Olive Dun: #20, morning and afternoon
Dark-Brown Caddis: #16, morning and afternoon

April 15–May 10
Quill Gordon: #14, afternoon
Hendrickson and Red Quill: #14, afternoon
Blue Dun: #20, afternoon
Green Caddis: #14 and 16, morning and afternoon
Grannom: #16, morning and afternoon
Blue Quill: #18, morning and afternoon

May 15–June 5
Blue-Winged Olive Dun: #14, morning and afternoon
Green Drake and Coffin Fly: #10, evening (spotty)
Slate Drake: #12 or #14, evening

June 5–July 10
Slate Drake: #12 or #14, evening
Light Cahill: #14, evening
Blue-Winged Olive Dun: #14, morning and afternoon
Yellow Drake: #12, evening

September 1–September 30
Rusty Brown Caddis: #14 and #16, morning and afternoon

Brodhead Creek

Monroe County in northeastern Pennsylvania contains some fantastic trout streams. Within a few miles of Stroudsburg you can fish on Pocono, McMichael, Big Bushkill, and Brodhead creeks. All streams present great fly-fishing, with many hatches and plenty of stocked, holdover, and streambred trout. Fly-fish on any of these in late April, and you'll likely fish over a tremendous Hendrickson hatch that lasts for a couple hours in the afternoon. Fish these same waters on a late-May morning, and you'll probably fish over a super Blue-Winged Olive hatch.

Progress and immigration from New York and New Jersey have caught up with Monroe County. Land prices are rising. The quantity of posted waters increases annually as more private fishing clubs develop. More and more fishermen fish on less and less water, putting undue pressure on the remaining precious public-access streams.

In addition to being subject to all the problems associated with a booming local economy, the Monroe County streams have been slow to recover from a calamitous flood caused by Hurricane Diane in 1955. After that flood the Corps of Engineers channelized much of the Brodhead just above and below the PA 191 bridge. Studies by the Pennsylvania Fish Commission in cooperation with the Brodhead Chapter of Trout Unlimited showed an alarming decrease in the wild trout population in the channelized area. In an effort to improve habitat on the Brodhead, the chapter has placed more than 400 tons of boulders in the stream. The results of this effort have been rewarding—a recent survey shows that the trout population has increased tenfold after installation of the boulders. But there's more work to do, and the chapter plans additional work days to further improve the stream through their Restore the Brodhead project.

Don Baylor met me on the Brodhead recently. We fished the upper end of the open water near Analomink. The Brodhead reminds me of a small Beaverkill. The streambed contains many huge boulders, small rocks, gravel, and sand. Siltation problems so common on our southeastern streams appear minimal here. The Brodhead contains an abundance of productive pocket water with stocked, holdover, and streambred trout. The upper ends of many of the pools contain productive deep riffles.

Don and I fished the Brodhead on a hot June evening after the air temperature had topped out at 91 degrees. The water temperature at 7:00 P.M. registered 71 degrees. Nothing much happened until dusk. This often typifies activity on hot summer evenings. At dusk hundreds of Sulphur

Don Baylor conducts many studies of aquatic life on the Brodhead Creek.

Duns emerged. Still more Sulphur Spinners returned to the water to deposit fertilized eggs. In a productive area ahead of us only two trout occasionally rose to this feast. Don hooked a heavy fourteen-inch holdover brown, while I looked on for rising trout. None showed. We left the stream well after dusk. I've experienced many instances like this one, where a tremendous hatch or spinner fall occurs and few or no trout rise.

From Analomink downstream to the Delaware the Brodhead presents six miles of open water. Just below Stroudsburg the stream enters an inaccessible gorge. Effluent from two plants pushes a heavy load of treated sewage into the lower three miles of stream. Two other excellent trout streams, McMichael and Pocono creeks, join the Brodhead in Stroudsburg. Both waters contain hatches similar to those found on the Brodhead.

Local fishermen have labeled certain areas on the stream. Going downstream you'll find PA 191 (High Bridge), the area channelized after the flood; Whirlpool; Stokes Avenue; Stokes Mill; and Moose Lodge. Above Analomink the water is posted. A mile above that town you'll see the Paradise Branch enter the main stem. The Brodhead Forest and Stream Club posts this lower part of the branch and the main stem in that area. The Henryville Conservation Club controls the Paradise Branch upstream, and the Parkside Anglers the main stem upstream. Were it not for these private clubs, the Brodhead in that area would be more highly developed, and fishing in the open section below would suffer. PA 447 parallels the upper part of the stream, and a paved secondary road the lower half.

The Brodhead contains an enormous supply of Hendricksons that appear from mid- to late April. Recently Don Baylor has seen Tricos on the Brodhead in August. Add to these a dozen or more other heavy hatches, and you see why fishing the hatches on the Brodhead can be rewarding.

Best Times to Fly-fish:

April 15–May 5
Little Blue-Winged Olive Dun: #20, morning and afternoon
Quill Gordon: #14, afternoon
Hendrickson and Red Quill: #14, afternoon

May 5–June 10
Tan Sedge: #14, afternoon and evening
Sulphur Dun and Spinner: #16, evening
Gray Fox and Ginger Quill: #12 and #14, afternoon and evening
March Brown: #12, morning and afternoon
Blue-Winged Olive Dun: #14, morning
Slate Drake: #12 and #14, evening
Light Cahill: #14, evening
Pink Lady: #14, evening

June 10–July 1
Sulphur Dun and Spinner: #18, evening
Cream Cahill: #14 and #16, evening
Yellow Stonefly: #14, evening

July 1–September 30
Light Cahill: #14, evening
Cream Cahill: #14 and #16, evening
Slate Drake: #12 and #14, evening
Trico: #24, morning
Yellow Stonefly: #14, evening
Olive Sedge: #14 and #16, evening
Tan Sedge: #14 and #16, evening

Big Bushkill Creek

Fly-fishing-Only Project—6 miles; on the Ressica Falls Scout Reservation property except 200 yards on each side of the falls.

As early as 8:00 A.M. the temperature approached 70 degrees. Don Baylor and I registered at the Boy Scout headquarters at Ressica Falls before fishing on the Big Bushkill. We parked our car at the designated lot and hiked downstream two miles to fly-fish a section below Piano Pool.

Don prefers fishing the Big Bushkill early in the morning. He's had a lot of success using stonefly nymphs on this boulder-strewn stream, which is filled with several stonefly species. These nymphs remain active in the morning.

We entered the stream where a heavy riffle flowed into a six-foot-deep, fifty-foot-long pool. I checked the water temperature on this late-June morning, and at 9:00 A.M. it registered 69 degrees. Any productive fly-fishing on this hot summer morning would be short-lived. Don hooked a couple browns and a brook trout at the tail of the pool and missed two at the head.

Above the pool lay a half-mile of deep pocket water. Don picked up several more trout on a caddis pattern. A few Blue Quills emerged rapidly from the surface, along with a hodgepodge of stoneflies. In the backwater Cream Cahill spinners lay spent from their final egg-laying ritual the night before. Both Don and I picked up trout in that stretch before the heat and humidity got to us and we quit.

Don often fishes the Big Bushkill earlier in the season. The stream holds an exceptionally heavy Blue Quill hatch the third week in April. If the water has warmed sufficiently, the Blue Quill and the Hendrickson hatches can last for hours, with plenty of rising trout. At about the same time Don fishes when Grannoms appear on the surface. Don says that Grannoms vary in color on the Big Bushkill and that there are light and dark phases of the species. The stream also holds abundant March Browns and Blue-Winged Olive Duns.

Like the brown-stained Tobyhanna, the Big Bushkill flows from the

Pocono Plateau. The Bushkill warms rapidly in the summer. Upstream it contains more than a half-dozen impoundments with top-water releases that considerably warm the water below.

The Bushkill's streambed has every kind of rock, from huge boulders to small stones. Wading this uneven surface can be hazardous. There's about six miles of fly-fishing water on the Scout reservation. The farther downstream you hike the less likely you are to meet other fly-fishermen. Some of the stretches have been named: the Firestone, Little Falls, Piano Pool (shaped like a piano), and Chapel Pool (the Boy Scouts hold worship services nearby). If you don't mind hiking, you can fly-fish in an isolated area with plenty of stocked and some holdover trout. PA 402 crosses the stream at Ressica Falls.

Best Times to Fly-fish:

April 15–May 5
Blue Quill: #18, morning and afternoon
Quill Gordon: #14, afternoon
Hendrickson and Red Quill: #14, afternoon
Grannom (light and dark phases): #14, morning and afternoon

May 5–June 10
Tan Caddis: #14, afternoon and evening
Gray Fox and Ginger Quill: #12 and #14, afternoon and evening
March Brown: #12, morning and afternoon
Light Cahill: #14, evening
Slate Drake: #12 and #14, evening

June 5–July 1
Gray Caddis: #14, evening
Blue Quill: #18, morning and afternoon
Light Cahill: #14, evening
Yellow Stonefly: #14, afternoon and evening
Little Green Stonefly: #16, afternoon and evening
Cream Cahill: #14 and #16, evening

Dyberry Creek

Delayed Harvest Fly-fishing Only—1 mile; from the Widmer property line about one mile below Tanner's Falls downstream to Mary Wilcox bridge, SR 4007.

The summer of 1988 was especially unkind to the Dyberry. Hot weather, droughtlike conditions, and urban development have taken their toll. Stream temperatures now often rise well into the 70s and stay there too long. Trout search out small spring-fed tributaries to survive. If these fish find a cool spring, and if a gray heron or raccoon doesn't find them, they might live through the season. A few trout do hold over in some of the deeper pools on the main stem. The twenty-foot-deep pool just below the dry General Edgar Jadwin Dam holds trout all year long. Another pool just above the delayed-harvest stretch that Rick Eck of Honesdale tagged the Five Pounder Hole holds trout through the summer. But much of the main stem of the Dyberry contains little cover and slow, shallow water, and warms quickly in the summer.

The Dyberry needs a host of stream improvements the way a seedling needs water. This once-great trout stream contains many sections with long, shallow pools with some riffles and pocket water between. Devices like log jams, rocks, and gabions would help rejuvenate the stream. In 1984 several fly-fishermen in the area formed a Pike-Wayne Chapter of Trout Unlimited. This group hopes to construct improvements under the Adopt-a-Stream arm of the Pennsylvania Fish Commission.

Another hazard to trout in the stream comes in late May when lamprey eels by the thousands move up the Delaware, into the Lackawaxen River, then into the Dyberry. These parasites latch onto any trout or pickerel they can find.

You reach the Dyberry from PA 191 north out of Honesdale, where it enters the Lackawaxen River. The section above the fairgrounds contains productive water for early-season fly-fishing, with plenty of Quill Gordons in mid-April. Upstream a blacktop road off PA 191 crosses the Dyberry at Day Bridge. The pool at Day Bridge is deep and productive. Just across the bridge another paved road to the right parallels the upper part of the main stem. Two miles above Day Bridge you'll cross the Mary Wilcox Bridge. The delayed-harvest, fly-fishing-only section begins at the bridge and goes upstream one mile.

Travel another mile upstream, and you'll see the East Branch on your right and the West Branch on your left. You can park in state game lands to fish either branch. Tanner Falls lies one mile up the larger West Branch. This area contains spectacular scenery, deep pools, and a good early trout population. The East Branch begins in Upper Woods Pond. This impoundment holds the only kokanee salmon in the Commonwealth.

Hatches begin early on the Dyberry and continue through much of the fishing season. Rick Eck says the Blue Quill (*Paraleptophlebia adoptiva*) and Quill Gordon often appear before the season begins. You can take advantage of these early hatches on the delayed-harvest area.

Mid-April and late May hold the most productive hatches. After the Blue Quills and Quill Gordons, you'll see a good hatch of Hendricksons on the Dyberry. In mid- to late May March Browns and Gray Foxes emerge by day and Sulphurs in the evening. In early June two down-wings, the

Yellow Stonefly and Dark-Blue Sedge, bring trout to the surface. Even as late as September you'll see Blue Quills, Slate Drakes, and a size-22 Blue Dun on the water.

If Honesdale native Rick Eck and other members of the newly formed Pike-Wayne Trout Unlimited Chapter have a choice, they invariably choose to fish the Delaware or Lackawaxen Rivers over the Dyberry. Therein lies part of the problem: why place stream-improvement devices on the Dyberry when the fantastic Delaware is only ten miles away?

Best Times to Fly-fish:

April 15–May 5
Blue Quill: #18, morning and afternoon
Quill Gordon: #14, afternoon
Hendrickson and Red Quill: #14, afternoon
Grannom: #14, morning and afternoon

May 12–June 10
Sulphur Dun and Spinner: #16, evening
Gray Fox and Ginger Quill: #12 and #14, afternoon and evening
March Brown: #12, morning and afternoon
Slate Drake: #12 and #14, evening
Yellow Stonefly: #14, afternoon and evening
Dark-Blue Sedge: #12, evening

June 15–August 1
Blue Quill: #18, morning and afternoon
Slate Drake: #12 and #14, evening

September 1–October 30
Blue Quill: #18, morning and afternoon
Little Black Caddis: #16, morning and afternoon
Little Blue Dun: #22, morning and afternoon

Four

STREAMS OF
Southeastern Pennsylvania

Southeastern Pennsylvania—who would think that fly-fishermen could catch healthy, heavy, native brown trout only a few miles from the Philadelphia city limits? Who would believe, in this urbanized area, that some great mayfly hatches like the Sulphur appear? Who but the anglers who fish these streams regularly would believe that caddis flies still appear on southeastern streams in excellent numbers?.

Despite their unexpected excellence, however, the streams of the southeast have encountered a number of serious problems—some of which will determine whether these waters will continue to hold trout and provide anglers hours of recreation. Problems of growth will decide whether man and his environment can coexist in any sort of harmony in this region. Housing developments, industrial parks, road construction, and farming near headwaters produce enormous siltation problems on local streams. Look at Ridley, Darby, and Valley creeks as examples. Ridley and Darby become coffee colored after a moderate rain. This siltation problem affects the hatches on these streams drastically. Take a walk along Darby Creek. In one pool you'll notice a car's fender, in the riffle above maybe a discarded barrel, farther upstream you'll see a shopping cart—all dumped into the stream. Valley Creek exemplifies the hazards of chemical pollution. What has man done to his precious environment?

Wayne Poppich, of King of Prussia, says that the trout streams of southeastern Pennsylvania are on the brink of disaster. Moreover conditions in the southeast have implications for the rest of the state. How man deals with the problems of pollution and population in this area will determine how streams in the rest of the state survive in the future. If these hard-pressed waters in the southeast survive our onslaught, then the future for trout fishing for the entire state appears bright. If these streams finally succumb to man's so-called progress, however, can others be far behind?

Regional, county, state, and national parks have become the salvation

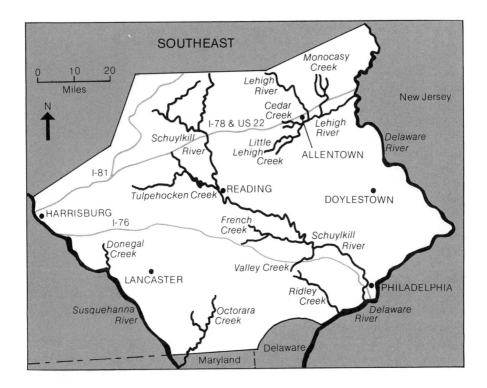

of many of the southeastern streams, a number of which lie within or have their headwaters in these protected areas. Some of Valley Creek's best fishing is contained within Valley Forge National Park; Ridley Creek holds a state park and an arboretum in its headwaters; and the Little Lehigh and the Tulpehocken run through extensive park systems. Interested sportsman and nature groups in the southeast provide another important ingredient to the stability of these streams. The Delco Manning and Valley Forge chapters of Trout Unlimited have undertaken many environmental projects dedicated to the protection and preservation of streams in their vicinity. They need your help to protect the future of these waters.

With all of its problems, however, southeastern Pennsylvania indeed boasts some exceptional trout fishing and some great opportunities for matching the hatch.

Valley Creek

No-kill Zone—Valley Creek and its tributaries.

What great history this stream holds! Just a little over 200 years ago the lower end of Valley Creek sheltered Washington's discouraged, desperate Continental Army. Some of the most productive pockets and pools on the stream lie within a few feet of Lafayette's headquarters during the Revolutionary War. The very spot you're fishing could be a spot where Washington, Lafayette, or one of their soldiers crossed. Three miles of the lower end of Valley Creek lie within the boundary of Valley Forge National Park.

But all is not well with this fantastically productive brown trout stream. Wayne Poppich, of King of Prussia, who has a deep, sincere affection for this stream, has seen it receive two doses of cyanide over the past ten years. Five years ago Valley received another shot of pollution. This time Conrail spilled PCBs into the stream. When the pollution occurred the state stopped stocking the stream. As with Spring Creek in central Pennsylvania, which also became polluted, the halt to stocking Valley became a blessing in disguise, however. Hordes of early-season anglers looking for recently stocked trout have vanished.

Yes, thousands of streambred browns inhabit this limestone stream located only minutes from Philadelphia. But as with Spring Creek, entirely too many trout die after swallowing an angler's live bait and hook. Why doesn't someone in authority protect this valuable resource by allowing only artificial lures on Valley Creek?

Poppich has said that if Valley Creek were located in central Pennsylvania, environmentalists would be more aware of the stream's value; because it's located in a sprawling metropolitan area, it doesn't get the respect it deserves. "Only because of its limestone aquifer has Valley Creek been able to withstand the ravages of man," says Poppich. "If the same exploitation happened to Ridley, French, or Darby they'd be dead streams."

The Valley Forge Chapter of Trout Unlimited of West Chester has devoted thousands of man-hours to the preservation of the fishery on this stream. They have built channeling devices on Little Crabby Creek. A system of baffles allows spawning trout to migrate upstream. The local Trout Unlimited chapter also filed suit in one of the recent pollution incidents and works with the Pennsylvania Department of Environmental Resources to remedy calcium sedimentation and warm-water discharge into Valley from a quarry site.

Trout Unlimited, Green Valley Association, and the Open Land Conservancy also received cooperation recently from the Trammell Crow Company when the latter planned to divert one of Valley's tributaries, Little Crabby Creek. After Trout Unlimited talked with Trammell Crow, the company hired the architectural firm Curtis, Cox, Kennerly, and Weston to design a new stream channel that would accommodate trout. This shows what can happen when companies and environmentalists cooperate on a worthwhile project.

Although he's only been fly-fishing for a few years, Chip Swarner catches some nice brown trout on Valley Creek in Valley Forge Park.

This limestone stream has summer water temperatures that rarely exceed 70 degrees. Valley Creek is twenty to thirty feet wide, and many anglers on it catch streambred brown trout over fifteen inches long.

Joe Petrella, Jr., of Downingtown, Frank Swarner and his son Chip, of Glenmoore, and Wayne Poppich fly-fish regularly on Valley in the park. Joe's office is only ten minutes from the stream, and he regularly spends his lunch hour fishing. I met Joe, Frank, Chip, and Wayne on Valley one evening not long ago. Hundreds of Little Blue-Winged Olives emerged off the riffles from 6:00 P.M. until dark. At least six heavy trout rose in the pool Joe selected to fish. Joe often fishes when the Dark-Olive Caddis emerges, and he lands and releases heavy sixteen-inch browns during this caddis hatch. Wayne landed a twenty-inch brown on Valley last year. Twelve-year-old Chip Swarner is an excellent caster and fisherman. Chip hooked one trout that evening that broke his hook and landed another streambred brown over a foot long.

There's a total of thirteen miles of fishing on Valley and two miles on its tributary, Little Valley Creek. Valley Creek enters the Schuylkill River near the national park.

Will Valley continue to be a proud stream with some great streambred browns? Will the state or the federal agencies change the regulations on this fine stream to prohibit bait fishing? Only time and demands from interested groups will tell.

Best Times to Fly-fish:

April 1–April 30
Dark-Olive Caddis: #16, morning and afternoon
Little Blue-Winged Olive Dun: #22, afternoon and evening
Pale Gray Crane Fly: #20, evening
Pale Yellow Crane Fly: #20, evening
Blue-Winged Olive Dun: #16, morning and afternoon

May 10–June 15
Green Caddis: #16, afternoon and evening
Sulphur Dun and Spinner: #16, evening
Light Cahill: #14, evening

July 10–September 1
Trico: #24, morning (Little Valley Creek)(spotty)
Little Blue-Winged Olive Dun: #22, evening

September 1–October 15
Light Olive Caddis: #16, afternoon

Tulpehocken Creek

Delayed Harvest Artificial Lures Only—3.8 miles; from the first deflector below Blue Marsh Dam downstream to the covered bridge.

Dick Henry lives in Lebanon. By vocation he's been a skilled watch repairman for thirty years. For the past ten years he's been a regular contributor of writing on his fishing and hunting experiences to *Field & Stream*. On Tuesdays and Sundays you can find Dick, Ellwood Gettle, also of Lebanon, and Larry Gasser, of Fleetwood, fly-fishing on their favorite stream—the Tulpehocken. Recently Dick invited me to fly-fish with the trio on that stream, after more than a year of boasting about the quality of the fishing.

We scheduled a trip in early May to coincide with one of the Tulpe-hocken's heavy caddis hatches. It rained for several hours before we met and continued to pour as we planned the day's strategy. We arrived near the section the locals call the Red Bridge Pool. Dick decided to stay in the

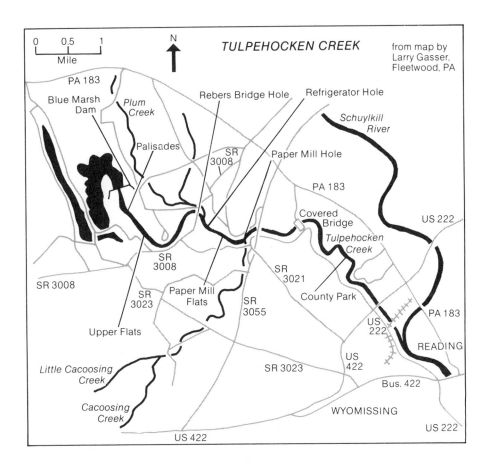

car and forgo any fly-fishing in the inclement weather. From time to time during the next four-hour fly-fishing episode, however, he'd leave the car and act as a kibitzer. Larry, Ellwood, and I gathered our fishing gear, donned our raincoats, and headed for the stream. It wasn't long before the action began.

"Whoee, did I ever miss a big one!" yelled Ellwood.

"There must be a half-dozen trout over fifteen inches long rising in front of me," bellowed Larry.

What a great day we experienced on that stream! Right in the middle of that early-May downpour, dozens of heavy browns and rainbows splashed the surface for Green Caddis adults, while others fed on emergers. Ellwood, Larry, and I braved the rain and stood in the water mesmerized by these large trout feeding freely on the caddis. Shortly Larry caught a brown trout that had been a planted fingerling just last year. Then Ellwood caught several heavy rainbows thirteen to fourteen inches long on a floating emerger pattern. All these trout, placed in the Tulpehocken just a few years before as fingerlings, fought viciously, unlike most recently stocked trout.

In checking the water in front of me I saw a size-16 bright-green caddis that had just emerged. I tied on a Deerhead Green Caddis that copied the natural closely. All three of us had a half-dozen to a dozen sporadic risers in front of us, and we yelled as we cast over these fish. The first few trout drifted in cadence with the drift of my imitation for a couple feet but refused the pattern. A couple nosed the pattern and refused it.

"Whoee, look at that monster rising in front of me!" yelled Ellwood.

Larry echoed his sentiments. Several fish over fifteen inches long splashed within feet of where he stood.

Intermittent rising continued for four hours during heavy rain. We finally quit at 4:00 P.M. after the three of us had landed more than twenty heavy browns and rainbows. These Tulpehocken trout strike slowly and very deliberately.

If you like large-stream fly-fishing and plenty of good-sized trout, you'll love the Tulpehocken. At many places the stream extends over 100 feet wide with many deep and deceptively fast flats. Many of the sections below the Blue Marsh Dam have been named by the locals. Downstream from the dam you'll find sections called the Palisades or Granite ⌐ool, Red Bridge Pool, Rebers Bridge, Refrigerator Pool, Paper Mill Flats, and the Water Authority. Guess how the Refrigerator Pool got its name? There's an old refrigerator in the middle of the hole.

What makes the Tulpehocken the top stream in the southeast? Until 1982 this section below the dam received legal-sized trout when it was stocked. In 1982 the state instituted a fingerling program. Annually they place 12,000 fingerling browns and rainbows in a five-mile stretch of the stream. In 1983 the state set special regulations on 3.8 miles of the water. On this delayed-harvest area only artificial lures can be used.

The Corps of Engineers cooperates fully with the state a⌐⌐ local sportsman's organizations to produce a tremendous fishery on the Tulpehocken. Jeff Omlor and Carl Warner work for the Corps, and if you call them between 8:15 and 8:30 A.M. they'll let you know the times of water releases for the coming day. The Corps uses bottom releases from the dam in July and August to cool the water below, providing an important ingredient in the successful trout fishery on the Tulpehocken. Dick Henry checked the water temperature at several locations below the dam on August 23 several years ago. Just below the dam he recorded a temperature of 68 degrees. Two miles downstream from the dam at Rebers Bridge he found temperatures around 81. Two miles below Rebers Bridge in the Picnic Area the water was 77. Because of the dam the water stays in good shape and doesn't discolor quickly after a storm.

The Tulpehocken Trout Unlimited Chapter has worked tirelessly to make the stream more productive by improving the water flow in the Water Authority Area with gabions and rock placements. This same dedicated organization monitors pH, water temperature, and invertebrates in the water at eight locations below the dam. They need your help to maintain this fantastic trout fishery.

The Tulpehocken, with its limestone base, contains a diversity of mayfly and caddis fly hatches. Caddis flies can be found almost daily on the stream from early April until September. Mayflies like the Trico and Sulphur also produce some excellent match-the-hatch fly-fishing. Larry Gasser says that the Trico spinner fall seems the heaviest at the Water Authority. Some days the Trico fall lasts for more than an hour with two and three separate falls. Sulphurs appear on the stream in early May and continue to emerge for several weeks.

The rainbows seem especially heavy and appear to have adapted well to their environment in the Tulpehocken. A fingerling rainbow planted two years ago might now be fifteen inches long and weigh well over a pound and a half.

Wading this large stream presents few problems. There is limited parking in some of the areas. The Berks County Recreation Authority owns much of the land along the stream. There's 3.8 miles of regulated water with two miles of open water below the delayed harvest project. A major tributary, the Cacoosing Creek, enters the main stem at Paper Mill Hole; another branch, Plum Creek, carries some sewage effluent. The Tulpehocken contains many long, flat sections. Trout are not spooky and often rise within feet of where you're standing.

Best Times to Fly-fish:

April 1–April 15
Little Blue-Winged Olive Dun: #20, morning and afternoon
Little Black Stonefly: #18, morning and afternoon

April 15–May 1
Little Blue-Winged Olive Dun: #20, morning and afternoon
Pale Olive Caddis: #16 or #18, midday
Tan Caddis: #16 or #18, midday
Yellow Crane Fly: #16, afternoon and evening
Brownish Gray Caddis: #14 or #16, evening

May 5–May 31
Black Caddis: #12, evening
Sulphur Dun and Spinner: #16, evening
Green Caddis: #16 or #18, morning and afternoon

May 25–June 30
Dark-Gray Caddis: #16 or #18, evening

June 15–July 1
Yellow Drake: #12, evening

July 1–September 30
Trico: #24, morning

August 10–September 1
Big Slate Drake and Rusty Spinner: #8, evening

September 15–November 1
Little Blue-Winged Olive Dun: #22, afternoon

Ridley Creek

Delayed Harvest Fly-fishing Only—1 mile; from the falls in Ridley
Creek State Park, downstream to the mouth of Dismal Run.

Barry Staats, Mary Kuss, and I planned a day of fly-fishing on one of the better suburban fly streams near Philadelphia, Ridley Creek. Barry has often boasted about the quality of fly-fishing on this stream so close to his Sporting Gentleman store, in Media. He's confirmed that the stream often contains rising trout and several decent mayfly, stonefly, and caddis fly hatches. Mary teaches fly-fishing classes at Barry's store. She's an expert caster, and she's familiar with the aquatic life of southeastern streams. Mary has been a fly-fisher since her sixteenth birthday and an accomplished caster for the past ten years. *The Philadelphia Inquirer* recently did a pictorial story on her fishing ability. Mary believes the three heaviest hatches on Ridley are the Sulphur in mid- and late May, the Little Black Stonefly in March, and the Light-Olive Caddis, which appears near the end of April. Watching Mary cast on the fly-fishing section of Ridley demonstrated her expertise for me.

Mary expressed concern that the put-and-take mentality of many area anglers is really strong. "Fishing pressure remains high on Ridley for a couple days after opening day and in-season stockings, then falls off dramatically," she explained.

Ridley Creek, in spite of the urban sprawl surrounding it, contains some holdover trout and acceptable water quality. Its main salvation lies with a 2,600-acre Ridley Creek State Park and the 700-acre Tyler Arboretum in its upper end. Dismal Run houses a trout nursery run by the Delco Anglers and Conservationists. This private stream flows through the arboretum's property. Barry claims that this small, cold tributary harbors some streambred browns. Upstream from the arboretum and state park are a golf course and farmland.

Ridley contains a heavy canopy of beech and sycamores through much of the seven miles of stocked water. At the lower end of the state park there's a one-mile delayed-harvest section that runs downstream to Dismal Run.

Ridley Creek begins in Chester County and flows southeast into Delaware County. It's located just west of Media off US 1. Ridley Creek Road and Knowlton Road parallel much of the water. The stream ranges from twenty to forty feet wide and contains many pools three to six feet deep, with some deep, productive riffles between. Water temperatures in July and August elevate into the high 70s. Trout look for springs or cool tributaries like Dismal Run or Jeffers Run during these hot spells. The state stocks the stream from the Colonial Plantation in the state park downstream to Rose Valley. There's a bicycle path that gives access to three miles of stocked stream in the state park.

Best Times to Fly-fish:

March 1–March 30
Little Black Stonefly: #14 and #16, morning and afternoon
Early Brown Stonefly: #12, afternoon
Tan Caddis: #14 and #16, morning and afternoon
Brown Caddis: #14 and #16, morning and afternoon

April 10–April 30
Little Black Caddis: #16 and #18, morning and afternoon
Little Blue-Winged Olive Dun: #20, morning and afternoon*
Hendrickson and Red Quill: #14, afternoon (spotty)
Quill Gordon: #14, afternoon (spotty)
Light-Olive Caddis: #16, morning and afternoon

May 12–June 15
Sulphur Dun and Spinner: #16, evening
Gray Fox: #12 and #14, afternoon
March Brown: #12, morning and afternoon
Blue-Winged Olive Dun: #14, morning and afternoon
Light Cahill: #14 and #16, evening*

September 15–October 15
Slate Drake: #12 or #14, afternoon

*Little Blue-Winged Olive Dun continues to appear from time to time until late September. Light Cahill appears until the end of August.

French Creek

Fly-fishing-Only Project—1.2 miles; from dam at Camp Sleepy Hollow downstream to Sheeder Road.

Leon Rosenthal, a dentist from Abington, has fly-fished on French Creek for more than forty years. Many changes have occurred in those years to this heavily fished yet productive trout stream just forty minutes from Philadelphia. Leon tells how development in the headwaters has greatly diminished this once-proud stream.

Mary Kuss, Barry Staats, and I arrived at the fly-fishing-only area at Sheeder Mill Road one day recently. I saw Steve Reifsneider of Pottstown checking the rocks for aquatic insects and went over to see what he found. There's an unusual diversity of mayfly, caddis fly, and stonefly hatches on French. Looking at several submerged rocks proved it. Examining two rocks Steve lifted in a riffle showed several mayfly species. As we checked the rocks a heavy downpour began. Surely there'd be no fly-fishing today. As quickly as it had begun, however, the rain ended and French Creek appeared no more discolored than before.

We glanced to the flat section below the bridge and saw trout feeding occasionally on a size-16 Olive Caddis. Barry and Mary headed down toward the rising trout. Barry tied on an appropriate imitation to match the emerging caddis, while Mary tied on a size-16 caddis pupa. Both Barry and Mary coaxed rainbows and browns to the surface for their patterns. The two landed a half-dozen trout on caddis imitations in an hour. Trout rose all morning, and most took a caddis pattern freely. Occasional Sulphur Duns appeared on this morning, May 6, a good week ahead of schedule.

French ranges from thirty to sixty feet wide and contains many deep runs, productive riffles, and pocket water. The state stocks approximately fifteen miles of the stream from St. Peters downstream to the village of Kimberton. The fly-fishing area runs from 100 yards above Sheeder Run Road upstream to Hollow Road, almost 1½ miles. Much of the stream contains a canopy of sycamores.

French Creek remains productive until early June. Temperatures after that time often rise into the mid- and upper 70s, and you'll find smallmouth bass where trout resided earlier. Steve Reifsneider has occasionally caught holdover trout.

French begins with water from Scott Run and Hopewell Lakes in French Creek State Park. The creek flows from Berks County southeast into Chester County, picking up tributaries like Pine Creek, Rock Run, South Branch, Beaver Run, and Birch Run before flowing through Phoenixville and emptying into the Schuylkill River. Its course is within forty minutes of Philadelphia. A blacktop road follows the stream to Kimberton.

Even with its shortcomings French maintains its stature as a good southeastern trout stream. Jack Mickievicz of Phoenixville says the stream contains an unusual diversity of mayflies but few spectacular hatches. If you're on the stream at the right time, however, matching the hatch can be rewarding. Hendricksons, Blue Quills, March Browns, Gray Foxes, Slate Drakes, and many more mayflies appear throughout the season. Caddis hatches become the fly-fisherman's salvation on French Creek. Even before the season begins Tan and Brown Caddis appear. Carry plenty of size-16 and -18 caddis patterns with you if you're fishing this stream.

Best Times to Fly-fish:

April 1–April 20
Little Black Caddis: #18, morning and afternoon
Little Tan Caddis: #18, morning and afternoon
Brown Caddis: #16, morning and afternoon
Olive Caddis: #16, morning and afternoon

May 10–June 10
Sulphur Dun and Spinner: #16, evening
Gray Fox: #14, afternoon
March Brown: #12, morning and afternoon
Light Cahill: #14, evening
Slate Drake: #12 or #14, evening

June 20–July 30
Little Blue-Winged Olive Dun: #20, morning and afternoon
Cream Cahill: #14, evening
Trico: #24, morning (spotty)

August 1–August 30
Cream Cahill: #14, evening
Trico: #24, morning (spotty)
Big Slate Drake: #8, evening
Perla Stonefly: #12, evening

Octoraro Creek

West Branch Octoraro Creek—Delayed Harvest Fly-fishing Only—
1.9 miles; from about 200 yards below PA 472 downstream to near
the second unnamed tributary below SR 2010.

Quaint Amish buggies plodded along the country road as we headed south from Lancaster. Pennsylvania Dutch country holds some exciting trout streams in this scenic section of Lancaster County. We first crossed the West Branch of the Octoraro on PA 472. At that point Black Rock

The West Branch of the Octoraro near Quarryville in Lancaster County. Des Kahn picks up a trout during a Sulphur hatch.

Gorge begins. This unusual, spectacular gorge with huge rocks has been classified as an outstanding geological site by the state. Just below that point a delayed-harvest section begins and continues downstream for two miles. A heavy canopy shared much of the upper end of the West Branch. Pennsylvania also includes the Octoraro in its scenic-river system. Just being on this stream evokes satisfaction and contentment.

At the lower end of the fly-fishing project I recently met Don Whitesel, of Millersville, Desmond Kahn, of Newark, Delaware, and Jim Leonard, of Claymont, Delaware. It's only a forty-five minute drive from Newark to the Octoraro. All three fly-fish the Octoraro frequently. Jim and Des know the hatches well. Desmond recently received his degree from the University of Delaware in insect ecology.

At first glance the Octoraro reminds you of a central-Pennsylvania limestone stream, especially in the meadow where we chose to fish. We fished the stream on a cool mid-June evening. The Octoraro water that evening registered a cool 60 degrees. Desmond assured me that the temperature often rises into the high 70s on hot summer days. All three have caught holdover trout on the stream.

By the time we arrived on the stream a few Cream Cahill Spinners were in the air. Jim Leonard said these spinners had appeared in fair numbers the past couple evenings. Jim and I selected Light Cahill patterns, while Desmond chose a Sulphur compara-dun, and Don fished a Light Cahill wet fly. Just at dusk a few remaining Sulphur Duns emerged. In two hours on this tranquil stretch of the Octoraro the four of us caught eighteen trout—trout hooked in the middle of June—in southern Lancaster County. The delayed harvest on this stream meant a good supply of trout until mid-June.

The delayed-harvest area contains some good holding water with deep riffles and small pools. The stream here ranges from fifteen to twenty feet wide, but some long, flat sections widen to twenty-five to thirty feet. The Southern Lancaster County Sportsmen's Association and the Donegal Chapter of Trout Unlimited have placed many valuable improvement devices throughout the stream.

The Octoraro has been hit with two floods within the past thirty years. These floods, plus intensive upstream farming, cause a serious siltation problem on the drainage system.

The West Branch begins near Nickle Mines. As it flows south it adds Meetinghouse Creek, Bowery Run (stocked), and Stewart Run (stocked), before it enters Octoraro Lake. The East Branch ranges from twenty to thirty feet wide and contains some deep pools. It begins near Christiana, adding Williams, Buck, Valley and Officers runs, and Valley Creek. Farther downstream the East Branch picks up additional volume with Knott, Ball, Knights, Bells, Coppers, and Muddy runs before it joins the West Branch in Octoraro Lake. PA 472 crosses the West Branch, and paved roads off that route parallel the stream. PA 896 crosses the East Branch, and secondary roads approach much of that branch. If you're in the Lancaster area don't miss this small, scenic, productive trout stream.

Best Times to Fly-fish:

March 15–May 5
Early Brown Stonefly: #14, morning and afternoon
Blue Quill: #18, morning and afternoon
Hendrickson and Red Quill: #14, afternoon (very spotty)
Black Quill: #14, afternoon
Little Black Caddis: #18, afternoon and evening
Cream Caddis: #16, afternoon and evening

May 10–June 10
Green Caddis: #14, afternoon and evening
Sulphur Dun and Spinner: #16, evening
March Brown: #12, morning and afternoon
Blue-Winged Olive Dun: #14, morning
Gray Drake (*Siphlonurus quebecensis*): #14, evening
Light Cahill: #14, evening
Slate Drake: #12, evening
Brown Caddis: #16 evening
Cream Cahill: #14, evening

June 20–July 10
Yellow Drake: #12, evening

July 10–September 1
Trico: #24, morning

August 10–August 31
Big Slate Drake: #6, evening

Donegal Creek

*Delayed Harvest Fly-fishing Only—2 miles; from 275 yards below
PA 772 downstream to T-334.*

Between Elizabethtown and Mount Joy in western Lancaster County lies a terrific limestone trout stream called Donegal Creek. The Donegal Fish and Conservation Association has worked for the preservation and upgrading of this stream. For years this group has had the good fortune to be headed by Ken Depoe. Through Ken's efforts the group has established a nursery on the stream and made hundreds of improvements on the water. Without these improvements Donegal Creek would be a shallow limestone stream with a few deep holding pools. With the dozens of man-made devices put in place by the association, the stream contains plenty of long, flat sections and small pools holding a good supply of trout. Ken says that before they installed the devices the stream ranged up to thirty feet wide and averaged six inches deep. Now the stream only extends fifteen feet across, but it averages two to three feet deep.

Donegal's water remains relatively cool through much of the summer. The upper end lacks any significant canopy to protect the stream, however. Ken says that after a few days of 90 degree weather the water temperature might rise into the low 70s; but by morning it's often back into the high 50s. When Don and Kathy Whitesel and I visited the stream on a June morning I checked the water temperature. Would you expect to see a 53-degree reading in the middle of June on a Lancaster County stream?

Much of the delayed-harvest area has a good canopy which shades the twenty-foot-wide stream all day. The upper end of the water flows through meadowland. Ken Depoe transported fertilized Trico eggs from Falling Springs near Chambersburg and placed them in Donegal Creek. The upper meadow now has a fantastic Trico hatch from early July through September.

The Donegal watershed causes dilemmas for the stream, however. The two major problems that prevent the water from being a top-quality trout stream are siltation and the high nitrogen content in the water—both caused by upstream farming. The stream devices have helped with the first concern, settling out much of the particulates. The water's high nitrogen content affects natural reproduction of trout. Ken recently placed fertilized eggs in the stream, but all died shortly after they came in contact with the nitrites.

Even though Donegal Creek has some problems, it's a great stream to fly-fish. Add a Trico or Sulphur hatch, and you'll experience a productive day.

Best Times to Fly-fish:

April 10–May 5
Little Blue-Winged Olive Dun: #20, morning and afternoon

May 10–June 10
Sulphur Dun and Spinner: #16, evening
Gray Fox and Ginger Quill: #12 and #14, afternoon and evening
March Brown: #12, morning and afternoon

July 1–September 30
Trico: #24, morning

Cedar Creek

What a fantastic, cool limestone stream! Two miles of Cedar Run flows through the Allentown park system—and it's open to fishing. Far-sighted officials acquired the stream bottom of Cedar and the Little Lehigh in

Allentown for the public to enjoy forever. The quality of life for all in the Allentown area is enhanced by their park system, the finest I've seen in Pennsylvania.

The state classifies 1.6 miles of Cedar as wild-trout water, and the creek holds an excellent population of streambred browns. Fish one of the productive pools, riffles, or flats near dusk on any summer evening, and the stream comes alive with rising trout. In late May these trout feed freely on Sulphur Duns and Spinners in the evening. From July 1 to October 1 you can fly-fish over fish rising to spent Tricos every morning. At almost any time you'll catch wary browns five to fifteen inches long. Like any resource these fish should be immediately returned so other fishermen can enjoy the same quality of fly-fishing.

In the park Cedar ranges from twenty to thirty feet wide. Its willow-lined, undercut banks provide plenty of cover for the wild trout population. The stream contains many pools, some long, flat sections, and productive riffles. About two miles of Cedar Creek run within the city park and some open water above PA 29 in a county park. Little Cedar enters the main stem in the city park. This tributary flows through Trexler Park and is closed to fishing. Below the park the state stocks a short section of Cedar Run. You can reach the stream off PA 29 onto Parkway Boulevard.

Best Times to Fly-fish:

April 1–April 30
Little Blue-Winged Olive Dun: #20, morning and afternoon

May 10–June 15
Sulphur Dun and Spinner: #16, evening
Light Cahill: #14, evening
Tan Caddis: #16, evening

July 1–September 1
Trico: #24, morning

Little Lehigh Creek

No Harvest Fly-fishing Only—1 mile; from just above Hatchery Road downstream to near the 24th Street Bridge. And Fly-fishing-Only Project—1 mile; from Lauderslager's Mill Dam upstream to T-508.

Last year Joe Kohler caught and released about 750 trout within ten miles of his Allentown home. He caught many of these trout on one of three limestone streams in the Allentown-Bethlehem-Easton area. Of the three streams, Joe fishes the Little Lehigh most often. He has studied the hatches thoroughly on the Little Lehigh and knows when the mayfly and caddis flies appear.

The Little Lehigh once displayed a great Yellow Drake hatch which it lost about thirty years ago. The hatch returned ten years ago, however, and is steadily improving. The Little Lehigh holds a few extensive hatches. Beginning in March Little Blue Olive Duns and Little Black Stoneflies begin emerging. By mid-May the evening surface fills with Sulphur Duns and Spinners, and Light Cahills. Mid-June and early July evenings aren't without their hatches. A closely related species to the Green Drake, the Yellow Drake, begins its annual appearance. From July to October Trico spinners appear every morning on the surface. The exact timing of the fall varies according to the air temperature and the time of year. On hot July and August mornings Tricos fall as early as 7:30 or 8:00 A.M. In early October this same species often falls spent onto the surface after 10:00 A.M.

Joe Kohler and his fly-fishing friends from the Little Lehigh Chapter of Trout Unlimited wait for an unusual evening spinner fall that appears the middle of August. The Big Slate and the Rusty Spinner (*Hexagenia atrocaudata*) frequent the Little Lehigh at that time of year. Joe waits until dusk to fly-fish a section below the catch-and-release area. That's the time when the big trout feed on the spent spinners.

In the Allentown City Park System you gain access to the Little Lehigh off PA 29 onto Fish Hatchery Road. One mile of water in the park, from the hatchery downstream, has a catch-and-release area. The nursery in the park has been developed and maintained by the City of Allentown in cooperation with the Trout Creek Fish and Game, Pioneer Fish and Game, and the Little Lehigh Fish and Game Protective Association.

The Little Lehigh flows about twenty miles before it enters the Lehigh River in Allentown. It begins near Topton Mountain in eastern Berks County and picks up Toad, Schaefer, and Iron runs before it enters the park. Just upstream from the Pennsylvania Turnpike the Little Lehigh has another regulated area, fly-fishing only. This area also runs for a mile.

The stream ranges from forty to sixty feet wide in the park and contains deep pools, productive riffles, and undercut, willow-lined banks. Many cool springs enter the park to help keep the water fairly cool throughout the summer. On a hot June afternoon at 4:00 P.M. I checked the water temperature at several points in the catch-and-release area. At the bridge near the hatchery I recorded 68 degrees. Downstream a mile and a half-hour later I found a temperature of 68 degrees. I checked the temperature on the Little Lehigh after three days of 90-plus-degree air temperatures.

The Little Lehigh Chapter of Trout Unlimited has placed over thirty gabions in the catch-and-release area. The state lists the Little Lehigh as a Class-B stream that contains some native browns.

With enormous development in the Allentown area it's amazing that the Little Lehigh is a productive stream. Recently authorities placed a sewage line along the stream. "It's remarkable how much abuse this stream can take and still hold up," Joe Kohler said.

Best Times to Fly-fish:

March 15–April 15
Little Black Stonefly: #16, afternoon
Little Blue-Winged Olive Dun: #20, morning and afternoon
Blue Quill: #18, morning and afternoon
Tan Sedge: #14, afternoon

May 5–June 10
Little Olive Sedge: #14 and #16, morning and afternoon
Sulphur Dun and Spinner: #16, evening
Light Cahill: #14, evening
Tan Sedge: #18, evening
Cream Cahill: #14, evening
Little Blue-Winged Olive Dun: #20, afternoon and evening

June 15–July 5
Yellow Drake: #12, evening

July 1–October 1
Trico: #24, morning
Big Slate Drake: #8, evening
Little Black Caddis: #18 and #20, evening

Monocacy Creek

Trophy Trout Project—1.9 miles; begins at Dam at Illick's Mills and runs upstream.

The Monocacy, Little Bushkill, Cedar Run, and Little Lehigh flow through highly developed areas of Pennsylvania. The Allentown-Bethlehem-Easton area is in the midst of an economic boom. With the increased development, people fear that one of the prized streams in the Lehigh Valley will be affected. The kind of incident we fear occurred on the Monocacy in June 1985. A chemical spill at the intersection of PA 512 and US 22 killed more than 30,000 fish in the Monocacy. Native brown trout made up a high percentage of the dead fish. Joe Kohler, of Allentown, feels that the spill did not affect the insect life on the stream, however. After the spill the Fish Commission decided not to stock the most affected area, from Illick's Mill Dam upstream, although they recently posted the area as trophy trout water.

Dr. John Hampsey, of Bethlehem, fly fishes on the Monocacy weekly during the season. He's a member of the Monocacy Chapter of Trout Unlimited and the Monocacy Watershed Association. Both organizations have been active in preserving the stream. Their major concerns are development along the bank and storm runoff control. Their goal is to control development along the stream and monitor developers during the building phase of a project. Recently the local Trout Unlimited chapter installed deflectors in the stream, the first of many planned improvements. The Bethlehem Parks Department cooperates fully with the chapter in their projects.

As with the Little Bushkill (near Easton), Cedar Creek, and the Little Lehigh, the Monocacy contains good hatches of Sulphurs and Tricos. Joe Kohler and John Hampsey look forward to mornings from early July well into October when Tricos appear in massive numbers on the Monocacy. On summer afternoons John relies on terrestrials such as ants and beetles. These, plus the green inchworm, work well all summer long.

There's about nine miles of fishable water on the Monocacy. The upper five miles is considered wild trout water, with 1.9 miles of trophy trout water. The lower four miles, including the part that flows through the city of Bethlehem, is stocked. The stream ranges from forty to sixty feet wide, has a good flow of limestone water, and remains fairly cool all summer.

Best Times to Fly-fish:

March 15–April 15
Little Blue-Winged Olive Dun: #20, morning and afternoon
Little Black Caddis: #16, afternoon

May 10–June 10
Sulphur Dun and Spinner: #16, evening
Light Cahill: #14, evening

July 1–October 1
Trico: #24, morning

Five

STREAMS OF
North-Central Pennsylvania

The home of the Brown Drake, the Green Drake, and the fabulous April trio—that's what the north-central streams mean to many Pennsylvania fly-fisherman. Travel to any one of dozens of streams in Lycoming, Potter, McKean, Tioga, Clinton, or Cameron Counties, and you'll meet prolific hatches like the Blue Quill, Hendrickson, and the Quill Gordon. Travel to many of these same streams in late May, and most of them exhibit the dynamic duo of Brown and Green Drakes and toss in some additional hatches like the Blue-Winged Olive and the Slate Drake.

But the north-central Pennsylvania streams hold much more than just a few hatches. Many of them contain Yellow Drakes and Tricos all summer. If only the water on these freestones remained cooler in July and August. Hatches like the Yellow Drake, Trico, Slate Drake, Sulphur, and others often emerge in 70-plus-degree water void of trout. Nevertheless, the head-waters of some of these streams contain cool water throughout the summer. The upper end of Kettle, Young Woman's Creek, Lick Run, the First Fork above Wharton, and the East Fork hold hatches and trout through August.

There's more to the north-central streams than just fly-fishing. They afford idyllic scenery with few other fisherman and towering mountains as a backdrop to crystal-clear trout streams. Travel up Pine Creek Valley or the valleys that embrace First Fork or Kettle, and you'll witness splendor and breathtaking beauty reserved for few other places in the East. If you haven't yet fly-fished on these streams, what are you waiting for?

First Fork of Sinnemahoning Creek

Visit the First Fork just below Wharton, where Bailey Run enters, and

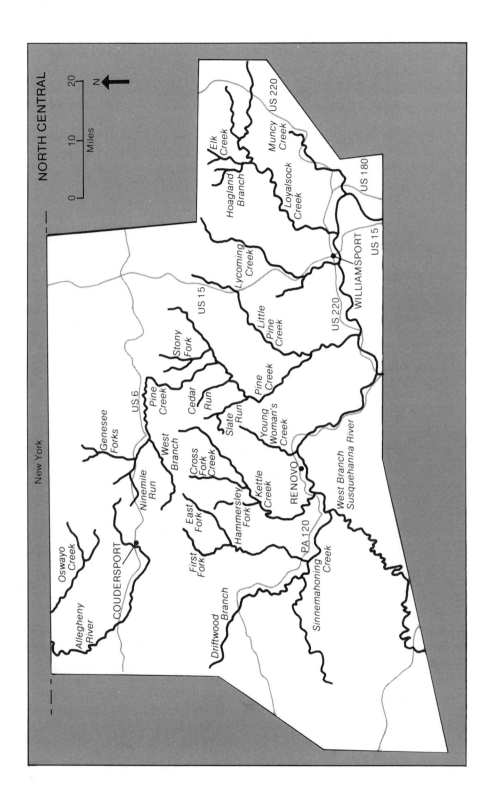

NORTH CENTRAL

N

Miles
0   10   20

New York

Allegheny River

Oswayo Creek

COUDERSPORT

Genesee Forks

Ninemile Run

US 6

Pine Creek

Stony Fork

West Branch

Cedar Run

Cross Fork Creek

First Fork

East Fork

Hammersley Fork

Kettle Creek

Slate Run

Young Woman's Creek

Pine Creek

RENOVO

Driftwood Branch

PA 120

Sinnemahoning Creek

West Branch Susquehanna River

US 15

Little Pine Creek

Lycoming Creek

Hoagland Branch

Elk Creek

Muncy Creek

Loyalsock Creek

US 220

US 180

WILLIAMSPORT

US 15

US 220

look downstream. If you didn't know better, you'd think you were fishing on a Montana stream. The scenery on this Potter County freestone is magnificent, and the early-season fly-fishing is often outstanding.

A typical Pennsylvania freestone stream, the First Fork warms quickly after the first of June. On that occasional year, however, when air temperatures average below normal, First Fork can be productive into July. Typically First Fork, especially below Wharton, is a marginal stream, while above Wharton cool water and a good supply of native browns produce excellent fly-fishing into June and July. There's five miles of high-quality water from Costello, where Freeman Run enters, downstream to Wharton. The East Fork of the Sinnemahoning is a major tributary of the First Fork, entering at the town of Wharton.

The First Fork above Wharton is a cold-water stream with plenty of pools and miles of fishable water. First Fork begins about eight miles northeast of Costello where Borie Branch and Prouty Run join. This small stream flows southwest to Costello, where it picks up an equal volume in Freeman Run, doubling the size of the main stem. Skip Gibson and I have witnessed tremendous Green Drake and Blue-Winged Olive Dun hatches two miles above Costello on the First Fork. Halfway downstream to Wharton, Big Nelson Run enters, and at Wharton the East Fork combines with the main stem to produce a much larger stream. In thirteen miles, from its headwaters to Wharton, First Fork increases in size threefold. Three miles below Wharton, Bailey Run links with First Fork, adding a shot of cool water in the summer. Two other tributaries which add volume to First Fork, Brooks and Lushbaugh runs, enter in the George Stevenson Dam. Below the dam the stream warms early, providing habitat for many smallmouth bass. The First Fork below Wharton is a typical large freestone stream with plenty of riffles, pocket water, and deep pools.

Hatches on the First Fork can be unusually spectacular, especially in April, May, and early June. Curt Thompson operates the Hemlock Campground near Wharton. He's written outdoor columns for the Coudersport *Leader Enterprise* on the hatches on the First Fork watershed. The Hendrickson remains his favorite hatch on the First Fork. It's not unusual for Curt to catch thirty to forty trout during a Hendrickson hatch. The First Fork also has all the typical April hatches, and in generous supply. Hatches imitated by the Blue Quill, the Quill Gordon, and the Hendrickson emerge from the middle of April until early May. Curt has fly-fished over April Blue Quills each afternoon for more than two weeks on First Fork.

Hatch intensity declines from early May until the third or fourth week of that month and then resumes with unbelievable diversity. With this resumption of hatches you'll witness the true character of First Fork. In quick succession hatches like the Brown Drake, Green Drake, Sulphur, and

Slate Drake fill the air in the evenings, while the Blue-Winged Olive, Gray Fox, and March Brown become air-breathing adults during the day. The problem here isn't whether there'll be a hatch, but rather which hatch or spinner fall the trout will favor. Often the dun or spinner you're prepared to copy doesn't develop into the dominant hatch of the day or evening.

The Slate Drake emerges in midevening, just when the Green and Brown Drakes subside. On the First Fork the Slate Drake imitation is particularly important. Here it copies at least three similar *Isonychia* species prevalent on the water from late May through October. Most of these are large-sized mayflies (size-10 to -14) that appear in the early evening. Don't fly-fish the First Fork from late May on without a generous supply of Slate Drake patterns and the White-Gloved Howdys. You can be certain duns have emerged if you see nymphal shucks on exposed rocks in the stream. At this time of year always examine the rocks for large brown-black nymphal shucks of recently emerged Slate Drakes. Inspect them carefully, and you'll be prepared for an evening hatch or spinner fall.

A healthy Brown Drake population lives in the First Fork. This species is truly an ephemeral mayfly. The dun and spinner appear above water for three to five days out of a year. Although it is a difficult hatch to meet, once you have succeeded you'll never want to miss it. The Green Drake often appears a few days before the Brown Drake. Above Wharton the Green Drake often appears throughout the daylight hours, making an entire day of matching this large mayfly a delightful challenge.

First Fork, East Fork, Little Pine, and Oswayo Creek are three of the few freestone streams in the north-central area that contain abundant Sulphur hatches. To match this hatch appropriately you need a size-18 Sulphur rather than the standard size 16. The Sulphur reigns supreme at the junction pool in Wharton, where East Fork enters. The Sulphur begins the third week in May and continues into early June, usually appearing just before dusk.

First Fork contains plenty of productive pocket water and riffles. That combination just below Bailey Run makes this section perfect for fishing the Brown and Green Drakes. Wading this big water can be treacherous, however, because of the huge boulders scattered pell-mell throughout much of the stream.

If scenery is important to you, and fishing over hatches is a bonus, try the First Fork of the Sinnemahoning or one of its productive tributaries. Ted Kulik, of the First Fork Lodge, in Costello, and Curt Thompson, of Hemlock Acres, near Wharton, know the hatches and the stream well. They'll be happy to share some fishing stories about the stream with you. Try the First Fork, especially from the opening of the season until early June. Almost from the beginning of the year the First Fork contains a generous share of productive hatches and plenty of hefty trout.

Best Times to Fly-fish:

April 20–May 5
Blue Quill: #18, morning
Black Caddis: #16, afternoon
Quill Gordon: #14, afternoon
Hendrickson: #14, afternoon
Tan Caddis: #14, afternoon and evening

May 5–May 15
Blue Dun: #20, afternoon and evening

May 15–June 5
Sulphur Dun and Spinner: #16 or #18, evening
Gray Fox: #12, afternoon
March Brown: #12, morning and afternoon
Green Drake and Coffin Fly: #10, evening
Brown Drake: #12, evening
Blue-Winged Olive Dun: #14, morning
Slate Drake: #14, evening
Light Cahill: #14, evening
Green Caddis: #14, evening
Rusty Caddis: #14, evening

June 20–July 5
Yellow Drake: #12, evening
Pale Evening Dun: #18, evening
Slate Drake: #14, evening
Sulphur Dun and Spinner: #16 or #18, evening

July 15–September
Trico: #24, morning
Slate Drake: #14, evening
Big Slate and Rusty Spinner: #8, evening

September–October
Slate Drake: #14, evening
Blue Dun: #20, afternoon and evening

East Fork of Sinnemahoning Creek

Avery Ripple lives in Costello five miles from the East Fork. He's fly-fished on the stream since World War II began. Avery has experienced good years on the stream, but recently he's seen some poor years. The past few years have been unkind to East Fork and other north-central streams, bringing acute drought and devastating summer heat. For the past two years Avery has quit fishing the branch before the Fourth of July. Will the stream return to its prior renown? Time and nature will tell. I remember the stream when the elements were kinder to it.

Skip Gibson and I first fished the East Fork fifteen years ago. Trout activity ended near noon that day on First Fork, so we headed up this major tributary for some afternoon fishing. Native brown trout abounded on this fertile mountain stream. All afternoon we caught these streambred fish. The native trout population in East Fork is so good that the Fish Commission has designated the middle part of the East Fork as a wild-trout stream. With that classification, and because some of this section is posted, the middle East Fork is not stocked. Above and below the wild-trout water East Fork still receives trout annually, however.

There's about ten miles of top-notch water on East Fork up to Conrad. A blacktop road from Wharton to Cherry Mills parallels the stream. Above Conrad the road becomes dirt. Upstream from Wharton, East Fork contains a heavy canopy for the first two miles. Above that you'll see fields and grown-over farmland interspersed.

East Fork contains many rock-filled pools, pockets, and riffles. Pools seemed to be separated by 200 to 300 feet of fast water above and below. The stream averages thirty to forty feet wide.

If you're so fortunate as to fly-fish on this stream in late April, you're in for a treat with some of the hatches. Blue Quills, Quill Gordons, and Hendricksons abound. Even into May you'll see Sulphurs in the evening and March Browns during the day. Check with Curt Thompson at the Hemlock Campground near Wharton on what's emerging on East Fork. Curt's fly-fished on East Fork when Green Drakes and Brown Drakes emerged. He says the lower three miles hold the most Brown Drakes.

On years in which the East Fork receives plentiful rains this stream can be spectacular. Don't miss it!

Best Times to Fly-fish:

April 15–May 5
Blue Quill: #18, morning and afternoon
Quill Gordon: #14, afternoon
Hendrickson and Red Quill: #14, afternoon
Great Stonefly (*Phasganophora capitata*): #10, day
Tan Caddis: #14, afternoon and evening

May 15–June 10
Sulphur Dun and Spinner: #16, evening
March Brown: #12, morning and afternoon
Light Cahill: #14, evening
Green Drake and Coffin Fly: #10, evening (spotty)
Brown Drake: #12, evening
Slate Drake: #12 and #14, evening
Pteronarcys Stonefly: #6, evening
Green Caddis: #14, evening
Rusty Caddis: #14, evening

Loyalsock Creek

*Fly-fishing-Only Project—3 miles; from Lycoming County Line
downstream to Sandy Bottom.*

The Loyalsock. What history this area contains! Look at the Whistle
Pigs, a club devoted to fly-fishing that has existed for more than a century.
It's probably the oldest such organization in Pennsylvania—possibly in
North America. The Whistle Pigs now claim the Loyalsock as their home
stream.

In years gone by, however, the club fished in western Clinton County,
on Young Woman's Creek. In 1887 a small group of trout-fishing devotees
took a train from Harrisburg and then a horse and buggy to their final
destination, Young Woman's Creek. These hardy souls camped in tents,
caught a good supply of brook trout, and became the nucleus of the century-
old trout club. They first called themselves the Pioneers of Fort Necessity.

On February 2, 1910, the group formally organized into a club. At
that time they changed their name to Whistle Pigs. Why not? They first
met, and continue to meet, on Groundhog Day.

In 1911 the Whistle Pigs relocated their "bivouac area" to the Hillsgrove
section of the Loyalsock. They continued to pitch tents near the creek until
1945. Finally, in that year, they struck a deal with the Ogdonia Fish and
Game Club, located three miles south of Hillsgrove. The Whistle Pigs now
use the quaint, native-chestnut-paneled lodge of the Ogdonia Club for their
annual gathering.

John Plowman, of Mechanicsburg, a third-generation Whistle Pig and
public-relations chairman for the unique organization, explained their common goal. "Our sole purpose is to enjoy the hatches of the Loyalsock and
Muncy watersheds in prime time."

Most of the twenty-five Whistle Pigs live in the Harrisburg area. They
claim among their notables the likes of the late Ned Smith. Many are
doctors, preachers, and other professionals.

The Whistle Pigs lined up at Ludy's Riffle on Loyalsock Creek.

In a hundred years any organization worth its salt will undoubtedly amass an array of cherished traditions and the Whistle Pigs have their share. The club screens potential members for two years before they're allowed to join. Each morning in camp someone wakes the members up with an early-morning serenade. The club does a great deal for the area and the Loyalsock. They strive to keep local streams open to all anglers, and they work with local sportsman's organizations and keep in touch with their Sullivan County neighbors of long standing.

If you see up to twenty-five crazy fly-fishermen, elbow to elbow on Ludy's Riffle above Hillsgrove in early June, you've met the Whistle Pigs.

The Loyalsock has shared a long and pleasant past with me, too. For years several of us began our meeting-the-hatch season on Loyalsock Creek. On numerous occasions in mid- to late April Dick Mills, Jim Heltzel, and I would travel from the Wilkes-Barre or State College area to be on the stream for the Quill Gordon and Hendrickson hatches in late April. As an added bonus the Blue Quill often appeared, with one or both of the larger mayflies. Some of those trips produced more snow flurries than mayflies, with extremely cold, winterlike air temperatures.

On many of these early trips we witnessed unbelievable hatches, but only occasionally would any trout brave the elements to surface for one of the dazed duns. Temperature readings on this water in mid-April often stay in the low to mid-40s. Often, by the time the Hendrickson appears, however, about the third week of April, the water temperature has risen above 50 degrees and dry fly-fishing comes into its own.

Although hatches like the Slate Drake emerge in heavy numbers throughout much of June, July, and August on the Loyalsock, however, the water warms quickly. By midsummer much of the lower three quarters of the stream becomes more smallmouth bass than trout water. Even the fly-fishing-only section at the Sullivan County line is marginal after mid-June. Furthermore, as the Loyalsock's temperature rises, the flow decreases dramatically. I checked the water temperature on the Loyalsock just below Laporte in the hot summer of 1988. The drought-plagued region had already had twenty-three days of 90-plus temperatures. The water in the upper end of the Loyalsock in early August registered an incredible 82 degrees. Look for cooler water by fishing below Big Bear, Little Bear, or Hoagland branches, Mill Creek, or one of a number of other tributaries. Denny Renninger has witnessed hundreds of trout holding in a small area in the main stream where cool springs enter.

The section of the Loyalsock around Hillsgrove has a respectable Trico hatch from mid-July into September. Above the bridge at Hillsgrove there can be some productive, albeit short, morning fly-fishing in July.

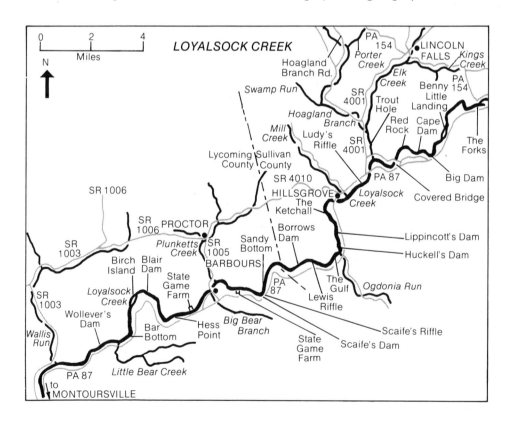

The Loyalsock contains abundant mayfly hatches, including a growing population of Green Drakes. Denny Renninger says that the Green Drake the past two years has appeared near Hillsgrove in numbers heavy enough to produce rising trout.

The stream also harbors excellent stonefly and caddis fly populations. In late April and early May stoneflies emerge in incredible numbers. This hatch is called the Great Brown Stonefly by the local fishermen. In addition to this stonefly, there's a good supply of the Early Brown Stoneflies in April and Light Stoneflies in early May.

The Loyalsock is a big stream, with its headwaters in Sullivan County near Lopez. Drainage from some of the old subbituminous mines in the area gives a slightly acidic character to the stream in the upper area. Above Lopez the water seems to be of higher quality, and native browns are abundant in some of the feeder streams. From Lopez to Forksville, however, the stream assumes a put-and-take identity.

The fertile Little Loyalsock, beginning near Dushore, enters the main stem at Forksville to produce a much larger stream and creates some twenty miles of prime dry-fly water extending downstream to Barbours. In that

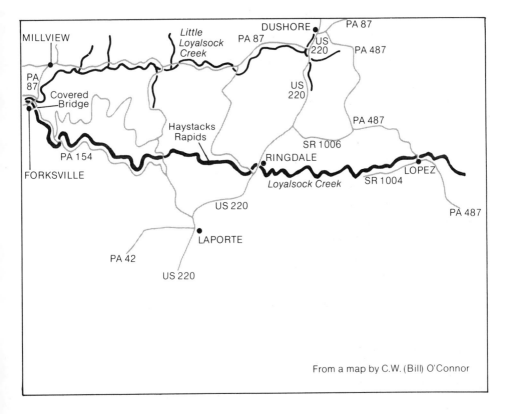

From a map by C.W. (Bill) O'Connor

section some excellent tributaries like Elk, Mill, and Plunketts creeks enter. All are freestone but add a supply of fairly cool water all summer long to the main stem. The best of the lot is Elk Creek and its main tributary, Hoagland Branch. The fly-fishing-only section on the Loyalsock begins at the Sullivan–Lycoming County line and goes downstream for about two miles. Below Barbours the water warms quickly in the summer.

On rare occasions the Loyalsock can be productive during June and July. Slate Drake patterns can be exciting to fish on these summer days in the riffles and pocket water. Wading is dangerous on some stretches, however, and the bottom is littered with various-sized boulders strewn helter-skelter about. Elevated water levels caused by spring runoff can produce treacherous footing, as well.

PA 87 parallels the Loyalsock from Montoursville to Forksville and the Little Loyalsock to Dushore. PA 154 follows the upper Loyalsock from Forksville to Laporte.

Best Times to Fly-fish:

April 18–May 1
Blue Quill: #18, morning and afternoon
Quill Gordon: #14, early afternoon
Hendrickson: #14, afternoon
Early Brown Stonefly: #14, morning and afternoon
Great Brown Stonefly: #12, morning and afternoon

May 5–May 15
Light Stonefly: #12 , morning and afternoon

May 20–June 15
Sulphur Dun and Spinner: #16, evening
Gray Fox: #14, afternoon
March Brown: #12, morning and afternoon
Green Drake and Coffin Fly: #10, evening (spotty)
Slate Drake: #12 and #14, evening
Blue Quill: #18, morning and afternoon
Chocolate Dun: #16, afternoon
Great Stonefly (*Phasganophora capitata*): #10, evening

June 22–July 10
Yellow Drake: #12, evening
Cream Cahill: #14 and #16, evening
Slate Drake: #12 and #14, evening

July 15–September
Trico: #24, morning (Hillsgrove area)
Slate Drake: #14, evening
Dark Slate Drake and Rusty Spinner: #8, evening (dun), dusk (spinner)

Hoagland Branch

What great memories Hoagland Branch and Elk Creek harbor for me! More than twenty years ago Lloyd Williams and Tom Taylor, of Dallas, and I fly-fished at the junction pool where Hoagland joins Elk. On that early June evening I saw my first great hatch of Light Cahills. Lloyd, Tom, and I caught and released three limits of trout, and more. The Cahill emerges in great numbers on the lower end of Hoagland Branch in late May and early June. By happenstance we selected one of those heavy-hatch evenings to fly-fish the junction pool. That night—that hatch—those rising trout—will forever remain a vivid triumph in our memories of productive fly-fishing trips.

I returned ten years later to the same pool, hoping to meet that same Light Cahill hatch. This time, six days into June, Slate Drakes supplanted Light Cahills as the hatch to match for the night. That second night proved the value of owning a good cache of White Gloved Howdy spinners. An eighteen-inch brown trout sucked in one of those size-12 maroon spinners that night.

Denny Renninger, of Hillsgrove, fly-fishes on Hoagland throughout the season. Just this past year in late April Denny caught more than two dozen trout on the stream on a Gold-Ribbed Hare's Ear wet and a Hendrickson dry fly. Hendrickson naturals appeared on the surface that afternoon, and Denny matched the hatch successfully. He's caught trout up to sixteen inches long on the branch and has seen trout up to twenty-one inches caught here.

Denny and I recently traveled Hoagland searching for trout and insects. We traveled up to the third bridge on Middle Creek Road, stopped, and checked a few spider webs on the bridge. By checking these webs you can often learn what insects have emerged from nearby streams recently. Denny and I noticed one lone male Trico trapped in one web. Certainly no hatch of Tricos appeared on this fifteen- to twenty-foot-wide freestone stream. Did the spinner come from the Loyalsock four miles below?

I delayed a planned trip to Wilkes-Barre for a day so I could search for Tricos on Hoagland and Elk Creek the next day. That morning I arrived at the stream a half-mile above its junction with Elk Creek. By 7:30 A.M. I noticed a few Trico duns, then dozens emerged. Within a half-hour that section of Hoagland boasted a heavy spinner flight. I headed down to Elk Creek and saw Trico flights from Hoagland down to the Loyalsock. If you hit the lower end of Hoagland or Elk in July or August, and the streams contain a decent flow and cool water, you'll be in for some late-season matching-the-hatch fly-fishing with Tricos.

Summer brings out the green inchworms on Hoagland. Denny Renninger uses these terrestrial patterns almost any afternoon he fishes here.

Hoagland Branch begins in northwestern Sullivan County where Fall

Run joins Hoagland Creek. Three miles downstream Porter Creek joins the main stem and forms Hoagland Branch. A few more miles downstream Swamp Run joins the main stem.

The state stocks four miles of Hoagland. The lower three miles of the stream flow through state forest lands. A dirt road, Hoagland Branch or Middle Creek Road, closely parallels the stream and crosses it four times in the lower four miles. At the bridges Hoagland forms some deep, productive pools. In addition to these pools the stream forms four or five other deep ledged pools very similar to those found on Cedar and Slate runs. Above the fourth bridge you'll find little access but plenty of streambred brook and brown trout. It's worth a hike into the upper end of the stream.

Hoagland Branch remains fairly cool throughout the summer. If you're fortunate enough to appear on the stream when the Light Cahill emerges on the lower end, you're in for a memorable evening of fly-fishing.

Best Times to Fly-fish:

April 15–May 5
Blue Quill: #18, morning and afternoon
Quill Gordon: #14, afternoon
Hendrickson and Red Quill: #14, afternoon

May 15–June 10
March Brown: #12, morning and afternoon
Light Cahill: #14, evening
Slate Drake: #12 and #14, evening
Gray Caddis: #16, afternoon and evening
Tan Caddis: #16, afternoon and evening
Little Green Stonefly: #16, afternoon and evening

July 15–September 1
Slate Drake: #12 and #14, evening
Trico: #24, morning

Elk Creek

Renninger's store in Hillsgrove acts as the local communications center for the area. The building contains a post office, a general store, and a sporting-goods store. Because it's the meeting place for many fishermen, Denny Renninger, the owner, hears many stories about lunker trout and often sees the evidence of a successful trip. Recently, in late July, a fisherman showed Denny three heavy trout, all over twenty inches long, caught on a local stream within a week. The angler caught all three lunkers on a stream within three miles of Hillsgrove—Elk Creek.

Elk contains most of the early-season hatches. Its main claim to fame, however, lies in its late-May and early-June hatches of Light Cahills and Slate Drakes in the evening. In addition, however, Elk, like the lower end of Hoagland Branch, holds a respectable Trico hatch from mid-July until September. Travel along the lower two miles of Elk any midsummer morning, and you'll see these tiny mayflies in their typical mating flight twenty feet above the surface. Select a morning when the stream has a reasonable flow and cool water, and you're in for some excellent late-season fly-fishing.

Elk begins near Camp Brule in southern Bradford County. The stream flows southeast and picks up the Second Branch just west of Eldredsville. Lloyd Williams lived near the upper end of Elk for years. He recounts stories of large streambred trout caught on the Second Branch. Access above Lincoln Falls is limited but worth the hike into this small stream. This area contains some productive pools. At Lincoln Falls, Kings Creek joins the main stem. The state stocks Elk from this point downstream to its mouth. From Lincoln Falls to Hoagland Branch, Elk flows through a small gorge. Access to this section is difficult. A half-mile below Hoagland Branch, Elk forms a large eight-foot-deep pool called the Trout Hole.

PA 154 crosses Elk at Lincoln Falls, and a blacktop road, Elk Creek Road, parallels the stream to the Loyalsock Creek. Elk ranges from twenty feet wide at Lincoln Falls to thirty to forty feet wide where it enters the Loyalsock. For its size Elk contains good, productive pools and great hatches. What about trout in the stream? Check with Denny Renninger in Hillsgrove—he'll tell you stories about Elk Creek trout.

Best Times to Fly-fish:

April 15–May 5
Blue Quill: #18, morning and afternoon
Quill Gordon: #14, afternoon
Hendrickson and Red Quill: #14, afternoon

May 15–June 10
Gray Fox and Ginger Quill: #12 and #14, afternoon and evening
March Brown: #12, morning and afternoon
Light Cahill: #14, evening
Slate Drake: #12 and #14, evening
Gray Caddis: #16, afternoon and evening
Tan Caddis: #16, afternoon and evening

July 15–September 1
Trico: #24, morning
Blue Quill: #18, morning and afternoon
Slate Drake: #12 and #14, evening
Light Cahill: #16, evening

Muncy Creek

Jeff Young, of Washingtonville, typically begins his fly-fishing year on Muncy Creek, his home stream. Jeff often meets with droves of early-season anglers on this freestone water. Last year he experienced one of those rare opening days when fly-fishermen can entice trout to the surface in mid-April. He caught a dozen trout that opening day on a size-18 Sid Neff Black Caddis, a size-14 Blue-Winged Olive emerger, and on a size-14 Quill Gordon cut wing.

In April the lower five or six miles of Muncy contain plenty of pocket water and a half-dozen deep pools, with a good flow of water. The creek, however, takes on a completely different look from late May through August. Scant summer rains often reduce it to a boulder-strewn small stream. Visit Muncy as we did in late June, and you'll probably see a stream that has barely a vestige of its heavy spring flow. Most of the remaining trout have moved into one of the deep pools or heavy riffles.

I visited this freestone stream recently with Jeff Young, Dave Rothrock, and his son, Dave Junior, of Jersey Shore. We arrived at one of the larger pools on the lower section of the Muncy near the town of Picture Rocks. Barely a trickle of water entered and exited the pool in front of us, but Jeff assured us that the pool, more than five feet deep and cool on the bottom, still contained a good number of trout. Even as we glanced at the pool, several trout began to feed on the surface. By 8:45 P.M. a respectable hatch of Yellow Drakes appeared on the surface. These mayflies would appear in heavier numbers the next week, but a few trout fed on the emerging duns and falling spinners. Dave Junior tied on a Light Cahill to copy the Yellow Drake and caught several trout on that as he had earlier on a green inchworm pattern. On that hot evening, with the water temperature at 74 degrees, I would have wagered that we wouldn't see a trout—but we did.

Jeff says the lower end of the Muncy contains several large pools. These pools contain cool springs and a good supply of trout all season long.

Upstream near Sonestown, in Sullivan County, the stream remains cooler in the summer and contains some streambred brown trout. You can fish the Muncy from Nordmont downstream to the town of Muncy. The stream varies in size from twenty feet in the Nordmont area to fifty to sixty feet wide in the Hughesville–Picture Rocks area. Until mid-May almost any section of the stocked stream can be productive. From mid-May to September, fly-fish around one of the cool, deep pools.

Muncy drops precipitously from Sonestown to Picture Rocks. When traveling US 220 you'll note several fairly flat areas followed by steep inclines. This rapid fall followed by a gradual fall, provides good holding water and a variety of hatches.

Best Times to Fly-fish:

April 15—May 5
Little Blue-Winged Olive Dun: #20, morning and afternoon
Blue Quill: #18, morning and afternoon
Quill Gordon: #14, afternoon

May 15—June 15
Green Caddis: #14, afternoon and evening
Sulphur Dun and Spinner: #16, evening
Gray Fox and Ginger Quill: #12 and #14, afternoon and evening
Light Cahill: #14, evening
Slate Drake: #12 and #14, evening
Little Green Stonefly: #16, afternoon and evening
Hendrickson and Red Quill: #14, afternoon

June 15—July 5
Light Cahill: #14, evening
Yellow Drake: #12, evening

Cedar Run

*Trophy Trout Project—7.2 miles; from the confluence with Buck Run
downstream to the mouth (at the town of Cedar Run).*

When you think of an isolated, untouched, pristine stream teeming
with streambred brown trout, some over twenty inches long, Cedar Run
comes immediately to mind. This acclaimed cold-water tributary enters
Pine Creek at the town of Cedar Run in Lycoming County. Its headwaters,
however, originate twelve miles upstream, just northwest of Leetonia, in
Tioga County.

Cedar Run is a spectacularly picturesque stream, replete with deep
gorges dripping with spring water throughout the year. But beyond that
Cedar has some excellent hatches and fine fishing for the first half of the
season. During the later half of the season, from mid-June through August,
however, water flow is often low, and trout become extremely wary. After
Pine Creek water warms in early June, thousands of migrating browns and
rainbows inhabit the first couple pools on Cedar, forced into the colder
water from the 70-plus temperature of Pine below. These lower holding
pools literally become black with trout which are almost impossible to catch.

Cedar often greets the new fishing season in April with the bevy of
fine hatches so common on many of the north-central streams. Select one
of the impressive, deep pools on this stream near midday. The true merit
of fishing over a hatch demonstrates its worth here, with plenty of Blue

Quills and rising trout. At this time in April synchronous hatches of Quill Gordons and Hendricksons appear. It's often a fairly predictable event, with Blue Quills arriving first, Quill Gordons next, and Hendricksons last. You sometimes find yourself fishing to successive hatches for three hours or more!

Cedar Run is an exceptionally cold stream. Often when the first hatches of the year appear they do so in 45- to 50-degree water. This cold water, plus the likelihood of high water, often work in to discourage trout from surface feeding. On those occasions when few trout surface, use a Quill Gordon wet fly or a Hendrickson or Blue Quill nymph. If you're fortunate enough to fish Cedar in April, when fly-fishing conditions are right, you're in for some exciting fishing.

Like most other north-central streams Cedar takes a break in early May from its previous hatch intensity. But when hatches resume in late May, they do so with incredible vigor. In quick succession insects like the Blue-Winged Olive Dun, Blue Quill (*Paraleptophlebia mollis*), Gray Fox, and March Brown emerge much of the day.

Evening is not without its hatches this time of the year, either. For in the same period when the daytime hatches appear, the Brown Drake, Slate Drake, and Green Drake move toward the surface in the evening. Fly-fishermen have an added incentive to fish the entire day on Cedar in late May—hatches during the day and evening.

About the middle of June, Cedar evolves into a typical summer free-stone stream with low, crystal-clear water and extremely alert trout. Times like these call for a twelve-to fifteen-foot leader with a 6X or finer tippet.

Cedar Run shelters some huge brown trout, many of them fish that have migrated upstream from Pine Creek. Some, however, are resident fish. My son, Bryan, and I spent a couple days on Cedar several years ago. It was a Saturday morning in late May, and a sporadic hatch of Blue-Winged Olives rode the surface. I caught several small trout from seven to twelve inches long. All of a sudden from 100 yards upstream I heard Bryan shout, and I saw him hold up a brown trout over twenty inches long. I rushed upstream to get a better look at the lunker Bryan held above his head. It measured twenty-two inches long and weighed about five pounds. Bryan, although he was only fifteen at the time, quickly placed the trout back in the water to fight another time for another fisherman.

Cedar's tributaries hold plenty of brook and brown trout. Branches like Fahnstock Run and Mine Hole Run, both entering the main stem from the northeast, possess an abundance of streambred trout.

At its widest point Cedar is about thirty feet wide, but much of the stream is considerably narrower. Wading can be treacherous, because of deep, boulder-filled pools and hidden rocky ledges. More than seven miles of the lower end of Cedar have been designated as a trophy trout project similar to the one located on Big Fishing Creek in Clinton County; only two trout over fourteen inches long from this section may be kept during the regular season.

Cedar is a picturesque stream with many hatches and some fine trout. A winding dirt road off PA 414 parallels the stream along its entire length. Don't miss an opportunity to fish on this scenic water.

Best Times to Fly-fish:

April 20–May 5
Little Black Stonefly: #16, afternoon
Blue Quill: #18, morning and afternoon
Quill Gordon: #14, afternoon
Hendrickson: #14, afternoon
Gray Caddis: #16, afternoon and evening
Dark-Olive Caddis: #16, afternoon and evening
Green Caddis: #16, afternoon and evening

May 1–May 15
Little Yellow Stonefly: #16, morning and afternoon
Tan Caddis: #16, afternoon

May 20–June 15
Blue Quill: #18, morning and afternoon
Blue-Winged Olive Dun: #14, morning and afternoon
Green Drake and Coffin Fly: #10. evening
Brown Drake: #12, evening
Slate Drake: #14, evening
Yellow Stonefly: #14, afternoon and evening
Little Green Stonefly: #16, afternoon and evening

Little Pine Creek

It's difficult to single out one trout stream in Pennsylvania as your favorite. For early-spring fly-fishing, however, one stream that would be near or at the top of my list is Little Pine Creek. What earns any stream the reputation that it's the best or the finest? First, for fly-fishermen at least, the stream must harbor a diversity of aquatic insects, and they must appear in abundant numbers. As we'll see later, Little Pine satisfies these preconditions well. Further, an ideal trout stream should flow with water cold enough all summer to hold trout. Little Pine's temperatures above the dam near Waterville are usually below 70 degrees all summer. A final requirement: the model stream should not depend entirely on a stocking program for its fish population but should hold its own supply of streambred trout. Both native brown and brook trout widely inhabit the water of Little Pine.

With all that going for it, does Little Pine have any disadvantages? It has. Like many freestone streams Little Pine changes into a typical low-water fishery in July and August. Pools that were once too deep can now be waded; riffles that earlier held rising trout now contain only minnows. Huge boulders and submerged hemlock trunks, once hidden from view by the spring runoff, are exposed by the shallow summer water.

Little Pine experiences frequent flooding, especially in the Carson Flats area. Channel changes occur annually. Last year's pools might be this year's riffles and vice versa.

When any stream or river has the descriptive adjective "little" in its name, you immediately perceive it as water that is slight. Not Little Pine: in some areas the stream is more than forty feet wide.

The stream begins several miles above the small town of English Center where Texas and Blockhouse creeks join. An excellent private fishing club called the Texas Blockhouse owns most of the water above English Center.

Open fishing begins just a half-mile above English Center and extends downstream about twelve miles to Waterville. Several stretches just below English Center are posted, but most of the stream remains open for public fishing. The state has impounded part of the water (Little Pine Creek Dam) about five miles above Waterville. The water below the dam is a typical warm-water fishery created by a dam having a top-water release. It rapidly becomes marginal for trout after early June.

The most productive area for fly-fishing is the section from just above the dam upstream for about five miles. Part of this section, called Carson's Flats, produces fine hatches throughout the year. It's not unusual during the last two weeks of April to witness hatches like the Little Blue-Winged Olive Dun, the Blue Quill, the Quill Gordon, and the Hendrickson emerging simultaneously. Fred Templin and Lambert Swingle once accompanied me on a memorable early-season trip to fly-fish in the Carson's Flats area. In late April on Little Pine you often experience three hours of superb fly-fishing over countless rising trout. Even with water temperatures just barely above 50 degrees, trout rise freely to the struggling duns. Trout no one would have guessed were there an hour before the hatch started ravenously gorge themselves on the first plentiful supply of food that season.

But there's more to the character of Little Pine than the first week of the season—much more. For there, when many of the north-central streams have few early-May hatches, you can meet and fish the Light Stone-fly hatching in enough numbers to generate an exciting day.

As with most freestone streams, however, Little Pine waits until the latter part of May to unleash some of its most abundant and spectacular hatches. In a period of less than a week you can find the Green Drake on the water both during the day and at night, thousands of Sulphurs emerging in the evening, March Browns and Gray Foxes on the water during the day, and an explosive hatch of Blue-Winged Olives appearing barely a couple hours after sunrise.

Even into June, Little Pine Creek has its better days, with carry-over hatches of Slate Drakes and Cream Cahills in the evening and some sporadic hatches of Blue-Winged Olives during the day.

Water temperatures in this freestone stream remain fairly respectable for trout fishing throughout much of June and July, but low-water conditions in midsummer normally produce extremely wary trout. The hour just before dusk is the preferred time to fly-fish after early June. Try a size-14 Slate Drake or a size-16 or -18 Cream Cahill tied onto a long leader with a fine tippet.

Late-season fishing on Little Pine is respectable, with sporadic Slate Drakes and small Blue-Winged Olives. With the approach of fall and cooler water, trout activity picks up considerably. As with so many north-central streams in Pennsylvania, though, Little Pine is most productive from mid-April until mid-June.

High spring runoff from snow melt and heavy rains can often create hazardous wading on Little Pine. Swollen rapids and pools are often impossible to cross. When waters subside, however, Little Pine presents few wading problems. The water resembles many north-central freestones with its mixture of sandbars and piles of small stones where flood waters once surged. Little Pine contains an inordinate number of productive pools with productive riffles and pockets above.

Access to the best water is easy: a blacktop road follows Little Pine Creek from Waterville to English Center.

Idyllic scenery and excellent water with plenty of pristine pools complete the setting of one of Pennsylvania's finest trout streams.

Best Times to Fly-fish:

April 18–May 5
Little Blue-Winged Olive Dun: #20, morning and afternoon
Blue Quill: #18, morning and afternoon
Quill Gordon: #14, afternoon
Hendrickson: #14, afternoon
Early Brown Stonefly: #12, noon
Grannom: #16, morning and afternoon (below the dam)

May 10–May 25
Light Stonefly: #12, morning and afternoon
Sulphur Dun and Spinner: #16, evening
March Brown: #12, morning and afternoon
Gray Fox: #14, afternoon

May 20–June 15
Slate Drake: #14, evening
Blue-Winged Olive Dun: #16, morning
Green Drake: #12, evening
Yellow Stonefly: #14, afternoon and evening
Little Green Stonefly: #16, afternoon and evening
Light Cahill: #14 and #16, evening

June 15–July 5
Light Cahill: #16, evening
Slate Drake: #14, evening

Pine Creek

What Pennsylvania stream contains more than sixty miles of trout water, ranges from 100 to 200 feet wide, and holds huge pools and eddies, some more than a half-mile long? What stream possesses mile-long productive riffles? Pine Creek. Nevertheless, fishing Pine Creek can be disturbing and troublesome. Pine can be one of the best and yet one of the most frustrating waters in the Commonwealth. This Jekyll-and-Hyde stream can literally change from good to bad in minutes. Fish Pine Creek in early May when the Cream Caddis is in the air, and you can truly become disenchanted with the water. Yet fly-fish any of the same stream from Waterville up to Galeton when the Brown Drake or Gray Fox emerge and you can experience a once-in-a-lifetime event.

Part of the reason Pine can be capricious is its marginal water temperature, despite tremendous hatches during much of the summer season. Brown Drakes, Blue-Winged Olives, and others sometimes appear in water well above 70 degrees. On these occasions heavy hatches and spinner falls prevail, but few trout rise in the warm water.

Pine has another problem as well. Tom Finkbiner, of the Slate Run Tackle Shop, and Mike O'Brien, of Williamsport, have lamented the alarming decrease in some of the hatches on the lower half of the stream over the past two years. Tom says that the Brown Drake and Gray Fox have appeared only sporadically below Blackwell in that time. What has happened? Look at an earlier indicator of water quality, the Hendrickson. For years the Hendrickson has only appeared in heavy numbers above Blackwell. The demise of all three hatches below Blackwell leads to only one culprit—Babb Creek, which enters Pine at Blackwell. Years ago the Babb Creek area employed hundreds of workers mining coal. Mine acid fills the stream continuously, even though these mines closed years ago. Future generations will suffer the consequences of man's inconsiderate destruction of the land and water.

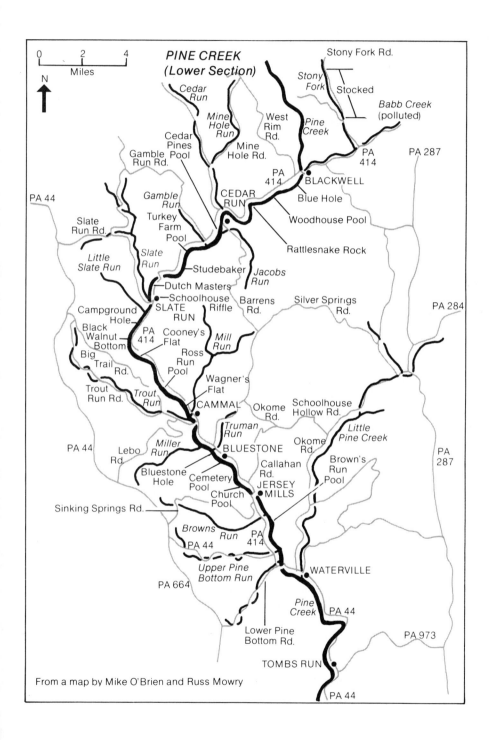

PINE CREEK
(Lower Section)

From a map by Mike O'Brien and Russ Mowry

If you encounter warm water on big Pine, try one of its productive tributaries, where temperatures usually remain in the 60s throughout much of the summer. When Pine heats up, thousands of trout migrate to one of the cooler holding pools on Cedar, Slate, or Trout runs, or to one of a dozen more smaller feeders.

The most eventful time on Pine Creek, if the water temperature is cooperative, is the last two weeks in May. Within a couple weeks you can fish over hatches like the Gray Fox, the Slate Drake, the Brown Drake, the Blue-Winged Olive Dun, the Light Cahill, and the Green Drake; and over spinner falls like the Ginger Quill, White-Gloved Howdy, Brown Drake, Dark-Olive Spinner, Coffin Fly, and more. Most of the trout in Pine Creek are stocked, but there is an occasional holdover and plenty of lunkers.

The Little Blue-Winged Olive Dun has not been affected by the mine-acid drainage from Babb Creek. This species (*Dannella simplex*) appears for a few weeks around the middle of June. If the water remains cool, you're prepared with a size-20 pattern, and you're on the stream in the morning, you're in for some excellent match-the-hatch fly-fishing.

Pine Creek is a large freestone stream, more like a river than a creek. From April to early May the water is usually high and cold, with temperatures between 45 and 60 degrees.

Pine warms quickly, however, and without the benefit of cold limestone springs or any heavy canopy to shade it, it becomes marginal trout water early in June. Were it not for the cold water of the tributaries, Pine Creek would be totally a put-and-take stream. Dave and Dana Poust, of Tombs Run, have reported seeing hundreds of dead and dying trout in Pine Creek when the stream warms in early July. What a great stream this would be if a bottom-release flood-control dam were constructed in the gorge just above Blackwell.

Pine Creek passes through some of the most scenic areas in Pennsylvania. Much of the stream is accessible by car on PA 44 near Waterville, and on PA 414 above. Some heavy hatches and large trout inhabit the area from Cedar Run downstream to the hamlet of Jersey Mills. Much of the stream here flows within 100 yards of the road. In this twenty-mile section of water you'll find the typical moderate sections at the head of the pool, a characteristic long slow pool or eddy, a tailout, then pocket water, followed by a moderate section or riffle at the head of the next pool. Many of the pools and sections, like the Dutch Masters near Slate Run and the Cemetery Pool, have been affectionately named by the local fishermen.

Above Galeton in eastern Potter County, Pine Creek is a cool, moderate stream. In this area the Hendrickson reigns supreme, with some of the heaviest hatches I have ever witnessed. Above Galeton the stream ranges from forty to fifty feet wide and contains a good supply of streambred brown and brook trout. For the first ten or fifteen miles Pine flows east adding Ninemile Run, Genesee Forks, and Phoenix, Elk, and Long runs to its flow.

At Galeton, Pine is impounded. The dam, plus marginal water entering from the West Branch, warms the water below. The West Branch at one time was a fantastic trout stream, but today the dam on Lyman Run creates marginal water on the lower six miles of the West Branch. US 6 parallels much of the upper part of Pine Creek from Ansonia to Walton.

At Ansonia, just west of Wellsboro, the stream picks up volume from Marsh Creek and heads south, forming the extensive, picturesque Pennsylvania Grand Canyon. Pine exits the gorge fifteen miles downstream, just above Blackwell. Early in the season high water brings out plenty of rafters and canoeists on this upper area. It's difficult to fly-fish because of this river traffic on many April and May weekends.

At Blackwell, Pine adds Babb Creek to its volume. Earlier I indicated that Babb carries heavy pollution originating from abandoned coal mines. This mine acid also affects some of the hatches on Pine for many miles downstream. Hendricksons, which are prevalent above Blackwell, become sporadic below. Not until the stream travels another thirty miles does the Hendrickson regain its hatching stature. From Blackwell ten miles downstream Pine picks up additional volume from Trout Run flowing in from the east and Cedar Run from the northwest. These tributaries, and just about all others, harbor good supplies of streambred brown and brook trout.

Pine travels southwest, adding Slate Run and Gamble Run in the next six miles. The section from Cedar Run to Slate Run has spectacular hatches, plenty of heavy riffles with deep pools below, and some heavy trout.

From Slate Run, Pine heads south, picking up Mill Run and another Trout Run at Cammal. This eight-mile section also produces some heavy hatches and large trout. From Cammal, Pine flows ten miles, picking up Miller, Browns, and Upper Pine Bottom runs before Little Pine enters at Waterville. The state plants no trout below Waterville, but many of the stocked rainbows migrate downstream for miles, and fishing in this lower area around Tombs Run can be productive with the onset of the Hendrickson hatch in late April.

Many hatches appear in incredible numbers throughout the year on Pine. Almost from the beginning of the season mayflies, caddis flies, and stoneflies appear. It's not unusual the first week of the season to witness the three early gray hatches somewhere on the stream. The Blue Quill often is the heaviest hatch of the three, but in some areas the Hendrickson emerges in dense numbers too.

Unlike many state streams, which pause for a respite around the beginning of May, Pine displays one of the greatest caddis hatches in the East, the Cream Caddis, at that time. Caddis adults can be seen for more

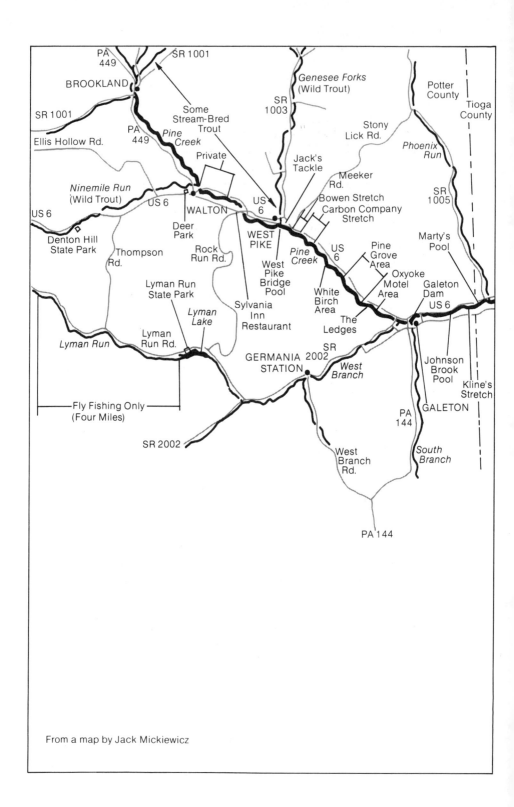

From a map by Jack Mickiewicz

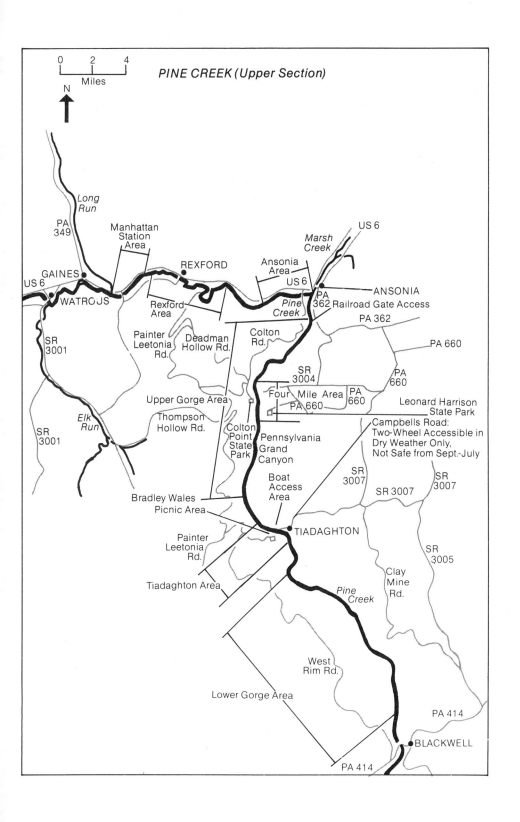

PINE CREEK (Upper Section)

than a week, appearing like blizzards from the past winter. Fly-fishing over this hatch, however, produces mixed results.

Spend an afternoon from May 18 to May 25 on Pine, and you'll probably encounter the Gray Fox. This mayfly usually appears sporadically from afternoon until early evening. Numbers are high, and the mayfly is sizable enough to promote some excellent dry fly-fishing.

Just about the time the Gray Fox diminishes in intensity, the Blue-Winged Olive takes over. At about the same date, but in the evening, appear hatches like the Brown Drake, Green Drake, and Slate Drake. If you have never witnessed a hatch of Brown Drake mayflies, you're in for a special treat. On the two or three evenings a year when these substantial insects emerge or when their spinners fall, you'll behold one of nature's finest ephemeral displays.

Even though conditions on Pine deteriorate during much of the rest of the season, hatches continue almost without interruption. Throughout late June and July mayflies like the Yellow Drake, Pale Evening Dun, and even the Trico appear on the water. Check the water temperature closely after early June—you might be fishing over a tremendous hatch with only smallmouth bass and fallfish surfacing.

Check with Tom Finkbiner, at Slate Run Tackle Shop, for the latest information on hatches on Pine. Tom keeps a daily diary of the hatches on Pine and Slate Run.

Best Times to Fly-fish:

April 20–May 5
Hendrickson: #14, afternoon (best below Waterville and above Blackwell—extremely heavy just above Galeton)
Blue Quill: #18, morning and afternoon
Quill Gordon: #14, afternoon (spotty)
Gray Caddis: #16, afternoon and evening
Dark-Olive Caddis: #16, afternoon and evening
Cream Caddis: #14, afternoon and evening
Black Quill: #14, afternoon (spotty)

May 20–June 10
Gray Fox: #12, afternoon
March Brown: #12, morning and afternoon
Sulphur Dun and Spinner: #16, evening
Blue-Winged Olive Dun: #14 and #16, morning
Brown Drake Dun and Spinner: #12, evening
Green Drake and Coffin Fly: #10, evening
Slate Drake: #12, evening
Light Cahill (*S. ithaca*): #14, evening
Chocolate Dun: #16, afternoon
Gray Drake: #14, afternoon

June 15–July 1
Sulphur Dun and Spinner: #18, evening
Little Blue-Winged Olive Dun: #20 morning and afternoon
Yellow Drake: #12, evening

July 15–September 1
Trico: #24, morning

Lycoming Creek

Mike O'Brien, of Williamsport, provides fishing tours and on-stream instruction to hundreds of fly-fishermen annually. After mid-June Mike and his long-time fishing buddy Wally Larimer, of Clearfield, fish after dark. Often Mike and Wally begin fly-fishing just as I'm leaving the same stream. The two have had some bizarre experiences in their quest for lunkers at night. They've encountered bats, herons, beavers, and snakes. Once Wally led Mike off a twenty-foot-high bank in the pitch black. But they have fun—and they catch an unusual number of heavy brown trout in the summer. Mike recently caught a lunker brown measuring 27 inches and weighing 7½ pounds on a night fishing trip in north-central Pennsylvania.

Recently an angler telephoned Mike and asked him where he could go night fishing. Mike suggested an area on the Lycoming Creek above Trout Run. The next morning that same fisherman friend called Mike back and thanked him. He caught two heavy brown trout both about eighteen inches long after dark on the Lycoming. After mid-June the best fly-fishing on the Lycoming is relegated to the hour before dusk—or as Mike will tell you, after dark.

If you're like me and prefer the more conventional daylight hours for catching trout, then try the Lycoming when one of its major hatches appears, especially early in the season.

Dick Mills, of Lehman, and I hit the Lycoming one late-April day. We fly-fished on a section at the bridge near Bodines just as a heavy Hendrickson hatch appeared and just after some Quill Gordons ended their daily appearance. The water in late April was exceptionally high but not off color, and we both looked for rising trout feeding to the second hatch of the day. Periodically one of us would spot trout rising for Hendricksons, but not in the numbers you'd expect given the intensity of hatch. Each trout that did rise did so almost imperceptibly, and we had difficulty spotting them. Dick continued to look for rising trout, while I switched to a weighted Hendrickson Nymph. This pattern in a size 12 or 14, with its dark-brown body, is deadly during a hatch of naturals. I picked up a couple trout just below a riffle leading to a deep, undercut pool and missed a couple more. Trout fed sporadically on the surface for a couple hours, but the Hendrickson Nymph continued to be productive well after the hatch had subsided.

My next trip to the Lycoming took place later that same season, near the end of June. In the area where Grays Run enters, the high water I'd found in the spring had been replaced by extremely low, crystal-clear water. Huge rocks and boulders, hidden by the snow melt in April, appeared in full view and dotted the pool. On my way up to Grays Run that evening I stopped at several convenient locations and checked the water temperature. The Lycoming recorded temperatures in the low 70s—marginal water for trout. Some of the Lycoming from Grays Run upstream, however, contains cooler water and some great late season fly-fishing. Just below where Grays Run enters, the Lycoming registered 67 degrees—just right for fishing a hatch in the middle of the summer.

Nothing much happened until near dusk. Various Light Cahill Spinners danced above the fast stretch at the head of the pool, but none of them even came close to the surface. Just before dusk, however, several large Yellow Drake duns appeared, then more. Only a couple of trout fed on the dozen or so laggards in the half-light just before dusk. One of the two trout that did rise, though, proved to be a sixteen-inch brown that had eluded the hooks of many previous bait fishermen.

The Lycoming is a typical north-central Pennsylvania freestone, with high, clear water in the spring and low, crystal-clear water during the summer. It has plenty of shallow riffles and deep pools. Locals favor the Camp Susque Pool a few miles above Trout Run. It is a fairly open stream, conducive to fly-fishing, with some great hatches, and good water in its upper sections. And it's readily accessible by car for the fly-fisherman who's willing to travel a few miles.

The stream begins near Grover in southwestern Bradford County, picking up volume from Sugar Works Run, Mill Creek, Roaring Branch, Rock Run, and Pleasant Stream before it meets Grays Run at Fields Station. Grays Run contains a 2½ mile fly-fishing-only section. This tributary also contains many great hatches, including a respectable Green Drake. The Lycoming continues south through the town of Trout Run, where it picks up a good brook trout stream with the same name as the town. The stream travels southward another thirteen miles before it enters the North Branch of the Susquehanna River at Williamsport. There are about twenty miles of good trout fishing before the stream becomes marginal near Trout Run.

Lycoming Creek was hit hard by Hurricane Agnes in 1972. Take a ride along its course, and you'll still find many gnarled railroad tracks and damaged bridges, demonstrating the power of the flood waters.

The Lycoming is a rocky stream with some large boulders. Wading in spring can be hazardous. Try fishing the Lycoming above Trout Run. If you plan a late-season excursion, try the stream just below one of its larger tributaries, where you're assured of cool water. Or, if you're a night fisherman like Mike O'Brien and Wally Larimer, try the Lycoming after dark.

Best Times to Fly-fish:

April 18–May 1
Blue Quill: #18, morning and afternoon
Quill Gordon: #14, afternoon
Hendrickson and Red Quill: #14, afternoon
Early Brown Stonefly: #12, noon

May 1–May 10
Olive Dun Caddis: #16, afternoon and evening

May 20–June 10
Tan Caddis: #16, afternoon and evening
Gray Fox and Ginger Quill: #12 and #14, afternoon and evening
March Brown: #12, morning and afternoon
Slate Drake #12, evening
Blue-Winged Olive Dun: #14, morning
Light Cahill: #14, evening
Cream Cahill: #14 and #16, evening

June 23–July 5
Blue Quill: #18, morning and afternoon
Yellow Drake #12, evening
Cream Cahill: #14 and #16, evening

Slate Run

Francis Branch Tributary to Slate Run Fly-fishing-Only Project—
2 miles; from mouth upstream to Kramer Hollow.

Main stem—Fly-fishing-Only Project—7.0 miles; from mouth
upstream to confluence of Cushman and Francis Branch.

Ah, the Good Old Days! In the early 1900s several anglers who fished the Francis Branch, one of the tributaries of Slate Run, reported that they caught a "bushel" of trout from twelve to fifteen inches long. For the next fifty years, Slate experienced an onslaught of anglers who kept their catch, particularly in the 1950 season. Regulations on Slate Run had changed the year before, and liberal limits took their toll on the trout population in the stream. Reports told us that the outlook for fishing on Slate Run in 1951 were bleak. Because the future looked dismal for Slate, a new group formed to protect the stream. The leaders of the Slate Run Sportsmen, Kurt Bonner, L. W. Fetter, Eddie Haines, and Grant Larimer, believed that Slate Run should become a fly-fishing-only stream. What foresight this group had! Were they well ahead of their time?

Mike O'Brien claims Slate as his second home. He first started fly-fishing on the stream at the age of six. He's fly-fished on the stream for

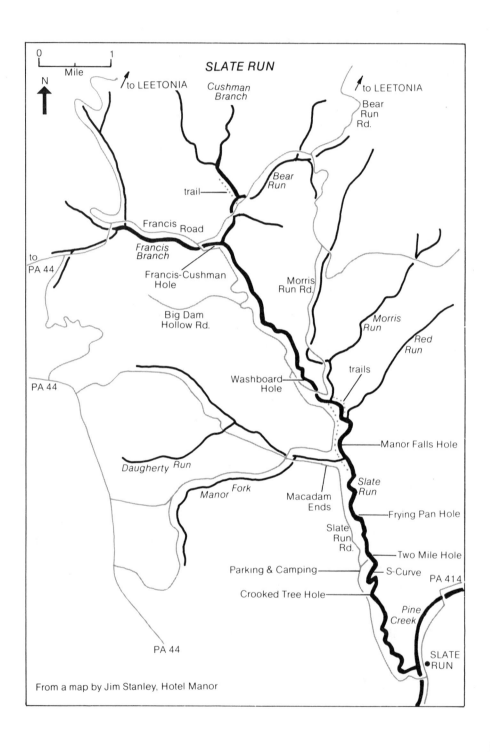

SLATE RUN

0 _____ 1
Mile

N

to LEETONIA

Cushman
Branch

to LEETONIA

Bear
Run
Rd.

Bear
Run

trail

Francis Road

Francis
Branch

to
PA 44

Francis-Cushman
Hole

Morris
Run Rd.

Big Dam
Hollow Rd.

Morris
Run

Red
Run

PA 44

Washboard
Hole

trails

Manor Falls Hole

Daugherty Run

Slate
Run

Manor Fork

Macadam
Ends

Frying Pan Hole

Slate
Run
Rd.

Two Mile Hole

Parking & Camping

S-Curve

PA 414

Crooked Tree Hole

Pine
Creek

PA 44

SLATE
• RUN

From a map by Jim Stanley, Hotel Manor

more than thirty years. Today, through the Slate Run Tackle Shop, Mike provides on-stream fly-fishing instruction on this water.

From the mid-1960s on, Mike has consistently fished this tremendous freestone stream for forty-five to fifty days each year, camping out on the stream for weeks at a time in some years. He relates that in those early years he and others would fish the water for a week without seeing another fisherman or hearing another car. Those quiet, deserted days have vanished forever. Slate Run now has a large following, but the stream still holds a sizable native brown trout population. The main stem and most of the tributaries also hold a good supply of brook trout.

Mike recently took me to one of his favorite stretches on Slate Run, where Manor Fork enters. We fished this section on a hot July afternoon. The water temperature on the main stem registered 72 degrees. Within an hour on this hot, mid-summer afternoon Mike caught three native brown trout ranging from ten to fourteen inches long. He caught them on his own ant imitation, which he's dubbed the O'Brien Deer Hair Ant. It's an effective terrestrial with a white poly post that you can actually see on the water.

Several years ago the Fish Commission did a survey of the trout population of many of the streams of Pennsylvania. Slate Run was found to possess an unusually high number of trout. On first glance at Slate Run, however, you might appropriately question the high esteem reserved for this piece of water. It's not much different from hundreds of other Pennsylvania streams. Indeed, much of Slate is difficult to reach—some of it being accessible only by hiking in to a steep gorge. It's a freestone stream with extremely variable water levels throughout the fishing season. But, as the state survey found, Slate contains a hefty supply of native brown and brook trout, some of them well in excess of twenty inches. Part of this concentration of trout is owing to an exceptional supply of mayflies, stoneflies, and caddis flies.

Slate Run flows about ten miles southwest of Cedar Run and contains just about the same species of insects that the latter does. Even with its poor access, however, Slate gets much more fishing pressure than Cedar, because of its reputation. Fishing pressure is highest on the lower few miles, just before Slate enters Pine Creek. Upstream the number of fishermen diminishes, and the scenic beauty of this spectacular stream blossoms.

Slate begins in southwestern Tioga County, with the juncture of Francis and Cushman branches. The stream then flows south-southeast, picking up additional volume from four other feeder streams, including Manor Fork, the largest. Slate enters Pine Creek twelve miles downstream at the town of Slate Run. You can reach the stream by traveling north on PA 414 to the town of Slate Run. Turn left, cross the bridge over Pine Creek, and proceed onto secondary roads which parallel much of the stream. Most of

Slate Run lies in a deep gorge, and there are only a few access points and trails to the stream. Once there, however, you'll find the experience is well worth the effort.

Hatches on Slate Run often coincide with the first week of the season. With any break in the weather you can witness Blue Quills and Quill Gordons that first week, followed closely by female Hendricksons and male Red Quills a couple days later. Slate also contains the common early-April stonefly hatches. Gray Foxes and Green Drakes appear on this pristine freestone water just after they debut on Pine. Hatches occur throughout the season, with Blue-Winged Olives emerging in late May and June; Tricos in July and August; and Slate Drakes, Blue Quills and Little Blue Duns interspersed with other hatches from late May into early October. Slate Run, at times, is a veritable hotbed of hatching activity.

Slate Run is a small stream with extremely clear low-water conditions throughout the summer. If you plan to fish the Trico hatch on the lower end of Slate in July, use a long leader and a fine tippet.

The stream is a series of rapids, moderate-flow stretches, and pools, with rocks as numerous as the trout. Many of the pools on this famous water are named. (See map.) The lower 7 miles of the stream from the Manor Hotel upstream are designated as fly-fishing-only water.

Slate Run has a reputation for poisonous snakes during July and August. Because I hate snakes, and because of the numerous early hatches on the stream, I most often fish the water in April. The dilemmas often faced then concern which of the hatches the trout are feeding on and what imitation to try. Often by 11:00 A.M. Blue Quills in a size 18 already rest on the surface, and trout seem to enjoy these tasty small naturals. Just prior to the time the Blue Quill appears, and for a short time thereafter, use a small, dark, brownish-black nymph and imitate the movement of the natural up from the bottom. Trout often swirl, then hit the nymph on almost every cast. Wet flies too, like those copying the Quill Gordon, perform well the first couple weeks of the fishing year. Some of the finest fly-fishing of the year occurs the first couple weeks of the season in Pennsylvania, especially on fertile streams with plenty of hatches, like Slate Run.

Slate can be treacherous to wade, with high water in the spring and with rocks and boulders strewn pell-mell on its bottom. Every once in a while you'll come across rock ledge in the stream, which also can be difficult to circumnavigate. Slate Run contains plenty of deep pools with productive riffles above. Try the stream either the last week in April or the last week in May for an exciting experience with plenty of hatches, rising trout, and impressive scenery thrown in as a bonus.

Tom Finkbiner, at the Slate Run Tackle Shop, can give you the latest information on the stream. Tom provides a log of all the hatches on Slate Run, Cedar Run, and Pine Creek from the beginning of the season. You'll

Mike O'Brien holds a heavy streambred brown trout caught at the Manor Falls Hole in late July.

also see a chalkboard in his shop showing which hatches are appearing and when and where. Tom updates the hatches weekly. He and his wife, Debbie, even provide a telephone hotline to update fly-fishermen on stream conditions and hatch information.

Best Times to Fly-fish:

April 20–May 5
Little Black Stonefly: #16 afternoon
Blue Quill: #18, morning and afternoon
Hendrickson: #14, afternoon
Quill Gordon: #14, afternoon
Early Brown Stonefly: #12, noon
Gray Caddis: #16, afternoon and evening
Dark-Olive Caddis: #16, afternoon and evening
Green Caddis: #16, afternoon and evening

May 5–May 15
Light Stonefly: #12, morning and afternoon
Tan Caddis: #16, afternoon and evening
Little Yellow Stonefly: #16, morning and afternoon

May 20–June 15
Gray Fox and Ginger Quill: #12 and #14, afternoon and evening
March Brown: #12, morning and afternoon
Sulphur Dun and Spinner: #16 and #18, evening
Yellow Stonefly: #16, afternoon and evening
Blue-Winged Olive Dun: #14 and #16, morning
Green Drake and Coffin Fly: #10, evening
Slate Drake: #12 and #14, evening
Light Cahill: #14, evening
Blue Quill: #18, morning and afternoon
Little Green Stonefly: #16, afternoon and evening

June 15–July 1
Olive Caddis: #16, evening

July 15–September
Blue Quill: #18, morning and afternoon
Trico: #24, morning

Kettle Creek

*Catch-and-Release—1.7 miles; from about 500 feet below PA 144
bridge upstream.*

Anyone who has fished north-central Pennsylvania streams has heard
stories about the tremendous fly-fishing on Kettle Creek. Early-season anglers talk about impressive, prolific Blue Quill and Hendrickson hatches.

Midseason fly-fishermen wait for the two drakes, the Green and the Brown, to appear in the evening or the Blue-Winged Olive in the morning. What great memories these hatches on Kettle arouse in many fishermen!

Kettle, after some meager years, has regained some of its preeminence. Hatches on the stream continue to produce spectacular dry fly-fishing the first 2½ months of the season. Part of this proliferation of hatches might be credited to Kettle's average pH of 7.3. Most other north-central streams carry pH values of from 6 to 7 (7 is considered neutral).

Phil Baldacchino, at his Kettle Creek Tackle Shop, displays dozens of pictures of stocked and holdover trout twenty to twenty-five inches long caught annually on the stream. Nevertheless temperatures in the 70s and low water in July and August continue to prevent Kettle from becoming an all-summer stream.

Phil recently spent some time with me on Kettle. He showed me stream-improvement plans projected by the Kettle Creek Chapter of Trout Unlimited. This group plans many channel diversions to obtain a more concentrated flow on the stream. Today much of Kettle has tree-lined banks. These trees, however, seldom shade the flowing water. The projected channels are designed to concentrate the water along the banks so it can be shaded for part of the day. The TU chapter has already accomplished a great deal along the stream. Once in place, these devices should hold more trout year-round.

Kettle, which can be reached from Renovo on PA 144, is a fairly long stream, about thirty-five miles from its headwaters just northeast of Germania to the Susquehanna River, a few miles west of Renovo. It's a clean, clear, freestone stream that contains alternating rapids and pools throughout its course. The creek broadens into a moderate-sized stream at Oleona, where Little Kettle joins the main stem. Fishing is worthwhile most of the season from the headwaters downstream to a point a few miles below Ole Bull State Park. Between Ole Bull Park and the town of Cross Fork almost two miles are designated as a catch-and-release area. This regulated area contains a good supply of fifteen-inch trout throughout the season. From the catch-and-release area downstream Kettle transforms quickly into marginal water, with temperatures too high for trout much of the summer.

Ten miles below Cross Fork, Kettle flows into the Alvin Bush Dam. Water below this impoundment contains some heavy trout. Bottom releases from the dam cool the water below for several miles. About three miles below the dam some mine acid enters Kettle. Two major tributaries to the stream, Cross Fork and Hammersley Run, enter near the Potter-Clinton county line. Other tributaries, like Trout Run, contain good native-trout populations and provide a shot of cool water to the main stem.

From Leidy upstream the locals have named many of the pools on

Kettle. All of these areas hold many trout—some throughout the season. At Leidy there's the Leidy Bridge Hole. Herman Hole, a slate-lined pool, lies a couple hundred yards upstream from Leidy. Above that are the Walters Run Pool and the Pittsburgh Hole. Cool water enters the latter from three springs. Above the Pittsburgh Hole lie Weed Run, Proctor Pool, and Adams Hole. Phil Baldacchino believes that the Adams Hole produces the best hatches and the best dry fly-fishing on all of Kettle.

Kettle has a diverse group of impressive hatches almost from the beginning of the season. Two years ago we experienced an unusually warm early part of April. On the opening day, April 19, I checked the water temperature of Kettle Creek just above where Cross Fork enters. I was surprised at the 52-degree reading recorded at 10:00 A.M. It was still early in the day, and the warm weather would raise the water temperature even higher by midday. I prepared for the possibility of an opening-day hatch by including, in addition to my usual opening-day collection of Muddlers and Wooly Buggers, some Blue Quills, Quill Gordons, and even some Hendrickson dry flies and nymphs.

Within a half-hour Blue Quills emerged in what seemed to be almost endless numbers, followed within an hour by an average Quill Gordon hatch. Very rarely do you experience top-notch dry fly-fishing opening day, but on that occasion trout rose throughout the stretch. Bait fishermen, in frustration, cast directly over some of the rising fish, which had already abandoned spinners and assorted other baits for naturals on the surface. Never have I experienced such an opening day on Kettle, with trout rising freely over several hours. Trout after trout readily took first the Blue Quill and later a Quill Gordon dry.

Kettle also has some exceptional later hatches. The Gray Fox hatch, although sporadic in the third week in May, is respectable enough to encourage trout to the surface. But the annual appearance of the Brown and Green Drakes on Kettle near the end of May heralds a week of great fly-fishing over rising trout. Neither of these two species appears as large as the same species on Pine—but nevertheless the Drakes create some great fly-fishing in late May.

Phil Baldacchino has developed a spectrum of poly blends to match each and every hatch found on Kettle Creek. Phil has experimented with these blends, which he calls Hatching Mayfly®, for years.

Plan a trip to the north-central streams like Slate Run, Cedar, Pine, and Kettle. Try to schedule the excursion in late April or late May for some superb fly-fishing over abundant, diverse hatches. Check with Phil Baldacchino at the Kettle Creek Tackle Shop for an update on the hatches and fishing conditions.

Best Times to Fly-fish:

April 20–May 5
Little Blue-Winged Olive Dun: #20, morning and afternoon
Blue Quill: #18, morning and afternoon
Quill Gordon: #14, afternoon
Hendrickson: #14, afternoon
Early Brown Stonefly: #12, noon

May 15–June 5
Gray Fox: #14, afternoon
March Brown: #14, morning and afternoon
Green Drake and Coffin Fly: #10, evening
Brown Drake: #12, evening
Slate Drake: #14, evening
Blue-Winged Olive Dun: #14, morning
Light Stonefly: #12, morning and afternoon
Sulphur: #18, evening
Little Green Stonefly: #16, afternoon and evening
Chocolate Dun and Spinner: #16, evening

June 20–July 5
Yellow Drake: #12, evening
Slate Drake: #14, evening
Chocolate Dun and Spinner: #16, evening
Cream Cahill: #14 and #16, evening
Little Green Stonefly: #16, afternoon and evening
Golden Drake: #12, evening
Blue Quill: #18, morning and afternoon

July 15–September
Trico: #24, morning
Blue Quill: #18, morning and afternoon
Slate Drake: #14, evening

Cross Fork Creek

*Fly-fishing-Only Project—5.4 miles; from Bear Trap Lodge
downstream to the Weed property.*

Phil Baldacchino spends many days matching the hatches on Cross
Fork. He lives only five miles from this productive stream. Phil's been on

Cross Fork hundreds of times in the past ten years. He's fished while Hendricksons, Blue Quills, and Quill Gordons have appeared in enormous numbers. He's witnessed trout rising to the impressive Green Drake on this stream.

I too have enjoyed the hatches on Cross Fork. My first trip came about purely by chance. About twenty years ago I traveled from my home 150 miles to fish Kettle Creek. We experienced a heavy downpour the night before that turned Kettle muddy and bank-high. I drove downstream to the town of Cross Fork, crossed the stream with the same name, and noted that it too was high, but not off color. Fishing this unfamiliar water topped any other strategy I had, so I headed upstream a few miles.

The farther I traveled up the dirt road paralleling part of the stream, the more intrigued with this water I became. Cross Fork is a small stream, replete with plenty of pools harboring native brook and brown trout. In most areas the stream is only fifteen to twenty-five feet wide in spring and less than that in July and August.

This first encounter occurred near the end of May. I had scheduled the trip hopeful the Green or Brown Drake would appear on Kettle that evening. Now that hope disappeared with the poor fly-fishing conditions on Kettle. I got out of the car in midafternoon to explore on foot more of this new water on Cross Fork. Not far from the car, in a well-shaded pool with much of its water flowing under a far bank, I noticed a large mayfly appear—then another. Soon, a couple trout seemed to move out from underneath the bank and start chasing duns on the surface. Now several more sizable mayflies struggled on the surface. I started chasing the mayflies in an attempt to identify this afternoon bonus. Finally I caught one, glanced at its cream body and barred wings, and concluded that Green Drakes had set off this feeding frenzy. Now more Drakes rested on the surface in the pool, and trout responded to this impressive source of food by feeding in the middle of the afternoon.

I wasn't too surprised by this afternoon hatch of Green Drakes. Small streams with heavy canopies often harbor afternoon hatches of this species. On Big Fill and Vanscoyoc runs in central Pennsylvania, and on Cedar Run in north-central, Green Drakes emerge all day.

Experiencing a spectacular hatch on a new stream with responsive trout proved too much for me. I ran back to the car, assembled my gear, and headed back to the stream. As I walked along a trail leading to Cross Fork, I hurriedly tied on a size-10 Green Drake pattern. At the stream I witnessed more than a dozen native trout taking duns from the surface. Nearly every trout took my pattern that day, a far cry from one of those frustrating Green Drake days on Penns Creek, for example, where you're often fortunate to catch one or two trout. In the middle of the afternoon on Cross Fork in late May, trout took that Green Drake pattern for several hours.

Cross Fork begins in southern Potter County near Cherry Springs Park.

It flows almost directly south and picks up additional volume from feeder streams like Boone Run, Bolich Run, Little Lyman Run, Yocum Run, Windfall Run, and Elk Lick Run before it enters Kettle Creek. Some of these tributaries, including Windfall Run, hold excellent populations of brook trout.

Improved dirt roads parallel much of the twenty miles of water on Cross Fork. A dirt road on the north side of the stream off PA 144 gives access to the lower end, and another dirt road on the south side of the stream parallels much of the upper water. There's 5.4 miles of fly-fishing-only water on the stream. Why not declare the entire Cross Fork watershed a catch-and-release area?

Best Times to Fly-fish:

April 20–May 5
Blue Quill: #18, morning and afternoon
Hendrickson: #14, afternoon
Early Brown Stonefly: #12, noon
Quill Gordon: #14, afternoon

May 10–June 5
Little Blue-Winged Olive Dun: #20, morning and afternoon
Sulphur Dun and Spinner: #16, evening
Gray Fox: #14, afternoon
March Brown: #14, morning and afternoon
Green Drake and Coffin Fly: #10, evening
Blue-Winged Olive Dun: #14, morning
Light Cahill: #14, evening
Slate Drake: #12 and #14, evening

June 5–June 20
Blue Quill: #18, morning and afternoon
Slate Drake: #14, evening
Light Cahill: #14, evening
Cream Cahill: #14 and #16, evening

July 15–September
Trico: #24, morning
Slate Drake: #14, evening

Hammersley Run (Fork)

Back in 1982 the state stocked the lower end of Hammersley Run for the last time. They found in a survey that this stream held a respectable native brook and brown trout population and felt it no longer needed additional fish. What has happened to the stream since that last stocking? Unwary stocked trout gave way to cautious, discriminating wild trout. Fewer anglers fish the stream since the native trout have become less easy to catch. But the trout are there, and some of the hatches are heavy. If you enjoy small, pristine streams loaded with streambred browns and brook trout, you'll enjoy a day on Hammersley Run. Good water quality, some heavy hatches, and a wild population make this a great place to fish.

Hammersley Road, dirt, parallels the lower two miles of the stream. Above that point the only way to reach this stream is on foot. The state recently declared the watershed a wilderness area. There are some large trout on the main stem and on the tributaries, which join about three miles upstream from the mouth.

You'll notice stream-improvement devices two miles upstream, placed there by the Cross Fork Sportsmen, Kettle Creek-Tamarack Sportsmen, West Clinton County Sportsmen, and the Kettle Creek Chapter of Trout Unlimited. Some of the improvements have withstood seven years of high spring waters.

Recently Phil Baldacchino, of the Kettle Creek Tackle Shop, and I traveled up the lower four miles of Hammersley. Phil and I noticed dozens of wild trout and the absence of any kind of worn path along the stream. Almost every stretch contained several undercut banks and rock-ledge pools. Phil declares that if you hit this small water when a hatch appears, the stream comes alive with rising native trout. Hammersley contains a good hatch of early-season mayflies. On occasion in late April you can fish over one of three hatches for several hours.

Bell and Nelson branches flow from the northwest and Hammersley Fork from the north to form the main stem near the Clinton County line.

If you enjoy small-stream fly-fishing, solitude, scenery, native trout, and some good hatches, you must try Hammersley Run.

Best Times to Fly-fish:

April 15–May 5
Blue Quill: #18, morning and afternoon
Quill Gordon: #14, afternoon
Hendrickson and Red Quill: #14, afternoon

May 12–June 10
Sulphur Dun and Spinner: #16, evening
March Brown: #12, morning and afternoon
Blue-Winged Olive Dun: #14, morning
Light Cahill: #14, evening
Slate Drake: #12 and #14, evening
Green Drake and Coffin Fly: #10, evening
Little Green Stonefly: #16, morning and evening

Young Woman's Creek

Fly-fishing-Only Project—5.5 miles; from State Forest property line
upstream to Beechwood Trail.

Back in 1962 Tom Forbes extolled the virtues of catch-and-release fishing in an article on Young Woman's Creek included in the popular booklet, *100 Trout Streams*. After many interviews with fly-fishermen, Tom concluded that this stream was a true paradise, with plenty of good-sized trout. In his story Tom didn't examine the other important ingredient that contributes to making Young Woman's a model trout stream: great hatches. Tom talked about the Left Branch of the creek which enters the main stem two miles above North Bend. The Left Branch no longer holds a catch-and-release area. More than five miles of the Right Branch are now set aside for fly-fishing-only, however.

Although the main stem and the Left Branch are typical small mountain streams with riffles separating pools of various lengths, the water has a good hatch diversity and a good population of brown and brook trout. In the fly-fishing-only section you'll probably catch native brook trout up to a foot long and streambred brown trout up to fifteen inches long, with an occasional lunker near twenty. The state stocks the Left Branch and sections on the Right Branch above and below the five-mile fly-fishing-only area.

Rich Meyers, of Pottstown, fly-fishes on Young Woman's just about every weekend. Rich caught his first trout thirty-four years ago on Hyner Run, just a few miles from Young Woman's Creek. He's fly-fished Cedar Run, Slate Run, and Young Woman's Creek since 1961. Rich has observed, identified, and photographed many of the mayflies on the stream. Several of his mayfly photos hang in Tom Finkbiner's store and at the Manor Hotel, both in Slate Run. Rich has studied Sulphur nymphs and the way they emerge. As a result of these observations he's developed an emerger pattern with an enlarged yellow thorax which works to perfection during the hatch.

Rich says that the two best hatches for him on Young Woman's are the early Blue Quill and the Sulphurs in mid-May. He fishes a Blue Quill for the first two weeks of the season.

In mid-May Rich fishes the Sulphurs, Green Drakes, and more Blue Quills. He's seen two Sulphur species, *Ephemerella rotunda* and *Ephemerella invaria*, emerge simultaneously on Young Woman's Creek. Green Drakes also emerge in heavy enough numbers on the stream to make this hatch rewarding to fly-fish. Often Rich sees a second Blue Quill (*Paraleptophlebia mollis*) appear at the same time the Green Drake does. During any of the prolific hatches on the stream Rich often catches twenty or more rising trout.

Rich Meyers lands a brook trout in late October. The fly-fishing-only section on Young Woman's Creek holds good populations of native brown and brook trout.

You'll also see plenty of stoneflies on this water. You'll encounter Little Black Stoneflies, Little Yellow Stoneflies, Little Green Stoneflies, the large *Pteronarcys*, and the Dark-Red Stonefly. The Little Black Stonefly appears as early as late March. Rich matches the Dark-Red Stonefly with a size-12 or -14 Red Quill wet fly.

Young Woman's Creek has an advantage few of its sister streams in north-central Pennsylvania can claim. In addition to exhibiting many of the hatches found on Kettle, First Fork, and Pine, Young Woman's retains its cool water year-round. Its heavy canopy of oak, maple, and pine protect much of its freestone surface from the heating effect of the summer sun. Temperatures rarely exceed 70 degrees except in extreme heat or drought.

There's little trouble wading either branch of the stream except when there's high water in the early season from snow melt. Small, medium and large boulders clog the bottom and produce some pools on this small stream which are indescribably picturesque.

Young Woman's Creek contains a lot of unproductive water, too. The fly-fishing-only area contains few large pools. Stream-improvement devices strategically placed throughout the Right Branch would make the stream even more productive.

Don't miss fishing this outstanding north-central Pennsylvania stream. You can reach Young Woman's Creek on a blacktop road off PA 120 at North Bend. There's a dirt road that follows the Left Branch.

Best Times to Fly-fish:

March 15–April 18
Little Black Stonefly: #16, afternoon

April 18–May 5
Dark-Red Stonefly: #12, noon
Little Blue-Winged Olive Dun: #20, morning and afternoon
Blue Quill: #18, morning
Quill Gordon: #14, afternoon
Hendrickson: #14, afternoon (spotty)

May 5–May 15
Light Stonefly: #12, morning and afternoon
Tan Caddis: #16, afternoon and evening

May 15–June 5
Gray Fox: #14, afternoon
March Brown: #14, morning and afternoon
Sulphur Dun and Spinner: #16 and #18, evening
Dark-Green Drake: #8, afternoon and evening
Green Drake and Coffin Fly: #12, evening
Slate Drake: #14, evening
Blue Quill: #18, morning
Pink Lady and Light Cahill: #14, evening
Little Green Stonefly: #16, afternoon and evening
Little Yellow Stonefly: #16, afternoon and evening
Pteronarcys Stonefly: #8, evening
Dark-Blue Quill: #20, evening

June 15–July 10
Slate Drake: #14, evening
Blue Quill: #18, morning
Sulphur Dun and Spinner: #18, evening

July 10–August 30
Slate Drake: #12 and #14, evening
Blue Quill: #18, morning and afternoon

Stony Fork

The chilly morning air quickly warmed under the high late-April sun. For weather, this second day of the season would prove to be a tremendous improvement over opening day, with its flurry-filled skies. Today I planned to arrive at Stony Fork about ten miles south of Wellsboro by early afternoon to check some of the early-season hatches.

Traveling down the paved secondary road that parallels Stony Fork, then onto a dirt road at Draper, I wasn't impressed with the character of the stream. The upper five miles of Stony flow through open pastureland and capture plenty of sunlight to warm the water in the summer. Once I hit state gamelands and the wooded section, however, the complexion of the stream changed dramatically. In this area rock-ledged pools, some more than ten feet deep, seemed common. Here the stream resembled another piece of water not more than six air miles away, Cedar Run.

I pulled into a parking lot about two miles upstream from one of Stony's major tributaries, Painter Run. The state stocks no trout below Painter, because this branch pours mine acid into the main stem. Ten cars were parked in the area, and fishermen lined all the productive spots on the twenty-foot-wide stream. I became intrigued with the character of this miniature Cedar Run and hiked downstream a half-mile in an attempt to avoid the hordes of bait fishermen.

I arrived at another deep pool that had evidently been stocked recently. Five or six other fishermen had come before me to this picturesque pool, so I moved downstream another 100 yards, now just exploring the water. When I arrived at this lower pool I noticed a half-dozen trout feeding in front of three bait fishermen. They saw my fly rod and encouraged me to try to catch these trout. I scanned the surface of the pool, saw hundreds of Blue Quills drifting in the eddy, and tied on a size-18 copy of the natural.

The pool had a heavy canopy of hemlocks, and a shadow covered its surface. I had difficulty picking up the drift of that size-18 imitation. On the first cast a heavy brown hit the fly. Soon Quill Gordons joined the Blue Quills, and trout began taking the larger morsel. I quickly tied on a size-14 copy, because it would be much easier to see than the size 18. For more than two hours Blue Quills, then Quill Gordons and Blue Quills, paraded across the surface of that small pool, and fish continued to rise throughout the episode. Two hours and twenty trout later I headed back to the car. What a day with the Blue Quill and Quill Gordon!

Gary Hall, of Wellsboro, fly-fishes on Stony often during the season and says that it contains some excellent hatches through much of the early and midseason. There are a few Green Drakes and even some Brown Drakes on this picturesque stream. Gary says that the stream contains some holdovers and hears reports about twenty-inch lunkers in some of the deeper pools.

Because of the open farmlands upstream, Stony Fork often warms into the high 70s in July and August. The best area to fish is the four-mile stretch above Painter Run. Stony can be reached at Wellsboro. Turn off PA 660 onto the Stony Creek Road. This blacktop parallels the upper half of the stream. At Draper a good dirt road follows the stream to Painter Run.

Best Times to Fly-fish:

April 15–May 1
Early Brown Stonefly: #12, morning and afternoon
Blue Quill: #18, morning and afternoon
Quill Gordon: #14, afternoon
Hendrickson: #14, afternoon (spotty)

May 15–June 5
Gray Fox: #14, afternoon
March Brown: #12, morning and afternoon (spotty)
Green Drake: #10, afternoon and evening (spotty)
Brown Drake: #12, evening (spotty)
Slate Drake: #14, evening
Blue-Winged Olive Dun: #14, morning
Blue Quill: #18, morning

June 20–July 15
Slate Drake: #14, evening

Oswayo Creek

Dr. Peter Ryan practices dentistry in the beautiful Potter County town of Coudersport. On Thursdays, Sundays, and any other time he can find an excuse, he becomes Pete Ryan, fly-fisherman.

After a frustrating day of fishing the Trico on the LeTort in south-central Pennsylvania, Pete headed to the Oswayo just twelve miles from his home in Coudersport. He was anxious to fly-fish this cool, productive free-stone and its Trico hatch—and he was now on his home territory. Forty trout later later Pete headed back to Coudersport satisfied with the hatch, the rising trout, and with the pattern he used to match the hatch.

Only a handful of fly-fishermen frequent the Oswayo regularly. One fly-fisherman who knows the stream and its hatches well is Stewart Dickerson, of Shinglehouse. When one of a dozen hatches appears, he fishes the stream four or five times a week. In mid-April Stewart spends any afternoon he can fishing the prolific Blue Quill and Hendrickson hatches. Often the Hendrickson appears for two weeks on the Oswayo.

By mid-May Stewart spends evenings on the Oswayo near Clara Creek, fishing the prolific Sulfur Dun and Spinner. This hatch lasts for three or four weeks. By late May a fantastic Green Drake hatch appears on this excellent stream. Stewart recalls many evenings when matching the ephemeral Drake produced dozens of heavy trout.

The last hatch of the Oswayo's season, and the smallest, appears for almost two months. Pete Ryan, Stewart Dickerson, and Vic Howard fish the Trico hatch, frequently with fantastic results.

Drive twelve miles north of Coudersport on PA 49 and PA 44, and you'll enter the scenic Oswayo Valley. The Oswayo stands out as one of the top trout streams in the state. Deep, pristine pools about every 100 yards, with some productive moderate stretches between, consistently cool water throughout the season, and some of the most abundant hatches in the state make this premier trout water.

The South Branch follows PA 44 and joins the main stem at Coneville. This bushy tributary contains stocked trout and ranges from fifteen to twenty feet wide at most places. Whitney Creek joins the South Branch near Coneville. The South Branch warms considerably in the summer with water temperatures sometimes above 70 degrees.

The Oswayo's main stem flows from a state fish hatchery through the village of Oswayo and meets the South Branch at Coneville. Many springs from the upper end cool the main stem above Coneville all summer long. This upper section ranges from fifteen to twenty feet wide and contains many pools and a great Trico hatch.

From just below the village of Oswayo downstream almost to Clara Creek, the Fish Commission classifies the main stem as wild-trout water. This section needs no additional trout. It contains plenty of streambred brown trout, some over twenty inches long, and a few brook trout.

Below Coneville, Clara and Elevenmile creeks enter the main stem. Elevenmile gets some stocked trout at its lower end. The state stocks trout on the main stem from Clara Creek to Sharon Center. In this area the Oswayo widens to forty to fifty feet, with some pools over ten feet deep, great hatches, and plenty of large trout.

Since the Oswayo contains a good supply of streambred brown trout, it's important to leave the stream the way you came—without any creeled trout. If this stream is to remain a consistently top-quality water, each fisherman must return his entire catch.

Will Pete Ryan ever travel south to fish the Trico again? Why should he, with the Oswayo so close to home?

Best Times to Fly-fish:

April 15–May 1
Blue Quill: #18, morning and afternoon
Quill Gordon: #14, afternoon (spotty)
Hendrickson: #14, afternoon

May 10–May 20
Grannom: #12 or #14, morning and afternoon

May 20–June 5
Sulphur Dun and Spinner: #16 and #18, evening
Gray Fox: #14, afternoon
March Brown: #12, morning and afternoon
Green Drake and Coffin Fly: #10, evening
Brown Drake: #12, evening (spotty)

June 20–July 10
Yellow Drake: #12, evening

July 15–September 15
Trico: #24, morning

Allegheny River

I had an entire day to spend on the Allegheny River in late April. At noon snow flurries filled the cold, early-season sky. The water temperature at this section, five miles below Coudersport, registered 48 degrees. If only the air would warm the water a few degrees, maybe a Hendrickson hatch would appear.

About 3:00 P.M. I checked the temperature a second time and again recorded a 48-degree water temperature. Probably no hatch would appear, I decided. Almost as soon as I returned the thermometer to my fishing vest, I noticed a few Hendricksons appear on a moderate stretch just above me. Soon dozens, then hundreds, then thousands of dazed Hendricksons and Red Quills drifted to the eddies and pools below. Almost immediately a half-dozen trout began feeding in unison in the moderate stretch where the duns first appeared. More than a dozen trout joined in on the surface food in the pool below. The trout were extremely selective—maybe a dozen duns floated over each feeding fish before it rose. After countless casts with a size-14 Red Quill imitation over a riser, it *might* take the dry fly. Soon Hendricksons covered the pool, but trout still only surface-fed sporadically. Maybe the cold water slowed the metabolic rate of the trout, and they needed little nourishment.

This Hendrickson and Red Quill hatch on the Allegheny might be one of the subspecies that Caucci and Nastasi discuss in *Hatches II* (Winchester Press, 1986). A size-14 imitation seems a bit large for the hatch on this river. These insects also looked somewhat darker than other Hendrickson hatches.

Three other fishermen arrived in the midst of the hatch. These bait-fishermen/part-time-fly-fishermen noticed the number of trout rising and quickly headed back to their car for their fly rods.

"What are they taking?" they yelled.

"A Red Quill," I said.

"Don't have any of those," they replied.

The tremendous hatch continued uninterrupted for two hours with thousands of duns now covering the surface. With the air temperature below 50 degrees no duns took flight. At 5:00 P.M. I quit. Trout continued to rise sporadically, but the icy water and cold air numbed my fingers. Even under those adverse weather conditions, and with extremely selective trout, I landed fifteen fish during that spectacular hatch.

The Allegheny River contains much more than just a sensational Hendrickson hatch. Vic Howard, of Coudersport, fly-fishes on the river frequently. He recently retired from teaching to devote full time to fly-fishing. After the Hendrickson, Vic often travels to the river for the March Brown, Sulphur, Green Drake, or Brown Drake hatches in late May.

Even into late June he finds some worthwhile hatches on the Allegheny river. About that time the Yellow Drake appears just at dusk. Early in August, Vic says, the natural imitated by the Big Slate Drake tied on a size-6 hook appears on the Allegheny in numbers. Vic fishes much of the river and vividly recalls many stories of lunker browns caught during the Green and Brown Drake hatches.

Vic and Pete Ryan fish the Allegheny frequently. They both belong to the local Trout Unlimited chapter, appropriately named God's Country. The chapter provides one of the few volunteer watchdog organizations dedicated to protecting the water quality of the river. The chapter has developed some stream improvements on Baker Creek, a tributary to the Allegheny.

The Fish Commission stocks about twenty-seven miles of water from Port Allegheny eleven miles upriver above Coudersport. Above the flood-control project in town the river is thirty to forty feet wide. This upper end above Coudersport harbors a good supply of holdover and streambred brown trout. Baker Creek and Peet Brook flow into the Allegheny above town.

In Coudersport a tremendous wild trout stream, Mill Creek, enters the Allegheny. US 6 and PA 44 follow Mill Creek to its headwaters. If you have some time and want to fish on a small, productive stream with wild trout, try Mill Creek.

From Coudersport, the Allegheny flows west-northwest and picks up additional flow from Dingman Run, Reed Run, Trout Brook, Laninger Creek, Fishing Creek (stocked), Card Creek, and Sartwell Creek before it enters Port Allegheny. Below Coudersport the river widens to fifty to sixty feet, with many deep pools and productive moderate stretches.

Water temperatures above Coudersport and a few miles below remain low all summer long. Below Roulette, however, the river's temperature rises in the summer, and warm-water fish species compete with the stocked trout.

PA 49 follows the Allegheny above Coudersport, and US 6 parallels the river from Coudersport to Port Allegheny.

If you like large-water fly-fishing with plenty of trout and some great hatches, try the Allegheny River.

Best Times to Fly-fish:

April 15–May 1
Early Brown Stonefly: #12, morning and afternoon
Blue Quill: #18, morning and afternoon
Quill Gordon: #14, afternoon
Hendrickson: #14, afternoon
Black Quill: #14, afternoon

May 10–May 20
Grannom: #12 or #14, morning and afternoon

May 20–June 5
Sulphur Dun and Spinner: #16 and #18, evening
Green Drake and Coffin Fly: #10, evening
Brown Drake: #12, evening
March Brown: #12, morning and afternoon
Light Cahill: #14, evening
Blue-Winged Olive Dun: #14 and #16, morning

July 20–July 10
Yellow Drake: #12, evening

Stewart Dickerson, Vic Howard, and Pete Ryan wait for the Hendrickson hatch on the Allegheny River below Coudersport.

July 15–September 1
Trico: #24, morning

August 10–August 20
Big Slate Drake: #8, evening

Genesee Forks

Jack Mickievicz lived and worked in Phoenixville in southeastern Pennsylvania for years. On weekdays he operated Jack's Tackle, but on weekends he left southeastern Pennsylvania for God's Country, Potter County. Jack finally succumbed to the scenic beauty of the West Pike area of Potter County. He moved his sporting-goods store onto one of his favorite streams, Genesee Forks. Now Jack can leave his store, rechristened Jack's Tackle and West Pike Outfitters, walk across US 6, and begin fly-fishing.

In addition to Genesee Forks, Jack fly-fishes several other local wild-trout streams, including Ninemile Run, Phoenix Run, and the upper end of Pine Creek. He prefers these smaller streams because he believes few other fly-fishermen visit them. From past experience he knows that these small streams boast a good supply of streambred brown and brook trout up to fifteen inches long, with an occasional lunker over twenty. Jack's favorite streams flow into Pine Creek between Galeton and Walton near US 6 and hold excellent stonefly, caddis fly, and mayfly hatches.

Caddis flies like the Grannom and Little Black Caddis abound in these streams. Even into August Jack has found the Cinnamon Caddis emerging on Genesee Forks.

Genesee Forks also harbors many mayflies. It has many of the early hatches but also some of the later ones: Tricos, Slate Drake, and Blue Quills in July and August. Don't expect the density of hatches on Genesee Forks that you'd witness on Pine below, however.

I followed Jack one day on the Genesee Forks to better understand his techniques for mastering small-stream fly-fishing. He fly-fished every inch of productive pocket water and pools in a one-mile stretch. On these small streams Jack uses a seven-foot graphite fly rod with a seven- or nine-foot leader. As the fly drifts across pockets of varying velocity he constantly mends the line to obtain a longer drift.

The water temperature on Jack and my early-season trip on the Genesee Forks stayed at 40 degrees throughout the day. Jack attempted to coax trout to the surface with a Royal Coachman, Quill Gordon, Hendrickson, and several other dry flies. Only occasionally would a trout rise in this cold water for the fly, but one that did was a hefty foot-long streambred brown.

Was Jack discouraged with his lack of success on Genesee Forks that day? Not Jack. He fly-fished Genesee Forks throughout the succeeding summer and caught plenty of brook and brown trout up to fourteen inches long. If you like solitude, wild trout, and some great hatches, try Genesee Forks. Be prepared with some caddis patterns and even some Green Drake imitations if you're there around the end of May.

The stream is brush lined at many places and difficult to fly-fish. It's about twenty feet wide with pools positioned about every 100 yards. Throughout its length Genesee Forks contains many overhanging trees and brush and pools filled with logs, sticks, and twigs. You'll find no fishermen's path along this stream. Few fishermen ever fish the Forks much above where it enters Pine at West Pike.

A secondary road off US 6 from West Pike to Loucks Mills parallels the stream for eight miles. Genesee Forks has one major tributary, California Creek, which enters at Loucks Mills.

Best Times to Fly-fish:

April 15–May 1
Blue Quill: #18, late morning and afternoon
Quill Gordon: #14, afternoon
Hendrickson: #14, afternoon
Early Brown Stonefly: #12, morning and afternoon

May 15–June 5
Gray Fox: # 14, afternoon
March Brown: #12, morning and afternoon
Slate Drake: #12 or #14, evening
Light Cahill: #14, evening
Green Drake and Coffin Fly: #10, evening
Blue-Winged Olive Dun: #14 and #16, morning

June 5–July 1
Light Cahill: #14, evening
Slate Drake: #12 or #14, evening

July 15–September 1
Blue Quill: #18, morning and afternoon
Trico: #24, morning
Slate Drake: #12 and #14, evening
Little Blue-Winged Olive Dun: #20, morning and afternoon
Cinnamon Caddis: #10, evening

Ninemile Run

Just 100 yards from the rustic Shiloh Lodge flows Ninemile Run, a major tributary of upper Pine Creek. Ninemile's headwaters begin just across US 6 from the Potato City Motor Inn, at an elevation of 2,500 feet. It flows east for nine miles before it joins Pine Creek at Walton. Flowing in the opposite direction, toward the west, is Mill Creek.

There are about six miles of excellent fishing on Ninemile for brook and brown trout. A study by the Fish Commission recently showed a good population of streambred browns from ten to twelve inches long and brook trout six to ten inches long.

Fly-fishing Ninemile presents many challenges. In the lower mile of water the stream contains a heavy canopy of hemlocks and beeches. In open meadows you'll find brush-lined banks and beaver dams. Here you find your fly on a bush or tree as often as it is in the water. At no place is the stream wider than fifteen feet. Fallen trees, logs, and twigs form impenetrable log jams. All this makes for challenging casting.

The water temperature in Ninemile rarely exceeds 70 degrees even in July. Wary trout scare easily on this wild-trout stream, and a low profile is a prerequisite.

Near the end of May this diminutive stream presents its pièce de résistance, the Green Drake. When these large mayflies struggle to become airborne on this small stream, trout seem to lose their timidity and feed voraciously on the insects.

Ninemile contains plenty of hatches other than the Green Drake. In late April Blue Quills, Quill Gordons, and Hendricksons appear.

Best Times to Fly-fish:

April 15–May 1
Blue Quill: #18, late morning and afternoon
Quill Gordon: #14, afternoon
Hendrickson: #14, afternoon
Little Black Caddis: #18, morning and afternoon

May 15–June 5
Gray Fox: # 14, afternoon
March Brown: #12, morning and afternoon
Green Drake and Coffin Fly: #10, evening
Brown Drake: #12, evening
Slate Drake: #12 or #14, evening
Light Cahill: #14, evening
Blue-Winged Olive Dun: #14 and #16, morning

June 5–July 30
Light Cahill: #14, evening
Slate Drake: #12 or #14, evening

July 15–September 1
Slate Drake: #12 and 14, evening
Trico: #24, morning

Driftwood Branch, Sinnemahoning Creek

Delayed Harvest Fly-fishing Only—1 mile; from the Shippen Township Building downstream to near PA 120 west of Emporium.

For several years Craig Hudson, of Emporium in Cameron County, has issued a standing invitation for me to fly-fish with him on the Driftwood Branch. Craig, now an accomplished fly-fisherman, operates the Fisherman's Attic for fly-fishermen out of the basement of his Sixth Street home in Emporium.

Craig, Mark Campbell, Don Perry, and Tom Barton met me at the Driftwood Branch just a few miles above town in the delayed-harvest area. Don and Craig belong to the local Trout Unlimited organization, called the Jim Zwald Chapter. Don currently heads the group, which diligently acts as a watchdog on local trout-stream concerns. The group urged the Fish Commission to change its regulations from "artificials" to "flies only" on the delayed-harvest area of Driftwood and placed at least six stream-improvement devices in the regulated water.

Even as we approached the forty-foot-wide water, we saw Green Drakes emerge. Craig indicated that they had begun to appear the night before. Within an hour, at 6:00 P.M., a major hatch of Drakes had developed. Hundreds of struggling duns, ranging from size 8 to 12, appeared on the surface, and many of the trout in this well-stocked area responded with splashing rises.

All five of us began the expected ritual, casting Green Drake dry flies over the rising trout. Several browns, brooks, and rainbows inspected, even nudged my pattern—but I had no true strikes. Dozens of trout still rose throughout the pool and riffle above. Then on one cast Craig's Drake dry fly sank, and a trout struck. I began purposely sinking my pattern just beneath the surface and had five strikes on five casts. As often happens with Green Drake hatches, trout chase the emerger and ignore the dun on the surface.

By 8:00 P.M. Ginger Quill Spinners appeared over the riffle at the head of the pool. Craig, Tom, Don, and I switched to appropriate patterns, waiting for the spinner fall. It happened almost at 8:30, and trout occasionally took our imitations. Tom, Craig, and Don yelled, "Tuna," every time they hooked a trout with the Ginger Quill. "Tuna" resounded up and down the valley repeatedly until the spinner fall subsided near 9:00 P.M.

What an evening on the Driftwood Branch! Thousands of Green Drakes on the surface; a few Coffin Flies appearing at dusk; thousands of Black Caddis emerging near dusk; and the fitting climax, the Ginger Quill spinner fall.

The Driftwood Branch contains many aquatic insects with outstanding match-the-hatch fly-fishing. Craig says that Hendricksons the past year appeared in huge numbers. The stream also contains an enormous hatch of Brown Drakes that appear near the end of May. Within the past few years these drakes have even emerged above Emporium. The hatch and spinner fall lasts for four of five days on the Driftwood Branch. Craig Hudson says that one Trout Unlimited member who has fly-fished many central-Pennsylvania streams believes that the Brown Drake hatch near Emporium appears in larger numbers than does the Green Drake on Penns Creek.

The Green Drake hatch seems to move upstream, like the one on Penns Creek. About five days after it first appears at Driftwood, it emerges at Emporium, twenty miles upstream. The Little Green Stonefly appears just at the end of the Green Drake hatch and becomes an important stonefly to copy almost the entire month of June.

The Driftwood Branch begins in northeastern Elk County. It flows southeast into Cameron County, where it picks up Bobby Run, Cooks Run,

Clear Creek, and North Creek. West Creek joins the main stem in Emporium, and Portage Creek on the east end of town. Above Emporium water temperatures remain fairly low throughout the summer but sometimes rise into the 70s. When temperatures in the main stem rise, trout migrate to one of the cooler tributaries.

Above Emporium Driftwood Branch ranges from twenty to forty feet wide with some productive riffles and pools up to five feet deep. Here you'll find some streambred browns and plenty of holdover trout. Below Emporium the Driftwood Branch flows south and adds tributaries like Canoe Run, Hunts Run, Stillhouse Run, and Sterling Run. Sterling Run enters the main stem at the town by the same name and adds a small amount of mine acid to the branch. Driftwood Branch joins the severely-polluted Bennett Branch at Driftwood forming the Sinnemahoning Creek.

Below Emporium the Driftwood becomes a large stream, widening to 100 feet. Deep pools, heavy riffles, and long, flat sections dominate the lower end of the stream. After June the lower end warms rapidly and becomes a warm-water fishery. In total there's about forty miles of stocked stream.

The locals have named many of the pools and sections on the Driftwood Branch. Above Emporium there's the Township Building, Dodge Hollow, Deflectors, Hertlein, Steel Dam, Fairgrounds, Water Company Dam. Below Emporium you'll find the Y, Mallorys, Friendly Garden, German Rocks, Memorial Springs, Coke Oven, Canoe Run, Cameron Hotel, and Tunnel Hill.

Above Emporium the delayed-harvest area runs for a mile. This regulated stretch needs to be extended upstream a mile or two, to encompass areas where several cool tributaries enter the main stem. In July and August water temperatures in the regulated area often rise above 70 degrees. Trout move out of the delayed-harvest area upstream to one of the cooler tributaries. Here bait fishermen lie in wait for these helpless trout. If the Fish Commission enlarged the delayed-harvest area, these trout could be caught and released all summer long.

Best Times to Fly-fish:

April 10–May 5
Early Brown Stonefly: #12, afternoon
Little Blue-Winged Olive Dun: #20, morning and afternoon
Blue Quill: #18, morning and afternoon
Quill Gordon: #14, afternoon
Hendrickson and Red Quill: #14, afternoon
Green Caddis: #16, afternoon and evening
Grannom: #16, afternoon and evening

May 12–June 5
Sulphur Dun and Spinner: #16, evening
Gray Fox: #14, afternoon
March Brown: #12, morning and afternoon
Light Cahill: #14, evening
Green Drake and Coffin Fly: #10, evening
Brown Drake: #12, evening
Blue-Winged Olive Dun: #14 and #16, morning and afternoon

June 1–June 25
Light Cahill: #14, evening
Little Green Stonefly: #16, afternoon and evening
Golden Drake: #12, evening
Slate Drake: #12 or #14, evening

Six

STREAMS OF
Central Pennsylvania

Central Pennsylvania is blessed with plenty of limestone caverns, limestone springs, and limestone water. This area of the state is a haven for tremendous mayfly hatches and large streambred brown trout. Who hasn't heard of Penns Creek, Spruce Creek, or even Elk Creek? These are just a few of the great streams in central Pennsylvania.

Some of the area's once-polluted waters have reemerged into prominence as top trout waters in the East. The Little Juniata River, for years a stream heavily polluted with tannic acid and upriver sewage, is now free from those contaminants. Spring Creek, once noted as one of the top ten streams in the East, fell victim to various doses of raw sewage and harmful chemicals over the past twenty years. It too has made a gallant attempt to regain some of its earlier brilliance. Both streams now harbor respectable hatches of several mayfly and caddis fly species along with an abundant supply of brown trout.

We'll explore more than nineteen central-Pennsylvania trout streams and their tributaries. Try some of these top-notch waters on your next fishing trip.

The Little Juniata River

Miscellaneous Waters Special Regulations—from mouth of Bald Eagle Creek (near Tyrone) downstream to the confluence of the Little Juniata River and the Frankstown Branch, Juniata River, near Petersburg.
No closed season on trout—Daily limit opening day of trout season to Labor Day—8 trout; day after Labor Day to succeeding day of trout season—3 trout.

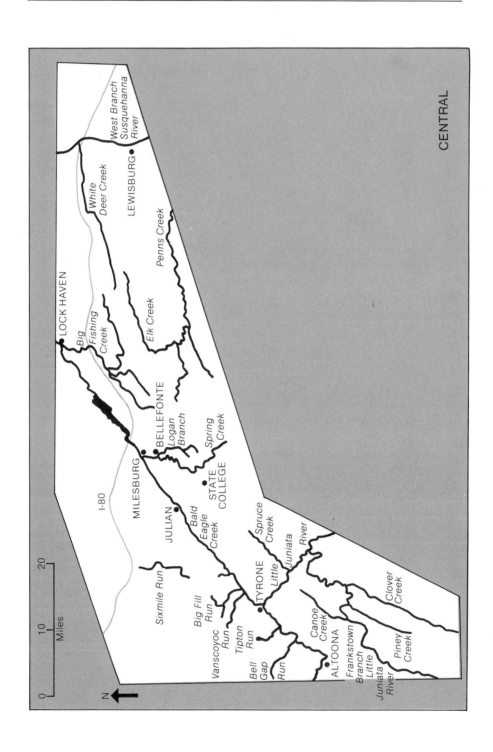

CENTRAL

It's been more than fifteen years since Mark Davis first took Larry Wilson and me to a certain new fishing spot. The evening occurred shortly after Hurricane Agnes had devastated central Pennsylvania. It was a late-July evening when we drove to the town of Spruce Creek to fly-fish or at least survey a new stretch of water called the Little Juniata River. Scars and erosion remained from the recent flooding. Huge uprooted trees lined the bank just below Spruce Creek—giant oaks and maples that had been growing near the stream for fifty years or more. The flooding had subsided more than two weeks before, but the water was still high and a bit off color—this was no time to fly-fish on a new river. We walked below Espey's farm and commented on the ravages of the flood.

Herm Espey greeted us as we passed his recently flooded farmhouse. He told us that Joe McMullen's trout hatchery just a couple miles up Spruce Creek had collapsed under the added volume of water, and that many of the hatchery trout had made their way down the Juniata. We scanned the river while Herm talked to us. Trout displaced from the tributary above seemed eager to feed on any surface natural available. In the barn pool immediately below the Espey farmhouse possibly twenty trout rose to a variety of insects. There were no other fishermen on the river that evening—at that time few anglers even knew the Little Juniata River existed as a productive trout fishery. We decided to fish.

Almost every cast with a Light Cahill caught trout ranging from fifteen to twenty inches long, and Mark, Larry, and I were the only three enjoying this tremendous success.

It didn't take long for the word to get out that the Little Juniata had blossomed into a tremendous trout haven. Two weeks after our first introduction other anglers began to appear on the water like new hatches of mayflies. These anglers seemed to keep every trout they caught. Within a couple years after its rejuvenation, and partly because anglers killed many of the trout they caught, the Little Juniata's trout population had declined precipitously. Thanks to the foresight of the Pennsylvania Fish Commission's policy of annually stocking fingerling trout, the river has recovered part of its previous productivity, but now the majority of trout caught by anglers average six to ten inches long. Unless and until the Fish Commission places the river under some special regulations governing size of fish taken, small trout won't have a chance to mature on the Little Juniata. Even with the fishing pressure it now receives, however, the river is a top Eastern trout stream—it even compares favorably to many streams and rivers found in the Midwest and West.

In contrast, until the late 1960s the Little Juniata was almost an open sewer filled with various and sundry malodorous pollutants. With the addition of sewage-treatment facilities for several municipalities and reduced effluents from an upstream paper mill in the mid-1960s, water quality began to improve dramatically. Water that was brown and rancid in the early '60s became clean and pure by the early '70s. Within a few years this once-polluted water became pure enough for abundant mayfly and caddis fly hatches.

Hatches take place on the the Little Juniata from early May until late October. The river contains few April hatches. It has no Quill Gordons, no Hendricksons, and very few Blue Quills. In fact few mayflies emerge on this river until the middle of May. Nevertheless during the first week in May the Green Caddis and some Yellow Caddises appear. Some unbelievable fly-fishing occurs then with imitations of these caddis. The most effective patterns are sinking ones that copy the emerger. Tie a grayish-green body with a turn or two of grouse hackle on a weighted size-14 wet-fly hook, and the imitation becomes one of the most productive patterns of the year. Caddis flies of various sizes and body colors continue to appear much of the season on the Little Juniata. Other patterns with brown and tan bodies take on importance in June and July.

But you haven't seen anything yet. The most productive hatches on the Little Juniata take place from mid-May until mid-June: the Sulphur, Light Cahill, and some Gray Foxes appear nightly throughout that period. Hatches of Sulphurs are so heavy and so abundant that large brown trout move to the surface to feed. Whenever I get a call from Bob Shoup, Allan Bright, or Ed Gunnett in the middle of May, I know what their message will be. They call when the most prolific hatch of all first appears on the Juniata. Usually, during the first couple days that the Sulphur appears, it does so in the late afternoon or early evening. But as time progresses and the days warm, the hatch appears near dusk.

Just when you expect insect activity to diminish in late June, enough Yellow Drakes appear on the slower pools at dusk to create feeding activity. When many fishermen have abandoned the sport for another season, Cream Cahills and White Mayflies emerge in August. Even into September and October you're apt to witness fishable hatches like the Slate Drake and the Blue Dun. These last two hatches appear in the afternoon in late September and early October.

Within the past couple years the Little Juniata has added some new hatches to its inventory, suggesting that the water quality may still be improving. Great hatches like the Green Drake, the White Mayfly, and Trico have increased in numbers abundant enough for productive fly-fishing. Great swarms of flying ants also appear on the Juniata for almost a week in late August. These ants usually appear on the water throughout the afternoon and evening around August 25 and can produce some exciting fishing—if you're prepared.

The Little Juniata River flows south from Tyrone to Petersburg in central Pennsylvania. Upriver from Tyrone the main river is marginal at

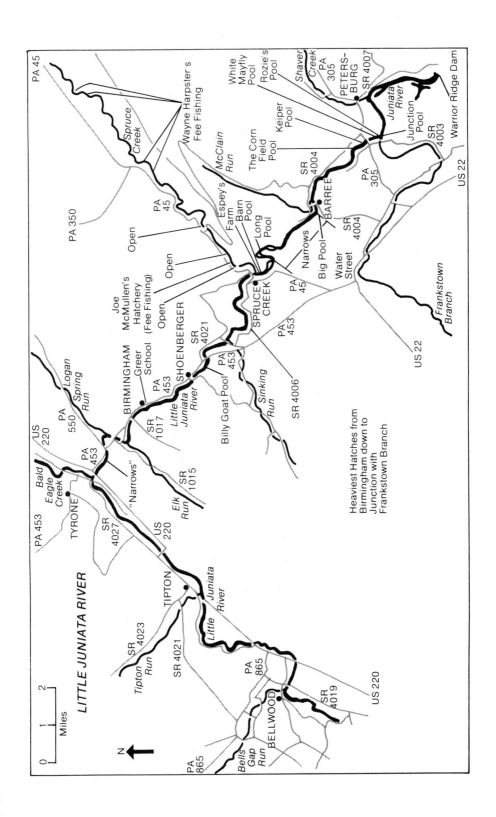

LITTLE JUNIATA RIVER

N

0 1 2
Miles

PA 45
Spruce Creek
Wayne Harpster's Fee Fishing
White Mayfly Pool
Rozie's Pool
Shaver Creek
PA 305
SR 4007
PETERS-BURG
Juniata River
Junction Pool
SR 4003
Warrior Ridge Dam
McClain Run
The Corn Field Pool
Keiper Pool
SR 4004
BARREE
PA 305
SR 4004
US 22
PA 350
PA 45
Open
Espey's Farm
Barn Pool
Long Pool
Narrows
Big Pool
Water Street
Frankstown Branch
Open
Open
Joe McMullen's Hatchery (Fee Fishing)
Open
SPRUCE CREEK
PA 45
PA 453
US 22
SHOENBERGER
SR 4021
PA 453
Sinking Run
SR 4006
Heaviest Hatches from Birmingham down to Junction with Frankstown Branch
Logan Spring Run
BIRMINGHAM
Greer School
PA 453
SR 1017
Little Juniata River
Billy Goat Pool
PA 550
PA 453
US 220
Bald Eagle Creek
"Narrows"
SR 1015
Elk Run
PA 453
TYRONE
SR 4027
US 220
Tipton Run
SR 4023
TIPTON
SR 4021
Little Juniata River
PA 865
Bells Gap Run
PA 865
BELLWOOD
SR 4019
US 220

best, except in sections where the main stem picks up productive tributaries like Bells Gap and Tipton runs, and a large tributary, the Bald Eagle. Downriver a few hundred yards from the town the river enters a narrows with high limestone cliffs. At this point, the Juniata becomes a limestone river. For the next ten miles, to the town of Spruce Creek, the river adds at least ten limestone springs of various sizes; these aid in keeping summer temperatures low and providing a moderate flow all season.

The Little Juniata is easily reached from Tyrone south for six miles via PA 453. From that point paved secondary roads parallel the stream to Spruce Creek. From Spruce Creek to Barree the only access is by foot. This latter section, about four miles long, contains some fifteen-foot-deep pools, productive riffles, heavy hatches, and plenty of wild trout. From Barree to Petersburg, about five miles, a paved secondary road again parallels the river. In this area the river expands and contains fewer small trout, but it has some lunkers over twenty inches. Pools are deep, and wading is dangerous in this lower end. PA 305 crosses the river near Petersburg, and 300 yards below, the Little Juniata joins with the Frankstown Branch to form the Juniata River. Here the two rivers form the upper end of Warriors Ridge Dam, a hydroelectric project. Trout fishing on the river is open year-round with a three-trout limit in effect from Labor Day until the opening of the season in April.

The river is a sizable one ranging from thirty to sixty feet wide with a moderate drop of about fifteen feet per mile. It contains many good-sized pools, some of them 100 yards or more long. Riffles and moderate water abound, and these sections teem with trout. Wading in the river is treacherous, and it's not uncommon to fall in at least once every season. The water hides countless medium-sized boulders covered with a slippery film. Some fast-water sections are impossible to cross or wade.

Fish the Juniata from mid-May through early June. Arrange to be on the river before 6:00 P.M. and you'll likely hit a bonus hatch of Light Cahills. Then wait until you witness the king of hatches around 8:30, the Sulphur.

Allan Bright's Spruce Creek Outfitters serves local fly-fishermen well with hatching information on the river. Tucker and Jean Morris run the Trout and Grouse Bed and Breakfast across the street from Allan's shop.

Best Times to Fly-fish:

March 1–April 1
Little Black Stonefly: #16, afternoon

April 15–May 1
Little Black Caddis: #16, afternoon (lower area of the river)
Blue Quill: #18, morning and afternoon (spotty)

May 5–May 15
Green Caddis: #14, afternoon and evening
Yellow Caddis: #14, afternoon and evening
Yellow Crane Fly: #20, afternoon and evening

May 15–June 15
Green Caddis: #14 and #16, afternoon and evening
Sulphur Dun and Spinner: #16, evening
Light Cahill Dun and Spinner: #14, evening
Gray Fox and Ginger Quill: #12, afternoon and evening

May 25–June 15
Sulphur Dun and Spinner: #16, evening
Green Drake and Shad Fly: #10, evening (spotty, but present two miles below Spruce Creek)
Light Cahill: #14, evening
Dark-Blue Quill: #20, early evening
Gray Fox: #12, afternoon and evening
Cream Cahill: #14, evening
Blue-Winged Olive Dun: #14, morning

June 20–July 5
Yellow Drake Dun and Spinner: #12, evening
Sulphur Dun and Spinner: #16 or #18, evening

July 15–September
Trico: #24, morning (spotty)
Little White Mayfly: #28, evening

August 22–September 1
White Mayfly: #16, evening
Winged Ant: #20, afternoon and evening

September 20–October 10
Slate Drake: #12, afternoon
Blue Dun: #20, afternoon

Elk Creek

A couple years ago Vince Gigliotti and Bryan Meck accompanied me to this small central-Pennsylvania limestone stream. We arrived at the stream at 11:00 A.M. on May 21. Late morning and early afternoon usually produce poor fly-fishing in late spring and summer, but meet a hatch on those days, and the fishing can be rewarding. That day on Elk Creek turned into a cloudy, misty day with the air temperature not rising much above

55 degrees. From the moment we arrived at the stream until we left at 4:00 P.M., Sulphurs appeared by the hundreds. They continued to emerge and struggle on the surface while trout fed continuously throughout the day In some pools as many as a dozen trout rose to the unending supply of naturals. Bryan and Vince caught more than fifty trout—beautiful brook and brown trout that rose all day long. Some of these trout measured over fifteen inches long. What great fly-fishing—right in the middle of the day! Of course that day's success can be attributed to the protracted Sulphur hatch. The cool, overcast conditions encouraged the hatch to appear early and the trout to feed.

Elk Creek is the largest tributary of Penns Creek, entering it at Coburn in eastern Centre County. Upstream from the junction Penns Creek heats up quickly and becomes marginal during the summer. Not so with Elk— the water temperature on this limestone stream stays in the 60s all summer long.

Elk Creek is not a sizable stream—it's no more than twenty feet across at its widest, and it's only about seven miles long. But that doesn't detract from its importance as a top eastern trout stream. Several years ago the Pennsylvania Fish Commission decided this stream was so productive that they placed it on their wild-trout list. Streambred brook and brown trout abound in Elk. They're not easy to catch, but with a good hatch the water comes alive with trout.

Hatches occur on Elk as early as opening day, when the Blue Quill appears. But Elk also harbors a major Sulphur hatch from mid-May until late June. Furthermore a sister species to the Sulphur (*Ephemerella dorothea*) appears well into July. March Browns appear along with Sulphurs in late May. Blue-Winged Olive Dun hatches appear daily, if only sporadically, in June and July. Blue Quills prevalent in July and August are often mistaken for Tricos because of their habitual undulating mating flight. Tricos are found only on the lower two miles of Elk. On this lower stretch Trico fall daily with few fly-fishermen taking advantage of this spinner fall.

Elk begins a few miles above Millheim, exiting from a limestone cavern. Just above Millheim the stream over the eons has created a gap through Brush Mountain. This narrows section is only a couple hundred yards long, but it contains some highly productive water and deep limestone pools. Below Millheim Elk becomes a typical pastureland stream passing through countless farms. Just above Coburn it picks up another outstanding limestone stream, Pine Creek. From Pine Creek downstream to Penns, Elk is a brushy, tree-lined creek. The upper end, from Millheim upstream, is paralleled by PA 445. A paved secondary road follows the creek from Millheim to Coburn. Because of its limestone origin Elk's water temperatures are usually ideal. Even in July and August the water seldom rises above 70 degrees.

If you've never fished this small, productive limestone stream, try it.

Fly-fish the stream in late May when you can be assured that a great hatch like the Sulphur will appear.

Best Times to Fly-fish:

April 20–May 1
Blue Quill: #18, morning and afternoon

May 15–June 5
Sulphur Dun and Spinner: #16, evening
March Brown: #12, morning and afternoon
Dark-Green Drake: #8, afternoon and evening
Green Drake: #10, evening
Blue-Winged Olive Dun: #14 and #16, morning

June 15–July 1
Pale Evening Dun (*Ephemerella dorothea*): #18, evening
Blue Quill and Dark-Brown Spinner: #18, morning and afternoon
Blue-Winged Olive Dun: #16, morning

July 15–September
Trico: #24, morning (found only on lower section)
Blue Quill and Dark-Brown Spinner: #18, morning and afternoon

Spring Creek

*No Harvest Fly-Fishing Only—1 mile; Lower boundary of Spring
Creek Hatchery grounds to the upper boundary of Fisherman's
Paradise. (No fish may be killed or had in possession.)
Miscellaneous Waters Special Regulations—From bridge at Oak Hall
above Neidig Brother's Limestone Co. to the mouth.
No-kill Zone—Unlawful to kill or possess any fish. All fish
caught must be immediately returned.*

I was lucky to have had the opportunity to fly-fish Spring Creek in 1954, when the legendary Green Drake hatch appeared in late May. How was I to know that I had just witnessed one of the last good hatches of Green Drakes that this limestone stream would ever display? Thousands of Coffin Fly spinners that last night emerged, as Green Drake duns greeted me on my first trip to this showcase of the East. Unfortunately, evil days were not far ahead.

Great crimes have been perpetrated on Spring Creek. In the late 1950s Spring received several doses of raw sewage, and many of the trout and most of the hatches vanished forever. Then in the '60s and '70s Spring endured additional pollution—this time from chemicals like Kepone and Mynex. Shortly after the last contamination the state decided to take the

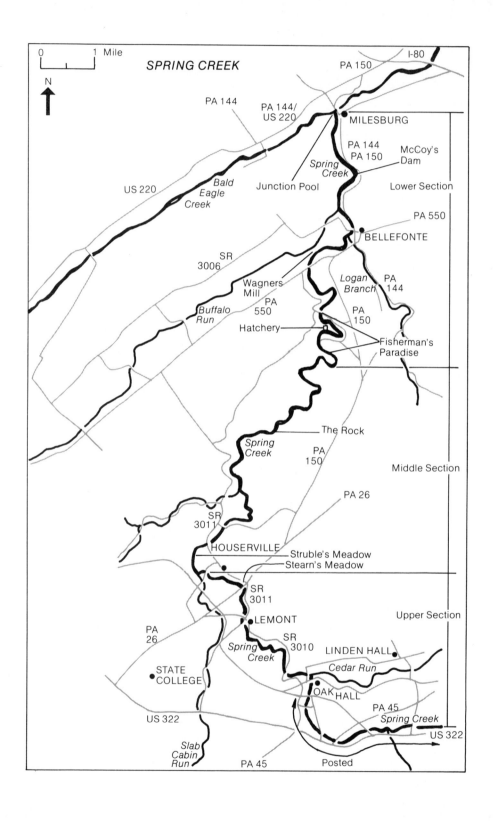

threatened stream off the stocking list and make it a "no-kill" stream. Guess what happened? Some of the hardier, more resilient tolerant hatches returned in abundant numbers, and the brown trout population multiplied. Now, ten years after the last trout was stocked in the water, Spring boasts an abundant number of hefty streambred browns. Spring Creek no longer harbors the Green Drake, Brown Drake, or the Yellow Drake, or for that matter many of the once-prominent hatches.

It's interesting to visit the Frost Museum at Penn State University, just five miles from Spring Creek. Here you can examine vials of mayfly species found in Pennsylvania, including the only remnants of the fabulous hatches Spring Creek once accommodated. Many of these vials house mayflies from Spring Creek before it fell prey to pollution—mayflies which will probably never return.

Luckily, all is not lost, for the stream or for the hatches. Spring Creek has valiantly made a comeback, and three good mayfly and a couple excellent caddis fly hatches now emerge annually. The Sulphur and Light Cahill seem to be somewhat pollution-resistant species. Both were the first two mayflies to appear on the Little Juniata after its bout with pollution, and both have remained on Spring in substantial numbers. The Sulphur appears on Spring from mid-May to mid-June. Sometimes when this species first appears in May it does so in the early afternoon. If you're lucky enough to be on the stream at that time, you can plan to fish over rising trout for several hours. Within a couple days of its initial appearance, however, the hatch resumes its normal emergence time, after 7:00 P.M. The Sulphur Spinner, with its tan body, can also be important to copy. The spinner is less predictable, since it sometimes appears before the dun, sometimes after, and sometimes is of no consequence at all.

The other pollution-tolerant mayfly, the Light Cahill, appears about the same time of year as the Sulphur but usually earlier in the evening. It's an added bonus to fly-fishing Spring Creek in late May, because you're consistently meeting and fishing over two hatches. The Cahill is larger than the Sulphur (the Cahill is a size 12 or 14, and the Sulphur is a size 16) and is a harbinger of the heavier hatch to come—the Sulphur.

The Trico hatch and spinner fall are extremely predictable on Spring Creek. The middle section of the stream is almost void of this species, but the upper and lower sections have dependable hatches and falls. The Trico falls in heavy numbers by the second week in July and continues to do so well into September. Spinner falls of this species occur between 7:00 A.M. and 9:00 A.M. on the hottest days and from 9:00 A.M. to noon in September. On warm, muggy mornings the spinner fall often lasts less than a half-hour.

There are three distinct sections of Spring Creek. The three are distinguished because of the different hatches and types of water in each. The upper section, from the source above Linden Hall downstream to Houserville, is a small meadowland limestone stream. The upper section of Spring has a different makeup of hatches from the rest of the stream. It harbors a good number of Sulphurs and a healthy Trico hatch, but it also has others not present below. Several species of Blue-Winged Olives (*Ephemerella cornuta* and others) appear daily in June and July in this upper section along with several Blue Quills and several Blue Duns (*Baetis tricaudatus* and others). Blue Duns, or Little Blue-Winged Olive Duns as they are also called, appear as early as March and April.

The middle section of Spring Creek, from Houserville downstream to the upper end of Fishermen's Paradise, was almost totally void of hatches for years, for it was this section that received the brunt of the worst pollution. Within the last couple years, however, several mayflies have feebly repopulated this area. The Trico now appears but not in the numbers it attains above or below, and the Sulphur and Light Cahill have also reappeared in limited quantities.

The lower section of Spring, from Fisherman's Paradise downstream six miles to the Creek's junction with the Bald Eagle Creek, is larger, more productive water. Hatches like the Sulphur, Trico, and Green Caddis become important again. Fisherman's Paradise, once a well-maintained and heavily stocked no-harvest, fly-fishing only section, has lost much of its previous notoriety.

Most of Spring Creek is readily accessible by car—much of the creek runs within less than 100 yards from a paved road. The upper end of the stream, from its source to Oak Hall, is posted water. A secondary road from the limestone quarry just below Oak Hall to Lemont parallels the upper end of the creek. PA 26 crosses the stream at Lemont, and PA 550 and 150 bring you close to the stream near Bellefonte and Milesburg.

Spring Creek has a relatively moderate flow with plenty of productive pocket water. The stream ranges from thirty to forty feet from bank to bank and is fairly easy to wade, although aquatic plants make wading difficult in some areas. Several excellent tributaries enter Spring Creek, and most of them contain streambred brown trout. Cedar Run, a typical pastoral limestone stream, enters Spring at Oak Hall. Downstream, just below Lemont, Slab Cabin Run enters. This too has native trout but was also the cause of much of the pollution; it was a minor tributary to Slab Cabin that carried effluents from the State College sewage plant. Two other important tributaries enter near Bellefonte. Logan Branch holds plenty of large trout and enters Spring in the center of Bellefonte. Buffalo Run, another important native brown trout stream, joins Spring Creek at the lower end of Bellefonte. All of the major tributaries of Spring Creek are productive limestone streams.

Since its inception as a no-kill stream, Spring Creek has made a remarkable recovery as a trout fishery, with plenty of healthy streambred browns. The entire stream from Oak Hall to its mouth is classified as a no-kill zone. Try fishing the stream from May 15 to June 10 for some exciting hatches and plenty of trout. Flyfisher's Paradise, in Lemont, can advise you about the conditions and hatches on the stream. Steve Sywensky, Dan Shields, and Dave McMullen know the area streams well.

Best Times to Fly-fish:

April 15–May 1
Blue Quill: #18, morning and afternoon
Little Blue-Winged Olive Dun: #20, morning and afternoon

May 5–May 20
Green Caddis: #14, afternoon and evening

May 15–June 10
Sulphur Dun and Spinner: #16, evening
Light Cahill: #14, evening

June 25–July 15
Blue-Winged Olive Dun: #14, morning and afternoon (upper section)

July 15–September
Trico: #24, morning
Blue Quill: #18, morning
Caenis: #26, evening
Pale Morning Dun: #22, morning

Penns Creek

Catch-and-Release—3.9 miles; from Swift Run downstream to J. J. Soper property line.

Fourth of July on Penns Creek, the famous but sometimes frustrating limestone stream in central Pennsylvania. By 10:00 A.M. the temperature had barely reached 58 degrees, and a fine drizzle fell. At the lower end of the catch-and-release section on this holiday, no one was fly-fishing except me. Two other fair-weather anglers had returned their gear to their cars seemingly disgusted with the depressing weather. I was the only nut remaining on the entire stretch of that productive water.

I put on a heavy jacket and headed up the abandoned railroad bed toward the R. B. Winter estate, where I entered the fabled waters. The water level was almost perfect even though it had rained for several hours and was still drizzling. As I often do when I first enter almost any trout

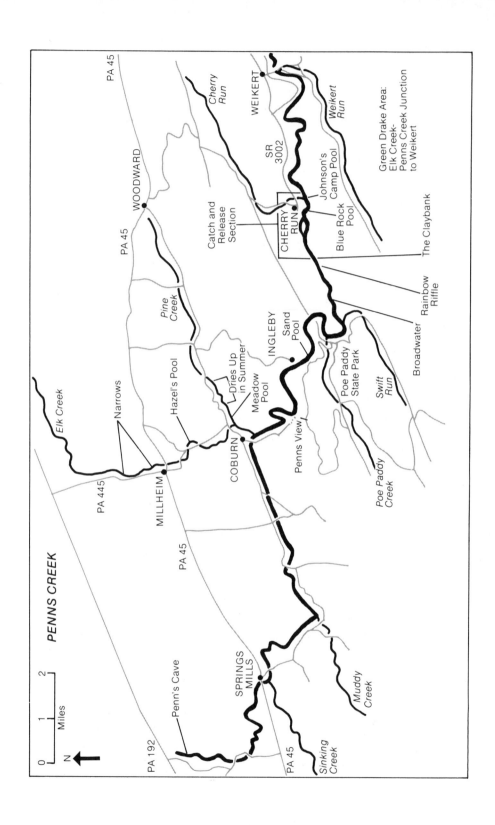

PENNS CREEK

N

0   1   2
Miles

PA 192

Penn's Cave

SPRINGS MILLS

Sinking Creek

PA 45

Muddy Creek

Elk Creek

Narrows

PA 445

MILLHEIM

Hazel's Pool

PA 45

COBURN

Meadow Pool

Dries Up in Summer

Pine Creek

PA 45

WOODWARD

PA 45

Cherry Run

Catch and Release Section

SR 3002

WEIKERT

Weikert Run

Green Drake Area: Elk Creek-Penns Creek Junction to Weikert

CHERRY RUN

Johnson's Camp Pool

Blue Rock Pool

The Claybank

Rainbow Riffle

Broadwater

Swift Run

Poe Paddy State Park

Poe Paddy Creek

Penns View

INGLEBY

Sand Pool

stream, I speculated that this might be one of the best fishing days I would ever experience. In this case, it was!

Swallows cruised near the water's surface, crisscrossing upstream, downstream, and across stream. Just in front of me thousands of Blue-Winged Olive Duns floated, half dazed, swirling around in an eddy. Normally this species (*Drunella lata*) takes off rapidly from the surface when emerging, but the unusually cold weather today prevented the duns from escaping quickly from the water. Five, ten, fifteen trout rose in a small riffle in front of me.

I quickly tied on a size-16 Blue-Winged Olive Dun, nervously finishing the improved clinch knot. The leader slipped out of the second loop, and I had to retie the knot. More and more duns emerged and added to the incredible number already resting on the surface. When it seemed like every trout in that section took my Blue-Winged imitation, I moved upstream. Ahead of me lay some moderate water with a boulder-strewn area at its head. Here maybe fifteen more trout lined up in a feeding lane and fed in a frenzy on the duns. At least ten of the trout in that stretch sucked in the dry fly. I continued upstream for about a half-mile, fishing every pool, riffle, and pocket that harbored rising trout. Remember, while this unbelievable fly-fishing over a hatch continued, not one other person took part in the excitement—not one other fly-fisherman shared this memorable experience. Three hours, sixty-five trout, and seven imitations later, I quit. Finally I had conquered Penns Creek.

What makes Penns Creek such an excellent trout stream? Hatches? Number and size of trout? Good water conditions all year long? Beautiful scenery? Plenty of open space to fly-fish? All of the above. What fly-fisherman hasn't heard of the great Green Drake on this hallowed stream? What fly-fisherman hasn't had reports of the lunkers caught during this hatch or following spinner fall? Penns Creek has received much notoriety in the last few decades, and much of it is warranted.

To many fishermen, including fly-fishermen, Penns Creek is a productive stream only until the Green Drake has finished its annual ritual, about the first week in June. Nothing could be further from the truth. You saw earlier that Penns contains some prolific, productive late-season hatches like the Blue-Winged Olive Duns in June and July. Few fly-fishermen take advantage of another late-June hatch, the Golden Drake. This mayfly (*Potamanthus*) appears nightly for a week on Penns near the end of June. Tricos succeed in July and August, and Slate Drakes are found well into October.

Superb fly-fishing develops early on Penns Creek. The lower section around Weikert has a decent Hendrickson hatch around April 21, and most of the stream contains a concentrated caddis fly, called the Grannom, about the same time. Joe Dougherty, of Lewisburg, has fished the Hendrickson hatch near Weikert for years. He says the hatch never gets extremely heavy, but still it brings plenty of trout to the surface. The Grannom on Penns can be as frustrating and unrewarding as the Cream Caddis is on Pine Creek. Thousands of caddis flies in the air this early in the season thrill many fly-fishermen but often don't persuade many trout into rising. Many times the air is filled with the large dark Grannoms on this fertile limestone stream, but no trout appear.

Penns Creek emerges from a limestone cavern at Penns Cave just a couple miles north of Spring Mills in Centre County. It is a cold, productive alkaline stream for the first five miles, but much of the water north of PA 45 is posted. From Spring Mills six miles downstream to Coburn there is access to most of the stream. The section, however, with the heaviest hatches and the largest trout is the fifteen-mile segment that extends from Coburn to Cherry Run.

Just upstream from Coburn, Penns is slowed by several small ponds and lacks any protective canopy. As a result this section warms quickly. But just a few hundred feet below Coburn, a cold limestone tributary, Elk Creek, enters. Elk injects a generous amount of cold water into the main stem, creating a great trout stream for the next twenty miles.

Access to the section from Coburn to Cherry Run is limited. You can reach the upper section by driving to the old railroad tunnel about three miles below Coburn, then hiking down the old railroad track. Or you can enter at Ingleby from the north or Poe Paddy State Park from the south, following the railroad upstream or downstream. Access from the Cherry Run section is no problem. A road parallels the creek down to Weikert. The section around Weikert is marginal. The Fish Commission has set aside a four-mile section near Cherry Run as a catch-and-release area. Fly-fishing on this part of Penns produces lunker trout during the Green Drake hatch.

Penns is most often renowned for its Green Drake hatch in late May. Fish the stream when the "Shad Fly" is on, and you'll meet hundreds of fly-fishermen on the water, each with his or her favorite pattern to match the upcoming hatch. It often happens when the Green Drake appears that five or six other significant aquatic insects arrive on the water at the same time. Anglers may become frustrated with this diversity of insects, but many continue to use the Green Drake even though trout are feeding on another phase of the same insect (like the emerging nymph), or are surfacing for a Light Cahill, Sulphur, Sulphur Spinner, Gray Fox, Ginger Quill, or one of many other species. More times than I care to remember I've quit the stream in disgust in these confusing circumstances. Like so many others who plan to fish the hatch, I use a Green Drake pattern no matter what else takes place that evening—a serious blunder when you're fishing the hatch on Penns Creek.

It's mid-June, however, and the hordes that have visited Penns are gone for another year. What happens now? You already know that Penns host a fantastic Blue-Winged Olive hatch. But it contains more hatches even later in the season. Slate Drakes (*Isonychia matilda*) emerge on many September afternoons in enough numbers to bring trout to the surface one more time. By that time of year the water is still in the mid- to high 50s in the afternoon, and the air is cooler. These cool days prevent the Slate Drake duns from their typical speedy escape from the surface. Fishing when this hatch appears can be your one last triumph of the season.

Penns drains six main tributaries. Sinking Creek enters at Spring Mills, adding tannic acid and warm water to the main stem. Sinking Creek's headwaters are in the boglike area of Bear Meadows. Downstream ten miles the largest and most influential tributary of Penns, Elk Creek, joins. In the Poe Paddy State Park area, Poe Paddy Creek and Swift Creek flow into Penns. At the lower end of the catch-and-release area Cherry Run, another excellent tributary, adds volume. A few more miles downstream Weikert Run enters.

Wading on Penns can be treacherous. In some areas deep pools lined with huge hidden boulders present obvious problems to the angler. Other sections, especially from Coburn downstream for about five miles, are easier to traverse.

The summer of 1988 was extremely unkind to Penns Creek. The state experienced more than thirty days with temperatures higher than 90 degrees. Joe Dougherty and I met in early October at the Blue Rock Hole in the catch-and-release area to fish for a couple hours. We saw dozens of Slate Drakes on the water and hundreds of Black Caddis, but no feeding trout—not one trout rose in two hours. Joe and I are convinced that the high water temperatures took their toll on the lower end of Penns Creek.

Try Penns after the hordes of fisherman have abandoned it for the season. Fish this famous stream in late June for the Blue-Winged Olive Dun in the morning or the spinner fall in the evening. You, too, will praise its hatches and trout.

Best Times to Fly-fish:

April 20–May 1
Grannom: #10 or #12, morning and afternoon
Blue Quill: #18, morning and afternoon
Hendrickson: #14, afternoon. (lower end)
Quill Gordon: #14, afternoon (spotty)
Little Black Caddis: #16, morning and afternoon

May 20–June 10
Chocolate Dun and Spinner: #16, afternoon (dun); evening (spinner)
Gray Fox: #12, afternoon and evening
Ginger Quill Spinner: #12, evening
Light Cahill: #14, evening
Sulphur and Sulphur Spinner: #16, evening
Green Drake and Coffin Fly: #10, evening

June 20–July 8
Blue-Winged Olive Dun: #16, morning and afternoon
Light Cahill: #14, evening
Yellow Drake Dun and Spinner: #12, evening
Great Stonefly: #10, afternoon and evening
Golden Drake: #12, evening

July 15–September 1
Trico Spinner: #24, morning (spotty)
Blue Quill: #18, morning
Caenis: #26, evening
Slate Drake: #12 and #14, evening

August 15–August 30
Dark Slate Drake and Rusty Spinner: #8, evening
White Mayfly: #14 and 16, evening (below Weikert)

September 15–October 15
Slate Drake: #14, afternoon and evening
Dark-Olive Caddis: #14, afternoon
Dark-Brown Caddis: #16, afternoon

Bald Eagle Creek (Julian)

For more than fifteen years I have begun the trout-fishing season on the Bald Eagle near Julian in central Pennsylvania. Normally my son, Bryan, Mel Neidig, Fred Templin, and a few other anglers join in that first-day ritual. All those years we have started the season with hundreds of other fishermen just below Julian. When 8:00 A.M. arrives, all of us cast our weighted Wooly Buggers and Muddlers into riffles and pools teeming with recently stocked trout. Meanwhile, the anglers near us cast assorted spinners, minnows, worms, salmon eggs, cheese, or anything else that seems to catch trout.

Opening day the past few years has seen warmer than usual water on the stream. This past year the water temperature at the start of the season was 52 degrees. Wooly Buggers proved to be effective early in the morning, but by 10:00 A.M. most of the trout in the section we fished had either been caught or frightened by the anglers' commotion. Soon the crowded stream emptied, and we sat back and decided what our next move should be.

While we sat on the bank a few Hendricksons began to emerge. Soon the few turned into an all-out hatch, with hundreds of duns on the pool in front of us. First one trout rose—the first of the year—then several joined in the search for food on the surface. Mel couldn't wait and quickly tied on a dry fly to imitate the emerging dun. One cast and he had a trout. Soon he aroused our interest with a second trout on the imitation. Within minutes all four of us tied on dry flies and began casting to rising trout, trout that were rising two hours before noon in the middle of April.

The hatch lasted for five hours that day, and trout continued to rise in concert with the hatch. All of us continued to catch trout throughout the afternoon. What an opening day on the Bald Eagle!

The Bald Eagle flows just five miles northwest of Spring Creek, but the two streams are very different. Water temperature on the Bald Eagle rises rapidly in the heat of summer, the stream loses much of its volume, and it holds few if any holdover trout. Spring Creek, on the other hand, remains relatively cool throughout the summer, retains a fairly constant water flow, and holds only streambred brown trout. Why the great discrepancy between these two neighboring streams? Spring Creek has been blessed with plenty of limestone springs, whereas the Bald Eagle is a typical flat freestone stream.

From Port Matilda to Milesburg, almost twenty miles, the Bald Eagle is a freestone stream that becomes a marginal trout stream in early June. What a pity, since this upper water has some fantastic late-summer hatches like the Yellow Drake, the White Mayfly, a Light Cahill (*Heptagenia marginalis*), and many, many Pale Evening Duns (*Heptagenia* species). On many occasions when the Yellow Drake appears in late June and early July, the water temperature approaches 80 degrees.

We saw earlier how the Hendrickson duns have caught many anglers by surprise on the opening day of the trout season and how those who were adequately prepared for a hatch experienced unbelievable dry fly-fishing. A 50-degree or higher water temperature on the creek provides a sure sign that the hatch will appear. Shortly after the Hendrickson appears, the Black Quill emerges on the slower sections of the stream. The Bald Eagle holds the only concentrated hatch of Black Quills in the area. Shortly after the middle of May the Gray Fox begins its sporadic appearance on the Bald Eagle. The large mayflies usually emerge in the afternoon, but on warm spring days they sometimes appear with a burst just at dusk. The spinner of the Gray Fox is the Ginger Quill. Predictable and heavy spinner falls occur nightly at 8:30.

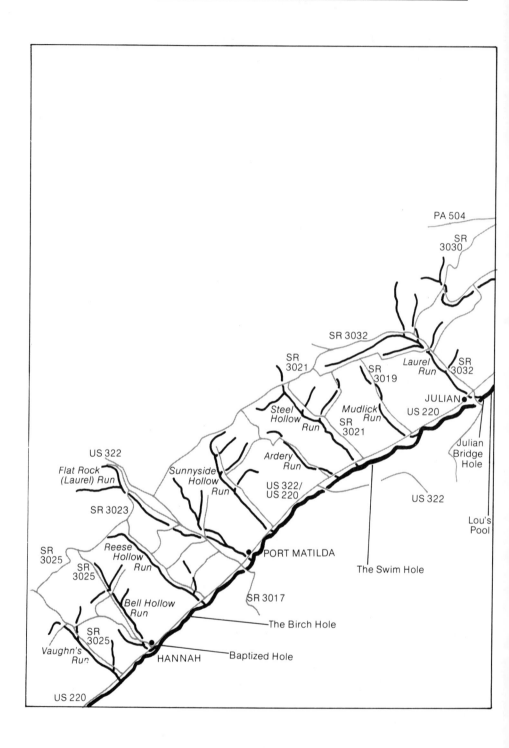

PA 504

SR 3030

SR 3032

SR 3021

SR 3019

Laurel Run

SR 3032

JULIAN

Steel Hollow Run

Mudlick Run

SR 3021

US 220

Julian Bridge Hole

US 322

Flat Rock (Laurel) Run

Sunnyside Hollow Run

Ardery Run

US 322/ US 220

US 322

Lou's Pool

SR 3023

SR 3025

Reese Hollow Run

SR 3025

PORT MATILDA

The Swim Hole

SR 3017

Bell Hollow Run

The Birch Hole

SR 3025

Vaughn's Run

HANNAH

Baptized Hole

US 220

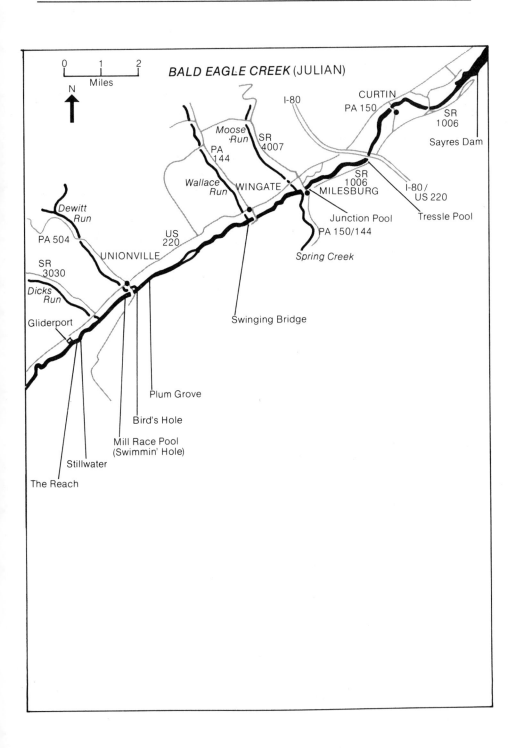

0 1 2
Miles

N

BALD EAGLE CREEK (JULIAN)

I-80

CURTIN
PA 150

SR
1006

Sayres Dam

Moose
Run

SR
4007

PA
144

Wallace
Run

WINGATE

SR
1006
MILESBURG

I-80/
US 220

Dewitt
Run

Junction Pool
PA 150/144

Tressle Pool

PA 504

US
220

UNIONVILLE

Spring Creek

SR
3030

Dicks
Run

Gliderport

Swinging Bridge

Plum Grove

Bird's Hole

Mill Race Pool
(Swimmin' Hole)

Stillwater

The Reach

The upper twenty miles of the stream flows within 200 yards of US 220. In this area the Bald Eagle is easy to wade and contains a bottom of compressed shale with few boulders. The stream ranges from twenty to thirty feet wide, with many deep pools but few fishable riffles. There are a few areas on this marginal upper section that provide cool water throughout the year. Cool mountain springs seeping from the Bald Eagle Mountain to the southeast provide some relief to the stream. And some fine tributaries with good supplies of brown and brook trout maintain low temperatures throughout the season. Travel up one of these branches in late July, and you'll likely see many trout that have migrated upstream from the Bald Eagle.

All the streams entering the Bald Eagle do so from the escarpment to the northwest, the Allegheny Plateau. Branches like Flat Rock Run (also called Laurel) at Port Matilda, Laurel Run at Julian, Dicks Run near Unionville, and Wallace Run at Wingate feed some cold water into the Bald Eagle.

When fishing the extensive Bald Eagle, your choices are simple. If you plan to fish the stream before mid-May, try the water from Port Matilda to Wingate. After the middle of May, fish the lower end near Curtin.

Best Times to Fly-fish:

April 10–April 20
Little Black Stonefly: #18, morning and afternoon

April 20–May 1
Hendrickson: #14, afternoon (appears in the morning and the evening if unusually warm weather occurs)
Black Quill and Early Brown Spinner: #14, afternoon

May 15–June 5
Pale Evening Dun: #16 and #18, evening
Gray Fox and Ginger Quill: #14, afternoon and evening (Ginger Quill reappears over the surface near 8:30 P.M.)
Slate Drake: #14, evening
Blue-Winged Olive Dun: #14, morning

June 5–September 1
Light Cahill: #14, evening

June 20–July 5
Yellow Drake Dun and Spinner: #12, dusk
Pale Evening Dun: #16, evening

August 20–September 5
White Mayfly: #16, evening
Dark Slate Drake and Dark Rusty Spinner: #6 or #8, evening (spinner) and dark (dun)

Lower Bald Eagle (Below Milesburg)

Since this section contrasts so remarkably from the Bald Eagle and Spring Creeks above, I've listed it as a separate stream.

During the summer of 1988 Commonwealth trout streams had to survive intense heat and ensuing drought. Over thirty days of 90-plus temperatures decimated trout populations in many of our trout waters. Penns Creek near Ingleby registered 80 degrees one afternoon and I logged 82 degrees one evening on the upper Loyalsock near Laporte. At the lower end of the fly stretch Bowman Creek, near Tunkhannock, warmed to 79 one evening. When temperatures on other notable Pennsylvania streams climbed to dangerous highs, the Bald Eagle never got out of the 60s.

That same hot summer John Randolph, of Harrisburg, and Bob Panuska, of Miami, Florida, met me on a late-August Saturday morning to fish a Trico hatch. For the past week I had kept John informed of the hatch and the heavy trout we caught on the Bald Eagle between Curtin and Milesburg.

John and several other fly-fishermen I told about that success questioned my report of the water temperature of the Bald Eagle so far below Spring Creek. Limestone springs and Logan Branch in the Bellefonte area cool the Bald Eagle below and make it a viable cold-water fishery all summer. Even on hot July and August days temperatures on this section rarely exceed 72 degrees. Few anglers fish the area after June, even fewer fly-fishermen. Access is limited, but this area contains some lunker brown trout.

John Randolph is a dedicated and expert fly-fisherman. John and Bob Panuska fly-fished their way through Williams College in Massachusetts. After college John became editor of the *Vermont Sportsman*, then joined the staff of *Fly Fisherman* as editor in 1979. This publication, with a circulation of 150,000, is the largest and best in its field. John has fly-fished in New Zealand, Canada, Venezuela, France, Greece, and all over the United States. You'll find him on almost any Pennsylvania trout stream, although he claims Clark Creek as his home stream.

I had bragged about the quality of the fishing on the Bald Eagle to John for weeks. He agreed to meet me the end of August. Murphy's Law would dictate that we not see any trout rising, miss the hatch and spinner fall, or encounter water too warm for rising trout. That didn't happen this time. The water temperature registered 60 degrees, Trico duns emerged as we entered my favorite stretch, and as we approached, we saw two rising trout. The only other thing that could go wrong now was that John and Bob wouldn't catch any trout.

Several trout rose sporadically as John and Bob moved into casting position. I looked upstream into the air and saw a dozen waxwings crisscrossing, catching Trico spinners thirty feet above the long pool.

Bryan Meck landing a brown trout during a Trico spinner fall on the Bald Eagle below Milesburg.

Even before the first female spinner hit the surface John hooked a heavy Bald Eagle brown trout. Soon he caught another brown about a foot long. Meanwhile, upstream, Bob missed two trout. All this action occurred before the Tricos hit the surface.

The Trico spinners fell in the space of a half-hour. The late-August morning sun heated the air quickly, and the spinners hastened their mating flight. On warm mornings Trico spinners fall in a much shorter span than on cooler ones. Nevertheless John and Bob had possibly fifteen trout rise in front of them. This all happened after the Bald Eagle had experienced the worst heat wave of the century. Moreover this rising occurred on open water where trout see everything from marshmallows to spinners. Ask John Randolph or Bob Panuska if the Bald Eagle withstood the summer of 1988.

If you want to see rising trout on the Bald Eagle, you've got to fish the hatches. Fish when the Sulphur, Trico, or Green Caddis appear. If you happen to be on this water when no hatch appears, use big wet flies and streamers. These sinking patterns work all season long in the deep pools the lower Bald Eagle contains.

Spring Creek joins the Bald Eagle at Milesburg and creates a totally different stream below. Because of the contribution of Spring Creek, the Bald Eagle from Milesburg to Curtin exhibits a completely different character from its upper twenty miles. Considered a limestone stream in its lower area, it receives a heavy alkaline discharge from Spring Creek. Unlike the upper part of the stream, this lower section rarely exhibits water temperatures above 70 degrees. It is a sizable stream, harboring many large brown and rainbow trout. You'll find many pools, some over five feet deep, and heavy, productive riffles are common. Above Spring Creek the stream ranges from twenty to thirty feet wide; on this lower end, forty- to fifty-foot-wide pools are common. Some of these pools are a quarter- to a half-mile long. Wading is more difficult with the heavier water and deeper pools.

I remember the first time I hiked upstream from Curtin to fish a section of the Bald Eagle not easily accessible. There was no angler's path along the bank to follow upstream—a certain indication that the stream lacked fishing pressure. Upstream about a half-mile large carp darted out from the shallows into deeper water. This is trout water? The subsequent events, however, convinced me that this section demonstrated some of the qualities of a incredibly underfished, top-quality trout fishery.

My first encounter with the stream occurred in mid-May at 5:00 P.M. Except for the movement of carp near the bank, the lower Bald Eagle seemed void of other fish. There was no surface activity for the first half-hour. Then it all began. First a few Sulphurs appeared, then a dozen or more swirled in the breeze in a back eddy just above me. A single heavy fish started rising to the sluggish pale-yellow duns. Soon a couple more sizable trout joined in the search for food on the surface. I cast a Sulphur Dun towards the first and seemingly largest rising fish. The dry fly drifted over the riser and disappeared in an instant splash. The lunker thrashed and turned, and in an instant the leader came flying back in my face. I lost that trout because I was excited and unprepared for the big trout living in the stream.

I tied on another Sulphur Dun, this time making certain that the improved clinch knot was fastened properly, and cast to the same general area where another trout now rose. On the third cast the fly landed two feet above the rising trout. The fish exploded when it felt the hook. Now more determined than ever to land the fish, I played it for a good ten minutes before I guided it into the net. A hefty twenty-inch brown had taken that Sulphur. When I unhooked the brown I noticed a second fly, another Sulphur pattern, in the other side of its mouth. Not only had I caught the trout, but I had also retrieved my previous fly, which this same fish had sucked in just a minute before. Never before and never since have I seen a trout that I had just missed hit again almost immediately. What excitement! In that pool that evening, just above Curtin, less than a half-dozen trout rose to that sparse hatch of Sulphurs, but all seized the size-16 imitation readily.

There are some paradoxes about this lower area of the Bald Eagle. The main one is the lack of extensive hatches. Only the Sulphur, Trico, and Green Caddis seem to appear in heavy enough numbers to bring trout to the surface. Often, even when hatches appear on the surface, few trout rise to them consistently. There's one section just below the Curtin Bridge, and another upstream a mile from the bridge, where trout seem to rise consistently during hatches. Unless there's a hatch in progress, however, a more prudent pattern selection often is a large wet fly or emerging caddis.

I suggested earlier that the Trico appears on this water from mid-July until late September. Select one of the long, slow pools during this spinner fall, and chances are you'll see rising trout. During the Trico spinner fall, rainbows especially seem to cruise while feeding on the small spinners. It's often difficult to pinpoint these fish and cast to them.

There are other mayflies on the lower Bald Eagle, like the Gray Fox and even a few White Mayflies, but the Sulphur and the Trico are the heaviest.

Although the section lacks many mayfly hatches, it does harbor many caddis fly species. Don't fly-fish here without plenty of Green Caddis patterns in sizes 14 and 16. Caddis appear on the Bald Eagle from early May until late September. During June and July trout chase the emerging pupae of the caddis and are active near the surface the first few hours after dawn.

Brown and rainbow trout over twenty inches long are common on this lower section. These large trout can best be taken on a large wet fly fished almost any time of the season or a dry fly imitating one of the few hatches. If your preference is dry flies, then fly-fish this lower section from the middle of May until early June from 6:00 P.M. to 9:00 P.M. Don't overlook this lower section.

Best Times to Fly-fish:

May 12–June 5
Sulphur Dun and Spinner: #16, evening
Green Caddis: #14, afternoon and evening
Gray Fox and Ginger Quill: #12 and 14, afternoon and evening (spotty)

July 10–September
Trico: #24, morning
Green Caddis: #14 and #16, morning
White Mayfly: #14 and #16, evening (spotty)

Bald Eagle Creek (Tyrone)

There's a section of the Bald Eagle-Tyrone near Vail that I fish often. It contains a pool about 100 yards long with a productive riffle above. I regularly visit this area in mid-April just before noon when I can depend on seeing the Blue Quill emerge. Thousands of these dependable mayflies appear in the riffle and drift to the pool below. Trout, eager to capture natural food, take the nymph and dun with regularity. Often during this hatch the pool comes alive with trout rising for every available dun. A size-18 imitation consistently performs well during this extensive hatch.

The Bald Eagle-Tyrone (we'll refer to it as BET) is a productive tributary of the Little Juniata River. Although it and the Bald Eagle near Julian begin in the same valley, the BET is better, having a healthy supply of native brook and brown trout. These two Bald Eagle Creeks have their headwaters in a swampy area a few hundred feet from each other. The BET, however, seldom has temperatures above 70 degrees all summer, as it drains two highly productive and sizable cold-water tributaries, Big Fill and Vanscoyoc runs. Both streams have a good supply of native brown and brook trout, and their summer temperatures rarely go above 65 degrees. Both tributaries flow into BET within a mile and produce a cold, productive larger stream about thirty feet wide. The BET is not lengthy. From its headwaters to its junction with the Little Juniata River it is barely five miles long; but the BET harbors many great hatches.

After an initial spurt of Blue Quills, Quill Gordons, and a few Hendricksons, few mayflies appear again until late May. Then within the span of a couple weeks mayflies like the Green Drake, Slate Drake, and by mid-June the Yellow Drake, produce rising trout.

Sulphurs too are important on the BET. This time the smallest of the three (*Ephemerella dorothea*) is the heaviest to appear. This size-18 Sulphur usually appears throughout most of the month of June, just at dusk. The Yellow Drake emerges on the BET in numbers equal to the hatch on the other Bald Eagle, but here trout feed on the Drakes freely since the water temperature in late June is usually in the mid-60s. As with many Pennsylvania streams, the BET is fished continuously from the beginning of the season until early June. For the remainder of the season the once heavily worn paths along the stream are restored to their natural appearance. Much of the best fly-fishing occurs after early June, however. Some of the water above the town of Bald Eagle is posted. US 220 parallels the BET near Tyrone. The BET is easy to wade and has only a few large boulders. The stream contains the characteristic riffle, pool, riffle, pool sequence. Try this stream in late June when the showpiece appears, the Yellow Drake.

Best Times to Fly-fish:

April 18–May 1
Blue Quill: #18, morning and afternoon
Quill Gordon: #14, afternoon
Hendrickson: #14, afternoon

May 15–May 30
Sulphur Dun and Spinner: #16, evening
Green Drake: #12, evening
Slate Drake: #14, evening

June 15–July 5
Pale Evening Dun and Spinner: #18, evening
Yellow Drake: #12, evening

September–October
Slate Drake: #14, afternoon

Big Fill Run

Until fifteen years ago the only massive Green Drake hatch I had ever witnessed was the famous one on Penns Creek. Then one late-May afternoon, at this diminutive six-mile-long stream guarded along its banks by shoulder-high rhododendron and a canopy of red oaks, I watched in astonishment as a hatch of these huge mayflies struggled to become airborne. This is the same stream where a year later I witnessed a hatch of March Browns. The stream? Big Fill in Blair and Centre counties.

Big Fill has some of the most concentrated and diverse hatches of any stream in Pennsylvania. It is small—only ten to fifteen feet wide at most places. Until a few years ago it was stocked heavily by the state and the Bald Eagle Rod and Gun Club from their cooperative hatchery. Recently the state declared Big Fill a wild-trout stream, and it is not currently stocked. Big Fill doesn't need any additional trout added to its supply. It has ample native browns and brooks well up into its headwaters. Some of the water on the lower end that was open to fishing prior to the stream's being reclassified is now posted.

Big Fill begins in extreme western Centre County and flows south to the town of Bald Eagle, where it crosses US 220. Three hundred yards below, it enters the Bald Eagle-Tyrone. PA 350 parallels the stream for about four miles. Above PA 350 hatches become sparse, although the supply of small native trout still persists. Even on the hottest days Big Fill temperatures rarely rise above the mid-60s. Fishing access to the stream is difficult because much of the stream is enclosed within a canopy of rhododendrons, hemlock, and a wide variety of other growth.

Hatches begin early in the season on Big Fill. By the second week of the season you'll find plenty of Blue Quills and Quill Gordons and see rising trout. Hendricksons don't seem to produce a heavy hatch on the stream, but you see them occasionally.

The heaviest and best hatches occur in the last week of May with the advent of the March Brown, Green Drake, Chocolate Dun, Sulphur, and Light Cahill. As with so many other small Commonwealth streams that have a heavy woodland canopy, Green Drakes often appear all day on Big Fill. Even into September this miniature stream contains viable hatches. Slate Drakes appear daily in limited numbers throughout much of September, even into early October.

Best Times to Fly-fish:

April 20–May 1
Blue Quill: #18, morning and afternoon
Quill Gordon: #14, afternoon
Hendrickson: #14, afternoon

May 25–June 5
March Brown: #12, morning and afternoon
Green Drake: #10, morning, afternoon, and evening
Chocolate Dun: #16, morning and afternoon
Sulphur: #16 and #18, evening
Light Cahill: #14, evening

September–October
Slate Drake: #14, afternoon and evening

Vanscoyoc Run

If you thought Big Fill was a small stream, then try to fish Vanscoyoc Run, just two miles southwest of the town of Bald Eagle. Much of the water above old US 220 is too narrow and too brush covered to fly-fish, but below the old route the stream holds several large pools, some excellent hatches, and a good trout population.

Green Drakes, Slate Drakes, Quill Gordons, Hendricksons, Blue Quills, and Dark-Green Drakes make up only a small portion of the potpourri of hatches found on this water, and on the main stem into which it flows, the Bald Eagle. Since the stream at its widest is less than fifteen feet across, select one of the pools or upstream riffles to fly-fish. Between the railroad and its merger with the Bald Eagle lie some productive pools with plenty of cool water throughout the summer.

Best Times to Fly-fish:

April 18–May 1
Blue Quill: #18, morning and afternoon
Quill Gordon: #14, afternoon
Hendrickson: #14, afternoon

May 20–June 5
Green Drake: #10, afternoon and evening
Dark-Green Drake: #10, afternoon and evening
Sulphur: #16, evening
March Brown: #12, morning and afternoon
Slate Drake: #14, evening

White Deer Creek

Delayed Harvest Fly-Fishing Only—2.5 miles; from Cooper Mill Road upstream to Union/Centre county line.

During my twenty-five years of service with the Pennsylvania State University I traveled extensively throughout the Commonwealth, frequently visiting all twenty university campuses. At least once a week I traveled I-80 east. I must have crossed White Deer Creek dozens of times before I finally gave in to temptation and exited the thruway at Mile Run to fish.

White Deer Creek is a small freestone stream located in central Pennsylvania's Centre and Union counties. The upper end, reached by an improved dirt road, contains a two-mile delayed-harvest fly-fishing-only section, heavily stocked and rewarding for the persistent angler. The stream in the upper area is tiny, and fishing it requires constant caution, a low profile, and a long, fine leader.

Although I-80 parallels White Deer Creek, much of the stream is relatively untouched by anglers after Memorial Day. Below the fly-fishing-only section are ten more miles of productive water with a diversity of hatches throughout the year and plenty of native brown and brook trout to complement the early stocking program. Fishing is decent to the town of White Deer, where the stream enters the Susquehanna River. Much of the stream is narrow, lined with rhododendrons, and almost impossible to fly-fish. White Deer contains some good pocket water, however, and adequate holding pools, especially for the heavy hatches that appear in spring.

One of the heaviest hatches on White Deer is also one of the earliest. The first Blue Quill of the year to appear does so in unbelievable numbers for such a small stream. Late morning and early afternoon in the third week in April, you can almost assuredly witness a hatch of these mayflies. Hendrickson duns and spinners often intermingle with the Blue Quills and Dark-Brown Spinners to produce some of the finest small-water fly-fishing in Pennsylvania. The Red Quill Spinners, the mating adult of the Hendrickson, perform their mating ritual in the late-afternoon and early-evening hours. And, there's more—the Quill Gordon also appears on this fertile freestone stream. On these early-season days carry patterns of the three duns and the Dark-Brown and Red Quill spinners: use the Dark-Brown Spinners in size 18 to imitate the adult of the Blue Quill; select the Red Quill Spinner to copy the images of the Hendrickson and Quill Gordon.

Occasional stoneflies and caddis flies continue to emerge on White Deer into mid-May. When mayfly activity returns after the earliest hatches, it does so with an exciting array of aquatic insects. First to appear after the respite following the Blue Quill, Hendrickson, and Quill Gordon is the large, sporadic March Brown. Since this species ordinarily appears throughout much of the day, it can be a boon to the persistent angler. Be prepared to wait for the March Brown to emerge, search for rising trout, and you'll be rewarded. The large naturals often start dashing toward the surface around 10:00 A.M. the third week in May. If you're fortunate enough to meet the hatch, you'll experience productive fly-fishing until late afternoon.

The Green Drake, a size or two larger than the March Brown, usually appears on White Deer around May 25 or 26. As the Drake does on so many smaller freestone streams, it emerges throughout much of the day, again making daylight fishing over large trout possible. (A heavy canopy of oaks, maples, and evergreens hide most of White Deer's surface from continuous exposure to sunlight.) Green Drakes appear sporadically throughout the day and into the evening, when another important species, the Sulphur, appears. Sulphur is a catch-all term used to describe dozens of yellow-bodied species ranging in hook size from 16 to 20. On White Deer the Sulphur *Ephemerella rotunda* requires a size-16 or -18 imitation to copy the size of the natural.

If you prefer wet flies and nymphs, you might try a Hendrickson nymph early in the season or a Green Drake or Sulphur nymph with its dark-brown body in late May. All are effective fish catchers at that time.

White Deer is a small stream. Its width ranges from fifteen to twenty-five feet. Wading, however, can be treacherous, because the stream hides plenty of huge boulders. Pools on the stream are small, but many of the riffles and pocket water harbor rising trout.

By late June White Deer evolves into a clear, freestone stream with extraordinarily wary trout. At this time you need a fine tippet on a long leader and a low profile. With these precautions trout can be caught all summer long on this relatively underfished and highly productive water.

Best Times to Fly-fish:

April 18–May 1
Blue Quill and Dark-Brown Spinner: #18, morning, afternoon, and early evening
Quill Gordon: #14, afternoon
Hendrickson and Red Quill Spinner: #14, afternoon and early evening

May 15–June 20
March Brown: #12, morning and afternoon
Gray Fox: #14, afternoon
Green Drake: #12, evening
Sulphur Dun and Spinner: #16, evening
Blue-Winged Olive Dun: #14, morning
Slate Drake: #14, evening

Big Fishing Creek

Trophy Trout Project—5 miles; from the bridge at Tylersville Fish Hatchery downstream to Fleming's Bridge at Lamar Fish Hatchery.

Pennsylvania probably contains dozens of streams with the same names. There are many Pine Creeks, Cedar Creeks, and Cedar Runs, Bear Creeks, and yes, quite a few Fishing Creeks. But none of the so-called Fishing Creeks is more productive, contains more hatches, and has consistently colder water all season long than does Big Fishing Creek in Clinton County. Big Fishing Creek originates near Loganton in southern Clinton County, then flows west and south for fifteen miles until it enters the Susquehanna River near Lock Haven. A few miles below Clintondale and a couple miles above Lamar, Big Fishing Creek enters a section affectionately called The Narrows by many fly-fishing enthusiasts. The narrows section is about four miles long and carries trophy trout regulations. This section is the most productive, but also the most heavily fished.

Special regulations end at the lower hatchery at Lamar. From this point almost to Mill Hall, Big Fishing Creek is classified as a wild-trout stream and receives no state stocking. It depends totally on natural reproduction for its trout population. This section, about seven miles long, has plenty of browns and brook trout and great hatches. From Cedar Run downstream

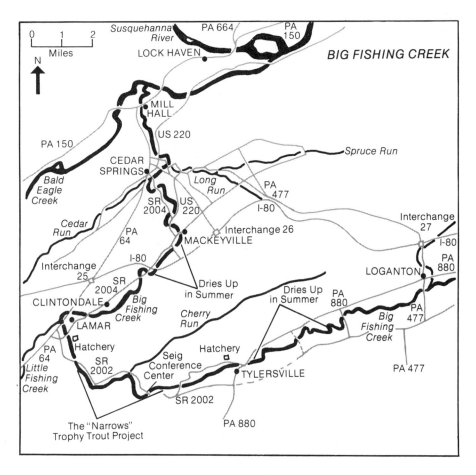

through Mill Hall, Big Fishing Creek is stocked with large numbers of trout annually. This section too has excellent hatches and is seldom fished after June.

Throughout its entire length Big Fishing Creek retains cool water all season long. Mid-July temperatures in The Narrows remain in the low 60s. Cool limestone springs create these ideal temperatures. Big Fishing Creek picks up additional cooling water below The Narrows from its limestone tributaries. In succession, going downstream, Big Fishing Creek picks up cooling water from Cherry Run (a freestone stream) in The Narrows, Little Fishing Creek at the town of Lamar, and Cedar and Spruce runs just above Mill Hall.

Big Fishing Creek reminds me somewhat of the Henry's Fork in Idaho because of the diversity and intensity of it hatches. The season begins almost immediately with the opening of the trout season. First-day fishermen are often greeted with the Blue Quill, Quill Gordon, and the Hendrickson.

Even during July and August Big Fishing Creek near Lamar holds good hatches and heavy trout.

But this limestone stream doesn't pause after the early hatches, as so many other Pennsylvania streams do. The third week of April produces a fantastic Black Caddis hatch which can be gratifying for the patient fly-fisherman. The most effective pattern for the caddis is the emerging-pupae imitation. During the hatch fish the pattern just under the surface. Trout sometimes swirl at the wet fly and miss it. There are plenty of other caddis species on the stream. Check the bottom of the stream, and you'll see all types of caddis larvae. Big Fishing Creek contains some massive Green Caddis larvae (*Rhyacophila* species) that measure twenty millimeters long. Many of these are bright green, and a green-bodied larval imitation on a size-10 hook works well.

The Sulphur begins early on Big Fishing Creek, almost the same day it first appears on the Little Juniata River. By May 13 or 14 the Sulphur is heavy enough to bring trout to the surface. This Sulphur has a distinct olive to its orange-yellow body. In my book *Meeting and Fishing the Hatches* I indicated many times that the size of insects of the same species varies from stream to stream. The coloration of insects, especially mayflies, also varies from stream to stream. The Sulphur emerges from The Narrows downstream until mid-to late June.

Big Fishing Creek is probably best noted for its Green Drake hatch, which appears about a week later than the one on Penns Creek. When the Drake appears in late afternoon and evening, any section of The Narrows is productive, and the trout seem to take the imitation more willingly than on Penns Creek. Fishing over the Drake during its peak emergence can be a three-hour event, and catching a dozen or more trout on the imitation is commonplace. As with Penns, however, when the word gets out that the hatch is on, dozens of fly-fishermen show up for the spectacle and crowd much of the suitable fishing space. The March Brown and the Sulphur emerge simultaneously with the Green Drake, so if you miss the Drake hatch you will probably see one of the two.

By mid-June Big Fishing Creek is still alive with insects. Yet to appear are several species of Blue Quills (*Paraleptophlebia* species), Slate Drakes, some Blue-Winged Olive Duns, Light Cahills, and a great hatch of Tricos beginning in mid-July. Tricos and Blue-Winged Olive Duns continue well into September. Dave Rothrock, of Jersey Shore, looks forward to the Slate Drake hatch on Big Fishing Creek. Dave's developed an excellent pattern for the nymph and finds it especially effective on this stream.

Big Fishing Creek is almost like three separate streams in its water conditions and hatches. Tricos, for example, don't appear on the upper section in The Narrows. They do, however, emerge from Mackeyville downstream, and for the patient late-season angler they can be a boon. Green Drakes and Blue Quills are most prominent in The Narrows. Therefore, even though this stream contains a great hatch of a given species, it's important to know just where that hatch occurs. Often the least productive section is that area just above Mackeyville where much of the stream moves underground in July and August.

Big Fishing Creek has a dependable Hendrickson hatch in The Narrows. For years this hatch has annoyed me because it appears often before the first week of the season, well ahead of its normal appearance on other local streams, and also because the body color of the local Hendrickson is much darker than that of other Hendricksons. The species has since been identified as a subspecies of the true Hendrickson.

The tributaries of Big Fishing Creek produce adequate hatches and harbor some large streambred trout. Cedar Run near Mill Hall has some Sulphurs and Tricos and a healthy population of streambred browns. Much of the stream is posted, however. Ask permission on this small limestone stream before fishing. Little Fishing Creek, which enters the main stream at Lamar, is heavily stocked by the state and holds a decent trout population all season. Little Fishing is a typical meadow limestone stream. If you were a gambler, you'd bet that the stream contains a heavy Trico hatch. It should, but it doesn't. There have been reports that this stream does hold some Green Drakes. Cherry Run, which enters in The Narrows section, is lined much of the way with rhododendrons, making it difficult to fly-fish, but it does contain some large trout.

Wading in much of The Narrows can be dangerous. The stream is filled with large rocks and boulders, and the bottom is uneven. The Narrows also has many deep pools and productive riffles. PA 64 crosses Big Fishing Creek at Lamar and numerous secondary roads take you within walking distance above and below.

You can spend weeks on Big Fishing Creek and still not know the true character of the stream. Try it almost any time of the year, and you will be impressed with the quality of the stream, the quantity of the hatches, and most of all with the trout population.

Best Times to Fly-fish:

April 15–May 5
Blue Quill: #18, morning and afternoon
Quill Gordon: #14, afternoon
Hendrickson: #14, afternoon
Black Caddis: #14 and #16, morning and afternoon
Blue Dun: #20, afternoon

May 12–June 5
Sulphur Dun and Spinner: #16, evening
March Brown: #14, morning and afternoon
Dark-Green Drake: #8, afternoon and evening (spotty)
Green Drake and Coffin Fly: #10, evening
Slate Drake: #14, evening
Light Cahill: #14, evening
Pink Lady: #14, evening
Green Caddis: #14, afternoon and evening

June 5–July 20
Little Blue-Winged Olive Dun: #20, afternoon and evening
Blue Quill: #18, morning
Blue-Winged Olive Dun: #14, morning
Sulphur Dun and Spinner: #16, evening

July 15–September 30
Trico: #24, morning (lower section only)
Blue-Winged Olive Dun: #14, morning
Blue Quill: #18, morning
Little Blue-Winged Olive Dun: #20, morning and afternoon
Blue Dun: #20, afternoon

Piney Creek

If you want to fish a real sleeper, try Piney Creek in Blair County. This small but exceptionally productive limestone stream is seldom fished after Memorial Day, and infrequently before that by fly-fishermen. Piney has many streambred brown trout over fifteen inches long. Because of its diminutive size and brush-cluttered banks, however, Piney can be difficult to fly-fish.

Piney is noted for three abundant hatches which occur over a good part of the season. Other than some Blue Quills and Blue-Winged Olive Duns, the first two notable hatches occur simultaneously in mid-May. Within a day or two of each other the Gray Fox and the Sulphur emerge. If you plan your trip accordingly, you can fish over hatches during the afternoon and early evening in the latter part of May and early June. Gray Foxes usually appear shortly after noon and sporadically the rest of the day. After 7:00 P.M. Sulphur Duns and Spinners appear. Theoretically various duns and spinners may be on the water any time from early afternoon until dusk. There's a two-week period from late May to early June where you're almost assured of fishing over at least two hatches.

To be a consistent stream, Piney should be productive late in the season, and it is, with a passable Trico hatch. Granted, many Pennsylvania streams exhibit much heavier Trico hatches, but the one on Piney is adequate. Besides, many other streams with Trico hatches suffer from marginal if not downright warm summer water. Not so with Piney, whose headwaters emanate from consistently cool limestone springs.

Piney is a small stream beginning just a few miles northeast of Martinsburg in Blair County and flowing northeast fifteen miles before it enters the Frankstown Branch of the Juniata River just west of Williamsburg. The lower half of the stream, beginning about six miles upstream from Williamsburg, offers good brown trout fishing. A secondary blacktop road parallels much of the lower water and PA 866 at the upper end.

Some anglers have reported excellent fly-fishing on the Frankstown Branch just below where Piney enters. This section is cooled somewhat by the flow from Piney, and it contains some Sulphurs. Piney picks up only one small tributary on its fifteen-mile journey to the Frankstown Branch of the Juniata River. What it lacks in tributaries it picks up in limestone springs. Wading is no problem on this fifteen-foot-wide stream. Piney has some deep pools and plenty of small pocket water and riffles where Sulphurs emerge. The Fish Commission maintains two access areas on the stream.

If you like fishing consistently cool water all summer long with a good supply of streambred brown trout, and limited but adequate hatches, and if you don't mind fly-fishing on a small, tree-lined limestone stream, then try Piney.

Best Times to Fly-fish:

March 1–March 31
Little Black Stonefly: #18, afternoon

April 1–May 1
Little Blue-Winged Olive Dun: #20, morning and afternoon
Blue Quill: #18, morning and afternoon

May 12–June 5
Sulphur Dun and Spinner: #16, evening
Gray Fox and Ginger Quill: #14, afternoon (dun) and evening (spinner)

July 12–September 15
Trico: #24, morning
Little Blue-Winged Olive Dun: #20, morning and afternoon

Clover Creek

Ed Gunnett, of Williamsburg in Blair County, invited me to fly-fish a stretch of his club's private water on Clover Creek a few years ago. It happened to be Memorial Day weekend, and Ed asked me to talk to his club's members on some of the hatches of Pennsylvania. We made certain that the talk and fishing demonstration ended by 7:00 P.M. so we'd have plenty of time to fish the Sulphur hatch so prevalent on this stream that time of the year.

Ed and I headed upstream a few hundred yards to the upper end of the club's posted water. Here we waited for the hatch to begin. Warm weather the past few days delayed the hatch until just before dark. When the Sulphurs appeared, they did so by the thousands on this twenty-foot-wide stream. Trout eagerly took our dry flies that evening, but the action only lasted for a half-hour. Then the hatch diminished, and total darkness set in. Before we quit, however, we had witnessed a tremendous hatch and seen maybe two dozen rising trout.

Clover has many of the same hatches as Piney. We saw that it contains a respectable Sulphur hatch, but it also holds a consistent Trico hatch on its upper end near Henrietta. The Trico combines with cool summer water in its upper end to produce dependable fly-fishing over rising trout every day. The Sulphur is the heaviest and longest hatch of the year on Clover, lasting for almost a month. Some Yellow Drakes appear in the latter part of June. In mid-October I've seen Ed Gunnett and Danny Deters fish over trout rising to Little Blue-Winged Olive Duns, on a day when 50-degree air temperatures delayed duns in escaping from the surface in their normal rapid fashion. Trout rose on Clover throughout the afternoon to dazed *Baetis* duns.

Piney and Clover are two fine limestone streams tucked in between Tussey and Lock mountains in southwestern Blair County. Piney Creek is the smaller of the two and lies five miles to the northwest of Clover Creek. These two little limestone streams make a good weekend trip for any fly-fisherman if he or she likes to fish new water with few other anglers.

Best Times to Fly-fish:

April 5–May 1
Little Blue-Winged Olive Dun: #20, morning and afternoon
Quill Gordon: #14, afternoon (spotty)
Blue Quill: #18, morning and afternoon

May 12–June 15
Gray Fox and Ginger Quill: #14, afternoon (dun) and evening
Sulphur Dun and Spinner: #16, evening

June 20–July 5
Yellow Drake: #12, evening

July 15–September 15
Trico: #24, morning (upper end)
Blue Quill: #18, morning and afternoon

September 15–October 15
Little Blue-Winged Olive Dun: #20, morning and afternoon
Blue Quill: #18, morning and afternoon

Spruce Creek

Catch-and-Release—0.5 mile; Pennsylvania State University Experimental Fisheries Area (about 0.6 mile above the village of Spruce Creek).

Joe McMullen holds a heavy trout taken from his private section of Spruce Creek.

Many consider George Harvey the greatest fly-fisherman in the country. He taught fly tying and fly casting to thousands of students and adults at Penn State University from 1934 to 1972 and coached two presidents—Eisenhower and Carter—on fly-fishing. George fished Trico hatches long before any of us knew the hatch existed; he saw his first Tricos in 1927. By 1935 he was fishing the hatch almost daily on Falling Springs. George was the first to effectively imitate the olive-green Trico dun. George recently revolutionized fishing the Trico spinner fall by adding Krystal Flash to the spent wings of the spinner.

Today, every morning from mid-July to late September, you find George fishing and studying the Trico hatch on Spruce Creek, as he has done since 1945. No one knows more about the Trico hatch and Spruce Creek than George Harvey. George has also experienced tremendous Green Drake, Sulphur, and Blue-Winged Olive Dun hatches on this fertile central-Pennsylvania limestone stream.

Spruce Creek over the past half-century has evolved into mostly private water. Several fishing clubs own about ten of the stream's fifteen miles, and several other areas around Franklinville contain private water posted by individual owners. Despite limited access, however, Spruce Creek is important because of the tremendous hatches on the stream which produce activity all season, and because there are four stretches of water open to public fishing. Besides, Joe McMullen and Wayne Harpster own sections of the stream, and they allow fee fishing. If you get an opportunity try either of these two stretches of private water.

Joe McMullen owns a half-mile stretch of Spruce one mile from its junction with the Little Juniata. This section contains plenty of five- to eight-pound rainbow and brown trout. Recently I met Kevin Daily, of Springdale, and Roger Rea, of Murrysville, on Joe's stretch of water. The two caught twenty trout over twenty inches long. Roger landed a twenty-five-inch brown trout that weighed 6½ pounds. If you don't have a lot of time to spend locating lunker trout, you might want to try one of these two sections of Spruce Creek.

Hatching activity begins early on Spruce, with the appearance of the Blue Quill and a sparse Hendrickson species in mid-to-late April. Blue Duns (*Pseudocloeon* species) appear in early May, making this one of the few Pennsylvania streams to provide a mayfly hatch at this time of the season. Spruce is best noted, however, for its hatches the last two weeks of May, when Green Drakes, Light Cahills, Sulphurs, Gray Foxes, Blue-Winged Olive Duns, and others appear.

The Green Drake hatch on Spruce is one of the earliest of the season, usually beginning about May 22. Thirty years ago the Drake hatch on Spruce was much heavier than it is today. I can remember evenings in late May when I had to stop along PA 45 to wipe the dead Coffin Flies (mating spinners of the Green Drake) off my windshield. Those times have long vanished, and the Green Drake is now downgraded to an abundant, but not an explosive hatch. Even now, however, when the Green Drake appears, it seems to bring every lunker to the surface.

Into July and August Spruce has more hatches. It contains a decent Yellow Drake in late June and an adequate Trico hatch beginning in mid-July. There are many other hatches on Spruce, including several species imitated by the Blue-Winged Olive Dun, a few White Mayflies, and multibrooded Blue Duns.

Spruce Creek is easily reached by PA 45. The stream begins about ten miles southwest of State College, where it emerges from a limestone cavern and enters a large holding pool. The stream then flows southwest through Franklinville, entering the Little Juniata River at the town of Spruce Creek.

As noted, Spruce has only a few sections open to public fishing. A half-mile section just above the Grange Hall at Baileyville is open. This water is extremely small, running through open pastureland. The only hatch of any consequence in this area is the Sulphur, which appears nightly from mid-May until early July. Some Blue Quills, Blue-Winged Olive Duns, and Little Blue-Winged Olive Duns also emerge on this stretch. The next open area downstream is the quarter-mile stretch at Colerain Park, about three miles above the town of Spruce Creek. This area is fished heavily by picnickers throughout the season. The Pennsylvania State University owns a half-mile section below Colerain Park that has been designated as a catch-and-release area. This water is extremely productive, contains plenty of native browns, and has abundant hatches. Just below McMullen's Hatchery at the edge of Spruce Creek (town) occurs the next open section, also catch-and-release, which holds many brown trout moving upstream in fall to breed.

About ten years ago the state stopped stocking the upper end of Spruce Creek. For years prior to that time they stocked a two-mile section at Baileyville. Many of the private sections stock their own trout—but Spruce doesn't really need any transplanting. It shelters a very healthy population of native brown trout.

On February 3, 1987, the lower end of Spruce Creek was polluted by a liquid-manure spill. The spill emptied into Warriorsmark Creek and entered Spruce just below Franklinville. Jim Bashline, who owns property on the affected stretch, says that the large trout actually jumped onto the bank when the spill passed his section of water. I fished the polluted area three months after the accidental spill occurred. Bashline pointed out at that time that trout had already moved back into the polluted area from upstream. The pollution seems to have had little effect on the hatches.

Even though most of Spruce Creek is posted, there is enough open water to satisfy the angler who wants to experience great hatches, plenty of wild brown trout, and hallowed waters. The best spot to fish is on the parcel owned by Penn State University.

Best Times to Fly-fish:

April 20–May 1
Blue Quill: #18, morning and afternoon
Hendrickson: #14, afternoon
Little Blue-Winged Olive Dun: #20, morning and afternoon

May 1–May 10
Blue Dun: #20, afternoon and evening

May 13–June 5
Sulphur Dun and Spinner: #16, evening
Gray Fox: #14, afternoon and evening
Green Drake: #10, evening
Slate Drake: #12 or #14, evening
Light Cahill: #14, evening
Blue-Winged Olive Dun: #14, morning and afternoon

June 5–June 20
Little Blue-Winged Olive Dun: #20, afternoon and evening

June 20–July 5
Yellow Drake: #12, evening
Blue Quill: #18, morning and afternoon
Blue-Winged Olive Dun: #16, morning and afternoon

July 15–September 30
Slate Drake: #14, afternoon and evening
Trico: #24, morning
Little White Mayfly: #28, evening
Blue Dun: #20, afternoon

September 30–October 30
Little Blue-Winged Olive Dun: #20, afternoon

Sixmile Run

Do you want to see a variety of hatches in a setting resembling a high-alpine bog? Do you mind fly-fishing on a small stream, only fifteen feet wide at its widest point? How about extremely clear pristine water and plenty of trout? Sixmile Run has it all.

Sixmile is a short, alder-lined stream with cold water all season long. It's located in northern Centre County near the old Philipsburg Airport. I still remember the day I disembarked from an Allegheny Airlines flight with a perforated Styrofoam coffee cup full of live western Green Drakes. I had captured a dozen of these mayflies just the day before on the Bitterroot River near Missoula, Montana and carried them in my luggage on the flight east. As soon as I left the airport, I headed to Sixmile Run and deposited all of the active mayflies in that stream. "What if they really take hold here," I thought. They didn't.

Even without my Montana Green Drakes, Sixmile Run hosts a broad variety of hatches. From the beginning of the season to October, aquatic insects abound. A few Hendricksons, and a lot of Blue Quills and Quill Gordons, emerge in late April, making Sixmile one of those fantastic north-central Pennsylvania streams with productive early hatches. But the activity doesn't stop there. Sixmile Run parades a variety of mayflies on its surface, including a prolific hatch of Blue-Winged Olive Duns and Blue Quills on late-May mornings. In the evening at the same time of year one of the lesser-known mayflies, the Pink Lady (*Epeorus vitreus*), appears.

Just when most anglers have abandoned the stream, the greatest surprise of all appears. Sixmile Run has an abundant hatch of Yellow Drakes.

Towards the end of June, around June 25, these large mayflies emerge in numbers heavy enough to entice any remaining trout to the surface. Look for any type of pool or slow water on the upper third of the stream, and you'll find the Yellow Drake. What's more, when the Drake appears, water temperatures on this creek are low enough for some decent fly-fishing. The Yellow Drake continues to appear nightly for a good two weeks on Sixmile before it declines. Heavy trout that have avoided early anglers' lures and live bait await anyone prepared for the Yellow Drake hatch.

Sixmile, as the name suggests, is an abbreviated stream. It begins on the Allegheny Plateau and flows directly north into the highly acidic Moshannon Creek. There are at least two impoundments on the upper end which are conveniently stocked with trout and which afford fly-fishermen plenty of casting room. A rutted dirt road parallels the entire length of the stream. PA 504, from Unionville to Philipsburg, intersects the stream at its midway point.

If you'd like to spend a day on a productive stream with plenty of early and mid-season hatches, and you don't mind fly-fishing a small stream, try Sixmile Run.

Best Times to Fly-fish:

April 18–May 5
Quill Gordon: #14, afternoon
Hendrickson: #14, afternoon (spotty)
Blue Quill: #18, morning and afternoon
Early Brown Stonefly: #12, morning and afternoon
Little Blue-Winged Olive Dun: #20, morning and afternoon

May 25–June 10
Pink Lady: #14, evening
Blue-Winged Olive Dun: #14, morning

June 20–July 10
Yellow Drake: #12, evening
Blue Quill: #18, morning and afternoon

Logan Branch

I first fly-fished on Logan Branch eighteen years ago. When I arrived at the stream that day, I almost turned around and went home. Why? Logan is a narrow limestone stream running through almost its entire length within a couple feet of a busy highway. Litter and debris tossed out of cars clutter the banks.

That first encounter with Logan occurred on June 13 at 6:00 P.M. A few Sulphurs had already appeared, and trout fed on the surface through the milky limestone water. More of these size-18 duns emerged, and more trout fed, especially in the short moderate stretches just above the abbreviated pools. No other fishermen appeared that evening. Sulphurs continued to emerge nightly on Logan Branch until early July.

Each year anglers catch several large trout over twenty inches on this miniature but extremely productive stream. Logan Branch contains only a few hatches, but the Sulphur is prolific enough for more than a month, and it produces some fine opportunities for matching the hatch. The stream harbors a decent Blue-Winged Olive Dun near the end of May, some Blue Quills, and some Little Blue-Winged Olives (*Baetis*).

Without a hatch to match, however, Logan Branch can be difficult to fly-fish. Check the rocks along the stream, and you find a plentiful supply of sowbugs and scud. If you plan to fish the stream when no hatch appears, you want to use an imitation of those isopods and fish the pattern on the bottom.

Logan slows its flow just enough on its way to Spring Creek to create many small, productive pools. At places along the stream you can almost jump across Logan—at many points it's barely fifteen feet wide. Logan develops from several springs near Pleasant Gap in Centre County. The stream flows north along PA 144 and enters Spring Creek six miles downstream at Bellefonte. Water temperatures remain fairly constant year-round because of Logan's limestone springs. If you're in the central part of the state in late May or June, and you don't mind fishing small water, don't miss this fertile stream.

Best Times to Fly-fish:

April 15–May 1
Little Blue-Winged Olive Dun: #20, morning and afternoon

May 15–June 30
Sulphur Dun and Spinner: #16, evening
Blue-Winged Olive Dun: #14, morning and afternoon

July 1–September 30
Blue Quill: #18, morning and afternoon

Tipton Run

Do you want to fly-fish for native browns and brooks on a picturesque mountain stream? Do you enjoy fishing over rising trout? If so, Tipton Run might be the perfect stream for you. Even before the trout season begins on this wild trout water, trout begin surface feeding on Early Brown Stoneflies. I've seen terrific hatches and rising trout on Tipton as early as April 3—a good two weeks before the stream opens for fishing.

Tipton Run flows southeast from its headwaters in Cambria County seven miles to the town of Tipton, where it enters the Little Juniata River. Most of its seven-mile trip parallels an improved blacktop road. Four miles upstream from its mouth lies the Tipton Reservoir. This large impoundment tends to warm the water below. Above the dam lie four miles of wild native brook trout fishing.

Below the dam pools, pockets, and riffles teem with both native brown and brook trout. The stream hasn't been stocked for years, as the state has designated it a wild-trout stream.

Best Times to Fly-fish:

April 1–May 1
Early Brown Stonefly: #12, afternoon
Little Blue-Winged Olive Dun: #20, morning and afternoon
Blue Quill: #18, morning and afternoon
Quill Gordon: #14, afternoon
Hendrickson and Red Quill: #14, afternoon (spotty)

May 10–June 5
Black Stonefly: #14, afternoon
Sulphur Dun and Spinner: #16, evening
Light Cahill: #14, evening

July 1–September 1
Blue Quill: #18, morning and afternoon

Bell Gap Run

Jack dams and other stream-improvement devices dot this stream in the Bell Gap valley floor. These slow Bell Gap Run only momentarily in its rush to meet the Little Juniata River three miles downstream. The Bellwood Sportsmen's Association, under the leadership of Dick Amrhein, Herb Jones, Chub Dillen, John Gunsallus, Don Johnson, Rick Sprankle, and Bob Slee, developed these stream improvements. Barren sections void of trout several years ago now hold recently stocked browns and rainbows and a fair supply of holdovers. But that's not all—the club recently established a cooperative nursery with the Pennsylvania Fish Commission. This nursery is one of 187 operated throughout the state by 154 different sportsmen's groups and husbanded by diligent volunteers. These cooperative nurseries released over a million trout and salmon during 1986-1987.

Bell Gap Run lies in a fragile watershed. Abandoned strip mines located around its headwaters still discharge silt into the stream all too frequently. Recent silt deposits cover much of the streambed, even in the lower sections of the stream below the reservoir. Tributaries like Bear Loop Run and Tubb Run are still affected by past mining practices in the area.

The state stocks four miles of Bell Gap Run below the reservoir. Add to this several stockings by the Bellwood club, and you see that the stream contains a good supply of trout. Above the reservoir are five good miles of native brook trout water that remains cooler in midsummer than the section below the reservoir. Temperatures on the lower end often rise into the 70s during July and August from water the reservoir warms.

In some years the stream releases a respectable Green Drake hatch; in others this same mayfly appears in diminished numbers.

The Bellwood club has also provided a small pond on its premises for kids under fifteen. They stock the dam with plenty of hefty trout for the youngsters.

Best Times to Fly-fish:

April 15–May 5
Little Blue-Winged Olive Dun: #20, morning and afternoon
Blue Quill: #18, morning and afternoon

May 20–June 10
March Brown: #12, morning and afternoon
Light Cahill: #14, evening

Canoe Creek

Ed Gunnett, of Williamsburg, called a couple years ago to encourage my son, Bryan, and me to experience the Green Drake hatch on a new stream in central Pennsylvania. I had vowed never to travel to Penns Creek again, because the drake hatch there draws a crowd and because I was frustrated with the hatch, as six or seven other mayfly species emerged with the Green Drake. Ed assured me that few fly-fishermen fish the Drake hatch on Canoe Creek, less than ten miles from Altoona, and also that few other species appear at the same time. I decided to give it a try.

We met Ed at the stream about two miles upstream from Canoe Lake. I had fished Canoe Creek several times before but not this late in the season. Low, clear water had already replaced the high spring waters.

As Bryan and I crossed a footbridge to meet Ed, Ed yelled, "They're on already."

We glanced upstream and saw a half-dozen duns struggling to take

The New Creek Area of Canoe Creek below the Canoe Creek Dam. The Blair County Chapter of Trout Unlimited has constructed many stream-improvement devices here.

flight. Several duns didn't make it—trout aborted their attempts to become airborne. Ed headed upstream and Bryan downstream to fish the hatch. I stood on the bridge, taping the hatch with my video camera. The hatch increased in intensity as 8:00 P.M. approached. Upstream from Ed, in a small riffle entering the pool, five trout fed on the duns. In short order he caught or missed all of the rising trout. Downstream Bryan experienced the same success with a Green Drake pattern. In a deep riffle below the pool at the bridge two trout rose for naturals. Bryan hooked both.

By 8:30 P.M. dusk had arrived, but Green Drake duns continued to appear. By now both Bryan and Ed headed to a long, deep pool 100 yards above the bridge. About every five minutes I heard Ed or Bryan yell that he had one on. What a great night! What a great Green Drake hatch! The hatch on Canoe Creek proved more rewarding than the one on Penns Creek because fewer mayflies appeared.

Ed Gunnett and Danny Deters often fish this overlooked stream in the summer. Although it's small, Canoe holds a good holdover trout population, even though anglers neglect it a few days after the hatchery truck has unloaded its last fish in the stream. The Green Drake hatch appears on Canoe Creek about a week ahead of Penns.

Canoe boasts hatches other than the Green Drake. Blue Quills early in the season produce some productive early dry fly-fishing. Sulphurs appear on Canoe from mid-May nightly into early June. Bob Beck, of Ruskin Drive in Altoona, has fly-fished Canoe for ten years. Bob often sees the Slate Gray Caddis emerging on Canoe at the same time the Green Drake appears. Bob says this down wing appears on the creek and on Canoe Lake.

Canoe Creek's headwaters begin in northeastern Blair County in Brush Valley. The upper end, flowing through state game lands, contains some streambred brown and brook trout. You have to hike in to the headwaters. There are about seven miles of fishable water in the game lands. Several beaver dams in this area warm the water and provide homes for pickerel rather than trout.

The state recently impounded an area of Canoe Creek a mile north of US 22. The state also stocks the lower section below the dam. This area, however, warms quickly in the summer, suffering from the dam's top release and from lack of any canopy. Just a few hundred yards below the dam New Creek enters the main stem. New Creek's temperature always stays five to ten degrees below that of the main stem. Many of the stocked trout move up the branch when the main stem warms. The lower end of New Creek contains some late-season Blue Quills and a few Tricos. Mary Anns Creek enters Canoe in the dam. This tributary holds a good number of native brown trout.

The Blair County Chapter of Trout Unlimited has installed several stream-improvement devices a few miles above the lake. Just below the dam, where New Creek enters, you'll see other devices installed by the local TU chapter.

A paved secondary road off US 22 at the town of Canoe Creek follows the upper section of stream up to the state game lands. You can reach the lower stretches by taking a paved road on the west side of the stream. The upper end is reached by a blacktop road on the eastern side. A dirt road gives access to two miles of the upper end off the blacktop road.

Best Times to Fly-fish:

April 15–May 5
Blue Quill: #18, morning and afternoon
Hendrickson and Red Quill: #14, afternoon (spotty)

May 12–June 5
Sulphur Dun and Spinner: #16, evening
Gray Fox and Ginger Quill: #12 and #14, afternoon and evening
March Brown: #12, morning and afternoon
Green Drake and Coffin Fly: #10, evening
Slate Gray Caddis: #12 and #14, evening
Light Cahill: #14, evening

June 20–July 5
Cream Cahill: #14 and #16, evening

July 10–September 30
Trico: #24, morning (spotty, just below the dam at New Creek)

Seven

STREAMS OF
South-Central Pennsylvania

Cool limestone waters abound in south-central Pennsylvania. Many south-central streams keep a constant cool flow all summer long. I've fly-fished successfully on these streams when summer air temperatures recorded 90-plus degrees. Different streams in the region also house the same aquatic insects. Just about all of them display Sulphur, Trico, and Little Blue-Winged Olive hatches. Only a few of the northern streams in the area house many Green Drakes, however.

Not all streams in this region boast limestone aquifers. York County has Muddy and Cordorus Creeks, which, though freestone in character, produce some fine trout fishing. Juniata County also contains some good trout streams with excellent hatches. East Licking and Lost Creeks have Green Drakes near the end of May.

LeTort Spring Run

*Limestone Springs Wild Trout Waters—1.5 miles; from 300 yards
above the bridge on Township Rt. 481 downstream to the Reading
Railroad Bridge at the southern edge of LeTort Spring Park.*

What fly-fishing history this magnificent limestone stream embraces! Visit the meadow by Charlie Fox's home on the outskirts of Carlisle, and you'll see initials of great fly-fishermen carved in a picnic table next to the stream. There Charlie Fox, Vince Marinaro, Irv Swope, Don DuBois, and many others casually met. These great anglers, and many others, spent hours near the table observing how trout fed and what they fed on. These observations on the LeTort led to tremendous fly-fishing innovations. Vince Marinaro has departed, but he's not forgotten. Just a half-mile upstream from Charlie's place, in a meadow, his friends recently dedicated a plaque in memory of Vince.

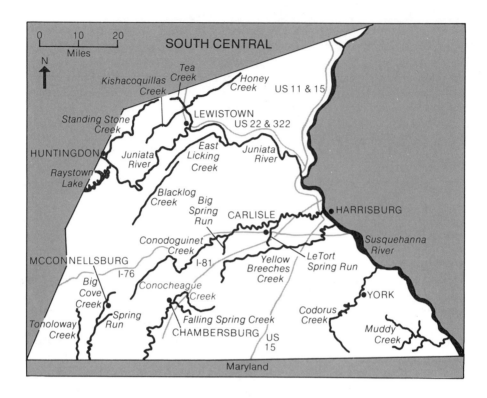

In 1978 the fine group of anglers who frequented the LeTort formed an organization called the LeTort Regulars. The name sounds like a group dedicated to the history of the Civil or Revolutionary wars. Not so. These anglers meet in an informal way not only to discuss all aspects of fly-fishing but also to dedicate their organization to the preservation of this fine limestone stream.

The regulars meet monthly with unusual camaraderie. Members of the association sound like a who's who in American fly-fishing: Lin Black, Don DuBois, Jack Eshenmann, Ben Felix, Larry Foster, Tom Henry, Jack Hunter, Lefty Kreh, Gene Macri, Andy McNeillie, Monroe Mizel, Gary Mortensen, Bill Porter, Gene Shetter, Norm and Rich Shires, Al Smeltz, Irv Swope, Tommy Thomas, Ross Trimmer, Gene Utech, Dave Wolfe, Sam Wilks, and Dave Williams (II and III).

The LeTort begins near Bonnie Brook, just a few miles south of Carlisle. It flows seven-plus miles through Carlisle before entering the Conodoguinet just northeast of town. A 1½-mile segment of the stream has been designated as limestone-springs wild-trout water. Throughout, the LeTort maintains a steady flow of cool limestone water and ranges from thirty to forty feet wide.

The LeTort has not been without its calamities. Intensive upstream farming with resultant runoff have added unwanted chemicals to the stream. In addition, urban development in the Carlisle area has outpaced that in many other areas of the state. Today a truck terminal is planned near the LeTort. Several years ago the stream received a shot of pesticides from upstream watercress farms. All have had a deleterious effect on the watershed. As a result both the mayfly hatches and the trout population have suffered.

Once on the LeTort, however, you're in for some challenging fly-fishing. Tricky variable currents with slower eddies on the right or left enter into long, smooth glides. Endless weedbeds of *Spirogyra*, watercress, and *Potamogeton* often prevent casting anywhere but in a small open channel near the center of the stream. The LeTort presents classic terrestrial water through most of the summer months. Add to this imitations of cress bugs and scud, and you'll likely match what a trout finds in the stream. Tricos, Sulphurs, and Little Blue-Winged Olives still appear, but not in past numbers.

Other interested citizens besides the LeTort Regulars look upon the LeTort as a national landmark. Recently the National Land Trust, of Media, Pennsylvania, has become interested in the preservation of this national shrine. This group is currently working with watershed landowners to provide an open area along the stream. Both the LeTort Regulars and the National Land Trust need our support and interest in preserving this prominent, historic limestone stream.

Best Times to Fly-fish:

April 1–May 1
Little Blue-Winged Olive Dun: #20, morning and afternoon

May 1–July 1
Sulphur Dun and Spinner: #16, evening

July 1–September 30
Trico: #24, morning

Big Spring Run (Creek)

Limestone Springs Wild Trout Waters—1.1 miles; from 100 feet below the source (Big Spring) downstream to the Strohm dam. NOTE: On the Big Spring Creek project only, two trophy trout of a length of 15 or more inches may be taken daily. Barbed hooks are permitted.

I prefer fishing a dry fly over wets, nymphs, and streamers any day. But Gene Macri, of Waynesboro, taught me an important lesson to re-

Allen Hepfer, of nearby Newville, holds a four-pound-plus rainbow caught on a cress bug on Big Spring Run.

member when fly-fishing on many of the south-central-Pennsylvania lime-stone springs like Big Spring Run. I tried several dry flies while Gene went on the bottom with a cress bug and light Sulphur nymph patterns. We fly-fished the section just below the hatchery that many locals refer to as the "ditch." In an hour Gene picked up several heavy browns, brooks, and rainbows. I stubbornly clung to my floating pattern throughout our trip to Big Spring, even after fishing for an hour without a strike. The moral: If you plan to fish any of these streams, take plenty of cress bugs and scud with you, and be prepared to fish on the bottom. (See Falling Springs, below, for more details.)

If you're properly prepared for a trip to Big Spring Run, you can experience an exciting day catching some hefty trout. In the short time Gene and I fished the ditch, we saw several fly-fishermen catch trout over three pounds. One rainbow, caught by Allen Hepfer, of Newville, measured twenty-three inches long and weighed over four pounds.

Big Spring Run begins halfway between Carlisle and Shippensburg just north of US 11. Back in the 1970s the state completed a hatchery where the spring emerges. Fishing's prohibited in the first 100 feet of the stream; the Fish Commission has designated this as a spawning area for brook trout. Below lies the ditch. Here you can see hundreds of brooks, browns, and rainbows—some over twenty inches long. The ditch, plus a mile of water below, constitute a section designated as limestone-springs wild-trout water. Regulations on this section differ from other limestone streams with the same designation, however. In Big Spring you *may* take two trout over fifteen inches long daily (in the designated section only). Please don't. Release these fish immediately so someone else can enjoy catching them later.

A couple miles below the hatchery the fish commission has constructed a weir to prevent browns and rainbows from moving upstream into an area designated as wild brook trout water. Above the weir and a small dam are flat, silt-filled shallows with little cover and few trout. A solution to this area just above the dam would be to narrow the streambed and add rocks and a canopy along the bank.

Mayflies and caddis flies appear on Big Spring Run. Gene Macri says that the middle part of the stream, a few miles above Newville, exhibits a decent Trico hatch from early July into September. There's also a Tan Caddis, according to Gene, which can be important to match early in the season.

Best Times to Fly-fish:

April 1–May 10
Little Blue-Winged Olive Dun: #20, morning and afternoon
Tan Caddis: #14 and #16, afternoon and evening

May 5–June 15
Sulphur Dun and Spinner: #16, evening

July 5–September 1
Trico: #24, morning

Yellow Breeches Creek

Catch-and-Release—1 mile; from Boiling Springs downstream to vicinity of Allenberry.

The Chambersburg bank thermometer registered 92 as we passed it on the way to the Yellow Breeches. Weather forecasters called for the temperature to rise above the century mark by 2:00 P.M. Certainly this fishing trip with Gene Macri, of Waynesboro, would prove unproductive. We headed to Boiling Springs and fished the short section of Boiling Springs Run below the dam. I immediately checked the temperature of this cold limestone stream—61 degrees. Gene and I fished the run for an hour, but our ultimate destination was to work our way downstream to the Breeches.

Boiling Springs Run cools the water in the Yellow Breeches below. That same day when the air temperature rose past 100 degrees, the section of the Breeches immediately below Boiling Springs Run produced some good dry fly and nymph fishing for Gene and me. How many other streams in Pennsylvania could you fish successfully on a 100-degree afternoon?

The Yellow Breeches begins near Lees Crossroads in southern Cumberland County. It flows east-northeast for about thirty miles before entering the Susquehanna River at York Haven. On its path to the Susquehanna, the Yellow Breeches picks up additional volume from tributaries like Mountain Creek, Spruce Run, Fishers Run, and Dogwood Run. Most of these enter the main stream from the south. Mountain Creek has recently experienced problems with acid rain. Near the Huntsdale Nursery the stream ranges from twenty to twenty-five feet wide. By the time it flows to Allenberry the stream runs from fifty to sixty feet from bank to bank.

The Yellow Breeches is easy to reach by car. PA 174 parallels much of the upper end of the Breeches, and Creek Road much of the lower end. The most heavily fished section is the one-mile catch-and-release area near Boiling Springs. The lower section, below Williams Grove, becomes marginal in summer. Sections above Boiling Springs Run also become marginal in July and August. Boiling Springs Run cools the Breeches for a mile below, making it productive through much of the summer.

Ask most fly-fishermen when they fish the Yellow Breeches, and many will say they visit the water when the celebrated White Mayfly appears in late August. Months after most anglers, including many fly-fishermen, have abandoned the hobby for another year, this laggard mayfly appears. This final observance of the fly-fishing year has almost a carnival atmosphere—similar to the Green Drake hatch on Penns Creek. Fishing access near Allenberry at the time of the hatch is at a premium, and the scene on the water is reminiscent of opening day—or at least the first few weeks of the season. As dusk progresses on these late-summer evenings, the White Mayflies emerge. They seem to do so later on the Yellow Breeches than on the Little Juniata River. Murmurs and outright yells from fly-fishermen up and down the stream signal the start of the hatch. Trout become active, acrobatic surface feeders during this concentrated activity. As with the hatch of Green Drakes on Penns Creek, the catch on the Yellow Breeches is not up to the standards you'd expect for the event, and the festivity often becomes more important than the catch.

Granted, this spectacular hatch stimulates many trout to rise, but the Yellow Breeches is more than a one-hatch stream. Just look at the diversity of hatches this water contains. (See Best Times to Fly-fish.) Many of the concentrated hatches occur in April, May, June, and July.

Gene Utech, of Huntsdale, is an expert wet-fly fisherman. He's fly-fished on the Breeches for years. Gene uses soft-hackle wets almost exclusively on this limestone stream. He agrees that fly-fishing on the Yellow Breeches can produce trout throughout the year.

Best Times to Fly-fish:

March 1–March 30
Little Black Stonefly: #16, morning and afternoon

April 15–May 1
Little Blue-Winged Olive Dun: #20, morning and afternoon
Blue Quill: #18, morning and afternoon
Hendrickson and Red Quill: #14, afternoon

May 12–June 15
Sulphur Dun and Spinner: #16, evening
Gray Fox and Ginger Quill: #12 and #14, afternoon and evening
Blue-Winged Olive Dun: #14, morning
Slate Drake: #12 and #14, evening

June 15–July 5
Cream Cahill: #14 and #16, evening
Yellow Drake: #12, evening
Trico: #24, morning

August 15–September 5
Big Slate and Rusty Spinner: #8, evening
White Mayfly: #14 and #16, evening

Falling Springs

*Limestone Springs Wild Trout Waters—2.4 miles; from near T-544
downstream to a wire fence crossing the Robert E. Gabler Farm
(near I-81).*

Twenty years ago I fly-fished a small, productive limestone stream near

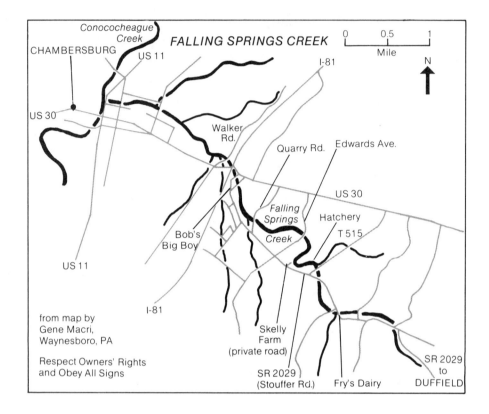

Chambersburg. I first fished with the late Vince Marinaro on Falling Springs in the middle of a heavy Trico spinner fall. It was early September, and the mayfly spinners appeared on the water almost as heavily as they did in late July. Vince uttered some language almost in a whisper, discouraged that so many trout rose to the Trico spinners but rejected his lifelike imitation. Barry Beck, Dick Mills, and I gathered around Vince to hear some wisdom on tricking these selective trout. Instead we heard nothing but grumbling. All four of us selected fishing spots nearby, tied on Trico imitations, and began casting to dozens of surface-feeding trout—and all of us experienced the same lack of success Vince was having. What was the problem? We all had size-24 dark-bodied Trico imitations; we were all using fairly lengthy leaders, about twelve feet long; and we had all tied on fine tippets, about .005 or 6x. Why were all of us experiencing frustration? It's a lot like the goose season on the Chesapeake in Maryland. For the first few weeks of the goose season, the birds fly within shotgun range; after those first few weeks the geese seem to fly higher, sensing trouble. Similarly, fly-fish over the Trico hatch in early July, and you'll likely experience more rises to your imitation, and more catches. Evidently trout become more discriminating as the season progresses. It's early October on Falling Springs, near noon. Guess what? Tricos still appear on this fertile stream until November. Falling Springs had the heaviest hatches of Tricos in the United States, but that was twenty years ago!

Gene Macri, of Waynesboro, asked me to meet him on the stream in early July one year. I was anxious to discuss the stream with Gene and to fish the famous Trico hatch after a hiatus of fifteen years. A few years ago Gene completed his master's degree at Shippensburg University. His research paper, "A Study of Falling Springs, A Limestone Trout Stream: The Invertebrate Fauna with Aspects of Geology, Land Use, Substrate Diversity, and Fishery," examined many aspects of the stream. (Gene publishes a newsletter entitled *Ecolines*. The newsletter examines different hatches, problems, and concerns with American trout waters. The newsletter can be ordered through Box 877, Waynesboro, PA 17268.) While completing his studies Gene spent 340 days on Falling Springs and found that the water has deteriorated significantly within the past ten years. Tricos, once so prevalent on the stream from late June through October, have dramatically decreased in numbers. The Sulphur hatches that appeared from late April until early September are now only about a fourth as abundant as they once were.

What has happened to this highly acclaimed stream? Siltation appears to have had a major role in the decline of Falling Springs. Many of the pools and riffles I remembered fishing with Vince, Barry Beck, and Dick Mills have filled in with silt. The Glory Hole, six feet deep twenty years ago, now barely holds three feet of water and contains a silt bottom. Intensive upstream farming, headwaters housing developments, and excavation for a sewage line in the early 1980s appear to have caused the siltation.

Also, the volume of water in the stream appears much less than it did twenty years ago. Some fishermen believe that digging the sewage line fractured a joint in the bedrock and allowed some of the water from Falling Springs to flow underground.

Gene Macri found in his study that Falling Springs contained at least four colors of Sulphur nymphs, ranging from pale tan to brownish black. He also found that Sulphurs and Little Blue-Winged Olives range from a size 14 in April to a size 20 for both in September. Many of us confuse the larger Blue-Winged Olive found in April with another species, when in reality it too belongs to *Baetis tricaudatus*.

Gene and I met at the Edwards Avenue bridge in Chambersburg at 8:00 A.M. When we gathered our gear and headed for the first pool below the bridge, we saw Tricos in the air. I tried a female Trico spinner, and Gene used a Trico nymph. Gene caught one trout on the nymph, then switched to a Trico spinner. A foot up the tippet he added a small lead shot. Yes, he fished the spinner imitation wet! The sunken spinner worked well. The sparse spinner fall that day discouraged trout from taking dead adults on the surface. Besides, trout rising for these diminutive mayflies would have expended more energy than they would have received in food value.

The Trico spinner fall lasted for a half-hour that July morning. Gene says that twenty years ago the same species would have fallen for one to two hours. I saw three trout rise for spinners. Years ago, when Falling Springs was at its peak, I would have seen fifty. After the feeble spinner fall subsided, Gene switched to a Sulphur nymph—light phase. This imitation had a body of ginger fur. It produced a few trout for Gene.

Falling Springs begins near Duffield, with part of it coming from a limestone cavern. It is an extremely small limestone stream. Wading is no problem; the stream is no wider than twenty-five feet at its widest point. Falling Springs flows northwest, entering the Conococheague Creek at Chambersburg. You can reach the stream by a secondary road near I–81 in Chambersburg. Four access points take you to the stream: Quarry Road, Edwards Avenue, Skelly Farm, and just below Fry's Dairy.

Falling Springs has only six miles of fishable waters, and some is posted. About midway up the stream is a 2.4-mile stretch of limestone-springs wild-trout water. You'll occasionally catch streambred rainbows over twenty inches long in this section. Water temperature remains fairly constant, ranging from 60 degrees in the summer to 46 in the winter.

The Sulphur hatch lasts for several months on Falling Springs. It begins in early May and continues well into September. Gene Macri found in his study that all of the Sulphurs were *Ephemerella rotunda*. Their predictable appearance just before dusk and their extensive hatching period make this sulphur an attractive hatch to fish and match.

Will Falling Springs ever regain its prominence as one of the top limestone streams in Pennsylvania? Will the Sulphur and Trico ever appear in their former numbers? Time and the efforts of concerned conservationists will tell.

Best Times to Fly-fish:

April 1–May 1
Little Blue-Winged Olive Dun: #16 to #20, morning and afternoon*
Little Black Caddis: #16 and #18, afternoon and evening
Tan Caddis: #14 and #16, afternoon and evening
Golden Caddis: #14 and #16, afternoon and evening

May 1–July 10
Sulphur Dun and Spinner: #16 to #20, evening**
Light Cahill: #14, evening

July 1–October 30
Trico: #24, morning

* Those *Baetis* that emerge early in the season are large; they become progressively smaller as the season progresses. These mayflies can be seen throughout the entire season.

** Those Sulphurs appearing earliest can be copied with a size-14 or -16 imitation. The hatch continues sporadically into August and September. These naturals are copied with size-18 patterns.

Muddy Creek

Fly-fishing-Only Project—2 miles; from SR 2032 bridge in Bridgeton up to Bruce.

John Taylor, Outdoor Editor of the *York Dispatch*, recently wrote an excellent article extolling the trout-fishing virtues of a southeastern York County stream. He's fished this water for more than twenty years, experienced some hatches on it, caught some heavy holdover brown trout, and likes the solitude of a stream so near a metropolitan area. Yes, Muddy Creek means much to John Taylor and many York County anglers.

In his story about the water, John wrote a detailed history of the efforts of some local anglers to maintain Muddy Creek as a respectable fishery. Years ago, he relates, a group of interested anglers became the Muddy Creek Trout Stocking Committee (MCTSC). The MCTSC ensures that all eight miles of the main stem receive trout. A problem was that much of Muddy Creek has little access by road, and some of the roads that approached it were poor. MCTSC struck an agreement with a company back in the 1950s to use a railroad that parallels the stream to stock it.

Muddy Creek presents some severe dilemmas that will test its ability to remain a viable trout stream. Siltation appears to be its main curse. Muddy suffers from severe doses of silt caused by upstream state and township road work, farming practices, and housing developments. Travel along the South Branch of Muddy Creek, and you'll see the siltation. Even minor storms quickly discolor the South Branch. During June, July, and August temperatures on Muddy and its branches often rise into the high 70s, causing cold-water fish to die or seek areas where cool springs appear.

Muddy Creek has no local Trout Unlimited chapter or other such organization to help protect it or improve it. John Taylor, in a recent column, suggested that York County residents form such an organization. Only three people indicated an interest. Unless and until local fly-fishermen protect this valuable resource, the future of Muddy will remain in question.

The North and South branches join at the small village of Muddy Creek Forks to form the main stem. The branches range from twenty to forty feet wide and contain plenty of moderately fast water with some deep pools below. The main stem runs from forty to sixty feet wide and contains plenty of long, deep pools. The state has designated a two-mile area near Bridgeton as fly-fishing-only water. One of the landowners on this stretch would like to revert the section back to an open area, however, so the future of the fly stretch seems to be in jeopardy.

March Browns, Gray Foxes, Sulphurs, and Tricos make up a large part of the mayflies on Muddy. Combine these with some caddis flies and stoneflies, and you can experience some good fly-fishing days on the stream. Many of the best fly-fishermen on the stream, like Fred Bridge, use nymphs almost exclusively. Check the rocks on any of the riffles, and you'll note a wide variety of nymphal life, including a good quantity of March Brown nymphs. That pattern should prove an effective selection for Muddy.

On its flow to the Susquehanna River, Muddy picks up tributaries like Toms Run (stocked), Bald Eagle Creek (stocked), Neill Run, Fishing Creek, Orson Run, and South Creek.

Best Times to Fly-fish:

April 20–May 5
Green Caddis : #16, afternoon and evening

May 10–June 5
Sulphur Dun and Spinner: #16, evening
March Brown: #12, morning and afternoon
Gray Fox: #14, afternoon
Blue-Winged Olive Dun: #14, morning and afternoon

July 10–September 1
Trico: #24, morning

Cordorus Creek

Delayed Harvest Artificial Lures Only—3.3 miles; from SR 3047 downstream to PA 116.

Brian Berger and John Taylor, of York County, drove me to this moderate-sized stream near Porters Sideling. Walk along this southern York County stream, and you'll note many weed-clogged pools, a hint of off-color, almost chalky water typical of many of the state's prime limestone waters. But check the water temperature on Cordorus in June, July, or August, and you're really in for a surprise. In the hottest part of the summer the water temperature in this part of Cordorus rarely rises higher than the low 60s—ideal for some late-summer fly-fishing.

But Cordorus Creek has no limestone aquifer. It's totally a freestone stream. Lake Marburg, a few miles above Porters Sideling, empties into the Cordorus. This lake contains a bottom release that maintains a productive tailwater fishery all year.

The stream holds a 3.3-mile stretch designated as a delayed harvest area. One landowner on this regulated stretch planned to close his property to fishing until the special regulations were posted. A major force in setting this stretch aside was Brian Berger, former area waterways patrolman. Cordorus only recently has been designated as a special project, but the quality of the fishery already is apparent. Already many Maryland anglers frequent the stream only a few miles from their border.

The Cordorus contains some good hatches. Fly-fish on any evening from May 12 into June, and you'll probably encounter many Sulphur Duns and Spinners. If you're fortunate enough to hit the stream on a cloudy, overcast day in mid- to late May, you're apt to witness Sulphurs emerging sporadically all afternoon, although the Cordorus exhibits its heaviest hatch of this mayfly shortly after 8:00 P.M. Fish this productive water for that hour just at dusk, and you'll have some excellent trout fishing. March Browns, Gray Foxes, and several other mayfly species add to the fly-fishing on the Cordorus.

Furnace Creek, Long Run, and the West Branch flow into Lake Marburg near Blooming Grove. These form the Cordorus, which flows north, picking up Oil Creek, and the South and East branches just southwest of York.

Cordorus Creek doesn't compare in size to other streams below dams with bottom releases, like the Allegheny River, Tulpehocken Creek, or Pohopoco Creek. The present stream ranges from twenty-five to thirty feet wide most places. It does, however, contain many pools five to six feet deep with short, productive riffles between.

The East Branch already has two dams—Lake Williams and Lake Redman. A third dam on this branch is planned upstream from the other two. This will further damage the trout fishery on this tributary.

Best Times to Fly-fish:

May 10–June 15
Sulphur Dun and Spinner: #16, evening
Gray Fox: #14, afternoon
March Brown: #12, morning and afternoon
Light Cahill: #14, evening

July 10–September 1
Trico: #24, morning

Kishacoquillas Creek

Lewistown area residents Denny Sieber, Bill Force, and dozens of other anglers who habitually travel to Penns Creek sometimes overlook excellent fly-fishing right in their own backyard on Kishacoquillas Creek. The Kish, as some of the locals call it, contains great hatches, heavy limestone water, and some large trout. But, like Rodney Dangerfield, it gets no respect. The local Trout Unlimited chapter meets within a couple feet of where the Kish flows, and yet the chapter's named the Penns Creek Chapter.

Walk along Kishacoquillas in early spring, and you'll meet plenty of bait and spinner fishermen. But after the last in-season stocking you'll have much of this large stream to yourself. The heaviest hatches and most productive water begin at Reedsville and continue downstream past Yeager-town. At Reedsville two other productive limestone streams, Honey and Tea, enter the West Branch of the Kish to form the main stem. When these three combine, the stream widens to forty to fifty feet, with plenty of deep pocket water. A mile below Reedsville the Kishacoquillas enters a mile-long section called the "narrows" by the locals. Similar to the narrows sections on Big Fishing Creek and Elk Creek, the section on Kish contains plenty of huge boulders scattered throughout the stream bottom.

The West Branch begins just west of Belleville in Mifflin County. On its twelve-mile trip to Reedsville the West Branch picks up several limestone tributaries, including Coffee. (Yes, Coffee, Tea, and Honey really are tributaries of the Kish.) Most of Coffee is posted, while much of Alexander Springs, another tributary, remains open to public fishing. Both branches range from ten to fifteen feet wide and contain plenty of streambred brown trout. Most of the West Branch around Belleville remains open to fishing—but some owners prohibit Sunday fishing. The West Branch flows east through Amish farmland to Reedsville. Some of the lower sections on this branch are posted and warm considerably in the summer. This branch ranges from twenty to forty feet wide with plenty of pools and productive riffles. Several years ago the West Branch received an ammonia spill that devastated the vertebrate and invertebrate biota. Even with the warming in the summer and the chemical spill the West Branch contains some hatches and heavy fish.

Travel through Reedsville or Yeagertown in mid- or late May and you will often see thousands of displaced Sulphur Spinners hovering above the roads. Fish the main stem in the narrows section in the evening at that time and you'll probably experience a great Sulphur hatch. Just prior to the Sulphur and during the hatch you'll also see many caddis on the Kish. Use a size-16 dark brown, green, olive, or tan body color to copy many of these insects.

The Kishacoquillas flows south from Reedsville, through Yeagertown, entering the Juniata at Lewistown. PA 655 follows the West Branch from Belleville to Reedsville, and US 322 parallels the main stem from Reedsville to Lewistown. Use waders and watch your step on the lower end of the stream.

Best Times to Fly-fish:

April 15–May 5
Grannom: #16, afternoon and evening

May 5–June 15
Green Caddis: #16, afternoon and evening
Olive Caddis: #16, afternoon and evening
Tan Caddis: #16, afternoon and evening
Sulphur Dun and Spinner: #16, evening
Slate Drake: #12 or #14, evening
Green Drake and Coffin Fly: #10, evening
Little Blue-Winged Olive Dun: #20, morning and afternoon

July 10–September 1
Trico: #24, morning

Honey Creek

Clouds of Coffin Flies filled the late-May air. The Green Drake hatch the previous night had been nothing short of spectacular. Fishermen from all around the Lewistown area met on Honey Creek to fly-fish during this sensational annual occurrence. But that happened thirty years ago—and that's how great fly-fishermen like Reed Gray, of Lewistown, remembers the last great hatches of this species on Honey.

The abundant emergences of the Green Drake, and others such as the Hendrickson, abandoned this once-fertile stream in the mid-1950s. Around that time some of the local limestone quarries washed concentrated limestone into the stream. Reed Gray and others feel that the concentrated limestone destroyed the mayfly population on Honey Creek.

Recent reports indicate that the Green Drake may be making a comeback and within a few years might again be abundant on the stream. Even now enough Drakes have returned on the lower end to create some fantastic fly-fishing for a few days in late May. Denny Sieber, of Lewistown, built a cabin near one of the tributaries of Honey, and fishes the stream frequently. Two years ago he witnessed a hatch of Green Drakes reappear on Honey. Enough emerged one evening to bring trout to the surface.

As with many central-Pennsylvania trout streams, much of Honey Creek's fame now rests with its Sulphur hatch. From mid-May into early June matching the Sulphur Dun and Spinner can still produce some exciting quality matching-the-hatch time.

Honey Creek begins near Reeds Gap State Park in northeastern Mifflin County and runs southeast to Reedsville, where it enters the Kishacoquillas. Two major tributaries, Treaster and Hovice, are freestone in nature in

Honey Creek near Lewistown is classified as a wild-trout stream.

their headwaters, but near Siglerville take on a limestone character. Near Siglerville, the Penns Creek Chapter of Trout Unlimited has installed numerous stream-improvement devices. They plan several more.

Upstream the state stocks these tributaries. Each branch ranges from ten to twenty feet wide. In the freestone headwaters, Reed Gray reports, several hatches emerge that are absent in the limestone water below. Typical fast water freestone mayflies like Slate Drakes and Quill Gordons are common on Treaster and Hovice, less so on Honey below. The branches like

Treaster, Hovice, Honey, and Laurel, which enters in the village of Honey Creek, flow underground in areas.

The state classifies Honey as a Class A Wild Trout Water, and the stream receives no stocked trout. Honey contains an adequate supply of streambred browns up to twenty inches long. The lower end of Honey ranges from thirty to forty feet wide and contains plenty of deep pools and many productive riffles. The main stem of Honey flows about five miles before it enters Kishacoquillas at Reedsville. A blacktop road parallels Honey from Reedsville upstream.

Best Times to Fly-fish:

April 20–May 5
Blue Quill: #18, morning and afternoon
Quill Gordon: #14, afternoon (headwaters)
Hendrickson and Red Quill: #14, afternoon (spotty)
Grannom: #14, afternoon

May 12–June 15
Tan Caddis: #16, afternoon and evening
Blue Dun (*Pseudocloeon*): #20, afternoon and evening
Sulphur Dun and Spinner: #16, evening
Blue-Winged Olive Dun: #16, morning
Gray Fox: #14, afternoon
March Brown: #12, morning and afternoon
Green Drake and Coffin Fly: #10, evening
Slate Drake: #12 or #14, evening (headwaters)
Little Blue-Winged Olive Dun: #20, morning and afternoon
Perla Stonefly: #12, morning and evening

July 15–September
Blue Quill: #18, morning and afternoon

Tea Creek

Reed Gray, of Lewistown, has fly-fished area streams for more than 50 years. One of the streams near his home he fishes frequently is Tea Creek. The state no longer stocks Tea Creek but it contains a good population of streambred brown trout. The native trout almost resemble salmon with their silver-sided bodies. What a pity this ten-to-twenty-foot-wide limestone stream doesn't contain a no-kill area. How can this small stream replace valuable trout killed in it? The stream flows cold all summer long with temperatures in the upper end rarely getting out of the 50s. Tea Creek would make an excellent stream in which to place some stream-improvement devices. At present most of the open water contains small pockets that could be improved by placing stone deflectors, log deflectors, tip deflectors, and gabions. There's only a mile of open water—all below US 322 in Reedsville.

Best Times to Fly-fish:

April 10–May 5
Blue Quill: #18, morning and afternoon
Little Blue-Winged Olive Dun: #20, morning and afternoon

May 12–June 10
Sulphur Dun and Spinner: #16 and #18, evening

July 10–September 1
Blue Quill: #18, morning and afternoon

East Licking Creek

East Licking Creek means a lot to Jim Gilson. He lives only a stone's throw away from the lower end of this Juniata County stream near Port Royal. He's been fly-fishing on the stream long before it was fashionable to fly-fish in Juniata County and is well acquainted with the water, its hatches, and the streambred and holdover trout it contains. Jim's one of those rare individuals whose avocation became his vocation. He and Dave McMullen have formed a business called Angling Fantasies that arranges trips for fly-fishermen to England, Scotland, Alberta, Alaska, western United States, and Pennsylvania.

But Jim keeps coming back to his roots—East Licking Creek. This mountain stream flows for more than twenty miles in an isolated, uninhabited, scenic valley. About halfway up the valley you'll see the Clearview Reservoir—the locals call it the Big Dam. Below the impoundment there's about ten miles of stocked water before the stream enters the Tuscorora Creek, which in turn enters the Juniata River at Port Royal. This lower end flows through some farmland and contains many long flat sections, some more than six feet deep. It warms in the summer, but contains some holdover trout. Several spring-fed streams like Johnstown Run enter this water, adding a limestone base to the last five miles. Drive above the dam on East Licking Creek Drive and you'll note an entirely different stream. Above the reservoir there's twelve miles of heavily forested water that rarely rises above 70 degrees in the summer. Even though it's heavily-canopied, this upper section presents few problems for the fly-fisherman. There's little brush near the banks to catch an errant fly. In this upper section you'll see plenty of rapids, riffles and small pools, a diversity of hatches, and many stocked and streambred trout. Jim Gilson feels that there are larger trout below the dam, but some natural reproduction above. The state developed the Karl Guss picnic area on this upper end.

Hatches on the two sections vary almost as much as the stream. On the lower end there's a decent hatch of Tricos, but the warm water in July and August often reduces the number of rising trout. On this same section Jim says there's a tremendous hatch of Big Slate Drakes in mid-August. The water above the dam harbors few of these huge *Hexagenia* mayflies. Few Green Drakes appear in the lower section, yet there is a fishable hatch upstream.

Even though East Licking Creek contains a diversity of hatches, Jim believes that the density of some of the hatches has declined noticeably in the past ten years. He says acid rain is the culprit. Below the dam the hatch density hasn't been affected because of the limestone springs entering the main stem.

Annually Jim catches sixteen- to twenty-inch trout on East Licking Creek on a variety of patterns. Some of the most effective copy *Stenonema* nymphs found in the stream. In July and August when hatches are scarce, Jim often resorts to terrestrials like the ant, cricket, beetle, or inchworm when he fishes above the dam.

East Licking Creek Drive parallels much of the water. It's paved upstream to the dam and dirt beyond. You can reach this access road just outside Mifflin from PA 35.

Best Times to Fly-fish:

April 10–May 5
Early Brown Stonefly: #12, afternoon
Blue Quill: #18, morning and afternoon
Quill Gordon: #14, afternoon

May 10–June 5
Sulphur Dun and Spinner: #16, evening
Gray Fox: #14, afternoon
March Brown: #12, morning and afternoon
Light Cahill: #14, evening
Green Drake and Coffin Fly: #10, evening
Little Blue-Winged Olive Dun: #20, morning and afternoon
Perla Stonefly: #12, afternoon and evening

July 10–September 1
Trico: #24, morning
Big Slate Drake: #8, evening

Big Cove Creek

Big Cove Creek, a respectable trout stream which few anglers fly-fish, begins near McConnellsburg and flows south just west of US 522. In its upper four miles Big Cove flows through open meadowland and averages twenty to thirty feet wide. Because of its lack of any canopy, this area warms quickly in the summer sun. The upper end of Big Cove would be much more productive with a system of stream-improvement devices, and an agreement with the farmers to keep their cattle out of the stream.

Near Big Cove Tannery, the main stem adds Back Run, Roaring Run, and Spring Run to its flow. Spring Run is a sleeper. This cold limestone stream contains some heavy hatches and a good supply of trout throughout the season. Spring Run above Webster Mills boasts a good Trico hatch from mid-July through September. During this period Spring's temperature often holds in the low 60s, but you'll see few fishermen on the stream in late summer. Spring Run, plus the next downstream tributary, Spring Creek, provide cool water to the main stem of Big Cove for a mile. The Fulton County Sportsmen's Association operates a cooperative nursery on the upper end of Spring Creek that supplies additional trout to Cove and other local streams.

From Big Cove Tannery the main stem contains a good canopy, with a generous green belt along the stream. Two miles downstream Cove enters Buchanan State Forest. Below this half-mile section Cove is almost inaccessible. Some cold springs from Dickeys Mountain enter the lower four miles, but the area still becomes marginal after June. Cove has a total of about fourteen miles of stocked stream.

Ed Lehman, of McConnellsburg, often fly-fishes the stream in October and November, catching dozens of trout. He's seen many holdovers on the main stem and heard of trout up to twenty-four inches long being caught on Cove. Steve Frey, another local fly-fisherman, recently caught a twenty-six inch brown trout in Cove on a Muddler Minnow. Yet few anglers fly-fish on Cove Creek.

Cove suffers from some severe problems. Bob Lynn, of McConnellsburg, has fly-fished on Cove since 1970. He's concerned that siltation has increased tremendously within the past few years. Intensive upstream farming on Cove, with open meadows and few trees, bode badly for the future. In addition poaching on Cove is widespread. Fishermen in the area think that they have to go home with their limit of trout. Unless and until local fly-fishermen form a organization devoted to conservation, area streams will continue to suffer.

Hatches appear on the stream from the beginning of the season until late fall. In late May and early June you'll encounter plenty of Light Cahills on Big Cove. Steve Frey, of McConnellsburg, has often fly-fished on the

Big Cove Creek near McConnellsburg holds a good Slate Drake hatch in late July.

stream when a prolific Blue-Winged Olive Dun appears in late May or early June. Fish Cove even in July and August, and you'll see a good supply of Slate Drakes appearing every evening. Add to this a good Trico hatch on Spring Run and on Big Cove one mile below Big Cove Tannery, and you can see that hatches continue almost uninterrupted throughout the season.

Cove above Big Cove Tannery flows through open meadowland. Below it ranges from thirty to fifty feet wide with plenty of undercut banks, productive riffles, and ledge-lined pools. US 522 gives access to the upper end, and PA 928 follows the stream below Big Cove Tannery.

Best Times to Fly-fish:

April 10–May 5
Little Blue-Winged Olive Dun: #20, morning and afternoon (Spring Run)
Quill Gordon: #14, afternoon

May 12–June 5
Gray Caddis: #16, afternoon and evening
Sulphur Dun and Spinner: #16, evening
March Brown: #12, morning and afternoon
Blue-Winged Olive Dun: #14, morning
Cream Cahill: #14 and #16, evening
Light Cahill: #14, evening
Slate Drake: #12 and #14, evening

June 22–July 5
Slate Drake: #12 and #14, evening
Yellow Drake: #12, evening

July 15–September 1
Trico: #24, morning (Spring Run and Big Cove Creek)
Slate Drake: #12 and #14, evening
Little Brown Stonefly: #16, evening
Little Blue-Winged Olive Dun: #20, morning and afternoon (Spring Run)
Light Cahill: #16, evening (Spring Run)

Blacklog Creek

John Gordon, of Huntingdon, caught ninety-eight trout on one June afternoon three years ago. Many of these trout ranged from six to twelve inches long, and all but a few were native browns and brooks. John, like a growing number of fishermen, returns most of his trout. He used a small spinner and promptly released all of the trout to fight for another fishermen at another time. He caught them on a stream few anglers ever fly-fish: Blacklog Creek in a secluded valley in Juniata and Huntingdon Counties.

Recently John and I met on Blacklog. We fished the upper end of the stocked area about twelve miles above Orbisonia. Here you not only find stocked trout but also many holdover trout and an abundant native-trout population.

The late-June day we selected to fish Blacklog could not have turned out to be a poorer choice. The stream level had fallen rapidly the week before, and by now Blacklog ran a foot below normal. Native trout scattered when we approached the bank. John used a small spinner, and I tied on a Cream Cahill, size 14. We alternated fishing pools on the ten-foot wide stream. We caught trout in almost every pool, even a few streambred browns. We headed upstream to fish the remains of a beaver dam abandoned several years ago. Blacklog contains many active and abandoned beaver dams in its twenty-mile flow. In one small pool I caught four heavy brook trout and missed two more. John agreed that there's an advantage to fly-fishing on small streams. After he caught one trout in a pool or riffle, other trout in that section refused his hardware. Not so with a dry fly.

Phil Stewart, of Allenport, fly-fishes Blacklog weekly throughout the season—one of the very few fly-fishermen on the stream. Phil often uses Bivisible or Adams patterns. He's caught some large holdover trout in October on Blacklog. Phil often fishes Blacklog with special success in late May, when a sporadic Green Drake hatch appears in the narrows just above Orbisonia.

Blacklog flows southwest from Juniata to Huntingdon County. It picks up few tributaries on its twenty-mile trip to Shade Creek, then into Augwick Creek near Orbisonia. Some of the upper ten miles of water are posted. Shade Creek enters near Blacklog, close to Orbisonia. This tributary seems to contain more hatches than Blacklog. I've seen a decent Black Quill hatch near the Catholic Church in late April on Shade Creek. Blue Quills appear every morning during the summer just below Shade Gap.

Although Blacklog flows in an isolated valley, it has a siltation problem that affects the hatches it contains. Silt flows into the main stem from poor road drainage and timbering in the headwaters. A secondary road parallels the stream from Orbisonia off US 522.

Best Times to Fly-fish:

April 15–May 5
Blue Quill: #18, morning and afternoon
Black Quill: #14, afternoon

May 12–June 5
Sulphur Dun and Spinner: #16, evening
Gray Fox and Ginger Quill: #12 and #14, afternoon and evening
March Brown: #12, morning and afternoon
Light Cahill: #14, evening
Green Drake and Coffin Fly: #12, evening (spotty)

June 15–July 5
Cream Cahill: #14 and #16, evening
Blue Quill: #18, morning and afternoon
Yellow Drake: #12, evening

July 10–September 1
Trico: #24, morning (very spotty)
Blue Quill: #18, morning and afternoon

Standing Stone Creek

Standing Stone has faced some major problems in the past few years. Like Spruce Creek just a few miles away, it suffered from a liquid manure spill into the main stem just above McAlevey's Fort. Within the past few years much of the East Branch, a productive tributary with a good population of streambred trout, has been closed. Standing Stone also suffers from major siltation from farming and, in the lower half, from warm marginal water. The last seven miles of stream become smallmouth bass water in late summer.

In spite of all of these difficulties, Standing Stone contains a good supply of stocked, holdover, and streambred trout. From Jackson's Corner upstream to Alan Seeger Park, you'll find native brook and brown trout. The farther you travel upstream, the higher a ratio of brook to brown trout you'll find.

Hatches on the stream often produce rising trout. By mid-April you'll probably encounter some Hendricksons. Even into late June you'll see trout feeding on Yellow Drakes and Cream Cahills. After early June try the upper end of the stream where water temperatures stay fairly low.

Standing Stone Creek begins above Alan Seeger Park and flows into the Juniata River at Huntingdon. There are about twenty-three miles of water between those two points. PA 26 parallels the lower sixteen miles of stream. A dirt-and-blacktop road to Alan Seeger Park gives access to the upper end of Standing Stone. An excellent tributary, Laurel Run, enters the main stem near McAlevey's Fort. Laurel Run holds a small impoundment, Whipple Dam. Above this lake you'll find plenty of streambred trout.

Best Times to Fly-fish:

April 15–May 5
Little Blue-Winged Olive Dun: #20, morning and afternoon
Blue Quill: #18, morning and afternoon
Quill Gordon: #14, afternoon
Hendrickson and Red Quill: #14, afternoon
Black Quill: #14, afternoon

May 12–June 5
Sulphur Dun and Spinner: #16, evening
Gray Fox and Ginger Quill: #12 and #14, afternoon and evening
March Brown: #12, morning and afternoon
Light Cahill: #14, evening
Slate Drake: #12 and #14, evening

June 20–July 10
Yellow Drake: #12, evening
Cream Cahill: #14 and #16, evening
Blue Quill: #18, morning and afternoon

Eight

STREAMS OF
Northwestern Pennsylvania

The streams of northwestern Pennsylvania present great contrasts. Small, productive streams like Thompson Creek, Hemlock Run, and Little Sandy Creek provide fly-fishermen with plenty of opportunities to fish the hatches. Large trout waters also flow through the northwestern sector of Pennsylvania. Oil Creek and Slippery Rock Creek present large water with some decent hatches, the Light Cahill in early June, for example. The largest potential trout water in the area, the Allegheny River below the Kinzua Dam, is in jeopardy. This big water with its lunker trout might revert back to a warm-water stream. It is imperative for all of us to see that this doesn't happen.

Thompson Creek

This beautiful stream contains great hatches. You can start early in the season with Blue Quills and Hendricksons; fish midseason with March Browns, Green Drakes, and Brown Drakes; and finish the season in early September with the Trico. Thompson Creek has them all. What a shame that this productive stream, with its many holdover and streambred trout, has a large section not open to the public. About three miles upstream from PA 8 there's a prime section of the stream, almost 1½ miles long, posted by the Titusville Rod and Gun Club. It's a pity this water can't be open to the public as a catch-and-release area.

Several years ago Jerry Honard, of Fairview, invited me to meet him on Thompson Creek. As regional director for Continuing Education at Penn State University, I traveled to the Behrend College in Erie at least once a month. On each of those trips I crossed Thompson Creek at PA 8. Each time I did I wondered about the fishing on the stream. Therefore it didn't take much coaxing to induce me to meet Jerry on Thompson Creek one late-July morning.

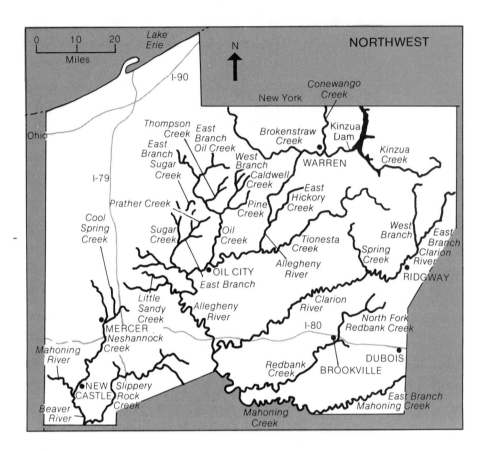

Jerry showed me jars of mayfly duns and spinners he'd collected over the years from Thompson Creek: March Browns, Gray Foxes, Hendricksons, and Brown Drakes. Other jars contained many other aquatic insects that I couldn't identify because their color had faded in the alcohol solution. I was impressed with the variety of insects Jerry had gathered on this water. What amazed me most was the collection of Brown Drakes. I had experienced this species on Kettle, First Fork, Pine Creek, and the Allegheny River, but I had not heard of it on Thompson Creek.

It was 8:00 A.M. by the time we gathered our gear for a morning of fishing. Jerry said to expect a respectable Trico spinner fall, so I tied on a size-24 female Trico spinner. By 8:30 A.M. the Trico spinners swarmed about ten feet above the fast water at the head of the pool where we entered the stream. While we waited for the spinners to fall, I checked the water temperature on this warm morning. The thermometer showed a 69-degree reading—higher than what I had expected this early in the day. We fly-fished on the lower end of the stream anyway, and Jerry assured me that upstream several miles the water would be cooler. Soon some female Tricos returned to the surface spent, and an occasional trout rose to the sparse food supply. For more than a half-hour only a few trout rose, and then the hatch ended as quickly as it had begun. Jerry and I had only three trout to show for our hour of watching and fishing, but we agreed that the unusually low water and elevated temperature evidently deterred trout from feeding.

As with so many other Pennsylvania streams, hatches on Thompson Creek have diminished in intensity the past few years. Is it because of upstream farming and siltation, or has this reduction resulted from natural causes?

As with many freestone streams, Thompson Creek warms in the summer. Despite this it harbors some holdover trout in its main stem and especially in its two major tributaries, McLaughlin Creek and Shirley Run. Thompson Creek is a relatively short stream, only about six miles long. It begins with the merger of Shirley Run and Hummer Creek, near the small town of Shelmadine Springs. Downstream Thompson picks up McLaughlin Creek—an extremely productive tributary. Thompson flows southwest and empties into Oil Creek at Hydetown. The upper end of the stream intersects PA 89, and the lower end crosses PA 8. A paved secondary road parallels much of the water.

Thompson's stream bottom contains mainly small rocks and shale and is not difficult to wade. Some of the pools are fairly extensive, and some of the riffles above are productive.

Do you want to experience some early-season success with the Hendrickson and the March Brown, and see the Brown Drake? Try Thompson Creek.

Best Times to Fly-fish:

April 20–May 1
Little Blue-Winged Olive Dun: #20, morning and afternoon
Blue Quill: #18, morning and afternoon
Hendrickson and Red Quill: #14, afternoon

May 20–June 5
Brown Drake: #12, evening
Gray Fox: #14, afternoon
March Brown: #14, morning and afternoon
Green Drake and Coffin Fly: #10, evening
Slate Drake: #12 or #14, evening
Light Cahill: #14, evening

June 15–July 15
Slate Drake: #12 and #14, evening
Cream Cahill: #14 and #16, evening

July 15–September
Trico: #24, morning

Caldwell Creek

*Delayed Harvest Fly-fishing Only—1.2 miles; from Selkirk highway
bridge downstream to near the Dotyville bridge.*

*West Branch of Caldwell Creek—Catch-and-Release—3.6 miles;
West Branch bridge upstream to Three Bridge Run.*

Jack Bush, of Erie, and I sat patiently by the stream, waiting for something to happen. In late April Caldwell Creek should have been alive with insect activity by early afternoon, and by 2:00 P.M. hundreds of Early Brown Stoneflies returned to the water's surface to complete their life cycle by laying eggs. As the stoneflies laid their eggs, dozens of Blue Quills escaped rapidly from the surface in the warm afternoon sun. Still no fish appeared. In a 100-yard section in front of me no trout rose to this increase in insect activity. Jack assured me that this water still contained plenty of trout, even though we saw cluttered remains of fish guts strewn about the stream bottom. By 2:30 P.M. Jack suggested we leave Caldwell Creek and head to Sugar Creek and the Grannom hatch on that stream. I suggested that we wait until 3:15.

About 3:00 P.M. the riffle ahead of me came alive with Hendricksons and Red Quills escaping rapidly in the warm spring air. With this assortment of hatches in the air and on the water, however, only two trout rose. I caught both surface-feeders on a size-14 Red Quill, and the pool and riffle above became quiet again. Probably the 48-degree water slowed feeding.

Jack suggested that we head upstream two miles to the delayed-harvest area. We parked the car at the lower end of the regulated stretch and walked upstream. In the first couple pools we saw about two dozen trout rising to Blue Quills and Hendricksons. Within a few minutes the Hendrickson hatch ended as abruptly as it had begun a half-hour before, but the Blue Quill continued for two more hours. In almost every pool Jack and I caught trout rising to a size-18 Blue Quill. Why so many trout rising in the regulated stretch and so few below? In the open water below most fishermen keep their catch. What a fantastic stream Caldwell Creek would be if the entire stream were catch-and-release water—or at least delayed-harvest.

Northwestern Pennsylvania fly-fishermen consider Caldwell a prime trout stream, one that maintains fairly cool temperatures all season. Caldwell contains plenty of holdover and a good supply of streambred browns and some brook trout in its headwaters.

Caldwell Creek in July is like most other state freestone streams: low and at some places marginal. There are, however, many springs feeding into the main stem, and fishing at those or just below them in late summer can be rewarding. Besides, this stream, on its West Branch, contains over 3½ miles of catch-and-release water, and the main stem includes more than a mile of delayed-harvest water.

Caldwell is a small stream, especially in midsummer, with a relatively moderate fall of fifteen feet per mile. The main stem begins near Torpedo and flows southwest along PA 27 to Titusville. The upper end can be reached via PA 27, the lower half by Dotyville and Flat Roads. An old railroad bed follows the stream near the regulated area. The main stem flows about fifteen miles before it enters Pine Creek, another trout stream, two miles west of Titusville. Pine Creek flows into Oil Creek near the Drake Museum in Titusville.

Caldwell exhibits many of the state's common hatches, including plentiful Blue Quills and Hendricksons in April. Often when these two hatches appear on this stream, snow flurries arrive as a last blast of winter. Blue Quills too dazed to take flight ride the surface from pool to pool. Water temperatures on these late-April days often hover near or below the 50-degree mark. If you're so fortunate as to be on Caldwell or the West Branch when the water temperature rises above 50, and trout rise to stunned mayflies, you'll probably experience tremendous fly-fishing.

March Browns and Gray Foxes appear on Caldwell during the latter part of May. Both species are large enough to bring trout to the surface of this small stream. Trout up to twenty inches long often surface feed to the Green Drake hatch common on Caldwell around the end of May. Even in late June, if you find cool water, Yellow Drakes appear in the evening for some good late-season fly-fishing. On those late-season mornings Blue Quills and Light Cahills appear daily on the West Branch, on the main stem, and on Pine Creek. Tricos appear every morning throughout the late summer.

Caldwell contains some unbelievably large pools for its size, and each seems to harbor a good supply of trout, especially those with undercut banks and logjams. Much of the stream has a good overhead canopy of hardwoods and hemlocks. In many areas the bank is lined with thick groves of alders, making fly-fishing frustrating. Although Caldwell is lined with rocks, wading is fairly easy.

If you enjoy small and moderate streams with many large trout and some good hatches, try Caldwell or its main tributary, the West Branch. Both have special-project water to ensure an adequate supply of trout through much of the season.

Best Times to Fly-fish:

April 18–May 5
Early Brown Stonefly: #12, afternoon
Blue Quill: #18, morning and afternoon
Hendrickson and Red Quill: #14, afternoon

May 18–June 10
Sulphur Dun and Spinner: #16, evening
March Brown: #12, morning and afternoon
Gray Fox: #14, afternoon
Slate Drake: #12 or #14, evening
Green Drake and Coffin Fly: #10, evening

June 20–July 5
Yellow Drake: #12, evening
Blue Quill: #18, morning
Light Cahill: #14, evening

July 15–September 1
Trico: #24, morning

Sugar Creek

Jack Bush met me at Titusville on a cool late-April morning. We had come for a day of fly-fishing during the Grannom hatch. I hoped I'd planned the trip correctly so as finally to witness the heavy emergence and egg laying of the caddis fly I had heard about for years.

Jack fishes Sugar Creek almost continuously from mid-April until late November and knows the hatches on the stream well. In late April the Grannom constitutes one of the major hatches, and this is an excellent time to find rising trout—that is, if conditions like water temperature and flow are satisfactory.

When we met at the Pizza Hut in Titusville, Jack carried several vials full of insects with him. "They're on," he said.

"The Grannoms?" I asked.

"Yes, they started four days ago."

I examined the vials of preserved Grannoms, with their brownish-black bodies, tan-and-black legs, and dark, mottled wings and urged Jack to head to the stream.

We arrived at Bradleytown, gathered our fishing gear from the car, and headed for a pool behind the church. Hundreds of adult Grannoms greeted us as we followed the worn path to the creek. At the stream we saw thousands of caddis flies in the air and on nearby bushes, and dozens

Jack Bush, of Erie, releases a heavy brown trout caught during a Grannom hatch on Sugar Creek.

laying eggs on the water surface. But with all this food available, no trout rose in the deep pool and rapids in front of us. We continued to walk upstream, exploring more pools and pocket water for rising trout. In the next pool under a low-lying hemlock branch a solitary trout rose sporadically to the enormous supply of insects on the surface. Trout seemed lethargic because of the 46-degree water temperature and four days of intense feeding on the insects.

About 1:00 P.M. several trout began to rise to the Grannoms. Jack cast over the nearest downstream fish. He caught two of the five risers and saw two more look at his imitation and refuse it. We were both confused and dejected at the lack of rising trout during this heavy hatch, but caddis hatches are often disappointing. Only a steady flow of Grannom naturals on the water kept us on the stream.

We waited until 4:00 P.M. and headed upstream a couple miles above Bradleytown. Jack told me to hike downstream a half-mile and work my way back up to the car. The first pool I entered contained a half-dozen freely rising trout taking Grannoms. Each one took my size-16 Grannom on the first accurate cast. I lost the last trout in an overhanging alder on the far bank. I hurriedly tied on another down-wing imitation and headed up to the next productive-looking pocket. Here a holdover trout of about fourteen inches sucked in my imitation. Each pool upstream held two and three rising trout, and most took the imitation.

Jack fished upstream from the car and experienced the same success. He too landed a holdover about fifteen inches long. The surface action lasted for about an hour and then subsided. Pools and riffles that had earlier come alive with rising trout now were silent. Grannoms appeared in the air and on the water until dark, but few trout rose to this magnificent hatch after 5:00 P.M.

Sugar Creek begins in southeastern Crawford County and flows south into Venango County to the town of Sugar Creek, where it enters French Creek. There's a total of about twelve miles of stocked water on Sugar. Just west of Chapmanville, PA 427 parallels the creek to its mouth. On its way to French Creek, Sugar picks up volume from Little Sugar, a few miles above Bradleytown. At Cooperstown, Lake Creek enters the main stem, and a mile upstream the East Branch joins Sugar. In the Bradleytown area Sugar ranges from twenty-five to forty feet wide, with some productive runs, moderate pools, and a good supply of holdover browns. Some of these holdovers range from fifteen to twenty inches long. At Cooperstown, Sugar doubles in size and ranges from sixty to seventy feet wide, with long, deep pools and runs, some a couple hundred feet long.

Sporadic mayfly and stonefly hatches appear on Sugar throughout the year. Blue Quills and Early Brown Stoneflies often appear on the opening day of the fishing season. But in late April when the Grannom appears, it's time to fly-fish on Sugar.

Best Times to Fly-fish:

April 15–May 3
Early Brown Stonefly: #12, morning and afternoon
Blue Quill: #18, morning and afternoon
Hendrickson: #14, afternoon (spotty)
Grannom: #16, morning, afternoon, and evening

May 15–June 5
March Brown: #12, morning and afternoon
Green Drake: #10, evening (spotty)
Slate Drake: #12, evening (spotty)

July 15–September 1
Trico: #24, morning (spotty)
Slate Drake: #14, evening

Pine Creek

Pine Creek lies just to the southeast of Caldwell. It too contains plenty of sizable pools for holdover trout. Much of the section above Enterprise contains streambred browns, but below they are limited. The upper end, before Caldwell enters, ranges from thirty to forty feet wide, with the section above Enterprise about twenty feet wide.

The best time to fly-fish Pine is near the end of May. By that time most other anglers have vacated the stream, and the hatches bring up some large trout. With the Sulphur and Green Drake hatches, late May is an ideal time to fish this water. In June, Pine harbors Light Cahills in the evening and in September and October you can experience some late-season fly-fishing with a size-14 Brown Caddis.

Caldwell joins Pine near East Titusville. Below, Pine widens considerably to sixty feet in some areas. It enters Oil Creek near the Drake Well Memorial Park in Titusville.

Best Times to Fly-fish:

April 15–May 3
Early Brown Stonefly: #12, afternoon
Hendrickson and Red Quill: #14, afternoon
Blue Quill: #18, morning and afternoon

May 20–June 10
March Brown: #12, morning and afternoon
Green Drake and Coffin Fly: #10, evening
Sulphur Dun and Spinner: #16, evening
Light Cahill: #14, evening

September 15–October 1
Brown Caddis: #14, afternoon

Oil Creek

Delayed Harvest, Artificial Lures Only—1.6 miles; from Petroleum Center Bridge downstream to railroad bridge at Columbia Farm.

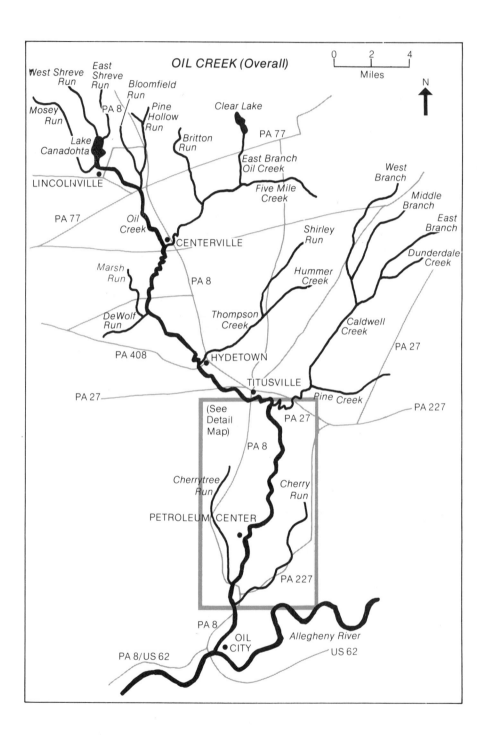

OIL CREEK (Overall)

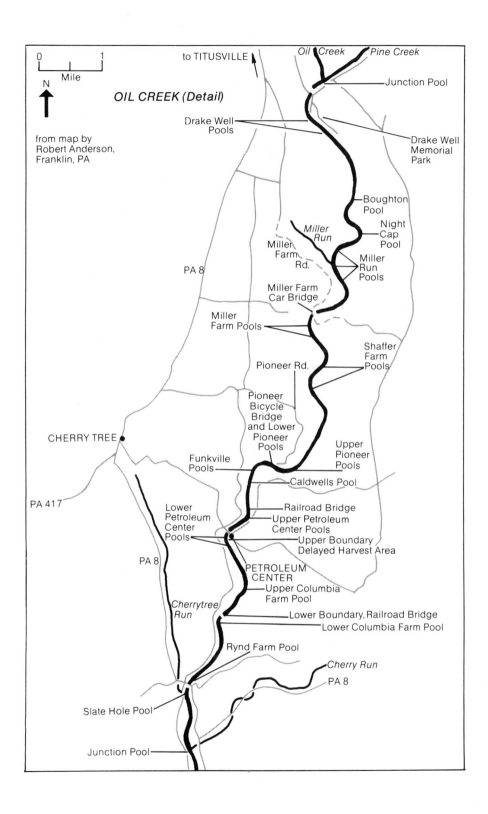

0   1
Mile

N

to TITUSVILLE

OIL CREEK (Detail)

from map by
Robert Anderson,
Franklin, PA

Oil Creek *Pine Creek*

Junction Pool

Drake Well
Pools

Drake Well
Memorial
Park

Boughton
Pool

Night
Cap
Pool

*Miller
Run*

Miller
Farm
Rd.

Miller
Run
Pools

PA 8

Miller Farm
Car Bridge

Miller
Farm Pools

Shaffer
Farm
Pools

Pioneer Rd.

Pioneer
Bicycle
Bridge
and Lower
Pioneer
Pools

CHERRY TREE

Upper
Pioneer
Pools

Funkville
Pools

Caldwells Pool

PA 417

Railroad Bridge

Lower
Petroleum
Center
Pools

Upper Petroleum
Center Pools

Upper Boundary
Delayed Harvest Area

PA 8

PETROLEUM
CENTER

Upper Columbia
Farm Pool

*Cherrytree
Run*

Lower Boundary, Railroad Bridge

Lower Columbia Farm Pool

Rynd Farm Pool

Cherry Run

PA 8

Slate Hole Pool

Junction Pool

It's one of the biggest trout streams in Pennsylvania. The state stocks more than thirty-three miles of water with 16,000 to 30,000 trout annually. It's more than 100 feet wide at many points and has plenty of deep, half-mile-long pools with productive, moderate riffles scattered between. It contains some locally named stretches like the Nightcap Pool. Sections of the stream have little vehicular access, unless you're willing to ride a bike or hike down a bike path. This bike trail follows the stream for fourteen miles of isolated beauty. Marshall Young calls the water Pennsylvania's Beaverkill. Most people, however, call it by its proper name—Oil Creek.

Don Foltz, of Lincolnville, and Marshall Young, of Union City, recently formed the Caldwell Creek Chapter of Trout Unlimited. Their goal for the organization is to preserve and even improve the quality of trout water in northwestern Pennsylvania. They have created stream-improvement projects on French Creek and plan to construct some on Caldwell. Their sister chapter, the Oil Creek Chapter, has proposed a delayed-harvest area on Oil Creek beginning in 1989. This stream would be fantastic, with its solitude, isolation, beauty, and massiveness, if only it contained a stretch that had a decent supply of trout through the early and midseason.

Weekly, throughout the season, Don and Marshall fly-fish on this extensive, underrated stream. A fishing trip with them often develops into a memorable experience. These two outstanding fly-fishermen, using a combination of emerging-pupa and dry-fly patterns, catch hundreds of trout annually. Almost from the beginning of the season you can find them on the stream matching a caddis fly or mayfly hatch on the water. Into July and August they fish Oil Creek, even though the water temperature sometimes rises into the high 70s. At this time of year Don and Marshall search the stream for cool springs or streams entering the main stem. Don has caught trout up to two feet long during the summer.

Oil Creek lacks many of the common mayfly hatches found on other Commonwealth streams. It has no Green Drake or Brown Drake. Consider, however, that it's not many decades since Oil was extremely polluted. From the 1880s until 1915 some companies discharged various pollutants into this potentially productive trout stream. Some companies poured acid into the stream, others floated logs down the water, and still others ejected shots of petroleum and refined gasoline into the stream. Oil Creek has recovered from these careless acts of man, but hatches remain sparse.

Caddis hatches often monopolize the surface activity on Oil Creek. These insects appear almost every day of the season. In May tan- and cream-bodied caddis predominate. Throughout the season emerging caddis pupae imitations work well on the stream. By late May some heavier hatches of mayflies appear. At that time Sulphurs provide some great dry fly-fishing. In June Light Cahills appear in the evening and persuade some heavy trout to surface feed. Marshall Young says the Big Slate Drake and the Rusty Spinner frequent the surface in mid-August. This huge mayfly dun usually emerges after dark, but the spinner can be found over riffles as early as 7:30 P.M.

Oil Creek begins near Don Foltz's home in Lincolnville, in northeastern Crawford County. Its tributaries are Mosey Run, West and East Shreve Runs, Bloomfield Run, and Pine Hollow Run. The East Branch, also stocked, joins the main stem at Centerville. On its trip south Oil Creek picks up additional volume from Thompson Creek at Hydetown and Pine Creek near Titusville. PA 8 runs parallel and within a mile of the area above Titusville and within a few miles of the area below.

Above Titusville, Oil Creek ranges from forty to eighty feet wide. After picking up Pine it widens to more than 100 feet in places. On its path to the Allegheny River at Oil City, the main stem adds Cherrytree and Cherry runs. Only four points allow access to the stretch from Titusville to Petroleum Center. You can reach the upper end at the Drake Well Memorial Park and the middle section by way of a poor dirt road, Miller Farm Road; near the lower end on Pioneer Road; and the lower end, Oil Creek State Park at Petroleum Center. A fourteen-mile paved bike trail runs along the creek from Titusville to Petroleum Center and also provides access. Picnic spots, resting areas, and historical markers dot the trail.

Wading on Oil can be extremely hazardous because of the slippery, coated rocks. Use a wading staff and chest waders to effectively cover the entire stream.

Best Times to Fly-fish:

April 15–May 5
Blue Quill: #18, morning and afternoon
Hendrickson: #14, afternoon
Green Caddis: #14, morning and afternoon
Brown Caddis: #14, morning and afternoon

May 15–June 10
Tan Caddis: #14, morning and afternoon
Gray Fox: #12, afternoon
March Brown: #12, morning and afternoon
Sulphur Dun and Spinner: #18, evening
Light Cahill: #14, evening

August 10–August 30
Big Slate and Rusty Spinner: #8, evening

September 20–October 10
Slate Drake: #10, afternoon

Slippery Rock Creek

Delayed Harvest Fly-fishing-Only—0.5 mile; from Heinz Camp
property downstream to ¼ mile below SR 2022 bridge.

How did this substantial stream get its name? Try wading it sometime, and you'll quickly see. This oversized stream contains a variety of rocks and boulders all covered with mud and organic matter and all bent on creating hazardous wading for the angler.

Tony Palumbo, of Hermitage, and Ted Fauceglia, of Sharpsville, travel to Slippery Rock Creek from their Mercer County homes at least a dozen times a year. They usually fish the lower end of the stream, which houses a delayed-harvest area. It's only a forty-five minute trip for them to this stretch. Frequently they meet many anglers on the section from the Pittsburgh area, only fifty minutes from Slippery Rock Creek.

Tony prefers the heavy pocket water in the regulated area and usually fishes caddis or crane fly patterns. His wet crane fly works exceptionally well on the stream. While Tony's fishing the heavy water, Ted moves downstream to one of the slow pools and uses midges. Both do well on Slippery Rock, each using his own style of fly-fishing. Midges, crane flies, and caddis flies make up important items on the trout's menu in Slippery Rock Creek.

Eighteen years ago Slippery Rock Creek received a super slug of mine acid after a heavy rainfall. Before the cloudburst only slight amounts of acid bled into the stream from abandoned mines. The heavy discharge killed most of the trout in the stream and decimated the aquatic life. The Department of Environmental Resources has since added a liming device near Harrisville to help alleviate the mine-acid problem on the stream. Tony says the hatches seem to get heavier each year. If you're on the stream around the end of May, you might even see the few Green Drakes that now emerge. Add to this several caddis flies, some Light Cahills, Sulphurs, Little Blue-Winged Olives, Brown Drakes in the upper end, and White Mayflies in late August, and you see that matching the hatch can be fun on Slippery Rock Creek. Tony says that the Little Blue-Winged Olives become important to match in April and September on this water.

Slippery Rock resembles the Little Juniata River in many spots. It even has cloudy water like the Little Juniata's, created by an upstream limestone plant that empties some of its effluent into the stream. Water temperatures rise above 70 degrees during June, July, and August. At those times trout look for one of the cool tributaries like the one just below Heinz Bridge or Hells Run upstream a half-mile. Here trout rest in the main stem just next to the bank and take advantage of the cool influx from the springs.

Slippery Rock begins in northern Butler County near Higgins Corners. It picks up Seaton Run, Blacks Creek, North Branch (stocked), McMurray

Run (stocked), South Branch, Long Run, Glade Run, Big Run, and Wolf Creek in Butler County. Continuing its flow southwest into Lawrence County, Slippery Rock adds Jamison Run, Taylor Run (stocked), and Muddy Creek. The stream enters the Beaver River near Jamison City. The state stocks the stream from Armstrong Bridge at the lower end of the delayed-harvest area upstream to a point just below PA 173 in Butler County—about fifteen miles.

On the lower end of the stocked water there's a delayed-harvest area accessible by the Heinz Camp Road. Here the stream averages 80- to 100 feet wide, with long, flat sections and some deep pocket water. Seven miles upstream from this point Slippery Rock flows through a gorge filled with huge boulders. This section is dangerous, and wading is extremely challenging. Upstream, where Slippery Rock crosses US 19, the stream narrows to sixty to seventy feet.

The delayed-harvest segment at the lower end of Slippery Rock is only a half-mile long. Additional length must be added to this regulated water. Since the stream is only a fifty-minute drive from Pittsburgh, the regulated section gets extreme fishing pressure, while the remainder of the stream seems void of fishermen. What a stretch this would be if the delayed area were extended upstream a couple miles.

You can get to the upper end of Slippery Rock via PA 108, PA 8, and PA 308. You can reach the lower end in Lawrence County off US 19 and US 422, and from secondary roads like Heinz Camp and Mountville roads. The stream has a siltation problem—it discolors quickly after a storm and stays off-color for several days.

Best Times to Fly-fish:

April 1–May 5
Little Blue-Winged Olive Dun: #20, morning and afternoon
Blue Quill: #18, morning and afternoon
Green Caddis: #16, afternoon and evening
Grannom: #16, afternoon and evening
Tan Caddis: #16, afternoon and evening
Dark-Olive Caddis: #16, afternoon and evening

May 10–June 10
Sulphur Dun and Spinner: #16, evening
March Brown: #12, morning and afternoon
Light Cahill: #14, evening
Brown Drake: #12, evening (upper end)
Slate Drake: #12 or #14, evening
Green Drake and Coffin Fly: #10, evening (very spotty)
Pteronarcys Stonefly: #6, evening

June 20–July 10
Yellow Drake: #12, evening

August 15–September 1
White Mayfly: #14 and #16, evening

September 1–November 1
Little Blue-Winged Olive Dun: #20, morning and afternoon

Neshannock Creek

Who would believe that the Neshannock Creek in Mercer and Lawrence Counties contains an abundant Brown Drake hatch? The same Brown Drake that you find on the Allegheny River, First and Driftwood forks of the Sinnemahoning, Kettle, and Pine creeks. The same mayfly that brings large trout to the surface to feed.

Near the end of May, Tony Palumbo, Ted Fauceglia, and I visited Neshannock Creek Outfitters, in Volant. Chris Horn, who manages the store, told us the Brown Drakes had appeared for the last three days on the stream. Ted and I rushed over to the bridge in Volant to see if we could spot any Drakes. Ted wanted to photograph a dun and spinner. I hoped that I would see the Brown Drake on Neshannock and authenticate it. As Ted and I walked to the bridge we examined several spider webs. Each web contained dozens of still-struggling Brown Drake duns and spinners. The Neshannock did contain a Brown Drake hatch, then, and from the number at the bridge, a sizable one. As with all other Eastern streams, the hatch of Drakes on the Neshannock lasts for three or four days.

The state stocks twenty-five miles of the Neshannock. There's an intense belief on the part of local fishermen that you catch and keep your limit. Consequently areas near stocking points like bridges see an undue amount of pressure, especially shortly after opening day and after in-season stockings. Fly-fishermen would do well to avoid these stocked areas and fish sections in between. Chris Horn and Wayne Edwards, of the Neshannock Creek Outfitters, have urged the Fish Commission to proclaim a two-mile delayed-harvest area from Leesburg Station downstream to the Volant Dam. Fly-fishermen would enjoy fishing over the Brown Drake hatch when the water still teemed with trout.

The Neshannock begins where Cool Spring and Otter Creeks combine at the eastern end of Mercer County. The stream then flows southwest through Mercer and Lawrence counties, picking up tributaries like Beaver, Pine, Indian, and Potter runs, and the Little Neshannock near Neshannock Falls. The Neshannock enters the Shenango River in New Castle. The water temperature on the Neshannock often rises into the high 70s and low 80s in late June, July, and August. When it does it quickly becomes a warm-water fishery.

"If you know where the springs are in late summer, you can find trout," Chris Horn said.

If you plan to fly-fish on this stream, check with Chris or Wayne and find out what hatches are appearing. They're knowledgeable about the stream and its hatches.

US 19 parallels the upper end of the stream, and Creek Road the middle section to Volant. PA 956 crosses the stream near Neshannock Falls. The Neshannock varies from a small stream above Volant, ranging from thirty to forty feet wide, to one over forty feet wide below.

Best Times to Fly-fish:

April 15–May 5
Tan Caddis: #16, afternoon and evening
Olive Caddis: #16, afternoon and evening
Dark-Brown Caddis: #16, afternoon and evening

May 12–June 10
Green Caddis: #16, afternoon and evening
Sulphur Dun and Spinner: #16, evening
March Brown: #12, morning and afternoon
Light Cahill: #14, evening
Brown Drake: #12, evening
Red Quill: #16, afternoon and evening
Blue-Winged Olive Dun: #14, morning and afternoon
Green Drake and Coffin Fly: #10, evening (spotty)
Slate Drake: #12 or #14, evening (continues later than June 10)

August 10–August 30
Big Slate Drake: #8, evening
White Mayfly: #14 and #16, evening

Cool Spring Creek

Delayed Harvest Artificial Lures Only—1.25 miles; from SR 2014
bridge upstream to the abandoned railroad grade.

If you get an opportunity to fly-fish on Cool Spring Creek in the delayed-harvest area, you'll notice plenty of work completed by the local Trout Unlimited group. The Neshannock Chapter provided access to the stream. Before the group completed their project, access to some stretches was difficult, but now it's merely a short walk along a path and some footbridges built by the organization's members.

Once you reach the stream you see plenty of trout, especially in the hole the locals call the Glory Hole. Here you'll probably see a dozen trout rising—especially if you get there before June 15. The stream contains some pools and short but productive riffles. In the regulated area the stream ranges from twenty to thirty feet wide and contains a good canopy of alders and hardwoods. Cool Spring does, however, warm into the 70s in the summer.

Who would believe that this small stream contains a decent Brown Drake hatch? If you're lucky enough to meet that hatch or the Little Blue-Winged Olive Dun in early June, you're in for some good small-stream fly-fishing. Cool Spring flows just east of Mercer and is reached off US 62 on Airport Road to McCullough Road then to Cool Spring Road. The state stocks five miles of water. The delayed-harvest area allows fishing with artificial lures.

Best Times to Fly-fish:

April 20–May 5
Green Caddis: #16, afternoon and evening
Brown Caddis: #16, afternoon and evening

May 15–June 5
Sulphur Dun and Spinner: #16, evening
Gray Fox: #14, afternoon
Brown Drake: #12, evening
Little Blue-Winged Olive Dun: #20, morning and afternoon
Slate Drake: #12 or #14, evening (continues after date listed)

Little Sandy Creek

Fly-Fishing-Only Project—1.3 miles; from SR 3024 at Polk
upstream to old bridge at Polk Center pump house.

In 1958 the Fish Commission poisoned Little Sandy Creek to kill all the brown trout in the stream. Some anglers and residents remember vividly that sorry day. They saw huge brown trout lying belly-up on the surface throughout much of the stream. For the next twenty years the state stocked only brook trout in this fertile freestone stream. What a crime was committed to this miniature insect factory!

In 1978, under pressure from the Neshannock Chapter of Trout Unlimited, the Fish Commission finally allowed the group to plant fingerling browns back in the stream. Tony Palumbo and Ted Fauceglia recall that initial stocking well. Tony proudly displays three large mounted brown trout—all taken from Little Sandy. Ted's an accomplished photographer. One of his most cherished photos shows a nineteen-inch brown that he caught on this stream.

For its size Little Sandy contains some massive and unusual hatches. This diminutive stream holds heavy, productive Quill Gordon, Blue Quill, Slate Drake, and Green Drake hatches, but it also houses a decent supply of Dark-Green Drakes that often appear concurrently with the Green Drakes. Members of the genus *Baetisca* also appear in numbers on the stream. Examine some of the exposed rocks in Little Sandy and you'll see evidence of these shucks from these humpback nymphs. If the need arises to match the *Baetisca*, use a Chocolate Dun in a size-12 or -14.

Little Sandy has a good number of holdover trout and streambred brown and brook trout. Temperatures seldom rise above 70 degrees on this heavily canopied stream. Heavy cover throughout and a narrow stream make casting a dry fly difficult.

Little Sandy begins just east of Lake Wilhelm in western Mercer County. The stream flows southeast to Polk, where it enters Sandy Creek. There are about five miles of stocked water. Above Polk the stream is narrow, about twenty to thirty feet wide, widening at Polk to thirty to forty feet wide. Throughout its length it contains a heavy covering of hemlocks, alders, and hardwoods. The stream contains plenty of small pools and productive riffles. The section near the old railroad bridge on the hospital grounds at Polk contains several deep, productive pools that harbor some large brown trout.

The last 1½ miles of Little Sandy have been designated as fly-fishing-only water. The Oil Creek Chapter of Trout Unlimited has placed many worthwhile stream-improvement devices in this regulated section.

The brown trout population has rebounded from the disaster that occurred in 1958. Little Sandy is home to many streambred and holdover browns.

Best Times to Fly-fish:

April 15–May 5
Little Blue-Winged Olive Dun: #20, morning and afternoon
Blue Quill: #18, morning and afternoon
Quill Gordon: #14, afternoon
Hendrickson and Red Quill: #14, afternoon
Grannom: #16, afternoon and evening
Beetle: #20, afternoon

May 15–June 10
Sulphur Dun and Spinner: #16, evening
Gray Fox: #14, afternoon
March Brown: #12, morning and afternoon
Blue-Winged Olive Dun: #14, morning and afternoon
Green Drake and Coffin Fly: #10, evening
Slate Drake: #12 or #14, evening
Dark Green Drake: #8, afternoon and evening
Light Cahill: #14, evening
Chocolate Dun: #12 or #14, evening

June 20–July 15
Slate Drake: #12 or #14, evening
Yellow Drake: #12, evening

Allegheny River—Below the Kinzua Dam

Miscellaneous Waters Special Regulations—0.75 mile below Kinzua
Dam. No closed season on trout. Daily limit—3.

The Allegheny River below the Kinzua Dam is a river that's searching for an identity. Will the eight miles from the breast downriver to the Warren Bridge be managed for trout, or will the stretch revert to a warm-water fishery?

The fate of this section rests with the Pennsylvania Fish Commission and the Army Corps of Engineers. Current indications from the commission are that the river will be managed to return to "historic flows and temperatures." The Corps attempts to maintain a summer temperature in the upper tailwater of 71 degrees.

What a pity the tailwater isn't a few degrees cooler! Look at the summer of 1988. Record heat and drought conditions devastated many of the state's streams and rivers. Only a handful of large-water trout survived this unusual summer. Fishermen had few choices if they wanted to fish for trout.

One of the very few large waters that held trout that summer was the Allegheny River. Now this important water may be lost to trout fishermen. The dam above contains miles of warm-water fishing, and more than 100 miles of the river below Warren hold warm-water species. And yet the Fish Commission insists that the eight miles below the dam can't be retained as a cold-water fishery. A productive cold water fishery on the Allegheny would bring untold anglers and dollars into the Warren area economy.

Hank Foradora, of Brockway, one of the anglers who frequents the Allegheny, is concerned about the future direction of the fishery. Hank hunts and fishes year-round. In fall and early spring you'll find Hank in the woods calling in a big gobbler. The rest of the year Hank fishes—much

The Allegheny River below the Kinzua Dam holds some lunker trout.

of that time on the Allegheny. He started fishing the river below the dam one year after the Corps completed it in 1965. He used live bait in February and caught browns over two feet long. Then Hank switched to fly-fishing in spring and summer. He's often caught rainbow trout up to eighteen inches long on a Picket Pin or other favorite pattern. Hank refers to any trout over eighteen inches long on the Allegheny as a "saw log." Hank and many other anglers who fish for trout express concern about the future of the river.

I had an opportunity to fish with Hank recently. After the usual cheerful send-off by his wife, Fedora, Hank, his son John, Bryan Meck, and I headed for the Allegheny, sixty miles from the Foradoras' Brockway home. We planned to be on the river before 8:00 A.M. John told me several weeks before that he had seen small mayfly spinners in the air early in the morning, and I wanted to identify them.

We arrived on the river and waded across near Putnam Eddy. Sure enough, small spinners began appearing at the head of the eddy shortly after we arrived. Soon Tricos filled the air. Then another species appeared, even smaller than the size-24 Trico. During all of this mayfly activity not one trout rose. Hank indicated that these trout were fickle, just like those on the Delaware River. The water temperature might have been the culprit. At 8:00 A.M. it registered 73 degrees—not good for an area several hundred feet below a bottom-release dam.

All four of us stood waiting for rising fish. Nothing happened. Finally Hank motioned for me to come downriver. He had spotted what he thought was a large muskie swimming just twenty feet out from him. I waded closer to the big fish, saw brown spots, and yelled to all three that it was a large brown trout. Hank and I agreed that this saw log would measure twenty-eight to thirty inches long and would weigh close to ten pounds. Bryan and John immediately cast dry flies, then wet flies, and finally streamers in front of the lunker.

Finally Bryan yelled, "I got him," and the fight was on.

The trout headed upstream, then toward the far shore, making Bryan's reel sing as the fish fought to free itself of the fly. Bryan waded towards the center of the pool until water poured in his waders. Now the trout surfaced near the far shore. Bryan was in his backing, which became tangled. With a final leap the monster said good-bye. Bryan sat stunned on the shore for fifteen minutes thinking what he would have done with this heavy brown trout. Would he have released it? This was certainly one of Hank's Allegheny River saw logs.

The Allegheny contains plenty of caddis throughout much of the season. Hank Foradora says that the Dark-Tan Caddis appears from mid-May until almost the Fourth of July. Abundant mayflies on the stretch include the Light Cahill, Trico, and Little Blue-Winged Olive Dun. Tricos and Little Blue-Winged Olives emerge many mornings from July through September.

The Allegheny River is easy to get to. PA 59 follows the river from US 6 at Warren.

Best Times to Fly-fish:

May 1–June 30
Dark-Tan Caddis: #14 and #16, morning and evening

June 1–July 10
Light Cahill: #14, evening
Little Blue-Winged Olive Dun: #20, morning and afternoon
Olive Caddis: #18, evening

July 15–September 30
Trico: #24, morning
Little Blue-Winged Olive Dun: #26, morning
Tan Caddis: #16, evening

North Fork, Red Bank Creek

*Delayed Harvest Fly-fishing Only—2 miles; from US 322 in
Brookville upstream.*

What a great stream this must have been years ago! Old-timers rave
about the fly-fishing on the North Fork back in the 1930s and '40s. Recently
the stream has suffered some setbacks. Acid rain, hot summers, and severe
drought have taken their toll. Fifteen years ago the North Fork experienced
a severe fish kill. Some anglers feel acid rain prompted the calamity. Visit
the stream almost any day in July and August, and you'll probably see that
the volume of water in the North Fork is but a trickle compared to its
strong flow in April and May. To make matters worse this often marginal
stream appears to receive entirely too many brook trout and too few brown
trout in its stocking program.

No road parallels the North Fork, so access is limited to bisecting roads.
Local fishermen have named many of these access areas after towns or
bridges. The state stocks upstream twelve miles from Brookville to the
Blowtown Bridge. In this upper area the North Fork flows slowly, often
forming sandy, tree-laden pools. Here you'll find tricky wading in swamps
and beaver dams in a stream about thirty feet wide.

Downstream about 1½ miles you'll find the next access area, Ryan
Road, or Jones Bridge. Here you'll see a half-dozen dilapidated log dams,
a good canopy over the stream, and tough fly-fishing. The next access,
Egypt Bridge, crosses the stream another 1½ miles below Jones Bridge.
This too contains a good canopy, high-velocity water, and a couple log
dams. Jones Bridge and Egypt Bridge lie on state game lands. The next
access below Egypt the locals have dubbed the Humpback Bridge. This
area contains deep, slow water.

The North Fork empties more than a dozen tributaries in its travels
to join the Red Bank Creek in Brookville. Some, like Clear, Craft, Shippen,
and Pekin runs, contain streambred brook trout. Others, like Manners Dam
Run, drain tannic acid into the main stem. You'll see farms on the upper
ends of many of the tributaries. A number of headwater streams have little

canopy, and consequently these branches warm rapidly in the summer.

Brent Rearick, of Brockway, believes that the best fly-fishing runs from the Richardsville Bridge downstream to the delayed-harvest area. Below Richardsville you'll find the Big Old Dam Access and the Moore Bridge Access, both maintained by the Fish Commission. A dirt road in Brookville gives access to the upper end of the delayed-harvest area. The regulated water begins at Brookville and runs upstream for two miles. You have to walk to reach the upper end of the project water. The lower end of the project water is located at the Water Works at Dick Park, in Brookville.

Despite its drawbacks the North Fork contains some good hatches. It's one of a handful of state streams that hold all three drake (*Ephemera*) hatches. Brent Rearick has fished the Green Drake hatch on the stream for years, and he follows the hatch upstream for a week. Brent has caught as many as twenty trout on some of his better nights on the stream. He's caught trout as large as sixteen inches during the Green Drake hatch. Later in the season ants and other terrestrials provide plenty of food for trout on the North Fork.

Brent's fly-fished the North Fork for nearly twenty years and feels the section below Richardsville would hold many more trout with some well-placed stream-improvement devices.

No surface mining occurs in the North Fork drainage area, although for years operators have tried to mine some of the valley's rich coal fields. If sportsmen and conservationists keep up their vigilance, the stream should continue to provide good hatches and fly-fishing for years. With some stream improvements and more brown trout North Fork could become even better.

Best Times to Fly-fish:

April 15–May 5
Hendrickson and Red Quill: #14, afternoon

May 12–June 15
Sulphur Dun and Spinner: #16, evening
Gray Fox and Ginger Quill: #12 and #14, afternoon and evening
March Brown: #12, morning and afternoon
Brown Drake: #14, evening
Dark-Tan Caddis: #14 and #16, evening
Green Drake and Coffin Fly: #12, evening
Light Cahill: #14, evening
Slate Drake: #12 and #14, evening
Little Green Stonefly: #16, afternoon and evening

June 15–July 31
Yellow Drake: #12, evening
Slate Drake: #12 and #14, evening
Cream Cahill: #16 and #18, evening

Clarion River

Mayflies once appeared on the Clarion River in enormous numbers. "Some snowstorms weren't that thick," says Sam Guaglianone, of Johnsonburg, about the hatches that once appeared in June.

Those once-heavy hatches have diminished alarmingly in the past four years. "There are still some hatches, especially just below some of the major tributaries, but not as heavy as they once were," Eugene "Brownie" Hoffman, of Brockway, says. "Below Millstone Creek there seems to be more than upriver."

What happened to the Clarion's hatches? Has sewage discharge, papermill effluent, mine acid, siltation, or oil and gas drilling caused the decline? Or maybe it's the increase in logging activity in the watershed. The cause is probably a combination of these factors.

Seven years ago the Pennsylvania Fish Commission placed a half-million fingerling trout in the Clarion River. Tom Crawford, of Falls Creek, and dozens of other trout fishermen began fishing the river the next year. Tom lives only twenty-one miles from the river, so he traveled to it almost every week throughout the fishing season. For the first three years after stocking, Tom caught trout in the Clarion—many times fifteen to twenty in an evening. The fourth year Tom caught a nineteen-inch brown, but most of his fish ranged from seven to fifteen inches long. Most of the trips were to the river just below Hallton, although he fly-fished much of the thirty miles of water from Ridgeway to Cooksburg.

Tom Crawford, and every other fly-fisherman I talked with about the Clarion River, said that the hatches and the fishing have declined noticeably in the past four years. Yet stories about successful trips continue to surface. Brownie Hoffman knows of a minnow fishermen who caught eight trout from fifteen to twenty-one inches long one day, and eight trout twelve to nineteen inches long on another trip in the Belltown area.

The Clarion River, however, presents a perplexity—why does it contain so few mayfly hatches? Look at the Delaware or the Susquehanna rivers in their upper reaches, and you'll see a diversity of mayfly species and an abundance of many of them. Not so with the Clarion River. In early June I searched for hours for adult mayflies on the surface of the stream and in the air and saw only a half-dozen. Caddis flies and midges provide necessary food on the river, but the lack of good mayfly hatches remains a mystery. Tionesta Creek lies twenty miles to the north, and it too lacks any sizable mayfly hatches, although it too is a large stream.

Do you like to fly-fish wide, big water? If so you'll like the Clarion. Do you enjoy fly-fishing slow stretches and slow, deep runs? The Clarion has these too. You'd expect the river to contain many fast stretches, but it doesn't. The river drops an average of three feet per mile on its trip from Ridgeway to Cooksburg. Near Ridgeway the river ranges from sixty to ninety feet wide. By the time it reaches Belltown, fifteen miles downriver, it widens to 200 feet.

You can travel miles up the river on dirt roads like River Road and Spring Creek Road before you spot a fisherman, and farther yet to see any fly-fishermen. This huge water gets little pressure, especially after Memorial Day. Temperatures in June, July, and August reach the 70s and you might find some good fly-fishing at the mouths of some of the cooler tributaries, like Bear Creek.

The main stem of the Clarion River begins near Johnsonburg, at the junction of the East and West branches. Both branches contain stocked trout from the northern Elk County line to Johnsonburg. Just below the junction of the East and West Branches, Powers Run enters the Clarion. Local fishermen consider this a good trout stream. Elk Creek, a polluted stream, enters in Ridgeway.

Below Ridgeway the river adds several stocked streams to its flow. It picks up Toby Creek, Big Mill, Bear Creek, Maxwell Run, Spring Creek, Callen Run, Millstone Creek, Clear Creek, Maple Creek, and Tom's Run before it flows to Cooksburg and under PA 36. Mill Creek has a one-mile fly-fishing-only section. All these streams are stocked.

Bear Creek contains a good hatch of Green Drakes, and Spring Creek has a decent hatch. Callen Run, entering the river at Heath Pump Station, holds decent hatches of Green and Brown Drakes. Big Mill Creek has a great Green Drake hatch around the end of May.

Not long ago Toby Creek poured mine acid into the Clarion. The stream has recovered thanks to the work of the Toby Creek Watershed Association, of Brockway. Recently the state placed fingerlings in Toby.

The Clarion is not without its problems, obstacles to its taking on the status of first-class trout water. I mentioned earlier that you'll encounter few hatches on the Clarion and often see few trout rise. If, however, you hit the stream when one of the caddis hatches appears, you're in for some exciting fly-fishing.

The watershed of the Clarion River experiences severe siltation. Wading on the river, even with its deliberate velocity, is treacherous. Each of the river's huge rocks and boulders is coated with a slippery substance.

Fishing the Clarion in the hot summer when the water is warm is relegated to an hour before dusk, at night, and early morning. When the river warms above 70, you'd expect to see the trout move up one of the colder tributaries as they do on Pine Creek, but they apparently stay in the river and in deeper pools with cool water on the bottom.

Another problem is pollution. A company has recently established a landfill in the Toby Creek area of the river. Although the operators have taken measures to safeguard the river, seepage is a threat.

The Clarion would be an excellent river for a no-kill area. At first this section might be only a mile or two long, but later it could be extended for several miles.

With the foregoing cautions in mind, and if you enjoy solitude and big-water fly-fishing, you should enjoy the Clarion River, especially if you like casting where few others fly-fish.

Best Times to Fly-fish:

April 15–May 5
Little Blue-Winged Olive Dun: #20, morning and afternoon
Hendrickson and Red Quill: #14, afternoon
Gray Caddis: #16 and #18, morning and afternoon

May 15–June 15
Green Caddis: #16, afternoon and evening
Gray Fox and Ginger Quill: #12 and #14, afternoon and evening
Brown Caddis: #16 and #18, evening
Light Cahill: #14, evening
Cream Caddis: #14, morning and afternoon

June 15–July 15
Light Cahill: #14, evening
Tan Caddis: #16, evening

Spring Creek

Tom Crawford, of Falls Creek, has fly-fished on Spring Creek for years. The stream has heavy fishing pressure from opening day to Memorial Day, then it becomes practically void of fishermen for the rest of the year. Bill Rowley of Ridgeway fishes the Parrish area, ten miles upstream from the Clarion River. Here he finds deep pools, heavy riffles, and a good supply of native brown trout.

Spring Creek has some decent hatches. One of the earliest and heaviest is the Hendrickson, which appears on the stream the last week in April. By late May you'll witness a sporadic hatch of Green Drakes throughout the day.

Spring ranges from fifteen to twenty feet wide in the Parrish area to thirty to forty feet wide just before it enters the Clarion River. If you plan to fish the stream in April, May, or October, try the lower end near the river. If you plan to fly-fish in June, July, or August, move upstream five to ten miles so you're certain of cooler water.

Spring Creek begins in northeastern Forest County with the combination of the East and Watson branches. The stream flows south, picking up Wolf Run at Parrish and Pigeon Run below. You can get to the stream on an improved dirt road, Spring Creek Road, at Hallton. A dirt road parallels the Creek for eight miles from Hill Run downstream to the Clarion River.

Best Times to Fly-fish:

April 15–May 5
Blue Quill: #18, morning and afternoon
Hendrickson and Red Quill: #14, afternoon

May 15–June 15
Yellow Caddis: #16, afternoon and evening
Green Caddis: #16, afternoon and evening
Sulphur Dun and Spinner: #16, evening
Gray Fox and Ginger Quill: #12 and #14, afternoon and evening
Green Drake and Coffin Fly: #10, evening (spotty)
Light Cahill: #14, evening
Brown Caddis: #16, evening

East Branch, Clarion River

What a fly-fisherman's paradise! Trout fishing and spectacular mayfly hatches flourished in the 1930s on the East Branch. Many area fly-fishermen called the fly-fishing area on this branch the Glen Hazel Paradise. Blackie Veltri, of Brockway, remembers those productive days well. Almost anyone could catch his limit of six trout over nine inches long on the stretch. By the late 1940s and early '50s, however, strip mining slowly contaminated the waters of the East Branch. The state no longer stocked trout in the river. In the mid-1950s the Army Corps of Engineers completed a dam on the Clarion tributary about eight miles upriver from Johnsonburg. This 100-foot-deep dam contained a bottom release. Nevertheless mine acid continued to pour into the watershed.

Showing great foresight, the Department of Environmental Resources (DER) in 1980 added a limer on one of the more visibly polluted tributaries, Swamp Creek. The river has slowly regained some of its former prominence. The state stocks the eight miles below the dam with legal-sized trout and fingerlings.

Where else in Pennsylvania can you fish over trout with water temperatures no higher than the mid-50s in July and August? The East Branch has returned through a cooperative effort of the Fish Commission and the work of the Corps of Engineers. Too many of us criticize the corps and the commission too readily. In this instance they deserve our praise for an excellent reclamation job.

Drive along the river above Glen Hazel, and you'll immediately notice strategically located stream-improvement devices scattered for miles. These devices should function as a model for groups interested in stream improvement. The Civilian Conservation Corps originally built these contraptions in the 1930s. The Fish Commission and Elk County have upgraded and maintained them since that time. Controlled releases from the dam protect these devices from the devastation of floods.

The East Branch flows out of the dam just above Glen Hazel. The dam's bottom release keeps the water below cool for its eight-mile trip to the junction with the West Branch at Johnsonburg.

The East Branch holds a few hatches. Recently Mike Veltri, of Reynoldsville, and I fly-fished on the stream. In one morning in late July, Mike and I saw a decent hatch of Blue Quills and Little Yellow Stoneflies and sporadic hatches of Green Caddis and Light Cahills. In two hours of fishing Mike and I picked up three browns over ten inches and dozens of fingerling brook and brown trout up to six inches long. If fishermen give these small trout a chance to grow, the East Branch will develop into a tremendous fishery.

Above the dam major siltation has damaged Sevenmile and Fivemile runs, Crooked Creek, and Middle Fork. Below the dam, because of the controlled bottom release, siltation is not a problem. Swamp Creek (entering in the dam) and Johnson Run empty varying amounts of mine acid into the branch. (See Chapter 11 for a more detailed discussion of the treatment plant on Swamp Creek.) Some of the East Branch tributaries contain good supplies of native brook trout.

The Glen Hazel Road parallels much of the stream from Johnsonburg to Glen Hazel. At Glen Hazel a dirt road leading to state game lands follows part of the upper two miles.

Congratulations to the Pennsylvania Fish Commission, the Army Corps of Engineers, and the Pennsylvania Department of Environmental Resources for a job well done. The East Branch has returned. Over time it will have a chance to develop into one of the top fisheries in the state.

Best Times to Fly-fish:

May 20–June 15
Sulphur Dun and Spinner: #16, evening

June 15–July 30
Light Cahill: #14, evening
Little Yellow Stonefly: #16, morning
Green Caddis: #14 and #16, afternoon and evening
Blue Quill: #18, morning and afternoon

August 1–September 1
Blue Quill: #18, morning and afternoon
Dark-Brown Stonefly: #16, morning and evening
Green Caddis: #16, afternoon and evening

West Branch, Clarion River

*Delayed Harvest Fly-fishing Only—0.5 mile; from intersection of
US 219 and SR 4003, upstream to Texas Gulf Sulphur Property.
Fishing permitted from east shore only. No wading permitted.*

Mike Veltri, of Reynoldsville, and I approached the West Branch of
the Clarion River on a cool, overcast late-July morning. We arrived at the
stream by 8:00 A.M. in anticipation of a Trico hatch. Mike said he had seen
a few Tricos on the West Branch and I wanted to experience this diminutive
hatch on another freestone stream.

We approached the delayed-harvest area of the West Branch with
much trepidation. We had just experienced two months of hot, dry summer
weather. Would there be any water or trout left in the stream? What would
the water temperature be on this fairly open stream?

When we arrived at the east bank of the water, I immediately lowered
my thermometer into the stream to check the temperature. Here, next to
an underground spring, the thermometer registered 62 degrees. We moved
downstream to obtain a more representative reading and found the water
at 65. The temperature and the water flow were a pleasant surprise.

Mike and I sat and waited for a Trico hatch. Only a very few appeared
that morning, but Slate Drakes and Dark-Tan Stoneflies emerged in good
numbers. Several trout rose to midges, and Mike and I noted more than
a dozen trout feeding. That's not bad for a delayed-harvest area a month
after you're allowed to keep fish.

The West Branch contains a half-mile of delayed harvest. In this area
you can fly-fish only from the east bank. You're allowed neither to wade
the stream in this section nor to fish from the west bank. This makes fly-
fishing extremely difficult and roll casting a necessity. Above the delayed-
harvest stretch some wading is allowed. Check the signs and regulations
before you start fishing.

Hatches on the West Branch seem more numerous than on the Clarion's main stem, with a good supply of Yellow Drakes, Light Cahills, March Browns, and Slate Drakes.

Sam Guaglianone says that in the upper reaches of this branch you can still find some streambred brown trout five to six inches long. The main stem is stocked from Johnsonburg upstream to the Elk County line, about eleven miles. The state stocks a main tributary, Wilson Run, for about eight miles.

The West Branch below Wilcox averages forty to fifty feet wide, with some deep runs, fishable riffles, and a few pools more than five feet deep. US 219 follows the stream from Johnsonburg to the Elk County line.

Best Times to Fly-fish:

April 15–May 5
Hendrickson and Red Quill: #14, afternoon

May 15–June 15
Sulphur Dun and Spinner: #16, evening
Gray Fox and Ginger Quill: #12 and #14, afternoon and evening
March Brown: #12, morning and afternoon
Light Cahill: #14, evening
Little Green Stonefly: #16, afternoon and evening

June 20–July 10
Yellow Drake: #12, evening
Slate Drake: #14, evening

July 15–September 1
Trico: #24, morning (very spotty)
Slate Drake: #14, evening
Dark-Tan Stonefly: #16, morning

Brokenstraw Creek

How many Pennsylvania streams do you know whose headwaters are considered a warm-water fishery while the lower half is stocked with trout? The upper half of Brokenstraw harbors plenty of pike and muskie, but from Spring Creek downstream to Youngville the state stocks thousands of trout annually. Two reasons for this atypical condition stand out. First, Brokenstraw changes from a slow, sluggish stream in its upper half to one with plenty of riffles and rapids in the lower reaches. Second, some cool tributaries, including Spring Creek, Blue Eye Run, and Little Brokenstraw, enter the main stem in the stocked section.

Spring Creek harbors a great Green Drake hatch and a good supply of Light Cahills around the end of May. It enters Brokenstraw at PA 426 and Cemetery Road. Blue Eye displays a good Hendrickson hatch in late April and a decent Light Cahill near the end of May. Blue Eye comes into the main stem near Garland. Little Brokenstraw enters the larger stream at Pittsfield. It warms in the summer, but the state stocks eleven miles of this branch.

Brokenstraw contains many long, flat, deep pools with some deep riffles in the lower half. At Garland the main stem ranges from forty to fifty feet from bank to bank and widens to sixty to eighty feet wide at Youngville. Until a few years ago the area near Garland contained a fly-fishing-only section.

The stream contains a few respectable hatches. In April it does on occasion display enough Hendricksons to allow fishermen to match the hatch. In May and June you will see some Sulphurs and Light Cahills. In mid-June the Yellow Drake appears. If the water temperature hasn't risen too high, you're in for some excellent fly-fishing on Brokenstraw when this drake appears.

Brokenstraw Creek begins in New York and flows south into north-eastern Erie County. It then flows southeast and picks up volume from tributaries like Hare Creek, Spring Creek, Blue Eye Run, Coffee Creek, Andrews Run, Mead Run, and Matthews Run.

Don Foltz, of Lincolnville, feels the best pattern on Brokenstraw is a Dark-Olive Henryville. He's even caught holdover trout in the stream on this pattern.

Wading the Brokenstraw can be challenging. It compares to the rigors of wading the Little Juniata River, Yellow Creek, Slippery Rock Creek, and others.

PA 426 follows the stream from Corry to Garland, and PA 27 and US 6 parallel the Brokenstraw to Youngville.

Best Times to Fly-fish:

April 15–May 5
Hendrickson and Red Quill: #14, afternoon
Dark-Olive Caddis: #16, afternoon and evening

May 15–June 5
Sulphur Dun and Spinner: #16, evening
Blue-Winged Olive Dun: #14, morning and afternoon
Light Cahill: #14, evening
Pteronarcys Stonefly: #6, evening
Slate Drake: #12 or #14, evening

June 15–July 10
Yellow Drake: #12, evening
Slate Drake: #12 or #14, evening

Kinzua Creek

When you look at this large freestone stream set in an isolated area of McKean County, you'd bet that it is one of the top streams in the state. If you fish the water, however, you may change your opinion. Kinzua has some water-quality problems that stem from a mud-and-tar bottom in its upper end caused by an old chemical plant. Near PA 59 the bottom of the stream is coated with a tarlike substance.

Kinzua contains some decent hatches, one of them quite unusual. It harbors some March Browns, Gray Foxes, and Slate Drakes, but it also contains plenty of mayflies in the genus *Baetisca*. The nymphs of these species act much like those of the genus *Isonychia*, both climbing out of the water and emerging on an exposed rock. I have never seen a pattern specifically imitating this species, but a size-12 or -14 Chocolate Dun would match the duns.

Both sides of Kinzua have dirt roads that closely follow the stream. The road on the stream's north side has deteriorated from use by logging trucks.

Kinzua has an undue amount of fishing pressure. It's located within the Allegheny National Forest and gets added pressure during the summer from campers. The stream averages forty to fifty feet wide at many places in its lower end and has a good canopy of pines and mixed hardwoods that hold down the water temperature. Don Foltz and Marshall Young catch streambred browns and holdovers in the Kinzua.

Kinzua begins near Mount Alton in McKean County. On its path south, then east, the main stem picks up dozens of small, cool tributaries, mostly entering from the north side of the stream. Runs like Threemile, Windfall, Wintergreen, Camp, Turnup, and Thundershower flow into the main stem. Just as Kinzua joins the Allegheny Reservoir, South Branch enters. South Branch is a good trout stream in its own right.

Kinzua can be reached at the lower end by PA 321, then National Forest Highway 122 (north side) or 321 (south side). Upstream US 219 crosses the stream at Tally Ho.

Best Times to Fly-fish:

April 15–May 5
Blue Quill: #18, morning and afternoon
Hendrickson and Red Quill: #14, afternoon
Tan Caddis: #16, afternoon and evening

May 15–June 5
Gray Fox: #14, afternoon
March Brown: #12, morning and afternoon
Slate Drake: #12 or #14, evening
Chocolate Dun: #12 or #14, evening

East Branch, Mahoning Creek

The East Branch of Mahoning Creek saw one of its first fly-fishermen in 1928. A hefty brook trout struck a Silver Doctor wet fly on Laurel Run one day that year, Laurel being one of the East Branch's main tributaries. Bob Davis, of Big Run, caught that trout, more than sixty years ago. He still fishes the East Branch and its tributaries, but now he matches the hatches on the water mainly with dry flies. Bob still lives just a stone's throw from this productive stream.

What hatches does Bob most often meet on the East Branch? Bobo, as his friends call him, usually waits until mid- to late May and fishes the two famous drake hatches on the stream. East Branch holds heavy hatches of both Green and Brown drakes. He finds the greatest number of Brown Drakes on the lower three miles of water and the Green Drake on the lower eight miles. Bob says the Brown Drake appears in unbelievable numbers near the water plant just a mile upstream from the town of Big Run.

The stream holds the third drake hatch also, the Yellow Drake. On many waters where the Yellow Drake appears, it does so in marginal water with water temperatures above 70 degrees. On the East Branch water temperatures normally cooperate with the fishermen, even when the Yellow Drake appears in mid-June.

The East Branch holds a good number of aquatic insects, a good number of holdover trout, and some natural brown trout reproduction. Two tributaries, Laurel and Clover runs, contain native brook trout. Bob Davis says that Clover flows about 10 degrees cooler than the main stem in the summer, and many stocked trout move up this tributary.

The quality of water on the East Branch and its tributaries at first glance might seem like an enigma. Ten years ago the streams in this watershed seemed destined for destruction from mine-acid seepage. Enter a local concerned-citizens group, the Allegheny Mountain Chapter of Trout Unlimited. This group, first formed by Al Gretz and Bob Davis, has policed area mining operations on the watershed. The Allegheny Mountain Chapter awarded Bob Davis its first Golden Reel Award for meritorious service to the club and the community.

Ten years ago you'd find the East Branch's water with a pH near 6— now the pH is near 7.2. Why? Liming by upstream strip miners has upped the pH, temporarily, on the stream.

The East Branch begins near Luthersburg in Clearfield County. The stream flows southwest into Jefferson County and enters Mahoning Creek at the town of Big Run. The state stocks the lower eight miles of water. Access to the stream is limited on the lower three miles. You can reach the lower mile on a paved road off US 119 at the north end of Big Run. The next access is three miles upstream at a bridge on a township road. Near the Clearfield County line the stream averages thirty feet wide, with haw-

Bob Davis has spent sixty years fishing one of his favorite streams, the East Branch of the Mahoning Creek.

thorn and alder growing next to the water. At the lower end near the water plant East Branch broadens to forty feet.

If you fish the East Branch in late May or June, you'll probably see Bob Davis there fly-fishing over one of the drake hatches. Enjoy the scenery, the quality of water, and the hatches on this stream. And if you see Bob or any member of the Allegheny Mountain Chapter of Trout Unlimited, thank him for his perseverance in keeping the East Branch of Mahoning Creek clean and productive.

Best Times to Fly-fish:

April 10–May 5
Little Blue-Winged Olive Dun: #20, morning and afternoon
Hendrickson and Red Quill: #14, afternoon
Tan Caddis: #14, afternoon
Brown Caddis: #14, afternoon

May 12–June 15
Sulphur Dun and Spinner: #16, evening
March Brown: #12, morning and afternoon
Green Drake and Coffin Fly: #10, evening
Brown Drake: #10 or #12, evening

June 15–July 10
Yellow Drake: #12, evening

July 15–September 1
Trico: #24, morning

September 1–October 1
Little Blue-Winged Olive Dun: #20, morning and afternoon

Tionesta Creek

The first two decades of the twentieth century were unkind to Tionesta Creek. "Black Creek" would have been a better name for the stream during these years of decadence. The water appeared black from the tannic acid and chemicals poured directly into it by chemical plants in Mayburg and tanneries in Sheffield.

Over the past few decades nature has revitalized this once-polluted creek. Insects in limited numbers now inhabit the stream. Trout stocked by the state can be found in most of the water.

The Tionesta drains a huge land area: the southeastern half of Forest County, much of southeastern Warren County, and a portion of southwestern McKean County and northwestern Elk County. Tionesta Creek warms quickly in the summer, but its watershed contains twelve branches and tributaries also stocked with trout. Many of these smaller streams hold trout all year long. Jack Bush, of Erie, fly-fishes on Two Mile Run in McKean all season long and catches trout.

The Tionesta near Kellettville is more a river than a stream. Here the stream averages sixty to eighty feet wide with plenty of deep runs and long holding pools. In the Kellettville–Mayburg–Porkey–Lynch area you'll see long riffles flowing into some deep pools and flats over 100 yards long. This section contains deep pools at Kellettville, Balltown, Minister Run, and Porkey. From Lynch upstream to Barnes the stream narrows. Near Barnes the South and West branches join to form the main stem. Both branches and many of the tributaries including Six-, Four-, and Two Mile runs, contain trout.

A beautiful rock-ledged stream, Bluejay Creek, enters the main stem near Lynch. This stream holds hatches like the Hendrickson, Quill Gordon, and Blue Quill found early in the season. Bluejay contains a heavy canopy of evergreens and hardwoods throughout its drainage area.

Dick Koval, of Brockway, has fly-fished the Tionesta for more than forty years. He cautions that you should not expect to see the variety and density of hatches on the Tionesta that you'll find on First Fork or Kettle. Early in the season you're likely to see a decent Hendrickson hatch appear and produce some rising trout. But caddis flies are the main source of food on the stream. Dick, however, has fly-fished when Light Stoneflies appeared in early May and when Slate Drakes emerged in early June. In both instances he's done well matching the hatch. Dick's caught trout up to eighteen inches long on the stream and has seen other anglers catch trout up to two feet long.

There's easy access to Tionesta. PA 666 parallels the stream from Kellettville to Barnes; at no point is the stream more than a couple hundred yards from the road. Below Kellettville the water warms early, the stream isn't stocked, and the Corps of Engineers has built Tionesta Lake. Below the lake the stream enters the Allegheny River at Tionesta. You'll cross the lower end on PA 36. If you enjoy large streams and scenic wilderness, and you don't mind fishing for stocked trout, you'll enjoy Tionesta Creek.

Tom Greenlee, at the Forest County Sports Center in Tionesta, knows the stream and its hatches well. Check in with him before you fish the Tionesta.

Best Times to Fly-fish:

April 15–May 7
Blue Quill: #18, morning and afternoon (spotty)
Hendrickson and Red Quill: #14, afternoon
Tan Caddis: #14, morning and afternoon

May 5–May 20
Light Stonefly: #14, morning and afternoon

May 15–June 15
March Brown: #12, morning and afternoon
Chocolate Dun: #12 or #14, evening
Light Cahill: #14, evening
Slate Drake: #12 and #14, evening

East Hickory Creek

Delayed Harvest Artificial Lures Only—1.7 miles; from Queen Creek Bridge downstream to Otter Creek Bridge.

East Hickory contains plenty of history, spectacular scenery, lots of native trout in its main stem and tributaries, and some great hatches.

The delayed-harvest area on East Hickory. This stream holds a good Green Drake population.

During World War I the Wheeler and Dusenberry Lumber Company operated a "fishermens' paradise" at the junction of Coalbed Run and Queen Creek. This tributary to East Hickory Creek teemed with trout. That same lumber company operated a railroad up East Hickory to supply its two sawmills upstream.

Ted Kiffer and his father before him have spent many days on East Hickory and all of its branches. Ted's dad remembers 1912, when state game authorities used the railroad to stock twenty deer brought in from Michigan. The railroad has long since ended operation, but the old grade, still visible along much of East Hickory, remains as a reminder of the activity the watershed once held.

Hike up Queen Creek, and you'll see huge blue spruce planted years ago. Near the headwaters on the main stem you'll find 400 acres of virgin white pine.

Ted Kiffer has fly-fished just about every mile of East Hickory and its many tributaries: Beaver Run, Queen Creek, Coalbed Run, Otter Run, and Middle Hickory Creek. His family has lived in the area since the War of 1812. Ted has caught eighteen-inch brook trout at the Saw Mill Dam on Beaver Run. He remembers the first time he resorted to fly-fishing in that dam. He used a telescoping steel rod and a snelled wet fly. The first time he cast the wet fly into the dam he saw a dozen brook trout race to take it. Now Ted often fly-fishes the main stem just above where Queen Creek enters. From this area upstream the main stem usually holds trout all season.

East Hickory boasts a good Hendrickson hatch and a superb Green Drake. Fly-fish this water in late May, and you'll see how spectacular the Drake can be. With the heavy canopy on much of the stream, Green Drakes emerge sporadically all day long.

East Hickory flows into the Allegheny River just ten miles north of Tionesta. PA 666 parallels the lower three miles of the stream. Above that a dirt road follows the stream up to Queen Creek. There's a 1.7-mile delayed-harvest area from the Otter Creek Bridge to the Queen Creek Bridge. Above the junction with Queen Creek access to the main stem is limited to trails and Allegheny National Forest Highway 119.

Best Times to Fly-fish:

April 12–May 10
Blue Quill: #18, morning and afternoon
Quill Gordon: #14, afternoon
Hendrickson and Red Quill: #14, afternoon

May 15–June 10
March Brown: #12, morning and afternoon
Green Drake and Coffin Fly: #10, evening
Light Cahill: #14, evening
Slate Drake: #12 and #14, evening

June 20–July 10
Blue Quill: #18, morning and afternoon
Slate Drake: #12 and #14, evening
Yellow Drake: #12, evening

Nine

STREAMS OF
Southwestern Pennsylvania

If you live in Pittsburgh or Greensburg and want to experience some great hatches and fish productive trout water, how far do you have to travel? Central Pennsylvania? North-central Pennsylvania? Neither one. You can stay in your own area and enjoy some of the finest fishing Pennsylvania has to offer.

The southwest presents diverse streams and rivers. Two of the best limestone streams in the state lie on the eastern border of the region. Cove and Yellow creeks contain abundant Green Drake and Sulphur hatches. Less than two hours southeast of Pittsburgh lies the extensive, prolific, always-cool Youghiogheny River. You can fly-fish on this water any time of the year and find it an excellent trout river. Travel a few miles below Confluence or upriver a couple miles above Ohiopyle, and you'll probably not see another fisherman.

You also have other streams in your area from which to choose: the Little Mahoning, Loyalhanna, and Laurel Hill creeks. All three become marginal by mid-June, but all three contain some unusual hatches and trout throughout much of the early season.

In the southwest you can experience Green Drake, Brown Drake, Trico, and many other hatches. On the Youghiogheny River you'll likely see caddis flies emerging all summer.

Would you like to fly-fish over streambred trout in the southwest? The two major limestone streams, Cove and Yellow, contain remarkable populations of native brown trout. Two of Loyalhanna's tributaries, Furnace and Laughlintown runs, even hold some streambred rainbow trout.

Southwestern Pennsylvania trout streams have their problems. Acid rain in the Laurel Highlands affects stream like the Loyalhanna and Laurel Hill. Mine-acid drainage affects the Casselman River and many others.

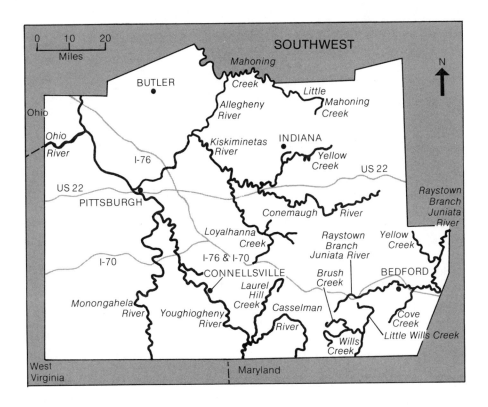

Loyalhanna Creek

*Delayed Harvest Artificial Lures Only—1.5 miles; from SR 0711
downstream to SR 2045.*

Russ Mowry lives near the Loyalhanna in Latrobe. He ties some of the
finest trout flies in Pennsylvania. His copies of the Brown Drake have gained
prominence throughout the Commonwealth as top producers during the
Drake hatch near the end of May. Russ, who runs Mowry's Fly Box, a fly-
fishing supply shop in Latrobe, normally concentrates his fly-fishing on
Pine Creek in north-central Pennsylvania. He does, however, on occasion
fish the Loyalhanna.

Ken Igo and Tim Shaffer, of Latrobe, accompanied Russ and me to
the creek recently. The late-March day turned out to be one of the first
warm days of spring. Early morning water temperatures in the low 40s
slowly rose to near 50 degrees by noon. Even at this early date occasional
Little Black Stoneflies danced above the surface, and gray midges by the
dozens rested in the back eddies on some of the slower pools. Both Tim

and Ken started the day with an unusual chartreuse-colored fly that the locals call the Green Weenie. It reminds me of the San Juan Red Worm that Mike Manfredo and I used on Montana's Big Horn River. The fly is nothing more than a piece of chenille looped at the tail, then wound around the shank of the hook to the eye. Others call it an inchworm pattern.

What trout would take this odd pattern, especially before any leaves appeared on the trees? Ken, Tim, and Russ proceeded to catch two dozen trout with the Green Weenie on the Loyalhanna that March morning.

Ken Igo knows the hatches on the Loyalhanna well. He says the Brown Drake, Green Drake, and Golden Drake are the most abundant on the stream, but those aren't the only hatches this water contains. Ken says that the stream harbors a decent Trico hatch from mid-July until September and adds that a respectable Sulphur hatch appears for a month or more during May and June.

The Loyalhanna has more than just mayflies. At least five separate caddis species appear in enough numbers to create some matching-the-hatch possibilities with down wings. Caddis with body colors of tan, yellow, green, cream, and brown emerge in May and June. Tie caddis patterns for this stream in sizes ranging from 12 to 16.

With its diversity of hatches, the Loyalhanna would seem to be a great stream all season long. In fact it is not, because water temperatures often reach 80 degrees in July and August. The stream contains some springs and several decent tributaries that temper the water of the main stem. Branches like Linn Run, Rolling Rock Creek (also called McGinnis Run), and Furnace Run flow into the Loyalhanna above Ligonier. Between Ligonier and Latrobe, Mill, Coalpit, and Fourmile runs add volume to the main stem.

The Rolling Rock Club owns and posts most of the Loyalhanna upstream from Ligonier. The Fish Commission stocks the stream from Ligonier downstream to Kingston Dam. The Lloydsville Sportsmen's Association and the Forbes Trail Trout Unlimited Chapter add more trout to the stream with their stocking programs. The Trout Unlimited Chapter recently built deflectors and other stream improvements on the Loyalhanna under the Fish Commission's Adopt-a-Stream Program.

The Loyalhanna flows out of the Laurel Mountains in Westmoreland County. It is a fairly large freestone, thirty to forty feet wide at most places. It contains some moderate pools, many rocks, and some productive riffles. Fishing pressure is high from early March until late June in the specially regulated section. This delayed-harvest area runs for 1½ miles from the PA 711 bridge in Ligonier downstream to the Two Mile Bridge. Fishing in this area is open year-round. All of the open ten miles of public water flow within feet of US 30, although parking in many areas of the stream is limited.

Best Times to Fly-fish:

May 12–June 5
Gray Fox: #12, afternoon
March Brown: #12, morning and afternoon
Sulphur Dun and Spinner: #16, evening
Green Drake and Coffin Fly: #10, evening (spotty)
Brown Drake and Spinner: #12, evening
Light Cahill: #14, evening
Blue-Winged Olive Dun: #16, morning and afternoon

June 5–June 25
Golden Drake: #12, evening

July 15–September 15
Trico: #24, morning

Laurel Hill Creek

Delayed Harvest Artificial Lures Only—2.2 miles; from Laurel Hill
State Park at B.S.A. Camp downstream to T-364.

Tim Shaffer, of Latrobe, has had only one trout mounted in his lifetime. That trout, a brown, came from a highly productive stream in southwestern Pennsylvania, Laurel Hill Creek. Tim recalls the day he saw the lunker feeding on terrestrials under a low-lying branch. Large trout always seem to find a difficult lie, and Tim tried several times before he got a perfect cast to that one. The ant drifted directly over the brown without any rise until it was a foot or so below the fish. The heavy trout then turned around, lunged at the terrestrial, and Tim felt the hit. About ten minutes later he netted and kept a nineteen-inch brown.

Nate Rascona and Ken Sarver, of Somerset, and John Sanner, of Rockwood, also fly-fish on Laurel Hill Creek frequently. Total the years these three have fished the stream, and you'll get well over 100. All three have also caught heavy trout on the stream. John landed a twenty-one-inch brown; Ken a twenty-incher; and Nate a nineteen-inch, three-pound fighter.

But Laurel Hill Creek has fallen on hard times the past two years. Rainfall in its headwaters has diminished drastically. At points along its flow Laurel Hill represents only a shadow of its former character. Laurel Hill experienced a severe fish kill in 1987—the second summer of inadequate rainfall. Walk along the stream in the delayed-harvest area in the summer months, and you'll immediately notice that the water level has dropped two feet below its height at spring runoff. At many points along the upper end the stream appears stagnant.

The Somerset County Fly Fishers have not given up on Laurel Hill, however. Along with Nate Rascona, Ken Sarver, and John Sanner the club's fifty other members have accomplished much with the stream. In particular they have worked for four years to get a delayed-harvest area designated. The stream now contains a specially regulated area in Laurel Hill State Park. Travel along this section of the stream, even in late June, and you'll see plenty of fishermen. And look at the trail that follows the stream along the delayed-harvest area. Unlike areas of the stream where few trout remain and paths have grown shut, the delayed harvest area even in late June remains well traveled and fairly heavily fished. If you walk along the stream even in low water conditions, you'll see that this section still contains a good trout population. It should. In addition to a heavy state stocking program, the Somerset Fly Fishers add some fourteen- to seventeen-inch trout. The Fly Fishers also monitor conditions on the stream and protect the delayed harvest from would-be poachers.

Much of the stream below Laurel Hill Lake becomes marginal trout water in early June, as a top release from the dam warms the water below. By the time it enters the Casselman River near Confluence, Laurel Hill becomes smallmouth bass water. Although the state stocks most of the stream, Laurel Hill in its lower end flows through open land and warms quickly. Many of the tributaries add a shot of cold water to the stream, however, and most are stocked by the state. Clear Run, Shafer Run, Jones Mill Run, Allen Creek, Blue Hole Creek, Fall Creek, and Sandy Run receive stocked trout. Although Jones Mill is small, it provides plenty of cool water to the main stem.

Because of its location just off the Pennsylvania Turnpike, Laurel Hill Creek receives heavy fishing pressure from Greensburg and Pittsburgh residents, especially in the delayed-harvest area. This area contains 2.2 miles of deep, flat sections alternating with small riffles. Casting a fly in this heavily canopied area enveloped with dead trees scattered about the banks is difficult. The delayed harvest begins at the upper end of Laurel Hill Lake (Old Forge Bridge).

Hatches on Laurel Hill have suffered from the recent drought. Still there are some Golden Drakes and Light Cahills in mid- and late June. In mid-March you can fish over the Little Black Stonefly.

Best Times to Fly-fish:

March 15–May 1
Little Black Stonefly: #16, morning and afternoon
Hendrickson and Red Quill: #14, afternoon (very spotty)
Cream Caddis: #14 and #16, afternoon and evening

May 12–June 5
Sulphur Dun and Spinner: #16, evening
Olive Caddis: #14, afternoon and evening
March Brown: #12, morning and afternoon
Gray Fox and Ginger Quill Spinner: afternoon (dun) and evening (spinner)
Blue-Winged Olive Dun: #16, morning and afternoon
Light Cahill: #14, evening

June 5–June 28
Golden Drake: #12, evening

Youghiogheny River

*Miscellaneous Waters Special Regulations—from reservoir to mouth
of river.
No closed season on trout. Daily limit opening day of trout
season to Labor Day—8 trout; day after Labor Day to succeeding
opening day of trout season—3 trout.*

In early April I scheduled a trip with Art Gusbar for late June on the Youghiogheny River. Art lives in Friedens, near Somerset, Pennsylvania. He agreed to share some of his hot fishing spots with me.

Between April and late June a heat wave unfolded in southwestern Pennsylvania, along with a severe drought. By late June the area had experienced seven days with 90-plus-degree temperatures. I called Art the day before the trip to make certain the river would still be fishable.

"Better bring your neoprene waders," Art commented. "The water temperature rarely rises above the low 60s."

Why does this 200-foot-wide river remain so cool from Confluence to Ohiopyle? Back in the 1940s the Corps of Engineers placed a dam on the river at Confluence. Someone had the foresight to build a bottom release on this 125-foot-deep lake. As a result, water released from the dam stays in the 50s to low 60s downriver for miles. Select any hot summer day, and you can fish in predictably cool water filled with rainbow and brown trout. Unlike the Delaware, which depends on cold water releases from upriver reservoirs, the Yough remains cool from a fairly constant flow throughout the summer. On hot summer days the water temperature averages 50 to 55 degrees at the release site.

Just below the lake two trout streams, Laurel Hill Creek and the Casselman River, enter. By the time both join the Yough they become marginal trout streams. For years the Casselman contained a heavy slug of mine acid. This situation has been corrected, and the lower mile or two is stocked.

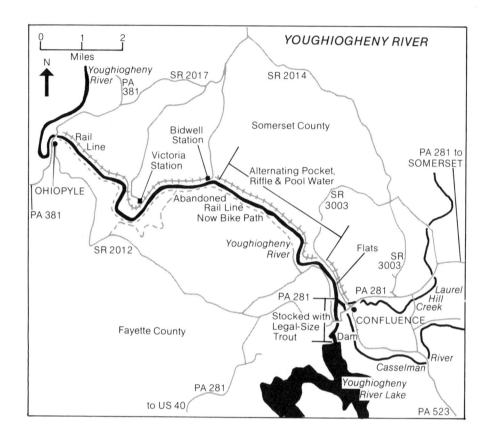

Cleaning up the Casselman has improved the hatches on the Yough below. For several miles downriver you can distinguish water from the Casselman on the east side of the stream from the Yough on the west side. There's a perceptible line or plume on the surface dividing the two.

The state stocks two miles of the Yough just below the dam with plenty of legal-size trout. They stock this section weekly into August. From this point to Connellsville the river depends on fingerlings planted annually. As an experiment the state placed the first fingerlings in the river in late August 1973. The program has continued, and now the state plants more than 100,000 fingerlings at Confluence and Ohiopyle annually. This mixture of browns and rainbows has adapted well to the river. Fingerlings from a June stocking average six to eight inches long by late summer.

If you plan to fish the Yough between Confluence and Ohiopyle, you have three choices: you can hike or bike down an abandoned railroad track or float the river. Thanks to the efforts of the Western Pennsylvania Conservancy, access via the bike trail will remain in public hands forever. Since there are nine miles of isolated river accessible by this trail, you won't see any crowd once you've traveled a couple miles below Confluence or a few miles up from Ohiopyle.

Once on the water you'll experience serious wading problems. The bottom contains square rocks, round rocks, huge boulders, and pebbles of all sizes. Each rock is well coated with a slippery surface prepared to take you off your feet at any moment. There are few places in the river where you have secure footing. Never wade the Yough without felts and a wading staff.

Under drought conditions the river was at least a foot lower than usual. Under normal conditions, many of the rising trout can be impossible to reach. Still, there's excellent trout fishing downriver to Connellsville, although access to the water from Ohiopyle to Connellsville presents major problems. You can raft down the whitewater and fish some of the slower eddies—but this is treacherous and I don't recommend taking expensive equipment with you. As we've seen there's plenty of water, good access, and very few fishermen from Confluence to Ohiopyle, but this nine-mile stretch contains some sizable pools over fifteen feet deep that are impossible to fly-fish. On the plus side some stretches in this area contain miles of pocket water that are productive most of the day.

Art Gusbar and I began fly-fishing on an area Art selected just a mile below Confluence, which represents a typical section of the Youghiogheny River. The water in front of us reminded me of many rivers I had fly-fished before—all of them Western. In front of us lay two-foot-deep pocket water with the typical drag problems associated with varying currents. Just downriver a fast, deep riffle led into a short, ten-foot-deep pool. Above us a 200-foot rapids flowed out of a half-mile-long, deep flat-water section. The river contains several other long flat, sections between Confluence and Ohiopyle. The water averages a moderate drop of eleven feet per mile between those two towns.

I struggled to keep my footing in the pocket water, but it didn't seem to bother Art. Shortly after we began fishing an intermittent Olive Caddis hatch emerged. The caddis takes on extreme importance in this river as a prime source of food for the trout. Many of last year's fingerlings made splashing rises at the emerging pupae. Art tied on an olive soft-hackle wet fly while I tied on a size-14 Olive Caddis dry. For the next two hours we saw several dozen trout rise to the caddis, and we caught twenty—all fingerlings. Art assured me that the Yough contained plenty of larger trout and that when we fished the flats upriver in the evening, we'd see these fish rise.

I spent much of the afternoon collecting aquatic insects. During that time I witnessed a sporadic hatch of size-20 or -22 Blue Duns and saw a few Light Cahills emerge in the pocket water in front of me. Caddis flies appeared in the heaviest numbers that afternoon, however. Art assured me that down wings take on tremendous importance on the river.

Art recommended that we move up to the flat section around 6:00 P.M., and we headed upriver a half-mile. Art felt this area might produce some mayfly activity that evening. Mayflies don't appear in heavy numbers on the Yough, although Art feels that these insects have increased in the past four years. Once on the flat water we waited for two hours for something to happen. Only a few Sulphurs and Light Cahills appeared on the surface—not enough to create any surface feeding. In those two hours of waiting and observing on this four-foot-deep flat water, we saw no more than two or three trout rise.

By 8:30 P.M. a few more mayflies had appeared. Some Sulphurs, Chocolate Duns, Blue-Winged Olive Duns, Light Cahills, and even a couple Slate Drakes paraded past us. Now several trout started feeding 100 yards above us. They fed in pods, as trout feed on some Western rivers. Art yelled, "They're feeding," and we both waded upriver after the rising trout. Soon two more pods of risers appeared. Within fifteen minutes Art and I had thirty to forty trout rising within our casting reach.

With just one trip to the river, I caught Yough Fever. I returned two weeks later to learn more about this fantastic trout water. Art Gusbar again accompanied me, along with Dave Bruner and Pat Docherty, both of Grafton, West Virginia. Pat is the Monongahela Resource Manager for the Army Corps of Engineers—a good fly-fisherman who provided me with information on the excellent job the Corps is doing on the Youghiogheny. On this second visit to the river we made an excruciating hike down the bike trail two miles below Confluence. By 2:00 P.M. the air temperature rose over the century mark. Certainly there'd be no trout fishing in the middle of this unbearably hot midsummer afternoon. When we arrived at the two-mile marker on the bike trail we headed for the river. Pat suggested that I check the water temperature. About four miles below the dam, on this extremely hot afternoon, the Youghiogheny along the shore registered 63 degrees! All afternoon the four of us caught trout—most in the six- to ten-inch category. All afternoon, also, we saw sparse hatches of Slate Drakes, Blue Duns, Light Cahills, and several caddis species. During that hot afternoon, when nobody should have attempted to fish, we caught trout.

The Youghiogheny River lacks one ingredient, however, without which it cannot be rated as a truly spectacular river—heavy mayfly hatches. Although we saw a smorgasbord of mayflies—seven different species—none appeared in numbers reminiscent of hatches on many other streams. Probably more Slate Drakes (*Isonychia*) emerge on the Yough than any other group of mayflies. Mayflies have increased on the river in the past few years, however. In a survey conducted by the Fish Commission in 1970 only two species were found below the dam. Now there are at least seven mayfly species indigenous to the river.

The best strategy for fly-fishing the Yough is to fish the fast pocket water and riffles during the day when the caddis emerge. In the evening move to one of the flats and wait for insect activity and rising trout. Don't quit too early; feeding may not start until dusk.

PA 281 takes you from Somerset to Confluence. Follow SR 2012 from Confluence to Ohiopyle to reach the lower end. It's only a forty-minute drive from Somerset and less than a two-hour drive from Pittsburgh to the Youghiogheny. Confluence and Ohiopyle lack overnight facilities, but Somerset has plenty of motels. If you have the time and enjoy solitude, you might want to hike or bike down the bicycle trail on the Fayette County side. Halfway between Confluence and Ohiopyle, about five miles downriver, there's another productive mile-long stretch of flat water at Bidwell Station that contains plenty of heavy trout. There are two bicycle-rental shops in Confluence.

Because of the cold water, hatches appear about three or four weeks later on the Yough than on other area streams. Slate Drakes appear in heaviest numbers in July. Yellow Drakes begin emerging in early July. The cold water also seems to affect the time of day when some of the hatches appear. We observed many Blue-Winged Olives emerging near dusk and Slate Drakes emerging in the afternoon.

Art Gusbar fly-fishes the river through much of the winter. The water in January and February averages 45 degrees just below Confluence. Art says that on many winter days he's seen tremendous midge hatches. Midges can be seen almost every day throughout the year on the river.

Are you tired of looking for productive cool water on big streams in the East in July or August? Are you longing to get away from the crowds? Or maybe you'd like to extend your season into winter. Either way, once you fly-fish this river you too will catch Yough Fever.

Best Times to Fly-fish:

April 25–May 10
Black Caddis: #16, afternoon

May 20–June 30
Olive Caddis: #14 or #16, afternoon and evening*
Blue Dun: #20 or #22, afternoon*
Sulphur Dun and Spinner: #18, evening*
Light Cahill: #14, evening*
Blue-Winged Olive Dun: #14, morning and evening*
Chocolate Dun: #16, afternoon and evening*
Gray Caddis: #16 afternoon and evening

July 1–August 15
Slate Drake: #12, afternoon and evening
Yellow Drake: #12, evening
Cinnamon Caddis: #14, afternoon and evening
Perla Stonefly: #12, morning

August 1–September 30
Blue Quill: #18, morning and afternoon
Dark-Gray Caddis: #18, afternoon and evening

*Hatches continue well after the ending date listed

Little Mahoning Creek

*Delayed Harvest Fly-fishing Only—4 miles; from SR 1034 at
Rochester Mills upstream to Cesna Run.*

"It's nothing but a ditch!" That's what a friend of Terry Powers calls the Little Mahoning Creek. But to thousands of anglers in western Pennsylvania and Ohio, this stream resembles an oasis in the middle of a desert.

The Little Mahoning flows north, then west through much of northern Indiana County. Many of the streams in this area and in the surrounding counties of Clearfield, Jefferson, and Armstrong have been ravaged by man's careless quest to mine coal. In the aftermath of these mining operations many streams in the area have suffered years of contamination from mine acid. The Little Mahoning, however, remains relatively free of the pollution from strip mining, although it does suffer from severe siltation, which in turn affects the aquatic life on the stream. Small upstream farms and strip mining contribute to this silting problem. Rocks and boulders through much of the stream contain a heavy coating of mud. Wading these mud-covered rocks can be challenging. Even small storms cause the water to discolor quickly.

The Little Mahoning begins near Deckers Point and flows north for ten miles, where it picks up a major tributary, the North Branch. In its headwaters the creek resembles a small, meandering farmland stream ranging from ten to twenty feet wide. Before it adds the North Branch, the stream enters a forested area. For the next seven miles a heavy canopy of mixed hardwoods and pines shades the water. The stream picks up additional flow from more tributaries, including Brewer Run, Broadhead Run, and Leasure Run, before the main stem flows through Rochester Mills. Special-Project water begins near Rochester Mills and continues upstream for four miles. The state stocks the stream above Smicksburg for fifteen miles. From Rochester Mills you can gain access to the stream by a dirt road that goes to Smithport. The locals have named many of the pools, especially in the fly-fishing-only stretch. There's a Millstone Pool, Gas Well Pool, and Swimming Hole Pool—among others.

Bob Davis, of Big Run, has fly-fished on the Little Mahoning for the past thirty years and knows the hatches on the stream well. He feels that along with a few caddis species, the March Brown and the Green Drake produce the heaviest hatches of the year. In contrast to many limestone streams like Penns Creek, the Green Drake on the freestone Little Mahoning produces plenty of risers and cooperative trout. Bob says that if you hit the Green Drake on the stream, you'll probably experience a great evening of fly-fishing.

Terry Powers, of Colver, and Dennis Horn, of Penn Run, met me on the Little Mahoning recently. Dennis spends his spare time fly-fishing on nearby streams and working with the local Ken Sink Chapter of Trout Unlimited. Beginning in 1982 this chapter, with the cooperation of the Fish Commission, installed twenty-six stream devices on the fly-fishing section of the Little Mahoning. These improvements still prevent bank erosion. Terry heads up the Western Pennsylvania Fly Fisherman's Association, in Barnesboro. This volunteer organization does much work on local streams to improve their quality. His organization recently installed stream-improvement devices on another Cambria County stream, Blacklick Creek.

"Henryville Special, Honey Bugs, and floating nymphs work well on this stream," Dennis said as we set out to fish. Terry tied on a Green Weenie, and Dennis a Honey Bug. I tied on more conventional patterns like the March Brown and Light Cahill.

Throughout the day March Browns emerged sporadically. After 3:00 P.M. a dozen Green Drakes appeared. The Drake here almost reaches the size of its counterpart on Penns and Yellow creeks. The dark-yellow abdomen of the Drake here, however, differs from the lighter belly of this species on most other streams.

We traveled upstream to be in place on the Swimming Hole for the last hour of fishing before dusk. Thousands of Great Red Spinners returned to the surface to lay their eggs, but only a handful of Coffin Flies reappeared. The Green Drake we had expected to materialize didn't—probably in another night or two the majority of these huge mayflies would emerge. Dennis caught more than a dozen trout that last hour on a gray floating-nymph pattern, while Terry experienced success with the Green Weenie. In a half-day's fishing the three of us caught more than thirty trout.

The Little Mahoning Creek is a ditch? Although it has a siltation problem and sparse hatches, the stream deserves a better designation. The delayed-harvest area teems with stocked trout and a few holdovers. To many area anglers the Little Mahoning Creek provides hours of fun and enjoyable fishing over a good supply of trout. If you're so fortunate as to hit the stream when the Green Drake appears, you're in for some top-notch fly-fishing.

Best Times to Fly-fish:

April 1–May 1
Little Blue-Winged Olive Dun: #20, morning and afternoon
Blue Quill: #18, morning and afternoon

May 12–June 10
Sulphur Dun and Spinner: #16, evening
Gray Fox: #14, afternoon
Light Cahill: #14, evening
Green Drake and Coffin Fly: #10, evening
Dark-Green Drake: #8, afternoon and evening
Slate Drake: #12 and #14, evening

July 15–September 1
Blue Quill: #18, morning and afternoon
Slate Drake: #12 and #14, evening

Yellow Creek

*Delayed Harvest Fly-fishing Only—1 mile; from mouth of Maple
(Jacks Run) upstream to Red Bank Hill.*

Nelson Hamel of Altoona, Carl Dodson of Martinsburg, and Bob Foor of Everett fly-fish Yellow Creek frequently. Carl's on the stream fishing nymphs from March until October. He's one of those treasured landowners who welcomes fishermen to fish his stretch of the stream at the lower end of the special-project water.

Bob Foor collected Green Drakes for a couple years on Cove Creek near his home and transplanted them to Yellow Creek near Loysburg in northern Bedford County. Years before, Yellow Creek had contained a respectable hatch of Green Drakes. That hatch had vanished on the stream in the mid-1950s. Recently, through Bob's efforts or through natural circumstances, the Drake has returned to this fertile limestone stream, where it has exhibited an outstanding hatch and spinner fall the last five years.

Nelson Hamel operates Nelson's Flies and Supplies, in Altoona. We fished the Green Drake on Yellow in late May. The Drake hatch on Yellow appears in heavy numbers, but trout have other food items on their menu at this time of year. On the stream at the same time the Drake appeared were Ginger Quills, Sulphur Duns and Spinners, and some Light Cahills. Some trout fed on the Ginger Quill, while others fed on emerging Green Drake nymphs just under the surface. Some regular fly-fishermen on Yellow during the Green Drake hatch tell stories of catching 50 trout per day and 200 in a four-day hatch.

Another great fly-fishing time on Yellow occurs near the end of April. At that time you'll find Blue Quills, some Hendricksons, and a heavy Green Caddis hatch on the lower end of the stream. Mid-May on Yellow Creek

Several local anglers discussing strategy on Yellow Creek before the Green Drake hatch appears.

also presents some fine hatches. Bob Foor caught forty trout on Yellow Creek last May 21 during a heavy but sporadic March Brown hatch.

Even into July and August this fertile insect factory harbors decent hatches. Tricos appear every morning, and if the water temperature remains cool, you can fly-fish over rising trout for an hour each morning. In August, Yellow also displays a White Mayfly hatch on its lower half. These late hatches often emerge in water that is in the 70s. Even into late summer fishing Yellow with terrestrials produces trout. Carl Dodson uses hopper imitations with yellow, green, or brown bodies.

Yellow Creek begins near Woodbury in southern Blair County. It flows south to Loysburg, where it enters the Loysburg Gap, then flows east to Hopewell, where it enters the Raystown Branch of the Juniata River. Tributaries include Hickory Bottom, Potter Creek, Three Springs, Beaver Creek, and Maple Run. The state stocks parts of the last four. There's a delayed-harvest, fly-fishing only section on the main stem from Maple Run upstream for a mile. This section accommodates a sizable number of fly-fishermen and should be extended upstream. Each part of the regulated area has been named by local fly-fishermen. From the top of the special-project water to the bottom you'll hear names like Red Bank (just above the regulated area), School House, Junk Pile, Slate Hole, Long Hole, Scout Camp, and Molly Gordon.

Yellow Creek gets its name from its coloration; it never really attains the clarity that some other limestone streams like Spruce Creek do. After a heavy rain it can stay off-color for five to seven days. This productive water contains plenty of holdovers and streambred browns. Matching the hatch for these wily browns often requires switching from one pattern to another, since you often encounter multiple hatches and spinner falls.

PA 36 parallels Yellow Creek from Woodbury to the lower end of the Loysburg Gap. Access below that is by blacktop at the New Frontier Restaurant. PA 26 parallels the last four miles of water. Wading in Yellow is tricky and hazardous. The stream contains deep pools, many productive riffles, heavy pocket water, and rapids in the Loysburg Gap area. Above Loysburg, Yellow averages twenty to forty feet wide; below, it widens out to forty to fifty feet. Just below Woodbury the state has designated a mile-long area as wild-trout water. As with so many of these Class A waters much of the wild-trout section on Yellow Creek has recently been posted (See Chapter 11). This area affords the open-pasture fly-fishing so typical of limestone streams, but, there are many native trout below and a good canopy in most places.

Best Times to Fly-fish:

April 15–May 5
Hendrickson and Red Quill: #14, afternoon (spotty)
Grannom: #16, afternoon

May 20–June 10
March Brown: #12, morning and afternoon
Green Drake and Coffin Fly: #10, evening
Light Cahill: #14, evening
Brown Drake: #12, evening

June 15–July 10
Yellow Drake: #12, evening

Cove Creek

Bob Foor lives in Everett, in Bedford County. He's a biology teacher and baseball coach for the local high school. Annually his biology classes take field trips to nearby streams to monitor water quality. Bob's students check pH, water temperature, and aquatic life in the streams. Bob's classes have adopted Cove Creek just south of Everett as one of their study streams.

Talk about an isolated valley, a beautiful limestone stream, and heavy hatches—Cove Creek has them all. Add to this a healthy supply of streambred browns and holdover trout, and you have all the ingredients for an excellent trout stream. Some landowners along Cove, however, have posted their property, a problem which seems destined to get worse along this stream. If you ask permission from some of the landowners, they might let you fish their property. This is an example of a stream to which the state should acquire access (see Chapter 11). The state stocks open areas of Cove up to the town of Rainsburg, although this limestone stream really needs no stocking, since it houses an excellent supply of streambred brown trout. Bob Foor has caught trout up to twenty-two inches long during the Green Drake hatch on Cove.

Ten years ago Bob transported Green Drake duns and Coffin-Fly spinners from Cove Creek to Yellow Creek in an attempt to establish a colony of that species there. He kept transporting adults for two seasons to Yellow Creek. Four years ago the Green Drake became a major hatch on Yellow, maybe in part because of Bob's work.

Cove Creek exhibits true limestone characteristics, with a pH near 8.2. The water temperature seldom rises above 70 degrees. Throughout its fifteen-mile flow additional springs add fresh shots of cold water to the main stem. Cove ranges from thirty to forty feet wide on its lower end. Ten miles upstream near Rainsburg, the stream narrows considerably. It contains many deep pools and heavy, productive riffles throughout. Cove is best fly-fished when a hatch or spinner fall appears on the water. Otherwise nymphs prove to be the proper choice. Much of the cold, spring-fed stream contains a good canopy to shade it from the sun. It does, however, flow through some open farmland.

Bob Foor and I recently visited Cove in late May. He wanted to show me the heavy Green Drake hatch it contains. By 8:00 P.M. Coffin Flies already appeared over the water, but the big surprise for me was the density of the Sulphur Spinners, which appeared as a cloud over every fast section we could see. As these clouds of spinners appeared, thousands of Sulphur Duns emerged. Cove exhibited its true fertility that evening—yet few trout rose. Several evenings before, a heavy thunderstorm had raised the level of the water by more than a foot.

Cove flows between Evitts and Tussey mountains just south of Everett in Bedford County. You reach the stream by crossing the Raystown Branch of the Juniata River at Everett, and traveling through Earlston on a blacktop road to the stream. PA 326 from Bedford gets you to the upper end near Rainsburg.

Best Times to Fly-fish:

April 10–May 5
Early Brown Stonefly: #12, afternoon
Blue Quill: #18, morning and afternoon
Quill Gordon: #14, afternoon
Hendrickson and Red Quill: #14, afternoon
Green Caddis: #16, afternoon

May 10–June 10
Sulphur Dun and Spinner: #16, evening
Gray Fox: #14, afternoon
March Brown: #12, morning and afternoon
Green Drake and Coffin Fly: #10, evening
Light Cahill: #14, evening
Blue Quill: #18, morning and afternoon
Brown Caddis: #14 and #16, late morning and afternoon

June 15–July 10
Slate Drake: #12 or #14, evening
Blue Quill: #18, morning and afternoon
Yellow Drake: #12, evening

July 10–September 1
Trico: #24, morning
White Mayfly: #14 or #16, evening

Wills Creek

August 13, 1984, looms dark in the history of Wills Creek, in Bedford and Somerset counties. On that day the entire valley in which Wills flows flooded. The headwaters of Wills near Callimont received six to eight inches of rain in two hours. As the swollen water moved downstream, it carried huge uprooted trees with it. These trees soon formed temporary dams along the narrow valley floor. When these dams burst, a sixty-foot-high wall of water cascaded down the valley. Hyndman endured the brunt of the flood. Much of the town lay under several feet of raging flood waters.

This flood destroyed aquatic life and killed the huge huge holdover brown trout formerly found on Wills. The flood scoured the streambed and today, five years later, the stream still suffers. Bob Bryant, of Hyndman, knew of a twenty-four-inch and a twenty-seven-inch brown caught before the flood on Wills. He's heard few reports of lunkers taken since. Mayflies— once present in heavy numbers—have returned but with much less density. As you walk up the valley floor, you can still see the scars from the flood: huge uprooted trees line the banks for miles, and boulders larger than cars lie helter skelter in the streambed.

Tony Stair, of Hyndman, Bryan Meck, and I visited the stream recently in early June to examine the water for insects. Tony lives just south of Hyndman and has fished Wills for most of his thirty years. His dad, Glenn, has fished the stream for more than thirty years. We visited the stream a mile below Fairhope.

By 8:00 P.M. huge *Pteronarcys dorsata* stoneflies mated in the air 100 feet above the stream. Never have I witnessed so many of these huge stoneflies egg laying at one time. In the hour just before dusk we may have seen more than a thousand of these monsters. Only on western streams have I encountered more stoneflies as large as this eastern species. The western *P. californica* is closely related to this eastern stonefly, and fly-fishermen out West call it the Salmon Fly. Mayflies also emerged. Dozens of Dark-Olive Spinners mated and laid eggs, along with Light Cahills, Ginger Quills, Slate Drakes, and hundreds of Sulphur Spinners. Three species (*Ephemerella dorothea, septentrionalis,* and *rotunda*) emerged just at dusk. Wills Creek has returned.

Earlier that day Tony took us to one of Wills's tributaries, Brush Creek. We fished for a short time at the Pack Saddle Bridge section. While we fished, 100 or more Green Drakes emerged, along with Light Cahills, Sulphurs, and Slate Drakes.

Wills Creek looks unlike any other stream in Pennsylvania. Wherever you fish on it, it reminds you of a fast-flowing western trout stream. Throughout, it's lined with huge boulders. The creek begins near Callimont at an elevation of 2,600 feet and falls 1,700 feet in fifteen miles. Each rock and boulder in the water contains a covering of slime and silt, so wading on Wills is dangerous. Many areas contain cascading rapids and few sizable pools. Dry fly-fishing on the stream above Hyndman encounters difficult cross currents. Below Hyndman the stream slows and forms deep pools. The Fish Commission at present doesn't stock below Hyndman, but this area would make a tremendous delayed-harvest section. Six miles below Hyndman, Wills flows into Maryland, where that state stocks the stream.

Many of Wills's tributaries carry native brook trout. Above Hyndman the state stocks Shaffer's Run, Brush Creek, and Laurel Run. In Hyndman, Little Wills enters the main stem. The state stocks six miles of this stream. Four miles below Little Wills, Gladdens Run enters. Gladdens has a good holdover trout population. Other branches on Wills not stocked are Gooseberry Run (some mine acid), Bore Mill Run (native brook trout), and Savage or Mountain Run (native brook trout).

You can reach the stream at Hyndman off PA 96. A paved secondary road follows the stream to Fairhope.

Wills Creek had survived the flood of a century. It's only a matter of time until its insect population and holdover trout increase in numbers.

Best Times to Fly-fish:

April 15–May 5
Blue Quill: #18, morning and afternoon
Quill Gordon: #14, afternoon

May 10–June 10
Sulphur Dun and Spinner: #16, evening
Gray Fox: #14, afternoon
Blue-Winged Olive Dun: #14, morning and afternoon
Light Cahill: #14, evening
Green Drake and Coffin Fly: #10, evening (spotty)
Slate Drake: #12 or #14, evening
Pteronarcys Stonefly: #6, evening
Tan Caddis: #14, evening

June 10–July 1
Sulphur Dun and Spinner: #16 and #18, evening
Slate Drake: #12 or #14, evening
Light Cahill: #14, evening

Raystown Branch, Juniata River

You'll often find Bill Thomas, of Thomas Chevrolet in Bedford, in Montana hunting for elk, in Quebec fly-fishing for salmon, and on the Chesapeake Bay goose hunting. When he's not on one of his excursions or at the car showroom, you'll find him fly-fishing near his Bedford home on the Raystown Branch.

Quite often Bill fly-fishes the lower end of Raystown until early June. At that time, when he fishes the branch, he does so about one hour before dusk or near dawn. The stream warms rapidly in summer and quickly becomes a warm-water fishery populated with smallmouth bass. At this time trout seek out the cooler springs and feeder streams scattered throughout the river.

If the water temperature cooperates, fly-fishing over a Trico spinner fall can prove productive on the Raystown Branch in July, August, and September. The White Mayfly appears in mid-August, and you can find some late-summer fly-fishing on Raystown—that is, if the temperatures cooperate. Bob Foor, of Everett, also says that there's a good Brown Drake downriver between Everett and Bedford.

Bill Thomas and his fly-fishing buddy Bill Masterson have fly-fished on the river for the past twenty-five years. They catch an occasional holdover on the lower end but feel the upper end holds more trout. They're both members of the Fort Bedford Chapter of Trout Unlimited. The area the two fish regularly near Bedford ranges from 80 to 100 feet wide and contains many slow pools, and long, flat sections, and a few productive riffles. Below Bedford the river widens considerably. Even though trout aren't stocked this far downriver, you'll find fish. The river near the Somerset County line averages sixty to seventy feet wide, with more riffles and cooler water. The state stocks twenty miles of the Raystown Branch from Somerset County downriver to Bedford.

The Raystown Branch begins near Macdonaldton in eastern Somerset County. It picks up Breastwork Run (stocked), Three Lick Run, Spiker Brook, Shawnee Branch, Buffalo Run, and Cumberland Valley Run before it enters Bedford. US 220 (Business) parallels the stream near Bedford, and PA 31 follows the river above town. Near Shawnee Park, about ten miles upstream from Bedford, the Raystown Branch flows through shale deposits. Since the upper Raystown flows through shale outcroppings, this area gets extremely low and warms rapidly in hot dry summers.

Best Times to Fly-fish:

April 15–May 5
Blue Quill: #18, morning and afternoon
Quill Gordon: #14, afternoon
Black Quill: #14, afternoon

May 15–June 10
Gray Fox: #14, afternoon
Light Cahill: #14, evening
Blue-Winged Olive Dun: #14, morning and afternoon
Brown Drake: #12, evening
Slate Drake: #12 or #14, evening
Cream Cahill: #14 and #16, evening

June 15–July 15
Yellow Drake: #12, evening
Cream Cahill: #14 and #16, evening

July 15–September 1
White Mayfly: #14, evening

Brush Creek

Tony Stair, Bryan Meck, and I arrived at the Pack Saddle covered bridge shortly after noon. Tony lives in nearby Hyndman, and he had bragged about the beauty and inaccessibility of this high-mountain stream. Because of the limited access to Brush, Tony doubted that many anglers fished more than the couple areas where roads crossed. At the time of day we approached I doubted that we'd see any hatches or trout rising.

Tony and Bryan fly-fished in the spectacular pool just below the covered bridge. Here you can see a picturesque waterfall flowing into a ten-foot-deep pool with a covered bridge in the background. The pool tailed out to two feet at the lower end.

All three of us were mesmerized by the waterfall and the beauty of the area. We didn't expect any hatch this early in the day. In a couple minutes, however, some Green Drakes appeared in the shallow riffle just below the pool. Soon a hundred or more Coffin Fly spinners appeared over the water. Then Slate Drakes, Light Cahills, and Sulphurs emerged with the Green Drakes.

Brush Creek contains some great hatches, but access is limited. The stream flows off the eastern slope of the Allegheny escarpment. Below Pack Saddle are three miles of heavily canopied water before you reach the next bridge at Bittners Mills. Upstream from Pack Saddle there's also limited access to this small stream, but the area is less densely forested than below.

Brush Creek begins in Somerset County where Panther and Hillegas runs join. Several of the tributaries of Brush hold good populations of native brook trout, and you'll find holdover trout in the main stem. Brush flows south for six miles before it joins Wills Creek near Fairhope. You can reach the stream from PA 96 at Hyndman, then take secondary blacktop roads to Fairhope, then to the stream. You can also reach the stream from Somerset off PA 31.

Try Brush Creek. The terrain is rugged, the scenery spectacular, and the hatches outstanding. Don't expect to park the car and take a leisurely hike to the stream; especially on the lower half much of the creek flows through a heavily forested narrow gorge where access is difficult.

Best Times to Fly-fish:

April 15–May 5
Blue Quill: #18, morning and afternoon
Quill Gordon: #14, afternoon

May 12–June 10
Sulphur Dun and Spinner: #16, evening
Gray Fox and Ginger Quill: #12 and #14, afternoon and evening
March Brown: #12, morning and afternoon
Green Drake and Coffin Fly: #10, evening
Light Cahill: #14, evening
Slate Drake: #12 and #14, evening

July–August 31
Slate Drake: #12 and #14, evening

TEN

TYING PATTERNS FOR
Pennsylvania's Hatches

By now you know a lot about the hatches you might encounter on the streams of Pennsylvania. You know where these hatches might occur and at approximately what time of the year they appear. Go to a sporting-goods store and attempt to buy some of the patterns I suggest to match these hatches, however, and you may face difficulty. Let me describe one of my early experiences trying to locate the proper fly pattern.

I started fly-fishing forty years ago in eastern Pennsylvania. Many streams in Schuylkill and Carbon Counties, including the Upper Swatara, Lower Swatara, Bear, Lizard, and Pohopoco creeks, saw me frequently. All of them have some hatches and good fly-fishing. The Lower Swatara near Rock contains some Pale Evening Duns throughout the summer. Bear Creek in lower Schuylkill County was a favorite of mine. It's a small stream coming off the Blue Mountain, flowing through Auburn, then into the Schuylkill River. Much of the creek is only a stone's throw from PA 895. In its headwaters it holds a good supply of small brook trout. I once found a long, slow pool on the stream three miles below Summit Station. Some local kids had evidently created it as a swimming hole, because it contained rocks neatly piled a foot or so high at the lower end. I passed by this dam one day and noticed several Yellow Stoneflies in the air, returning to the pool to lay their eggs for the next generation of Bear Creek nymphs. As I stood and stared at the insects, I saw six trout begin to feed in the impoundment. I got my fishing gear out of the car and tied on the only pattern I owned that looked anything like the bug in the air. That pattern, a Yellow Sally wet fly, proved to be the final inducement needed to encourage me to fly-fish. Trout took the pattern until it became ragged. The last half-hour the Sally contained only a yellow body—no hackle or tail. The questions then became, where did I get this fly, and where do I get another?

My total fly selection at the time amounted to no more than twenty wets and twenty drys—but that Sally had been the only light-colored fly in my box. Forty years ago there wasn't a store within thirty miles of Bear Creek that sold flies.

I was fortunate enough to have a neighbor who tied flies. I described the Yellow Sally to him, and he tied me several copies. Because of the difficulty of getting flies, and with the encouragement of this local tier, I started tying.

Those days of few fly-fishermen and even fewer flytiers have long passed. There are now dozens of top sporting-goods stores and thousands of flytiers in the state, and many of them tie specified patterns. Many of the best stores, and Trout Unlimited and Fly Fishing Federation chapters, sponsor fly-tying classes.

If you do tie, or if you're in the process of learning, you've probably acquired your fly-tying skills from several tiers. Maybe you've learned a method for tying wings from one tier, and faster technique for tying the whip finish from another. In my case George Harvey, one of the greatest fly-fisherman in Pennsylvania, taught me the basics at a conservation camp. Adding to that initial lesson were such flytiers as John Perhach, Dick Mills, Barry Beck, Joe Humphreys, Greg Hoover, and others. For me the end product of all of this instruction from a wide variety of experts is my own unique method of tying. The same will happen to you. Your method will become so personal that your patterns will display a character all their own.

We'll examine tying methods for down wings or caddis patterns, for nymphs, for terrestrials. We'll look at upright patterns for many of the common mayfly hatches, spent-winged imitations to copy the spinner falls, and some of the more important wet flies. Not all the patterns we've discussed previously are described here, but we'll cover more than enough to make those trips to the Commonwealth's streams successful ones.

Some New Tying Methods

Several years ago in the great magazine *Flyfishing the West* (now called *Flyfishing*) a writer alluded to the number of new patterns and tying methods which have come in vogue lately. He grouped new patterns and methods into three categories:.

1. Those new patterns which are not as good as the old standbys.

2. Those new imitations which are equal to, but not better than, the present patterns.

3. Those patterns which are truly revolutionary and are better than the present patterns.

In Group 1 the author listed the no-hackle flies, latex-bodied nymphs, and other patterns. In Group 2 he placed patterns like the Matukas and parachute dry flies. Guess what patterns he ranked in Group 3? None! I often say some patterns catch fishermen while others only catch fish. Following are some questions we should ask ourselves as fly-fishermen and tiers before we jump at every new pattern, method, or material that comes our way:.

1. Is the newer method of tying a known pattern easier for me than the older one?.

2. If the pattern is supposed to copy a natural insect, does the end product (the finished fly) copy the real insect more effectively than the old pattern did?.

3. Is the material recommended easy to obtain?.

4. Is the finished pattern relatively durable?.

5. If the new pattern is a floating one, does it float well?.

6. Does the new pattern catch trout? Moreover, does it produce over a wide range of waters and a good part of the season?.

With the above cautions in mind let me suggest some methods which definitely make tying some of the patterns much simpler. Look, for example, at the description for tying the Deer Head Caddis. We use the elementary concept that Keith Fulsher used to tie his famous bucktails, the Fulsher Minnows. You'll note another easy tying method we suggest for the Poly Beetle. We tie the pattern much as its forerunner, the Crowe Beetle, was tied, but we use multipurpose polypropylene. Look at the instructions for tying the Poly Beetle. We suggest you use black poly yarn instead of the normal black deer hair used in the Crowe Beetle. Deer hair splits readily. After a few strikes on the Crowe Beetle, the deer hair often comes apart. The Poly Beetle holds up better than the Crowe, floats as well, and takes less than a minute to tie.

Tying the Terrestrials

Surprising but true, the life cycle of many ants, especially those in the genus *Lasius*, is very similar to that of the mayflies we described in Chapter 2. The cycle begins with a swarming flight, mating, and death of the male. The female lives and lays her eggs. These flights or swarms of winged ants are very common in Pennsylvania toward the end of August, usually occurring in the afternoon and evening. On these late-summer days it's important to carry plenty of the winged-ant imitations in sizes 18 to 24 and with body colors ranging from black to ginger. To imitate the ant's wings use a light-gray or white strip of poly yarn, and tie it down wing between the two humps of the ant. Tie the two humps in the body of the ant with black or brown poly dubbing.

Ants, as well as crickets, grasshoppers, beetles, and other terrestrials, are important to copy and use on Pennsylvania's streams, especially in July, August, and September. As often as possible use poly as wings or body material for these floating patterns. Black poly is the best yarn for the body of the crickets, ants, and beetles, and an olive or pale-yellow poly for the body of grasshoppers. Poly is extremely buoyant and easy to use.

Caterpillars are another important terrestrial for your summer collection of patterns. I prefer those made of cork and colored with a permanent marking pen. Take a piece of cylindrical cork and test the marking pen to see the color you achieve. The marking pen produces a truer color with less shine than lacquer. To add legs to the terrestrial, start at the rear and palmer the hackle to the eye of the hook. Clip the top and bottom of the hackle to create a more lifelike imitation. Always carry plenty of green inchworm patterns on your summer fishing trips.

Tying the Down Wings

Caddis flies appear on Pennsylvania streams throughout the entire season. An ample supply of diverse patterns copying these insects can mean the difference between a frustrating and a rewarding day. Include hackle (or legs) on some but not all of your patterns. Those with hackle, called "fluttering caddis," ride fast water higher than a second type, the Deer Head Caddis.

The usual method for imitating wings on a caddis is to tie deer hair in by the butt just behind the eye of the hook. With this method of tying, the hair tends to roll, however, and it's difficult to achieve a smooth head on the imitation. Try tying instead a Deer Head Caddis; it is easier to tie, and the final product is a better copy of the natural. The end result resembles a smaller version of the Fulsher Minnow. To tie the Deer Head Caddis follow these instructions:

Begin by tying in a bunch of cut deer hair, just as with the fluttering caddis. Place the deer hair so the butts are facing toward the rear (not the front) of the hook, and the hair tips extend well out past the eye of the hook. Take your tying thread and wind it securely up over the deer-hair butts forward to the eye of the hook. Take a small piece of poly of the proper color, and dub it in just behind the eye. This little piece of dubbed poly becomes the chin of the caddis. Pull the tips of the deer hair back over the hook, and tie in about one fourth of the way back from the eye. Finish off with a whip finish, lacquer the head and thread, and you have a Deer Head Caddis. If the wings of the natural caddis you want to imitate are darker than the deer hair, use moose mane or darker deer hair.

Tying Spinner Imitations

Many female spinners die spent on the surface after laying their eggs.

Others, Sulphur Spinners and Ginger Quills, for example, sometimes ride the water with their wings upright, just like the duns of the species. Conversely, male spinners of many species never get close to the water, but meet the female, mate, and die over land. Knowing beforehand a mayfly's mating behavior helps when fishing the spinner fall. Since many of the spinners ride the surface for some distance with wings upright and not spent, it's important to include some of these upright patterns in your selection. There's a bonus to using an upright pattern as a spinner—the imitation is much easier to follow on the surface than is a spent-wing, especially at dusk. The upright version of the Sulphur Spinner performs well on the Delaware River during a spinner fall of the naturals.

Orvis and other top companies supply a good poly yarn for spent-wings. Use this same material to tie the pattern upright, but tie the poly in as you would with calf tail and divide.

In many of my spinner patterns I include a few strands of Orvis Krystal Flash with the poly spent-wings. George Harvey first recommended using this material in an article on the Trico in *Fly Fisherman* Magazine. Using a few strands of this material produces many more strikes.

Tying the Duns

Many new fly-tying methods and materials have come and gone since my *Meeting and Fishing the Hatches* was published several years ago. In that book I recommended using mallard quill wing to imitate the dark-gray wings so common on many emerging duns. These quill sections effectively copy the wings of all Blue Quill species, all of the Slate Drakes, the Quill Gordon, and all of the Olive Duns. When you use these wings on any pattern larger than a size 18, however, they tend to twist fine leader tippets. Dun hen hackle tips shaped with a wing burner, on the other hand, are much easier to tie and don't twist the line.

In the earlier book I recommended using poly for body material as much as possible. Today there are more varieties and colors of poly than ever before. Use the synthetic material in place of the natural quill bodies, because the poly is much more durable. How many times has a Red Quill, Ginger Quill, or a Quill Gordon body unraveled after catching a few trout? This won't happen with poly. Use dark-gray poly for the body of Slate Drakes, light brown for the Ginger Quill, and reddish brown for the Red Quill.

I haven't discussed compara duns or methods for tying them. Although these patterns are extremely effective, they don't hold up as well as hackled flies. Check the compara duns you tied last year, and see how straight the wings are now.

Tying Wet Flies

Wet-fly patterns copying the Quill Gordon and other early hatches are deadly in April. One of the most memorable trips I've ever made was a day on northeastern Pennsylvania's Mehoopany Creek. No dry fly or wet fly seemed to work that day, until I switched to a Quill Gordon wet. There were a few Gordons in the air, but no massive hatch. That didn't stop just about every trout in the particular pool from taking that wet fly.

Wet flies produce because they copy many emerging caddis and mayflies. They work exceptionally well in April and May and again in September and October.

The second hook number in the list of patterns at the end of this chapter refers to the wet-fly hook. Since in tying a wet fly you're tying a pattern you want to sink, use a less buoyant material than poly. Fur, wool, and some other body materials sink quickly, and they come in an assortment of colors for any wet-fly pattern. Use hen hackle for the tail and legs, and dark mallard quill sections for wings instead of the gray hackle tips suggested for many of the dry flies.

Tying Nymphs for Pennsylvania Streams

If you've looked carefully at the life cycle of aquatic insects in Chapter 2, you've already noted that mayflies, caddis flies, and stoneflies live most of their life below water as nymphs or larvae. Nymphs are available as food for trout a good ninety percent of their life. It's essential, then, that you imitate nymphs on occasion. These patterns work well before and during a hatch of the naturals they represent, when the naturals move toward the surface and begin emerging. You'll note in the tying directions that we suggest angora, opossum, or just plain fur as body material. All absorb water quickly and sink rapidly. Another material, called Ultra Translucent Nymph Dubbing and sold in many of the better fly-tying stores, is excellent dubbing material for nymphs. To make nymphs less buoyant, no matter what body material you use, you might want to incorporate some weight onto the body of the nymph. Just add a piece of lead wire and wind it around the hook to get the desired sinking action.

When we use the word "wings" in the tying descriptions for nymphs, we're really referring to the insects' wing pads, and when we list "hackle" in the instructions, we're referring to the legs of the insect. Tie in the wings about halfway back on the shank of the hook. Wind the tying thread over the tip of the wing section with the shiny side of the wing up and the butt of the section pointing back toward the bend of the hook. Leave the wing pad in that position until you've completed dubbing the front end of the body and have tied in the legs or hackle. Next take the proper soft hackle, and tie it in at the same place you tied in the wing pad. Finish dubbing the front part of the body, then wind the hackle over that. Trim the top part of the hackle, bring the wing pad up over the hackle, and tie it in at the eye.

You'll note that we recommend using cree or ginger-variant hackle quite often to copy the legs of nymphs and duns. Ginger-variant hackle normally includes dark- and light-brown shading on the same hackle; and cree contains cream, black, and brown barring. Both duplicate the multi-colored legs of naturals quite well. The cream variant provides a lighter hackle than the ginger variant.

The Tying Tables

In the tables below, you'll note under most of the pattern descriptions at least two hook numbers (not sizes). The first number refers to the hook used for tying the dry fly, and the second refers to a hook preferred for the wet fly. After these hook numbers we list the preferred sizes for the patterns. When more than one hook size is listed, the pattern in question copies more than one mayfly, or the mayfly copied varies in size from stream to stream.

Each pattern listed in the tables can be tied as a wet or dry fly. If you plan to tie a wet-fly version, then omit poly as a body material and use angora, fur, or another less buoyant substitute. Even if you use fur or angora, you may find it necessary to add weight to a wet fly.

In almost every pattern description we suggest the body be "dubbed." Dubbing, or placing small bits of poly between your fingers and actually rolling it on prewaxed tying thread, produces a realistic, buoyant body. Many mayflies, caddis flies, and stoneflies have an underbelly that is ribbed. Use a fine colored thread to mimic this natural ribbing.

We frequently refer to mallard-flank feathers in the pattern descriptions. These are the light-gray or off-white feathers, heavily barred, on the side of a mallard duck. They effectively copy the natural barring of the wings of many aquatic insects.

Poly yarn is another material used extensively in tying bodies of the patterns. It comes on a spool or card and resembles wool yarn. It's impossible to dub, but it's excellent for winding around the shank of the hook and especially well adapted for tying terrestrials. In light gray or white, poly yarn provides great wing material for spinner imitations.

The patterns listed in the following tables should copy just about all the hatches and circumstances you'll encounter on Pennsylvania's streams and rivers. We have not covered any attractor patterns like the Royal Coachman and Trout Fin. Because we've omitted them doesn't mean they're unimportant on Pennsylvania streams. When there's no hatch to match on the water and terrestrials and down wings won't work, then it's time to try an attractor.

You'll note we first list those patterns that copy mayflies. The first pattern listed copies the dun, the second the spinner, and the third the nymph. If a pattern copies more than one hatch, we suggest some of the species that the pattern imitates.

Following the tying descriptions for mayflies you'll find patterns for caddis dry flies, caddis larvae, and emerging caddis pupae. Next listed are some of the common patterns for stoneflies (floating) and nymphs, and finally some suggestions for patterns copying some of the state's terrestrials.

Mayfly Imitations

Blue Dun or Little Blue-Winged Olive Dun
  Copies *Baetis tricaudatus*, and *Pseudocloeon* species
  Thread: Dark gray
  Tail: Medium to dark gray hackle fibers
  Body: Gray muskrat or medium gray poly, dubbed; for the Little Blue-Winged Olive use olive gray poly
  Wings: On smaller sizes (20) use dark gray mallard quills; on larger sizes use dark gray hackle tips
  Hackle: Blue dun
  Hook: Mustad 94840, 3906, sizes 18 and 20

Rusty Spinner
  Thread: Dark brown
  Tail: Dark grayish brown hackle fibers
  Body: Grayish brown poly, dubbed and ribbed with fine tan thread
  Wings: Pale gray poly yarn, tied spent
  Hook: Same as above

Nymph
  Thread: Dark olive
  Tail: Wood duck fibers, dyed dark olive
  Body: Dark olive brown opossum
  Wings: Dark gray mallard quill section
  Hackle: Cree or ginger variant hackle, dyed dark olive
  Hook: 3906B, size 18

Blue Quill
  Copies all *Paraleptophlebia* species, and *Ephemerella deficiens*
  Thread: Dark gray
  Tail: Medium to dark gray hackle fibers
  Body: Eyed peacock herl, stripped or dark gray poly, dubbed
  Wings: Dark gray hackle tips
  Hackle: Light to medium blue dun
  Hook: Mustad 94840, 3906, size 18 or 20

Dark-Brown Spinner
  Thread: Dark brown
  Tail: Dark brown hackle fibers
  Body: Dark brown poly, dubbed
  Wings: Pale gray poly yarn, tied spent
  Hook: Same as above

Nymph
  Thread: Dark Brown
  Tail: Mallard flank feather, dyed dark brown
  Body: Dark brown angora, dubbed
  Wings: One dark gray mallard quill tied down
  Hackle: Dark gray
  Hook: 3906B, size 16 and 18

Blue-Winged Olive Dun
  Copies many *Drunella* (*Ephemerella*) species and *Dannella* (*Ephemerella*) like *cornuta, longicornus, attenuata, cornutella, lata, simplex, walkeri*, and others
  Thread: Olive
  Tail: Grayish olive hackle fibers
  Body: Light to medium olive poly, dubbed
  Wings: Dark gray hackle tips
  Hackle: Medium creamish olive
  Hook: Mustad 94840, 3906, size 14 to 20

Dark-Olive Spinner
  Thread: Dark olive or black
  Tail: Moose mane (dark brown)
  Body: Dark olive poly (almost black with an olive cast)
  Wings: Pale gray poly yarn, tied spent
  Hook: Same as above

Nymph
  Thread: Olive
  Tail: Wood duck
  Body: Dark brown angora tied over dubbed in olive opossum
  Wings: Brown turkey
  Hackle: Ginger variant, dyed olive
  Hook: 3906B, sizes 14 to 18

Quill Gordon
Copies species like *Epeorus pleuralis* and some *Rhithrogena* species
Thread: Dark gray
Tail: Dark gray hackle fibers
Body: Eyed peacock herl, stripped and lacquered
Wings: Wood duck or imitation wood duck, divided; or dark gray hackle tips
Hackle: Dark gray hackle
Hook: Mustad 94840, 3906, size 14

Red Quill Spinner
Use same pattern as spinner listed under Hendrickson

Nymph
Thread: Dark brown
Tail: Fibers from a mallard flank feather, dyed dark amber
Body: Dark brown fur or angora, mixed with a bit of lighter brown or amber
Wings: Mottled brown turkey, tied down over thorax
Hackle: Cree or ginger variant hackle (dark and amber mixed)
Hook: 3906B, size 14

Light Cahill
Copies diverse species like *Stenonema ithaca*, *Stenacron interpunctatum*, *Heptagenia marginalis*, and many others
Thread: Cream or tan
Tail: Cream hackle fibers
Body: Cream poly, fox fur, or angora, dubbed
Wings: Mallard flank feather, dyed pale yellow, divided
Hackle: Cream hackle
Hook: Mustad 94840, 3906, size 14

Light Cahill Spinner
Same as dun except omit hackle and add pale yellow poly yarn for wings. Tie them spent.

Nymph
Thread: Brown
Tail: Fibers from a mallard flank feather, dyed brown
Body: Dark brown angora yarn on top and pale amber belly, dubbed
Wings: Dark brown turkey
Hackle: Dark cree
Hook: 3906B, size 12

Slate Drake
Copies all *Isonychia* species in Pennsylvania
Thread: Black
Tail: Dark gray hackle fibers
Body: Peacock herl (not from eye), stripped; or dark gray poly, or muskrat, dubbed

Wings: Dark gray hackle tips
Hackle: One cream hackle tied in behind and one dark brown hackle tied in front
Hook: Mustad 94840, 3906, size 12 or 14

White-Gloved Howdy
Thread: Dark brown or maroon
Tail: Medium gray hackle fibers
Body: Dark mahogany poly, dubbed
Wings: Pale gray poly yarn
Hook: Same as above

Nymph
Thread: Dark brown
Tail: Three dark brown hackle with one side cut off
Body: Very dark brown angora or opossum
Wings: Dark gray mallard quill section, tied down over thorax
Hackle: Cree hackle, dyed pale olive
Hook: 3906B, size 10 or 12

Sulphur Dun
Copies *Ephemerella rotunda*, *invaria*, *septentrionalis*, and to a lesser degree *dorothea*
Thread: Yellow
Tail: Cream hackle fibers
Body: Usually pale yellow poly with an orange (and sometimes olive orange) cast
Wings: Pale gray hackle tips
Hackle: Cream hackle
Hook: Mustad 94840, 3906, size 16 and 18

Sulphur Spinner
Thread: Tan
Tail: Tan deer hair
Body: Female with eggs—yellowish tan poly; female without eggs—tan poly; male—bright red hackle stem, stripped and wound around hook
Wings: Pale gray poly yarn, tied spent (also tie some upright)
Hook: Same as above

Nymph
Thread: Grayish brown
Tail: Brown pheasant tail fibers
Body: Brown (ground color) fur
Wings: Dark gray mallard quill section, tied down over thorax
Hackle: Cree hackle
Hook: 3906B, size 14, 16, and 18

Red Quill and Hendrickson
Red Quill copies the male and the Hendrickson the female of *Ephemerella subvaria* and several closely related subspecies. In addition the Red Quill effectively imitates many spinners like *Ephemerella subvaria*, *Epeorus pleuralis*,

and the male spinner of *Ephemerella invaria* and *rotunda*
Thread: Brown
Tail: Medium gray hackle fibers
Body: Red Quill—reddish brown hackle fiber stripped of its barbules and wound from the bend of the hook to the wings. Hendrickson—tan poly, dubbed
Wings: Wood duck, divided. Optional on Hendrickson are gray hackle tips
Hackle: Medium gray hackle
Hook: Mustad 94840, 3906, sizes 14 and 16

Red Quill Spinner
Thread: Brown
Tail: Bronze dun hackle fibers
Body: Dark tannish brown poly, dubbed and ribbed finely with tan thread
Wings: Pale gray poly yarn, tied spent
Hook: Same as above

Nymph
Thread: Dark brown
Tail: Fibers from a mallard flank feather, dyed brown
Body: Dark brown angora, mixed with a bit of amber
Wings: Mottled brown turkey, tied down over thorax
Hackle: Cree hackle
Hook: 3906B, size 12 and 14

Yellow Drake
Copies *Ephemera varia*
Thread: Yellow
Tail: Tan deer hair
Body: Pale yellow poly, dubbed
Wings: Mallard flank feather dyed pale yellow, divided
Hackle: Pale yellow with a turn or two of grizzly in front
Hook: Mustad 94840, 3906, size 12

Yellow Drake Spinner
Thread: Yellow
Tail: Dark brown deer hair
Body: Same as above
Wings: Gray poly yarn, tied spent
Hook: Same as above

Nymph
Thread: Tan
Tail: Pale gray, trimmed
Body: Amber colored angora or opossum
Wings: Medium to light brown turkey
Hackle: Ginger
Hook: 3906B, size 10 or 12

Green Drake
Copies *Ephemera guttulata*
Thread: Cream
Tail: Moose mane

Body: Cream poly, dubbed
Wings: Mallard flank dyed yellowish green, divided
Hackle: Rear—cream hackle; front—dark brown hackle
Hook: Mustad 94831, 3906B, sizes 8 and 10

Coffin Fly
Thread: White
Tail: Light tan deer hair
Body: White poly, dubbed
Wings: Grayish yellow poly yarn, tied spent
Hook: Same as above

Nymph
Thread: Tan
Tail: Three medium brown hackle, trimmed and tied in
Body: Pale tan angora
Wings: Dark brown turkey, tied down and over thorax
Hackle: Cree
Hook: 3906B, or 9672, size 8 to 12

Brown Drake
Copies *Ephemera simulans*
Thread: Dark brown
Tail: Moose mane
Body: Yellowish brown poly, dubbed
Wings: Mallard flank feather, dyed yellowish brown, divided
Hackle: Rear—cream; front—dark brown
Hook: Mustad 94831, 3906B, sizes 10 and 12

Brown Drake Spinner
Thread: Dark brown
Tail: Brown hackle fibers
Body: Yellowish brown poly, dubbed
Wings: Gray poly yarn, tied spent
Hook: same as above

Nymph
Thread: Brown
Tail: Three light brown hackle, trimmed and tied in
Body: Tan angora or opossum
Wings: Brown turkey, tied down and over thorax
Hackle: Dark cree
Hook: 3906B, or 9672, size 10 or 12

March Brown
Copies *Stenonema vicarium*
Thread: Yellow
Tail: Dark brown hackle fibers
Body: Tan poly, dubbed and ribbed with dark brown thread
Wings: Mallard flank feather, dyed yellowish brown and divided
Hackle: One cream and one dark brown, mixed
Hook: Mustad 94840, 3906, size 12

Great Red Spinner
Thread: Dark brown
Tail: Dark brown hackle fibers
Body: Dark reddish brown poly, dubbed
Wings: Pale gray poly yarn, tied spent
Hackle: Dark brown with a turn or two of pale ginger mixed
Hook: Same as above

Nymph
Thread: Brown
Tail: Fibers from a mallard flank feather, dyed brown
Body: Same as Gray Fox above
Wings: Dark brown turkey, tied down over thorax
Hackle: Dark cree
Hook: 3906B, size 12

Gray Fox
Copies *Stenonema fuscum* and subspecies, and *Stenonema ithaca*, and others
Thread: Cream
Tail: Tan deer hair
Body: Cream poly, dubbed
Wings: Mallard flank feather, dyed pale yellowish tan, divided
Hackle: Cree hackle or one brown and one cream mixed
Hook: Mustad 94840, 3906, size 12 or 14

Ginger Quill Spinner
Thread: Brown
Tail: Dark brown hackle fibers
Body: Eyed peacock herl, dyed tan and stripped, or grayish brown poly, ribbed with brown thread
Wings: Gray hackle tips (conventional); or pale gray poly yarn, tied spent
Hackle: Dark ginger (conventional); or none with poly yarn wings
Hook: Same as above

Nymph
Thread: Brown
Tail: Fibers from a mallard flank feather, dyed brown
Body: Brown angora yarn, tied on top over cream. Tie in brown at tail, and dub in cream so that top (*tergites*) of body is brown and the belly (*sternites*) is cream
Wings: Dark brown turkey, tied down over thorax
Hackle: Dark cree
Hook: 3906B, size 12

Cream Cahill
Copies species like *Stenonema pulchellum* and *Stenonema modestum*
Thread: Cream
Tail: Cream hackle fibers

Body: Very pale cream (almost white) poly, dubbed
Wings: Mallard flank feather dyed very pale yellow, divided
Hackle: Cream
Hook: Mustad 94840, 3906, sizes 14 and 16

Cream Cahill Spinner
Thread: White
Tail: Pale cream hackle fibers
Body: White poly, dubbed
Wings: Pale poly yarn, tied spent
Hook: Same as above

Nymph
Thread: Olive brown
Tail: Light brown hackle fibers
Body: Dub pale creamish gray on hook, then tie pale brownish olive yarn in at bend and bring over top to wing case and tie in
Wings: Dark brown turkey
Hackle: Dark olive brown
Hook: 3906B, size 14 or 16

White Mayfly (dun and spinner)
(Since the female dun never changes to a spinner, I've listed one pattern for both phases.)
Copies *Ephoron leukon* and other similar species
Thread: White
Tail: White hackle fibers
Body: Female dun—creamish white poly, dubbed; male spinner—a couple turns of dark reddish brown poly at the rear, then white poly for the rest of the body, dubbed
Wings: Very pale gray hackle tips
Hackle: Cream (a turn or two of dark brown for the male spinner)
Hook: Mustad 94840, 3906, size 14 and 16

Nymph
Thread: Gray
Tail: Tannish gray hackle fibers
Body: Pale gray angora or opossum, dubbed heavily
Wings: Pale gray mallard quill sections
Hackle: Cream ginger
Hook: 3906B, size 14 or 16

Chocolate Dun
Copies species like *Ephemerella needhami*, and *Eurylophella* (*Ephemerella*) *bicolor*
Thread: Brown
Tail: Medium gray
Body: Chocolate brown poly finely ribbed with lighter brown thread
Wings: Dark gray hackle tips
Hackle: Tan hackle
Hook: Mustad 94840, 3906, size 16

Chocolate Spinner
Thread: Dark brown
Tail: Tannish gray hackle fibers
Body: Dark rusty brown poly, dubbed
Wings: Pale gray poly yarn, tied spent
Hook: Same as above

Nymph
Thread: Brown
Tail: Light brown mallard falnd feather
   fibers
Body: Light brown poly nymph dubbing
Wings: Dark gray mallard quill
Hackle: Brown hackle
Hook: 3906B, size 16

Dark-Green Drake
Copies species like *Litobrancha recurvata*
Thread: Dark gray
Tail: Dark brown moose mane
Body: Very dark slate poly, dubbed and
   ribbed with yellow thread
Wings: Mallard flank, heavily barred and
   dyed dark green
Hackle: Rear-tannish brown hackle; front-
   dark brown hackle
Hook: Mustad 94833, 3906B, size 8 or 10

Brown Drake Spinner
Thread: Brown
Tail: Brown hackle fibers
Body: Reddish brown poly, dubbed and
   ribbed with yellow thread
Wings: Pale gray poly yarn, tied spent
Hackle: Dark brown
Hook: Same as above

Nymph
Thread: Light brown
Tail: Three dark bronze hackles,
   trimmed and tied in
Body: Tan with a grayish cast angora, or
   opossum
Wings: Dark brown turkey
Hackle: Dark cree
Hook: 9672, size 8 or 10

Trico Dun
Copies all *Tricorythodes* species
Thread: Pale olive
Tail: Cream hackle fibers
Body: Pale olive green poly, dubbed;
   male—dark brown poly
Wings: Pale gray heckle tips
Hackle: Cream hackle
Hook: Mustad 94840, size 20 to 24

Trico Spinner
Thread: Dark brown
Tail: Female—short cream hackle fibers;
   male—long dark brown moose mane
Body: Female—rear one third is cream
   poly, dubbed and front two thirds is
   dark brown poly, dubbed; male—dark

brown poly, dubbed and ribbed with a
very fine light tan thread
Wings: White poly yarn, tied spent
Hook: Mustad 94840, size 20 to 24

Nymph
Thread: Black
Tail: Dark brown hackle fibers
Body: Dark brownish black fur
Wings: Dark gray mallard quill section
Hackle: Dark reddish brown
Hook: 3906B, size 22

Pale Evening Dun
Copies species like *Ephemerella dorothea*,
   E. septentrionalis, and many *Heptagenia*
   species like *H. walshi*, *aphrodite*, and
   others
Thread: Pale yellow
Tail: Cream hackle fibers
Body: Pale yellowish cream poly, dubbed
Wings: Pale yellow hackle tips
Hackle: Cream
Hook: Mustad 94840, 3906, size 16 to 20

Pale Evening Spinner
Thread: Cream
Tail: Cream hackle fibers
Body: Pale yellowish cream poly, dubbed
Wings: Pale gray poly yarn, tied spent
Hook: Same as above

Nymph
Thread: Brown
Tail: Dark brown pheasant tail fibers
Body: Dark tan ultra translucent dubbing
Wings: Gray mallard quill section
Hackle: Cree
Hook: Mustad 3906B, size 16 and 18

Pink Cahill
Copies female of *Epeorus vitreus*. Male
   dun is copied with the Light Cahill,
   size 16
Thread: Cream
Tail: Gray hackle fibers
Body: Pinkish cream poly for female and
   pale yellow poly for male, dubbed
Wings: Mallard flank feather, dyed pale
   yellow
Hackle: Cream ginger hackle
Hook: Mustad 94840, 3906, size 16

Salmon Spinner
Thread: Pink
Tail: Cream ginger hackle fibers
Body: Pinkish red poly, dubbed
Wings: Pale gray poly yarn, tied spent
Hook: Same as above

Nymph
Thread: Tan
Tail: Dark brown fibers from a pheasant
   tail
Body: Dub amber on the entire, tie in a

dark brown yarn at the bend of the hook and bring up and over and tie in at where you tie in the wings
Wings: Brown turkey section
Hackle: Several turns of a ginger hackle
Hook: 3906B, size 14

Caddis Imitations

Green Caddis
Copies many members of the genus *Rhyacophila*

Deer Head Green Caddis
Thread: Brown
Body: Medium olive green poly with a gray cast, dubbed
Wings: Medium brown deer hair tied in with butts pointing toward the bend of the hook and the tips of the deer hair extending out over the eye of the hook. Tie in hair securely near the eye of the hook, then wind thread one fourth of the way back towards the bend. Bend deer hair back and tie in
Hackle: If you prefer the regular fluttering caddis, you can tie as above and add a ginger hackle where you tie in the hair. Place a drop of lacquer on thread and finished head
Hook: Mustad 94840, 37160, size 14 and 16

Spotted Sedge
Copies *Symphitopsyche slossanae*
Thread: Tan
Body: Grayish tan poly, dubbed
Wings: Medium brown deer hair
Hackle: Ginger
Hook: Mustad 94840, 37160, size 14 and 16

Dark Blue Sedge
Copies *Psilotreta frontalis*
Thread: Dark gray
Body: Dark gray poly, dubbed
Wings: Dark grayish brown deer hair
Hackle: Dark brownish black
Hook: Mustad 94840, 37160, size 12

Grannom
Copies many species of the genus *Brachycentrus*
Thread: Black
Body: Dark brownish black to black poly, dubbed
Wings: Dark brown deer hair
Hackle: Dark brown
Hook: Mustad 94840, 37160, size 12 and 14

Little Black Caddis
Copies *Chimarra atterima*
Thread: Black
Body: Black poly, dubbed
Wings: Deer hair dyed dark gray
Hackle: Dark brown
Hook: Mustad 94840, 37160, size 16

Cream Caddis
Copies some *Hydropsyche species*
Thread: Tan
Body: Creamish tan poly, dubbed
Wings: Medium brown deer hair
Hackle: Ginger
Hook: Mustad 94840, 37160, size 14

Dark-Brown Caddis
Copies *Deplectrona modesta* and many other caddis species
Thread: Dark brown
Body: Dark brown poly
Wings: Dark brown deer hair
Hackle: Dark reddish brown
Hook: Mustad 94840, 37160, size 12

Caddis Larvae

Caddis Larva
Thread: Appropriate color (most often dark brown or black)
Body: Olive, green, brown, yellow, black, or tan fur dubbed and ribbed with fine wire, or use a rubber band of the appropriate color and tie in at the bend of the hook and spiral to the eye
Thorax: Dark brown fur, dubbed; or an ostrich herl, dyed dark brown wound around the hook several times
Hook: Mustad 37160, sizes 12 to 18

Emerging Caddis Pupa
Thread: Same color as the body color you select
Body: Olive, green, brown, yellow, black, or tan fur or poly nymph dubbing material
Wings: Dark mallard quill sections shorter than normal and tied in on both sides of the fly, not on top
Legs: Dark brown grouse or woodcock neck feather wound around the hook two or three times
Hook: 37160, sizes 12 to 18

Stonefly Imitations

Early Brown Stonefly
Copies species like *Strophopteryx fasciata*

Adult
Thread: Yellow
Tail: Short dark brown hackle fibers
Body: Dark grayish brown poly, dubbed; or peacock herl, stripped
Wings: Dark brown deer hair
Hackle: Dark brown
Hook: Mustad 94840, 3906, size 12 or 14

Nymph
Thread: Brown
Tail: Fibers from a brown pheasant tail
Body: Reddish brown ultra translucent dubbing
Wings: Brown turkey

Hackle: Brown
Hook: Mustad 3906B, size 12

Light Stonefly
Copies species like *Isoperla signata*

Adult
Thread: Pale yellow
Tail: Short ginger hackle fibers
Body: Pale yellow poly, dubbed and
ribbed with tan thread
Wings: Very light tan to cream deer hair
Hackle: Ginger
Hook: Mustad 94840, 3906, size 12 or 14

Nymph
Thread: Tan
Tail: Fibers from a mallard flank feather,
dyed brown
Body: Tan fox fur or nymph dubbing
Wings: Light brown turkey
Hackle: Cree
Hook: Mustad 3906B, size 12

Little Green Stonefly
Copies species like *Alloperla imbecilla*
Thread: Green
Tail: Short pale cream hackle fibers
Body: Medium green poly, dubbed
Wings: Pale gray hackle tips, tied down
wing
Hackle: Pale creamish green hackle
Hook: Mustad 94840, size 16

Yellow Sally
Copies species like *Isoperla bilineata*
Thread: Yellow
Tail: Short cream hackle fibers
Body: Pale yellow poly, dubbed
Wings: Cream hackle tips, tied down wing
Hackle: Cree hackle
Hook: Mustad 94840, size 14 or 16

Great Brown Stonefly
Copies species similar to *Acroneuria lycor-
ias*
Thread: Dark brown
Tail: Short dark brown hackle fibers
Body: Dark brownish gray poly, dubbed
and ribbed with yellow thread
Wings: Dark gray deer hair
Hackle: Dark brown
Hook: Mustad 94840, 3906, size 10 or 12

Nymph
Thread: Brown
Tail: Light brown hackle fibers
Body: Light brown fur or nymph dubbing
Wings: Brown turkey
Hackle: Light brown
Hook: Mustad 3906B, size 10

Acroneuria Nymph
Copies many species like *Acroneuria arida*,
abnormis, and *carolinensis*

Thread: Dark brown
Tail: Light brown hackle fibers
Body: Dark olive brown yarn, laid over
top of pale yellow dubbing fur
Wings: Dark brown turkey
Hackle: Cree
Hook: 3906B, size 10 and 12

Great Stonefly Nymph
Copies many species like the very com-
mon *Phasganophora capitata*
Thread: Tan
Tail: Soft ginger hackle fibers
Body: Dark cream below with darker
brown on top
Wings: Mottled turkey quill
Hackle: Cree
Hook: Mustad 3906B, size 8 and 10

Terrestrials

Poly Beetle
The Poly Beetle is tied exactly like the
Crowe Beetle, using black poly yarn,
however, rather than black deer hair.
On a size-16 beetle use 3 strands of
the yarn (about 3 match sticks thick).
Tie in the poly securely below the
bend of the hook. If you wish, tie in a
peacock herl at the bend of the hook
to imitate the Japanese Beetle. Wind
the tying thread up to the eye of the
hook, and wind the peacock. Pull the
poly up over the shank of the hook
and tie in securely just behind the eye.
Cut off the excess poly, but leave
some to imitate the head. You'll really
like this excellent pattern. It's simple,
realistic, and takes less than a minute
to tie. Tie on hook sizes 12 to 20.

Poly Ant
Body: Black poly, dubbed into two humps
on the hook with the rear hump being
a bit larger than the front one
Hackle: Add a black hackle after you
complete the rear hump and before
you start the front one

Ken's Hopper
Body: Yellowish olive poly, dubbed heavily
Head and wings: Use deer body hair dyed
yellow and tie in just behind the eye
as you would with the Muddler. Clip
the butts also as in the Muddler

LeTort Cricket
Body: Black poly, heavily dubbed
Wings: Black dyed goose quill sections,
tied down wing
Hackle: Deer body hair, dyed black and
tied in similar to the Muddler

Eleven

SOME PROPOSALS FOR BETTER FISHING ON
Pennsylvania Streams

Probably no other state organization in Pennsylvania has done as much good in its area of responsibility as has the Pennsylvania Fish Commission. With the remarkable foresight to classify streams in several categories, the commission, especially under the energetic guidance of its former chief, Ralph Abele, and the present executive director, Edward Miller, has accomplished some remarkable policy changes in the past decade. Many of these moves, thought to be revolutionary at the time, have benefited fly-fishing in Pennsylvania. Especially given the Commonwealth's considerable population and development, Pennsylvania can truly boast of its fine trout fishing. With the anglers' support, however, more can be done.

Pennsylvania has a large population of fly-fishermen. In a survey conducted for the Pennsylvania Fish Commission in 1977, ten percent of respondents indicated that they preferred to use artificial flies. That's almost 90,000 licensed fishermen using flies—in 1977. I'm certain that if a survey were conducted today the figure would be closer to twenty percent.

While preparing to write this book, I had the opportunity and good fortune to fly-fish with many of the state's finest anglers. Each one of them expressed concerns about his or her local streams and the future of fly-fishing as a sport in Pennsylvania. The suggestions that follow for improving the trout fishery in our state have evolved from these interviews and from visiting more than 150 Commonwealth streams and rivers.

Conduct Educational Programs

John Gordon, of Huntingdon, releases more than 400 trout per year, but he catches ninety percent of his trout on spinners. We often assume that hardware fishermen kill their limit. Why doesn't John? John realizes that if he wants to have quality fishing all season long, he has to return his trout. That argument's not too difficult to present to fishermen. Yet those of us who return trout and want others to do the same don't do a very good job of explaining the positive effects of releasing trout. Trout Unlimited, Fly Fishers Federation, and other interested groups must set up educational programs designed to instruct anglers about the advantages of catch-and-release fishing. These organizations should arrange discussions in schools, with sportsmen's organizations, and with the general public. The quality of fishing tomorrow depends on the number of trout returned today.

You can assist these organizations by joining and actively participating in their goal of better fishing.

Encourage Land Acquisition

What do Big Fill Run, Spruce Creek, Yellow Creek, Willow Run, Tipton Run, and Piney Creek have in common? They all contain sections considered Class A wild-trout waters. In addition, however, since that classification some sections of all of these streams have been posted. It appears that the state's classifying these streams was an open invitation for some landowners to post their water. As soon as some landowners found out that streams running through their property would not be stocked anymore, they posted their property. In the near future much of the wild-trout and stocked waters that remain open seem destined to be posted.

The state's Fish Commission does not have the money to purchase land. Access rights should be acquired, however. Money should be appropriated to the commission by the state legislature specifically for this purpose. This action would ensure good fishing in the future, because everybody's future depends on access.

Within a few years access to many state streams will be prohibited unless we act now. Pennsylvania streams are too important—too vital—to be restricted to a handful of users.

Promote Stream Improvement

Recently I visited an experimental stream-improvement site on Martins Creek in Bangor. Don Baylor and other members of the Brodhead Chapter of Trout Unlimited developed the program. Two years ago the chapter, in cooperation with the Fish Commission, conducted electrofishing surveys on two adjoining areas, each about 100 yards long. On the upper section the chapter did no stream improvement. On the lower section the chapter installed low-flow channel structures, upstream Vs, and gabion deflectors. In all the chapter installed about ten devices on the experimental section of Martins. Twenty months after the devices were in place, the Fish Commission again conducted electrofishing surveys in both areas. The area containing the stream devices held four times as many trout as did the unimproved area. Before the devices were installed both sections held an equal number of trout.

The Brodhead Chapter conducted another experiment—this time on their namesake stream. Brodhead Creek, devastated by floods, suffered channelizing by the Corps of Engineers. Channelizing decimated the native brown trout population on the stream. After the chapter changed the habitat in a previously channelized area through stream improvement, the number of wild brown trout in the project area increased from eleven to thirty-eight.

I have seen dozens of streams in the Commonwealth that could be improved in the same manner. Travel to the East Branch of the Clarion River, and look at the quality of the stream-improvement devices installed above Glen Hazel. These devices fulfill a need and make almost the entire stream in that area a productive fishery. The East Branch project deserves to be a showplace.

To date much of the stream improvement in Pennsylvania has been accomplished by the Fish Commission, sportsmen's groups, Trout Unlimited chapters, Fly Fishers Federation chapters, foundation grants, and youth groups. Streams near McConnellsburg, like Cove Creek and Spring Run, need habitat-improvement devices desperately, but there's no trout organization within miles. Consequently nothing will be done. A concerted effort must be made to acquire funds for worthwhile stream improvement.

The Adopt-a-Stream Program instituted by the Pennsylvania Fish Commission has done much to improve habitat in many areas of the state. This worthwhile project needs the support of all anglers. If you or your organization are interested in actively contributing to stream improvement, consult the Fish Commission.

Improving trout waters is only part of stream improvement. Richard Snyder of the Fish Commission adds that working with the landowner to keep livestock from the streams, diverting barnyard runoff, seeding badly eroded banks, and encouraging contour farming are also important. Without cooperation of the landowner stream-improvement devices are at best a Band-Aid approach.

Continue and Expand Stocking Fingerlings

The state stocks fingerlings in the Little Juniata River, Youghiogheny River, Clarion River, East Branch of the Clarion River, Tulpehocken Creek, Kettle Creek (lower end), Lehigh River, LeTort Spring Run (lower end), West Branch of the Delaware River, Slippery Rock Creek, and Stoneycreek River. Results from these placements in most instances have been outstanding. Ask any fisherman on the Little Juniata or the Tulpehocken what he thinks of the program. The vast majority agree that stocking fingerlings has been successful.

More streams should be added to the list of those receiving fingerling-stocked trout. Streams like the Cordorus Creek in York, the Allegheny

River below the Kinzua Dam, the Pohopoco Creek below the Beltzville Dam, and the Bald Eagle Creek below Milesburg should receive experimental plantings of fingerlings.

Encourage Studies on High-Acid Streams

Thousands of miles of potentially productive Pennsylvania trout water have been ruined by mine-acid drainage and acid rain. No longer are the experiments to combat these pollutants conducted only in the laboratory. State organizations, universities, and watershed associations now conduct viable, successful stream-site pilot programs that might eventually rehabilitate many of our present high-acid streams. Two programs now operating are on Linn Run and Swamp Creek. All fishermen should encourage their legislators to continue these efforts.

LINN RUN ACID-RAIN STUDY

From a fisherman's perspective Linn Run, which flows through eastern Westmoreland County, stopped being a trout stream in 1959. Many of the trout housed in a cooperative nursery on the stream, and the trout stocked by the state in preseason, died. Linn Run suffered from a high-acid environment; pH readings lower than five (7.0 is neutral) were common in April that year. Fish kills from preseason stockings forced the Fish Commission to delay stocking trout until May. The stockable length declined to only a few miles. The stream continued to deteriorate, and the state seriously considered taking it off the stocking list. The culprit in Linn Run's case wasn't mine-acid drainage but acid rain.

Linn Run emanates high on the Laurel Hill escarpment. This nearly 3,000-foot mountain collects pollutants blown east, which fall as acid rain. Rainwater with a pH near 4 enters the soil. This acid water leaches aluminum from the soil and flows into Linn Run and other nearby tributaries. Aluminum coats the gills of fish, interferes with vital body-salt regulation, and kills them.

Enter the Loyalhanna Watershed Association and Penn State University. Lysle Sherwin, executive director of the Loyalhanna Watershed Association, appealed to the university to see if they could help. In 1983 William Sharpe and David DeWalle, of Penn State's Environmental Resources Research Institute, initiated a proposal to locate well sites near Linn Run, among other goals. They hoped to locate wells near the stream that could produce water with a pH of 7 or higher. Sharpe and DeWalle asked hydrogeologist Richard Parizek to help with this phase of their project. The group located five wells. Charles Gagen, a graduate assistant with the project, coordinated and developed the experimental program. From April to June today, well water is pumped into Linn Run, elevating the pH of the stream during high-water, heavy-rain periods.

What has happened to Linn Run since the experiment began? The state now stocks trout again in preseason, adds brown trout to the brook trout, and stocks an additional mile upstream of the well sites.

Linn Run is still a put-and-take trout stream, and much work remains to rehabilitate it completely. Wild trout still must depend on access to less acid tributaries to survive year round. The well system is currently being operated jointly by the Loyalhanna Watershed Association and Linn Run State Park, making it the only nonexperimental acid-rain-mitigation project in Pennsylvania that is continuously operated by local organizations. Through the combined efforts of the watershed association and the university, and with the financial support of the Richard King Mellon Foundation, of Pittsburgh, a tremendous leap forward in acid-rain research has begun on Linn Run.

SWAMP CREEK TREATMENT PLANT

The East Branch of the Clarion River resembles a human being on a life-support system. Take the patient off the machine, and he or she suffers permanent damage or dies. Take Swamp Creek off the liming device and the East Branch Dam and the river below the dam suffer. The Department of Environmental Resources (DER) built the Swamp Creek Treatment Plant in 1970 as part of Operation Scarlift. The drainage area of this mine-acid stream flows through sections strip mined during and shortly after World War II. Generations to come will suffer the consequences of the devastation caused by man. Above the treatment plant Swamp Creek's pH averages 4. The water flowing out of the liming device registers a pH of nearly 9. The pH of the discharge just below the dam in the stream averages 6.5. Without the liming device the pH on the stream below would be lower and might not be able to support a great trout fishery. Swamp Creek empties into the East Branch Dam a mile below the treatment site. The East Branch flows out of the dam. The DER operates the device and deserves the gratitude of all fishermen and environmentalists.

The DER operates other mine-treatment plants in the state. The plant on Slippery Rock Creek near Harrisville differs from the Swamp Creek plant, since it adds a slurry to the water, while the Swamp Creek plant adds dehydrated lime. This procedure seems to be more effective on larger streams.

Dale Eury operates the Swamp Creek Treatment Plant for the DER. Recently I spent some time at the operation. The plant consists of a lime-storage tank or silo and an automatic feeder. Two feeders add dehydrated lime to the mine acid in the stream below. There's a mixing shaft in the stream that thoroughly mixes the lime with the mine acid. Downstream from the effluent you'll see the bottom of the stream covered with an iron precipitate that occurs after the pH is elevated. This area of precipitation often runs for a mile downstream from the plant.

Without the liming device Swamp Run would carry mine acid directly into the East Branch Dam. Currently the impoundment contains a good number of bass and deep-water lake trout. Below the dam the branch holds great numbers of fingerlings, as well as stocked and holdover trout. Mayfly, caddis fly, and stonefly hatches appear on the stream throughout much of the year. Would they still appear without the treatment plant above?

Thanks to Mike Bielo, Dale Eury of DER, and all others associated with the treatment plant, East Branch survives as a viable trout fishery. The treatment plant works. It's no longer just a pilot program, but an important alternative to mine- acid drainage in small streams.

LIVING LAKES PROJECTS

In 1986 a group of environmentally-conscious utility and coal companies formed a not-for-profit organization in Washington, D.C. called Living Lakes, Inc. This group devotes its energies to searching for techniques which will restore biological productivity to streams and lakes affected by acid rain. Living Lakes has funded several pilot projects in the northeastern states, including ones on McNerney and Gifford runs (tributaries of Mosquito Creek), Wolf Run (Centre County), Powell Creek, and Stony Creek (the last two in Dauphin County) in Pennsylvania.

Rainfall in many of the project watersheds registers a pH of 3.8 to 3.9. At present the five trial streams support few trout. Gifford Run sustains an average of one four-inch brook per pool. Living Lakes' goal is to elevate the pH on Gifford Run below the treatment site to 6.5. This higher pH should increase the number of aquatic insects and the reproductive success of trout, with a corresponding increase in the size and number of catchable trout.

Project coordinator for the five study streams is Dean Arnold, an aquatic ecologist at Penn State University. With the support of Living Lakes, Dean, Bill Skinner, Joe Gallagher, and helpers completed installing a Sweetwater Doser on Gifford Run in May 1988. Water piped from an upstream dam powers the mechanism, then drops to a mixing tank. Limestone is fed into the mixing tank by a worm-screw conveyor. The limestone mixes with the water through turbulence. A chute pours the treated water back into Gifford Run. Within a few yards the limestone not dissolved in the mixing tank has dissolved in the stream and begun to neutralize acidity. The storage tank above the conveyor holds thirty tons of limestone, enough for two or three months of operation. Since the total operation depends on gravity and water power, there's no need for electricity.

Pennsylvania contains some of the finest trout waters in the East and we can make our waters better. By encouraging studies and funding to rehabilitate some of the 1,700 miles of acid water in the state, and by protecting our waters through land acquisition, encouraging stream improvement, adding fingerlings to appropriate waters, and conducting educational programs, Pennsylvania can truly be the leader in fishery innovations—and in excellent trout fishing. We have accomplished much. We can do even more.

Index of Streams

Fish and Game Books Available from The Countryman Press

The Countryman Press, long known for its fine books on the outdoors, offers a range of practical and readable manuals for sportsmen and women—from fly tying to wild game cooking.

FISHING AND HUNTING

The Fisherman's Companion, by Frank Holan, $7.95
Getting the Most from Your Game and Fish, by Robert Candy, $16.95
Taking Freshwater Game Fish: A Treasury of Expert Advice, edited by Todd Swainbank and Eric Seidler, $14.95

FLY TYING

Bass Flies, by Dick Stewart, $12.95 (paper), $19.95 (cloth)
The Hook Book: A Guide for Fly Tyers, by Dick Stewart, $8.95
Universal Fly Tying Guide, by Dick Stewart, $9.95

COOKBOOKS

Fish and Fowl Cookery: The Outdoorsman's Home Companion, by Carol Vance Wary with William G. Wary, $10.95
Wild Game Cookery: The Hunter's Home Companion, Revised and Expanded Edition, by Carol Vance Wary, $12.95

OTHER BOOKS ON PENNSYLVANIA FROM BACKCOUNTRY PUBLICATIONS

Fifty Hikes in Eastern Pennsylvania, by Carolyn Hoffman, $10.95
Fifty Hikes in Central Pennsylvania, by Tom Thwaites, $9.95
Fifty Hikes in Western Pennsylvania, by Tom Thwaites, $11.95
25 Bicycle Tours in Eastern Pennsylvania, by Dale Adams and Dale Speicher, $8.95

Backcountry Publications offers many more books on canoeing, hiking, walking, bicycling, and ski touring in New England, New York State, and the Mid-Atlantic states.

Our titles are available in bookshops and in many sporting goods stores, or they may be ordered directly from the publisher. Please add $2.50 per order for shipping and handling. To order or obtain a complete catalog, please write The Countryman Press, P.O. Box 175, Woodstock, Vermont 05091.